The Complete Guide to
STATIONARY
GAS ENGINES

D1605477

Mark Meincke

MBI Publishing Company

First published in 1996 by MBI Publishing Company, 729 Prospect Avenue, PO Box 1, Osceola, WI 54020-0001 USA.

MBI Publishing Company books are also available at discounts in bulk quantity for industrial or sales-promotional use. For details write to Special Sales Manager at Motorbooks International Wholesalers & Distributors, 729 Prospect Avenue, PO Box 1, Osceola, WI 54020-0001 USA.

Library of Congress Cataloging-in-Publication Data
Meincke, Mark.
  The complete guide to stationary gas engines/Mark
  Meincke.
    p. cm.
  Includes index.
  ISBN 0-7603-0121-2 (pbk.: alk. paper)
  1. Internal combustion engines—History—Handbooks,
  manuals, etc.
  I. Title.
TJ755.M46   1996
621.43—dc20   96-14071

Photos by the author unless credited otherwise

On the front cover: This stationary gasoline engine was built by the International Harvester Company. *Randy Johnson*

On the back cover: Top: A Reeves engine. Bottom: A Rockford engine.

Printed in the United States of America

Contents

Acknowledgments

First, I must thank my family for their support over the past several years. Wendy, I deeply appreciated your love, understanding, and support. You have been the best proofreader a husband could wish for and without your help this book would not have been completed. Thanks must go to my father Eldon for the help and friendship that a son could only hope for. You have been an unrelenting companion during the long trips to collect reference materials. I must thank you once again, Dad, for being there at my side. The pride that I see in my mother Marilyn's eyes has pushed me to achieve my life pursuits. Thanks for giving me the drive and confidence I needed to complete this book. I love you all.

My friends Don Irvine, Ken Fildes, and Wayne Hawkins must be given a special thanks. Don, Ken, and Wayne have unselfishly shared their friendship and knowledge of gas engine history. They have also allowed me to use their personal reference libraries to enhance the content of *The Complete Guide To Stationary Gas Engines.*

There is a special friend of mine, Mr. Ben Romich, who has given me support on this project from its inception. Ben, your many suggestions during the past several years have been helpful. Thanks for contributing to the overall accuracy and content of this book.

Authors Glen Karch, C. Lyle Cummins, Jr., and Verne Kindschi must be mentioned for their cooperation, and unselfish sharing of their personal engine reference materials. Thanks to all three special men for their help and especially their support.

Motorbooks International took a chance with a first-time author, and it's important that I express my thanks to them for believing in me. Your confidence from the beginning has helped to make this project a success. The help, support, and guidance that Mr. Mike Dapper and my editor, Mr. Lee Klancher, showed throughout this project is appreciated far beyond any thanks that can be given here.

I have looked at thousands and thousands of engines during the research period for *The Complete Guide to Stationary Gas Engines.* The heyday of the old gas engine has passed, and the doors of the manufacturing plants have closed. The preservation of the remaining engines is necessary to insure future generations will understand the impact these machines made in our lives. We must pass this legacy of early gas power on to our future generations.

I, therefore, dedicate this book on stationary gas engines and their history to my family, friends, and every gas engine enthusiast!

—*Mark J. Meincke*

Introduction

The Complete Guide to Stationary Gas Engines is a reference guide for purchasing, identifying, and troubleshooting gas engines. Stationary gas engines are machines that were developed to convert liquid fuels, such as gasoline and kerosene, or gaseous fuel such as natural gas or coal gas, into usable power. Stationary engines can immediately be identified by the large flywheels that were part of their design. The height of stationary engine usage lasted about 70 years, with the greatest activity occurring from 1895 until 1930.

Today, the greatest interest in stationary engines comes from collectors and restorers. Thousands of antique power shows are held each year by clubs and antique power museums. Here, enthusiasts are able to view and show their stationary engines and related machinery. These shows provide the hobbyists with a place to purchase or trade old engines, literature, and books. Many times, current and out-of-print engine literature can be found during these exhibits. Spare engine parts and accessories are often bought and sold or traded while traveling through the flea markets set up at the show grounds.

The Complete Guide to Stationary Gas Engines started out as my handwritten log compiled during travels to Midwest gas engine shows. It was not long before my list of Ohio engines had grown to include well over 100. My log book grew to several volumes of handwritten data. Documentation on manufacturer's identification tags was recorded from engine museums. Information was collected from privately owned engines displayed at various gas engine shows during the past eight years. In addition, many magazines, books, journals, and original manufacturer's manuals dating from the 1880s were researched. An extensive list of over 3,400 engines from all over the United States has now been accumulated and included as a reference in this book. The list provides the manufacturer's name, city, state, engine name, and an approximate date when the company or engine was known to exist.

The history of the internal combustion engine from its inception to the time of the stationary engine is covered briefly. The history of explosive power will help you develop a better overall understanding of the ideas that were used and further developed to manufacture an efficient machine capable of producing rotary motion.

Basic engine design differed from manufacturer to manufacturer. Several early stationary engines are detailed, and specific engine design characteristics and operating methods are discussed at length. The stationary engine is broken down into its major parts, and each part is detailed and discussed. Many illustrations and photographs have been included for every major part. Fuel and cooling systems are covered to provide an understanding of the differences found from one manufacturer to another. Methods of ignition and governing engine speed are covered with detailed examples of their design and function. Commonly found engines, such as the IHC Mogul, IHC Famous, Sears and Roebuck Sparta Economy, and Fuller & Johnson engines are featured. Their engine design and operating methods are covered at length.

What was that engine used for? One of the most often asked questions about stationary engines has been addressed. The chapter on powered equipment details many early machines that were operated from power supplied by a stationary engine.

A special chapter in the book has been set aside to cover troubleshooting and maintenance of stationary engines. The evaluation of an engine prior to purchasing is included to prevent the prospective buyer from making unnecessary mistakes. An engine price guide was also developed to assist the hobbyist. A variety of engines are pictured and suggested prices are given for various horsepower models. Prices also take into consideration overall engine condition. The prices listed may vary considerably in some areas of the country. Please view this information with an open mind and realize that not everyone will agree. Over 350 photographs are included to provide assistance when trying to identify unmarked engines and also illustrate many different engine designs. The engine's maker and key information about the engine or its maker are featured with every photograph. Illustrations from original manufacturer's advertising has been photographed and inserted throughout the book to further document the stationary engine.

Near the end of the book, many resources have been included for hobbyists. Parts suppliers, engine services, and literature entrepreneurs are listed. Current books and magazines on the gas engine hobby, along with their unique content are provided for interested enthusiasts.

I'd like to encourage all engine enthusiasts to share information on American-made stationary gas internal combustion engines with me, by writing to Mark J. Meincke, c/o Motorbooks International, 729 Prospect Avenue, Osceola, WI. 54020-0001.

A Brief History of the
Internal Combustion Engine

The story of the internal combustion engine takes us back to France in the year 1678. A French chemist named Abbe d' Hautefeuille was the first inventor to propose an engine that functioned on explosive power. Hautefeuille suggested that with the use of gunpowder a piston could be driven through a cylinder and that this motion be converted to useful power. About 1680, Christian Huygens, of Dutch descent, was given credit for actually sketching an engine that operates on the explosive power theory. There is no known record of a gunpowder engine having ever been built, but it could be said that Abbe d' Hautefeuille's and Huygens' theories of explosive power were the conception of the internal-combustion engine.

Over 100 years would pass before the next attempt to design a workable engine would be documented. In 1791, Englishman John Barber patented a turbine engine that would fire on a mixture of gas and air. It was the force of the explosion acting on the vanes of the turbine that would be used to produce power from combustion. In 1794, Barber's fellow countryman John Street filed for a patent that describes an engine that would operate by mixing a liquid fuel vapor and air. This mixture was then to be ignited inside a cylinder by the open-flame method. However, the efforts of both Barber and Street failed to produce a working engine.

In 1799, French inventor Philippe Lebon worked on an engine design that would use coal gas for fuel. Lebon failed to develop any practical engine or application for his coal gas engine patents. Not until 60 years later would the Belgium-born Jean Joseph Etienne Lenoir finally design, develop, and construct the first known working example of an internal combustion engine. Lenoir's one-brake-horsepower engine of

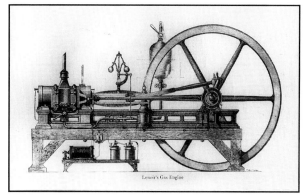

The Lenoir non-compressing engine appeared in 1860. It generated one horsepower and found limited commercial success. Reprinted with permission from *Internal Fire* © Society of Automotive Engineers, Inc.

1860 was built with a 5.5-inch-diameter cylinder and an 8.5-inch stroke. Naphtha and turpentine were used as the fuel. A mixture of fuel and air flowed into the combustion cylinder through slide valves similar to those used in steam engines. After the fuel was locked in the cylinder, an electrical spark ignited the fuel and air mixture. A water jacket around the combustion cylinder kept the heat of combustion from damaging the cylinder wall. Many design defects would lead to the engine's ultimate demise, in particular the huge quantity of fuel it consumed for the amount of work produced. Several manufacturers did, however, build engines of up to 12 horsepower using Lenoir's design. But the high cost of operating a Lenoir engine would take its toll, and the manufacture of Lenoir-designed engines was short-lived.

The Otto-Langen free piston atmospheric engine was developed in 1867. A slide valve with an open flame ignited the fuel charge inside the engine's combustion cylinder.

The Otto six-horsepower engine used a side shaft, tank cooling and a low-tension ignition system. This particular engine was built in 1894.

The four-cycle engine was first patented by French engineer Alphonse Beau de Rochas in January 1862. In his patent, the four specific strokes of the engine's piston were described. The first stroke is the intake stroke, which draws in a mixture of fuel. The second stroke is the compression stroke, which compresses the fuel mixture. At the end of the compression stroke and the beginning of the third stroke, the power stroke, the engine fuel is ignited. The fourth stroke of the piston is the exhaust stroke, which expels the exhaust gasses. Although Rochas had developed the modern four-cycle theory, he was unable to construct an engine that would function as he had described.

Probably the most famous name in early stationary engines is that of Otto. In 1862, a German named Nicholas A. Otto made his first attempt to build an engine. But, it was not until 1867, that Otto, with the help of Eugene Langen produced a working free-piston engine. This vertical engine used a charge of gas and air for combustion. The piston worked from the bottom of the engine in an upward fashion. The piston was held in place by a lever as the engine's cylinder filled with the fuel mixture. At the moment of ignition, the lever released, setting the piston in motion in the cylinder. When the fuel was ignited, it set the piston upward in the cylinder. On its downward stroke, the piston engaged with a rack gear that gave circular motion to the flywheel. The engine's normal running speed was 80–90 rpm. The Otto-Langen Atmospheric engine used about half the amount of fuel consumed by the Lenoir engine. Though this engine had its defects and limitations, it is the first engine that can be said to have had any real commercial success. A sizable number of engines were manufactured, and some have survived to this day. The Otto and Langen Atmospheric engine can be seen running at the Rough and Tumble Engineers club grounds in Kinzers, Pennsylvania. This is one of the oldest working examples of an internal combustion engine in North America. The engine is operated yearly during the club's annual antique power show.

The Brayton engine of 1873 was the first stationary gas internal combustion engine to be manufactured in the United States. This vertical engine used two cylinders, the first a working cylinder and the second a charging cylinder. Air and fuel were mixed at a ratio of 1:9. The engine compressed the fuel mixture to 74 pounds per square inch prior to ignition. This engine, while having two cylinders, only produced power from one working cylinder. The second cylinder was only used to compress the fuel mixture.

The first working example of a four-cycle engine surfaced in Paris, France, in 1878. The Paris Exposition provided the opportunity for Nicholas A. Otto to show the world his four-cycle engine. Otto had successfully designed and built an engine that used the four-cycle principles described in 1861 by Rochas. Otto's engine used a flame for ignition. A slide valve was used to admit the flame into the cylinder where the fuel mixture had been compressed. Once the flame made contact with the combustible fuel mixture, the gasses were ignited, and a power cycle was delivered to the engine. Several Otto engines are on display at the Coolspring Power Museum, located in Coolspring, Pennsylvania. The museum has several organized antique power shows each year. There, visitors will find the Otto engines operating as they did 100 years before.

The list of men working on the internal combustion engine seems almost endless. Gottlieb Daimler, Wilhelm Maybach, Carl Benz, and Rudolf Diesel were developing their ideas in Germany around the turn of the century. Rudolf Christian Diesel developed the first engine that used the theories of thermodynamics. Diesel's engines could ignite the fuel mixture without the use of spark or flame. Diesel would develop and construct engines that exerted extremely high pressure on the air mixture, to ignite the fuel mixture as it was injected into the combustion cylinder near the end of the compression stroke. Diesel's patents and engines laid the cornerstones for an entire industry based on the manufacture of diesel and semidiesel engines.

The two-cycle engine was credited to a Scotsman named Dugald Clerk. It was his engine of 1879 that demonstrated the two-cycle principles for which he is famous. This design provided a power stroke on each revolution of the engine. The value of two-cycle power would become apparent early in the boating industry. Over the years, thousands of two-cycle engines would be manufactured for marine use. The question of which engine design was better was debated throughout the industry. Two-cycle engines could be made lighter per horsepower than those of the four-cycle design. However, as the horsepower of the engine moved upward, the four-cycle engines were found to be more desirable. The two-cycle/four-cycle debate did nothing to stop the early industrialist from taking his dreams of producing the ideal engine and jumping head first into production.

The late 1870s and the 1880s were the formative years of early stationary and marine engines. As the 1890s came to an end, gas power began to push steam power into obscurity. By this time, the use of steam engines had long been embedded in all facets of American life. From the giant iron monsters of the Case and Avery tractor companies, to the huge blast-furnace blowing engines of the steel industry, steam was power. Steam engines could be found in almost any horsepower. However, an endless supply of water was needed for the production of steam. Also, these machines were not effi-

In 1893, Rudolf Christian Diesel built his first successful diesel engine. Reprinted with permission from *Internal Fire* © Society of Automotive Engineers, Inc.

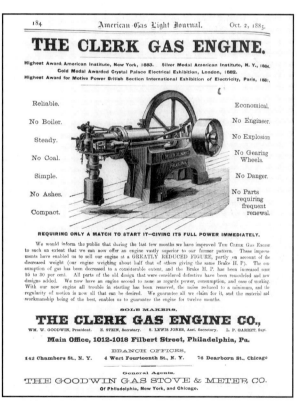

Dugald Clerk's two-cycle engine was developed in 1883. Two-cycle engines deliver a power stroke on each complete revolution of the engine. Reprinted with permission from *Internal Fire* © Society of Automotive Engineers, Inc.

cient users of fuel. Tremendous amounts of wood, coal, illuminating or coal gas, hay, or blast-furnace or coke gasses were burned to heat the water in the boilers. There was a need for more efficient, cleaner, smaller, lighter, cheaper, safer, and simpler sources of power.

Gas engines provided a versatile power unit that could be used to make many daily tasks more produc-

The Coal Handling Machinery Co. of Chicago manufactured the Cornell gas engine. This engine was typically used to power electric generators. The Cornell is a rare internal combustion engine.

The Brown Cochran Co. of Lorain, Ohio, as it appeared in 1905. This view shows the east end of the manufacturing plant with the Johnson Steel Co. in the background. Brown Cochran manufactured stationary and marine engines.

tive. Engines were found belted to pumps to water livestock. Grain was ground using the same power that would also irrigate fields. Wood for the winter heating season no longer needed to be cut by ax or handsaw. Log or buzz saws could be purchased, which would allow their owners not only to cut enough wood for themselves, but, at times, to have a surplus that could be traded or sold. Sawmill lumber for homes could be cut without the need of boilers. Rocks could be crushed, and milk could be separated. Gas engines provided individuals of limited budgets a power source they could afford. Engine size and simplicity would allow the portability needed to move gas-engine power to the job site. Industries, farmers, and small businesses were all eagerly looking for help from gas power. It was now up to men of industry to build them.

By 1900, engine companies would spring up in all areas of the country. Everyone with a better idea for a gas engine wanted their piece of the action. The Northeast seemed to have the largest concentration of manufacturers. It could have been that the availability of cast iron from the steel mills of the north was a great influence in their location. The waterways and railroads of the north helped to deliver the raw materials and ship the completed engines.

Many small companies such as the Coal Handling Machinery Co. of Chicago, which manufactured Cornell engines, were in competition with giants of the industry that had been in the agricultural manufacturing business several decades. By the early 1910s, competition and market saturation caused little-known companies such as the Brown Cochran Co. of Lorain, Ohio, to crumble, along with hundreds of others.

The Great Depression of 1929 turned the gas-engine business upside down. Mid-size companies such as Fuller & Johnson could not recover from the upheaval that the Depression brought. Doors of many obscure companies with less than a dozen employees closed overnight. The plethora of companies manufacturing the internal combustion engines would never approach what it had been before. The old saying that "only the strong survive" could have been written about gas-engine manufacturing companies that were able to overcome the Depression and keen competition to recoup their losses of the late 1920s and 1930s. A few engines continued to be manufactured into the 1940s, until the availability of electricity made electric-motor power the consumer's choice. IHC and Fairbanks Morse were among those companies that struggled through the hard times, surviving to today, although Fairbanks Morse no longer makes engines and IHC is now part of the Case Corporation.

The innovative men who built these engines in hundreds of small towns and cities made profound contributions to industry and modern life that will never be forgotten. Their efforts to improve the efficiency, performance, and reliability of the internal combustion engine set the stage for the continuing quest for a perfect engine.

Chapter Two

Basic Engine Design

The variety of engines that are found today on old homesteads or exist in private and public collections are evidence of the once-mighty single-cylinder engine industry. The study of antique engines reveals the evolution of engine design. It also illustrates that every manufacturer had unique interpretations of basic engine design. This becomes readily apparent as you examine the parts that make up an engine. For example, there are different methods and designs for ignition, cooling, carburetion, pistons, lubrication, governing, and timing. The ability to mentally break down an engine into its components is a valuable skill for every engine collector and restorer. With the thorough examination of engine parts, a greater understanding of overall engine design and function can be enjoyed. Your level of confidence will grow as you begin to understand how all these different parts interact and make a particular engine design unique. Let's begin our examination of these parts by looking at different methods of ignition.

Ignition Systems

Nondiesel internal combustion engines must have some device to explode the gaseous mixture taken into the cylinder. During development of early gas engines, generally three methods of ignition were used. The first method used an open flame and a slide valve to ignite the gaseous mixture within the engine cylinder. The second ignition method is commonly referred to as hot-tube ignition. The gaseous mixture was compressed into a hollow tube until the charge was ignited. The last method and the most reliable is that of electric-spark ignition. There were two types of electric-spark devices, igniters, and spark plugs. Hot tube and electric spark are the most common meth-

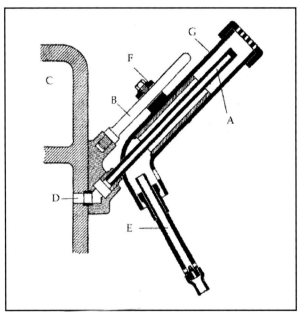

This is a diagram of a typical hot tube igniter. The hot tube parts are referred to as: A - hot tube, B - clamp rod, C - cylinder, D - fuel mixture passageway, E - Bunsen burner, F - clamp, and G - chimney.

ods of ignition used with stationary gas engines. We will begin with an explanation of hot-tube ignition.

Hot-Tube Ignition

Many different hot-tube ignition designs have been well documented. Larger engines generally had hot-tube arrangements that differed considerably from those of engines below 25 horsepower. I will limit this detailed examination to hot tubes that would typically be found on engines from 3 to 25 horsepower.

In the standard hot-tube design, the hot tube is connected to the engine's cylinder. A passageway al-lows the fuel mixture to pass from the cylinder into the body of the hot tube. As the piston moves toward top dead center of the compression stroke, it forces the fuel mixture up into the hot tube. As the compressed mixture travels deeper into the tube, it arrives at a point where the tube—which was preheated by a Bunsen burner or similar device inside the chimney—is hot enough to ignite the fuel charge.

Early hot tubes were made from platinum or porcelain. Platinum was very expensive. Porcelain could withstand constant contact with the open flame but was easily broken. Later, a less-expensive and more-durable design used a nickel alloy for the tube. Hot tubes were made in lengths from 6 to 12 inches. Hot-tube chimneys were normally made from cast iron and were lined with asbestos. Engine builders had many ways with which to fasten their hot tubes and chimneys to the engine. Some were tapped into the heads or cylinders; others were set or clamped in position. There were many different diameter chimneys, ranging in size from around 1-1/2 inches up to 2-1/8 inches. The asbestos lining helped maintain the hot tube's temperature and conserved on fuel needed for the Bunsen burner.

The Bunsen burner's flame is directed at the tube inside the chimney. As the flame comes in contact with the tube, the tube begins to absorb heat until it is cherry red in color. Preheating the tube normally takes about 10 minutes, after which the engine is ready to be started.

By adjusting the flame's point of contact on the hot tube, the point of ignition can be changed. Only experienced operators can regulate all the variables of hot-tube ignition and maximize engine output. Using his experience, the operator often needs to make adjustments while the engine is running to ensure top engine performance.

The variables associated with the ignition point made the hot-tube engine lose favor. The length of

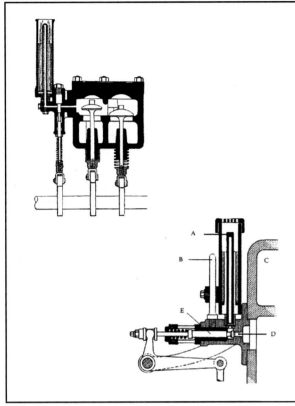

These two hot tubes use timing valves that control engine ignition. The valves are operated mechanically allowing the fuel charge to enter the combustion chamber at a predetermined moment during the engine's cycle. The parts are commonly called: A - hot tube, B - clamp rod, C - cylinder, D - fuel mixture passageway, and E - is the timing valve.

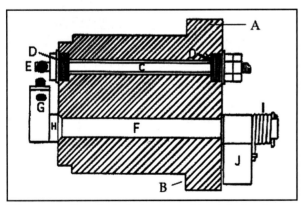

This cross section of a typical make-and-break igniter shows all of its major components. The igniter's parts are called: A - flange, B - gasket, C - stationary electrode, D - mica washers, E - stationary point, F - movable electrode stem, G - movable electrode stem point, H - collar, and I - coil spring.

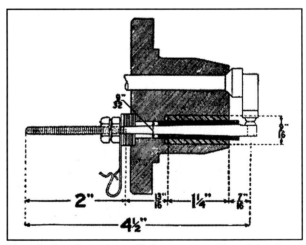

These igniter dimensions will give you some idea of the size of a typical igniter.

the tube used affects ignition timing, and the size of the tubing affects the heating requirement, as well as the amount of the fuel mixture being compressed into it. Tube temperature is critical for ignition. If the tube is not hot enough, the fuel simply does not ignite. The type of fuel used is also a factor in ignition, as different fuels ignite at different temperatures.

High-speed engines are not well suited for hot-tube ignition. The hot tube does not recover or keep up with engines running above 800 rpm because compression changes in the cylinder affect tube performance. As the fuel mixture's compression ratio changes, so does the ignition point. This causes the fuel mixture not to come in contact with the tube's ignition point, or it affects the engine timing cycle. As in all engines, the fuel mixture itself is critical to proper ignition. If the charge does not have the proper mix of air and fuel, the fuel mixture could not be ignited.

The hot-tube ignition system was improved over time to overcome some of the shortcomings of the device's design. One common way of improving the hot tube was to add a timing valve. These poppet-valve timing methods are more accurate and provide better results than results experienced with nonvalved engines. The valves open and close during the engine cycle, timing the fuel charge's entry into the hot tube. Not until just a split second before the point of igni-

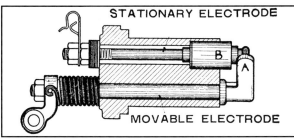

Pictured here in cross section is an International Harvester Co. make-and-break igniter. It is designed for use on their Mogul side-shaft engines. The igniter's movable electrode is shown at A with B showing its stationary electrode. The movable electrode is spring loaded.

The International Harvester Co. make-and-break igniter used on Mogul side-shaft engines.

Stover Igniter

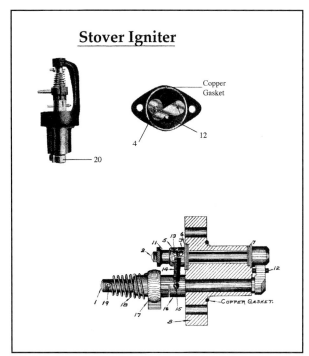

Many engines manufactured by Stover Manufacturing and Engine Co. were built with make-and-break igniters. Stover hammer-break igniters are illustrated here, showing the following parts: 1-movable electrode, 2-stationary electrode, 3-washer -stationary electrode, 4-platinum points, 5-stationary electrode nut, 6-mica washer, 7-mica washer, 8-igniter body (which was a casting), 11-thumb screw, 12-limit pin, 13-spring pin in the igniter body, 14-small igniter spring, 15-movable electrode taper pin, 16-movable electrode collar, 17-movable electrode spring sleeve, 18-large igniter spring, 19-movable electrode spring pin, and 20 - bearing.

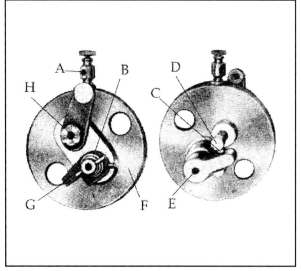

This illustration of the Galloway low-tension igniter shows the following parts of the igniter: A - electrical wire hold down, B - coil spring, C - point, D - stationary electrode contact rod, E-movable electrode, F - flange, G - pawl and H - stationary electrode.

This five-horsepower round-rod Galloway low-tension igniter was fastened to the engine with two stud bolts.

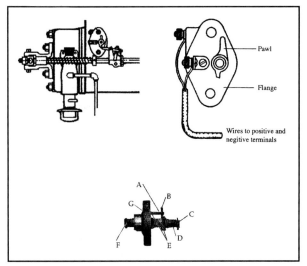

Pawl

Flange

Wires to positive and negitive terminals

A

B

G

C

F

E

D

This illustration shows the parts of a 1918 three-horsepower Fuller and Johnson Model N igniter. The parts are labeled as follows: A - stop pin, B - catch, C - movable electrode, D - coil spring E - binding posts (positive - negative), F - igniter points and G - igniter flange.

tion does the valve allow the charge to enter the hot-tube passageway. The timing valves are generally cycled from a side shaft on the engine.

The hot-tube igniter was the common device used to ignite the fuel mixture in early internal combustion engines, but this device was losing its place in engine manufacturing by the early 1900s as more reliable methods of ignition were beginning to be used. The use of the hot tube, however, did remain much longer than would be expected. These engines could still be found working in the oil and gas fields well into the late 1970s and early 1980s. Today, almost all of these engines have been relegated to the collectors and restorers, but there just might be a few waiting in the field to be found by an engine enthusiast.

Igniters

Igniters came in several different types. I will discuss three types of electric spark igniters in detail. First is the common hammer-type "make-and-break" igniter. The jump-spark igniter will be detailed second. The third device was called a wiper-break igniter.

Make-and-Break Igniter

The make-and-break igniter produces electrical spark for ignition by the sudden break or separation of the contact points. This simple mechanical unit was manufactured in many different configurations. A common place to attach an igniter on side-shaft engines is through the head of the cylinder. The igniter protrudes through the water jacket and cylinder wall and into the combustion chamber. The side-shaft engine was designed with a mechanical trip arm to separate the points of the igniter. Air-cooled engines not having a water jacket have a bore through the cylinder wall that accommodates the igniter. Vertical-engine manufacturers positioned the igniter on the side of the vertical cylinder. A vertical push arm working off the cam eccentric engages the trip mechanism on this engine. Throttle-governed horizontal engines have the igniter positioned on the working side of the engine. The igniter is mechanically tripped from the exhaust-valve control shaft. Many manufacturers designed a separate shaft or link arm to trip the igniter.

When started, the timing of the engine is set up with the tripping of the igniter points. The actual breaking of the points is done mechanically. Igniters also require the battery and coil or magneto to be at the peak of its cycle to produce a spark hot enough to ignite the fuel.

Let's examine the construction of a common igniter, beginning with the body of the unit. The body is flanged and fits into a hole in the cylinder wall. As the flange comes to rest on the cylinder or head wall, this positions the points within the combustion chamber. A gasket made of either copper or a combination of copper and asbestos is fitted to seal the igniter. This gasket prevents any leakage or escape of the combusted gases between the igniter flange and the combustion chamber. The stationary electrode passes through an oversized hole or bore in the igniter body. Mica washers are set in a counter bore to insulate the stationary electrode from grounding on the engine housing. Insulation around the stationary electrode is necessary to ensure a satisfactory electrical circuit. If the stationary electrode fails to remain insulated from the engine body, the igniter will ground out. If grounding of the igniter occurs, no electrical circuit will exist. The igniter will then be unable to furnish the engine with a spark to start the engine. One of the contact points is found on the inside end of the stem of the stationary electrode. The wire from the positive terminal of the battery and coil is attached to the opposite end of this electrode. The movable electrode fits through the other bore in the igniter. The bore is machined oversize, eliminating any binding of the movable electrode. This second contact point and stem are fastened to the inside end of the movable electrode. A collar serves as a spacer and fits a countersunk surface in the igniter body. Some igniter manufacturers used a mica washer in this area. The washer and countersink stop the escape of gases from the cylinder through the igniter body.

Adjustment of the movable electrode is important to maintain free movement. Any binding of the electrode will prevent the igniter from cycling properly. Two springs exert constant pressure against the pawl and igniter body to seal in combustion gases and provide the pawl with the proper tension to cycle the points. The springs also hold the points apart prior to the pawl being pushed by a moving rod. The rod pushing on the pawl closes the points and completes the electrical circuit. The pawl then cycles forward and begins to slip from contact with the pawl. During this time, the points remain closed. This pushing of the pawl tensions the springs in the opposite direction. As the rod continues through its cycle, it slips off the pawl. As contact is suddenly lost, the second spring snaps the pawl and movable electrode in the opposite direction. This violent rotation of the movable electrode and pawl creates the separation of the points. As the points break, a spark occurs. It is this spark that ignites the fuel mixture in the cylinder.

This description of the ignition process explains why it is called "make-and-break" ignition. The making of the circuit does not occur until just moments before the circuit will be broken. The points, which close or complete the electrical circuit, are only held closed long enough to charge the electrical circuit with energy so that when the points are separated, a spark will occur between them. This make-and-break design conserves electrical current and extends battery life. During much of the engine cycle, the circuit and the battery are at rest. Not until the points are closed does this system use any battery power or charge the coil with electrical energy. As soon as the points spark or the current is broken, the battery and coil are at rest until the points come into contact once again.

By loosening and tightening the movable electrode, the proper gap distance between the fixed and stationary points can be adjusted. All igniter points can be adjusted to the proper gap many times before needing replacement. When the points need replacing, the new points are installed through the same holes in the movable and stationary electrode stems. These points holes generally are smooth, requiring a tapered or pinned fit, but some manufacturers went as far as to drill and tap the points holes. After installing new points, filing, checking, resetting, and gapping of the points is required.

During the process of ignition, small amounts of the platinum (or other material used for points) are transferred from one point surface to the other. The

A 1918 three-horsepower Fuller and Johnson Model N igniter.

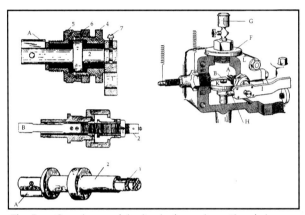

The Foos Co. wipe spark igniter is shown in sectional view. Foos igniters used a rotating point that wiped across the stationary point. This action cleans the contact and produces an excellent spark as contact is broken. A priming cup is used to deliver a small amount of gasoline directly into the igniter chamber. The parts that make up the Foos igniter are: A - revolving contact blade or point, B - stationary contact blade or point, F- removable cap, G - priming cup, H - thumb screw, I - revolving electrode spring crank, J - removable electrode, K - intake valve, 1 - revolving electrode spring crank, 2 - shaft, 3 - notch, 4 - male nut, 5 - male/female nut, 6 - lock nut, and 7 - screw.

metal transfer is caused by the burning away of the metal point during the electrical sparking of the igniter. By changing the current flow from one contact point to the other, the process can be reversed, extending point life.

Understanding the principles of make-and-break ignition is a good starting place when trouble-shooting your engine. By understanding these basic concepts of the electrical circuit and how the battery, coil, and igniter function, you will be able to cure many engine starting and running problems. The following specific examples are variations of make-and-break ignition that will help to further your understanding of this sparking device.

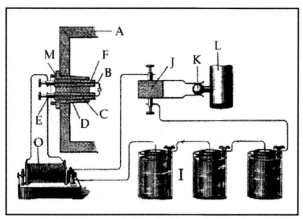

Jump spark igniters are designed with stationary electrodes. The spark must jump the gap that exists between the two electrodes to produce a spark. Several parts make up this type igniter and they are called: A - cylinder head, B - point, C - copper conductors, D - igniter body, E - wire terminal, F - porcelain insulator, I - batteries, J - spring contact, K - knob, L - rotating shaft or rod, M - jump spark igniter, and O - the coil.

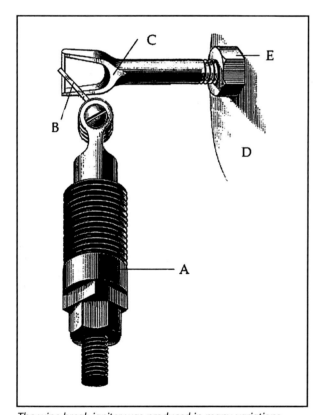

The wipe break igniter was produced in many variations. In this illustration the stirrup is attached to the piston and makes contact as the piston works back and forth. If the stirrup is unable to make contact with the spring contact no ignition will occur. This ignition method limited, or at least made it difficult for engine operators to advance or retard the ignition spark. The igniter's common parts are called: A - plug, B - helical spring contact, C - stirrup, D - engine head and E - lock nut.

Stover Make-and-Break Igniter

The Stover Igniter is a make-and-break design of igniter. This igniter uses an outboard bearing to support the movable electrode and prevent it from binding in the igniter body. A copper gasket is fitted into a recess cut in the flange of the igniter body. The gasket is then tightened between the igniter flange and the cylinder to seal in combustion gases. The points were made from platinum for an exceptionally long life. When adjusting this igniter, the manufacturer recommended setting it up with the points in the open, idle position. Stover specifications show that the point gap should be about 1/16 inch. Through the years, I have had some degree of success with points that are gapped from 1/16 inch to just over 1/8 inch, but you may need to experiment with this adjustment as you tune your engine. Normally, these early machines are pretty forgiving and adjustment is not that critical, so don't become intimidated if you feel that you have missed the adjustment by a couple thousandths.

Mogul Make-and-Break Igniter

The International Harvester Co. Mogul side-shaft engine igniter mounts in the cylinder head of the engine. Gaskets used on the inside of the igniter eliminate any leakage of the combustible fuel. The side shaft on the engine controls the igniter cycle, and a coil spring closes the points during each completed cycle of the engine. As the engine comes around to the power stroke, the linkage disengages and the igniter spring rotates back extremely fast, causing the points to separate. Quick breaking of the points is very important in order to ensure a hot spark with proper duration. After point separation, the spark is generated between the two point surfaces, causing the fuel to ignite.

The Mogul igniter as pictured was very solidly built. My experience with this engine testifies to the reliability of IHC's igniter. I have run a 4-horsepower, skidded Mogul engine for thousands of hours. The igniter has yet to fail. I'd wager that the engine has already had a few thousand more hours on it than I know about, too. If I've noticed any weak link at all, it is the hole in the pawl on the front of the igniter. As the adjustment rod has snapped back and forth through it countless times, the pawl seems to have suffered from abrasion, and the pawl's rod hole has enlarged somewhat. Not too bad for being 81 years old, as this engine was built in 1914.

Galloway Make-and-Break Igniter

The William Galloway Co. made another style of make-and-break igniter. When examining this device, the first difference noticed is that the flange is round. The movable electrode is operated by two springs. One spring remains in tension underneath the adjustment screw. This holds the points open until its tension is overcome by the rod that closes on the pawl. The coil spring attaches to the outside end of the igniter and begins to tension itself as the pawl is cocked by the actuating rod. After the rod disengages the pawl, the spring snaps the electrode shaft into reverse. The movable electrode and the pawl suddenly rotate back against a stop that is pinned through the movable electrode. This forces the movable electrode to separate the points, causing a gap to exist and a spark to jump between the two point surfaces. Sparking is once again induced, and ignition results.

The point-gap adjustment screw provides a mechanical stop that does not allow the points to be opened beyond the proper gap adjustment. Wires from the battery and coil are attached to a brass wire hold-down, on the stationary electrode. The stationary electrode on this unit is only a round piece of rod. Mica washers are used to insulate the stationary electrode from the engine casting. The movable electrode's platinum point makes contact with the round rod or stationary electrode to complete the electrical circuit. As wear or exchange of metal takes place, the round rod requires filing or dressing the same as any other contact surface or point. By maintaining the proper gap and providing the platinum point with good matching surfaces, optimum igniter performance is achieved. The ground wire from the battery is connected to a similar hold-down tapped into the flange of the igniter. It is important that these contacts and connection points are never loose. Loose wires or connections spell trouble when it comes to starting any engine.

Fuller & Johnson Make-and-Break Igniter

The Fuller & Johnson igniter was yet another make-and-break design. On this igniter, the movable electrode runs straight through the flange and body of the unit. A small, round rod, about 3/16 inch in diameter, is used to stop the travel of the movable electrode. That means the point gap has to be adjusted by moving the stationary electrode to the right or left. The stationary electrode has mica washers to insulate it from grounding on the engine. A brass stud was tapped into the side of the flange to accommodate the attachment of the ground wire. The wire from the battery/coil is fastened to the stationary electrode. Two springs are again used to activate the motion of the movable electrode. The rod comes into contact with this igniter from the underside and trips off the bottom of the unit, again causing the movable electrode to swing back and open the points. A hole was drilled through the flange and into the opening of the movable electrode to allow oiling of the electrode.

The igniter uses a flat gasket between its flange and the engine casting to seal the gases inside the cylinder. No recess was cut in this flange. By eliminating machine processes like this, even early companies showed signs of cost cutting in their manufacturing practices. After studying the pictures of the Fuller & Johnson igniter, you may conclude that this is a very

The spark plug is also used as an ignition device for stationary engines. Spark plugs require high-tension electrical current to force an electrical spark across the air gap created between the two stationary electrodes. Spark plugs have been made in thousands of different shapes and sizes over the years.

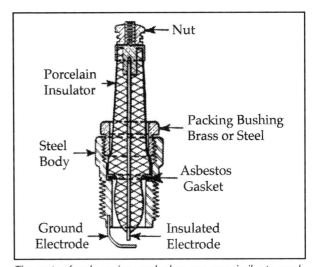

The parts of early engine spark plugs are very similar to spark plugs of today. An ignition wire is normally attached to the nut on the top of the spark plug. The spark plugs part names are: the nut, porcelain insulator, steel body, ground electrode, packing bushing (brass or steel), asbestos gasket and an insulated electrode.

simple design. Reliability and function, however, were not sacrificed.

Foos Make-and-Break Igniter

The Foos-designed igniter functions differently from any of the previously featured igniters. Wipe-spark igniters were commonly found on Foos engines, which were manufactured in Springfield, Ohio.

On the Foos wipe-spark igniter, the two electrodes are flat, and the points are made from spring steel. During operation of the Foos igniter, the movable electrode rotates until it comes in contact with the stationary contact. The movable electrode is put in motion by the cycling of the igniter rod. As the

A glass-cased Edison-Lalande battery is pictured here. Glass-cased batteries were very fragile. These wet-cell batteries produce sufficient current for low or high-tension ignition systems.

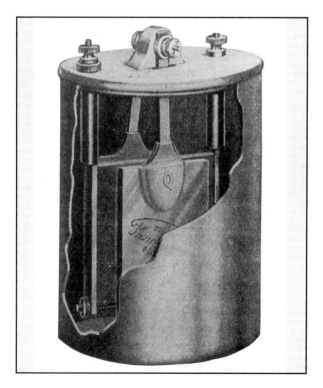

movable electrode rotates through its cycle, it presses down the stationary electrode, causing it to flex until the movable electrode slips off of the stationary electrode. This abrupt break or tripping action of the points creates the gap needed for the spark. At the very moment the points separate, a gap is formed, and the spark passed from one electrode contact surface to the other.

A disadvantage of using the spring-steel points inside the inlet chamber is the problems created by the extreme temperatures of combustion. This continual heating and cooling eventually damages the temper in the steel. Spring-steel points were not well tempered in these early years, and as the temper was lost, they had a tendency to break. However, there are some advantages to this design. The contact surfaces are kept clean by the constant wiping action of the points. This prevents the points from fouling, or at least makes it very hard to foul them.

The body of this igniter provides the engine owner with an access hole in the top of the igniter to service the points or contact blades. All of the components of this igniter can be removed from the cast igniter body for servicing. To advance the spark, rotate the thumb screw while the engine is running. Rotate it back in the opposite direction prior to starting the engine to retard the spark and prevent backfiring. The points are centered directly over the intake valve. This puts the points right in line with the fuel mixture's pathway to the cylinder. The priming cup is directly over a removable cup. Loading this cup with gas and then opening it allows the gas mixture to flood the inlet chamber. This charge of gas for starting the engine is then in position to be ignited. The revolving electrode consists of a shaft that holds the point or contact blade. The revolving electrode is insulated with mica to ensure that the electric circuit does not ground to the engine housing. The shaft is fitted with two replaceable graphite-filled bushings that hold the shaft in alignment and allow the shaft to turn freely. The revolving electrode crank is fitted with a spring, which engages in a notch in the electrode shaft. After the spring engages with the shaft, the shaft rotates with the crank arm. A screw holds the revolving electrode spring crank in contact with the revolving electrode shaft, and the screw fits into a notch cut in the shaft.

This elaborate igniter was very well designed and can give years of reliable service. The igniter body is a part of the engine casting. All the parts that make up the igniter are assembled through drilled and tapped bores and are adjustable from the outside of the engine by opening the top cap and unscrewing the assemblies. Parts can then be removed, repaired, or re-

Left
The enameled steel-cased Edison-Lalande and similar wet-cell or common storage batteries quickly replaced the fragile glass-cased battery.

placed, and a final check of the contact surfaces can then be made through the top cap opening.

We have discussed the common make-and-break igniters and several specific manufacturer's designs. We will now move on to the jump-spark igniters.

The Jump-Spark Igniter

The jump-spark igniter is a stationary igniter. The points remain at the gapped position and do not rotate or revolve. The body of the igniter is threaded into the head of a cylinder or through the side. This positions the platinum points well into the combustion space of the cylinder. Two holes were bored through the body of the igniter. Inserted in the bores are two porcelain insulators. By using the porcelain insulators, both points are insulated from the engine and one another. This sets up the electrical path for ignition spark. Two copper conductors run through the porcelain insulators of the igniter. Attached to the ends of the copper conductor are two platinum points. At the ends of the two points, a gap is adjusted to allow the spark to jump from one point to the other. It is this forced jump of the spark that gives this unit its name, the jump-spark igniter. The batteries furnish the coil with electrical current. The spring contact is located near the rotating shaft on the engine. As the shaft rotates with the engine, a knob on the shaft passes through the spring contact on every revolution. During the time that the knob is engaged with the spring, two sparks are generated between the points—the first spark coming with the initial spring contact, the second when the knob loses contact with the spring.

Several dry-cell batteries are commonly used in a series circuit to produce electrical current for stationary engine ignition. Dry-cell batteries of today are not much different than the 1.5-volt dry cells manufactured at the turn of the century.

This original battery box was supplied by the Galloway factory with its five-horsepower engine. The box held dry-cell batteries, an ignition coil, and hand tools for the engine. Many times, an electrical knife switch was attached to the outside of box for opening and closing the electrical circuit.

Many buzz coils were housed in wooden boxes. Buzz coils produce high-tension electrical current used for jump spark ignition. Tremblers control the ignition sparking cycles of the coil.

The American Type E-2 coil produces low-tension current. This design is typical of hundreds of coils that were produced for this purpose. Low-tension coils were made with an iron core around which hundreds of wraps of copper wire were then wound. The coil wires were then attached to the coil's two wire terminals.

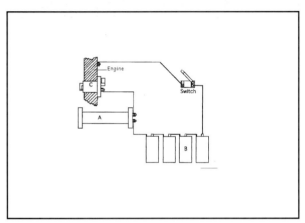

In order for any internal combustion engine to operate, an electrical spark must be delivered to the engine's combustion chamber. The electrical circuit and all components must be correctly connected to produce this spark at the precise time the engine requires it. In this illustration, a typical low-tension ignition circuit is shown. Low-tension ignition is generally used with engines equipped with hammer-break igniters. The major components of this low-tension electrical circuit are: A-the spark coil, B-a dry cell batteries, and C-the engine's make-and-break igniter.

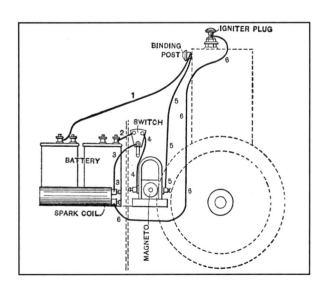

The knob on the engine's shaft is what times the engine. By rotating the knob, the spark can be advanced or retarded. This knob is usually attached to the valve shaft on a four-cycle engine and allows one spark cycle every two revolutions of crankshaft. On a two-cycle engine, the knob is usually attached to the valve crankshaft. Two-cycle engines require a spark cycle on every revolution of the crankshaft. This unit has no moving parts, so wear is minimal, but the points require constant attention and adjustment.

Wiper-Break Igniter

On the wiper-break igniter, a threaded plug is screwed into the cylinder wall of the engine, and a helical spring is attached to the end of the threaded plug. A nonconducting insulator runs through the

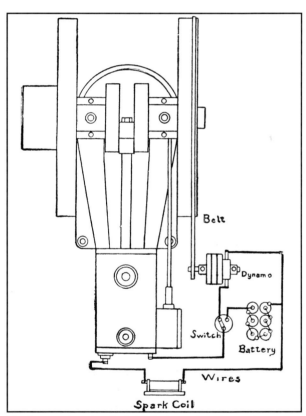

The low-tension electrical circuit shown here has a dynamo added to the circuit. This circuit uses dry-cell batteries, a spark coil, a two-position electrical switch and a dynamo connected to a make-and-break igniter. Use this wiring scheme when running an engine on a low-tension coil or switching it over to run on a dynamo.

Left
Another low-tension electrical circuit is detailed here. This system is made up of dry-cell batteries, a spark coil, a make-and-break igniter, a magneto, and a dual-position knife switch. Follow this wiring plan if you are using a low-tension ignition system and wish to switch from the battery and coil over to a magneto after the engine has started.

center of the plug and holds the spring shaft in alignment. It also keeps the spring shaft from grounding out on the cylinder. A threaded stirrup is fastened to the engine's piston by a lock nut. As the piston comes up in its cycle, the stirrup comes in contact with the spring. As the stirrup continues through the cycle, it loses contact with the spring, causing a spark to be created. This cycle happens each time the piston approaches the top of the cylinder. The return of the piston on the downward stroke causes the reverse to happen and another spark is generated. This spark, however, is not of any value to the engine. Wiper-break ignition is inefficient because it makes twice as many sparks as the engine can use, so batteries are depleted much faster using this type of ignition. Wiper-break ignition needs a powerful battery and coil to supply the igniter with the necessary current to produce this continual sparking.

Spark Plug Ignition

Spark plugs have passed the test of time. They haven't changed much in appearance in over 100 years. Plugs were used in two-, four-, and eight-cycle engines. Spark plugs can be found in the cylinder heads of almost every working internal combustion engine used today. They are found in everything from automobiles to weed wackers.

The spark plug's purpose is to supply an electric spark to ignite the fuel mixture. The spark plug is wired into the ignition system, and the spark jumps the air gap between the two nonmovable internal electrodes of the spark plug when the ignition system discharges.

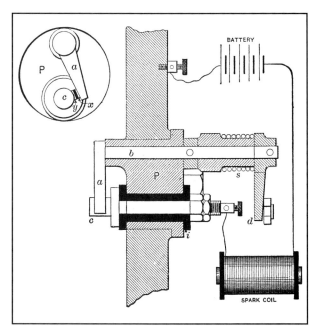

Illustrated here is a low-tension electrical circuit using a battery, spark coil, and a make-and-break igniter. Follow this wiring diagram when using mechanically tripped igniters.

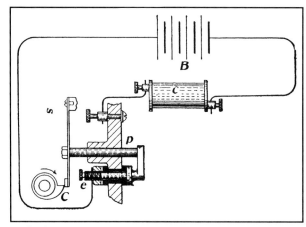

In this low-tension ignition circuit, batteries, a spark coil, a make-and-break igniter, and a crankshaft breaker are wired into the completed electrical circuit. The diagram shows that the crankshaft breaker is used to time the engine spark. As contact is made and broken at C, a spark is produced.

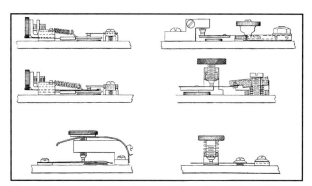

Shown here are six typical buzz coil trembler designs. The trembler can be adjusted as battery wears down and output decreases. By adjusting the air gap between the magnetic contacts in relationship to the batteries' power level, proper sparking qualities can be maintained throughout the batteries' life.

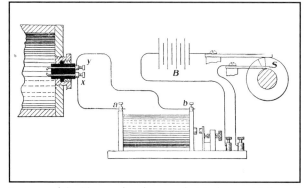

Jump spark ignition works when an electrical current is forced to jump an air gap. In this illustration, an ignition system that uses a buzz coil, crankshaft breaker, and a battery is featured. This is a very common high-tension ignition system. Refer to this diagram when wiring an engine for jump spark ignition.

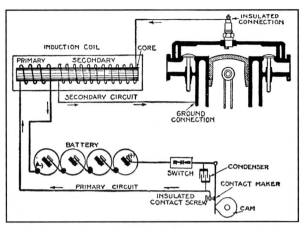

In this high-tension jump spark ignition system a spark plug, several dry-cell batteries, a single pole switch, a buzz coil, and a cam breaker are used. Notice that the batteries here are connected in a series circuit.

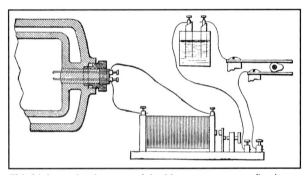

This high-tension jump spark ignition system uses a fixed electrode, wet-cell battery, buzz coil, and crankshaft breaker to complete the circuit. Generally only one wet-cell battery is necessary for this type of ignition system.

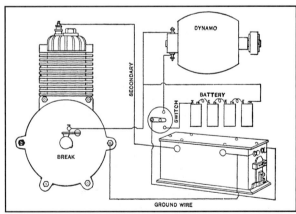

Jump spark ignition that uses a dynamo, dry-cell batteries, a buzz coil, a spark plug, a two-position knife switch, and a cam breaker represents a fairly complex electrical circuit for early stationary engines. Notice how the dynamo or the batteries and buzz coil can be use for ignition simply by throwing the switch from one circuit to the other. This allows the engine to be started on battery power, but once started it could be run using electrical current produced by the dynamo.

The spark plug's threaded body is found in various configurations but all have a threaded base. The threads serve three distinct purposes. First, threads provide a method of securing the plug into the cylinder head. Second, they seal the plug in the combustion chamber and keep gases from escaping during the operation of the engine. Third, they provide a method for grounding the electrical circuit.

The threaded surfaces are compressed against each other as the plug is tightened into the threaded port in the cylinder head. Tightening creates a good surface that does not corrode easily. This connection between the engine and spark plug creates the ground for the ignition circuit. Once the plug's base is secure against the cylinder, the grounded electrode completes the electrical circuit.

The insulated electrode connects to the coil or magneto wire by the threaded nut at the top of the plug. Through this insulated electrode the electrical charge flows. As the electrical field in the coil or magneto is collapsed, the current overcomes the resistance of the air gap between the electrodes and the electrical charge crosses over to the grounded electrode, causing a spark. This is the all-important spark needed for ignition.

Some spark plugs can be taken apart for cleaning. A gasket provides a seal between the two halves of the body and functions as a cushion for the porcelain insulator, to protect it from cracking due to over-

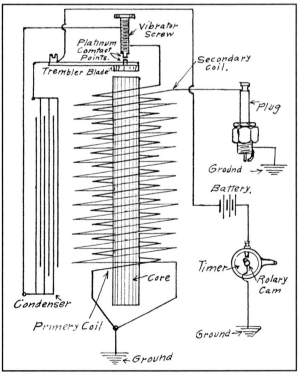

This high-tension jump spark ignition system used a battery, buzz coil, rotary cam timer, condenser, and spark plug to ignite the engine's fuel charge.

tightening. The plug need only be tightened enough to seal the insulator and the two halves of the body from leaking under compression. Insulators were usually made of mica or porcelain.

Electrical Systems

Hundreds of thousands of stationary engines employed make-and-break or jump-spark ignition. Low-tension electrical spark is produced by an igniter, spark coil, battery, knife switch, and connecting wires. High-tension or jump-spark ignition uses a spark plug, buzz coil, timer, battery, knife switch, and connecting wire. Magnetos, generators, or dynamos can be used in place of batteries. The sparks produced using high- or low-tension electrical current are each sufficient to ignite the fuel mixture in a stationary engine, but the components differ in each system. Being able to identify various parts of each system, and understanding how they function, will ensure that you can maintain and repair the engine's ignition system.

Batteries

Batteries are an important component in an electrical system. During the time stationary engines were being manufactured, batteries came in many different designs, sizes, shapes, and outputs. Edison batteries are examples of early wet-cell batteries. Zinc- and copper-oxide plates are suspended in a caustic-soda electrolyte to form the battery. Edison battery cases are made from glass, porcelain, and enameled steel. The positive and negative terminals are located on the ceramic cover. The top is removable, allowing the battery to be serviced by adding electrolyte or oil through a hole in the center of the cover. Edison batteries were supplied with a small bottle of paraffin oil

that was poured on top of the electrolyte. Paraffin oil prevents corrosion, slows the evaporation rate of the electrolyte, and suppresses the electrolyte's chemical action. The glass-jar Edison batteries are very fragile. Extreme care must be taken so that the battery is not damaged while in use. Traditional rectangular-shaped storage batteries were used during these early years as well. These batteries were much more durable than the glass-jar-style batteries. However, some of these storage batteries were also constructed of glass. To-

The Webster oscillating low-tension magneto is found on thousands of stationary engines. Permanent magnets are standard design for these magnetos. Webster magnetos are tripped mechanically, usually by the engine pushrod.

The Accurate low-tension magneto is equipped with a permanent magnet and drive gear. Magnetos of this type are normally driven at twice the engine's speed by a crankshaft pinion gear. A terminal can be seen on the opposite side of the magneto's drive gear. The ignition wire was connected from this terminal to the engine's igniter electrode.

The Motsinger Auto-Sparker produces electrical current as its armature is rotated. It can be friction- or belt-driven from an engine flywheel or crankshaft pulley. The Auto Sparker's speed had to be regulated below 1,200 rpm. It is equipped with a flyball governor to prevent it from overspeeding. Prolonged over-speeding will cause internal component damage.

day's 6- and 12-volt wet-cell car, truck, and marine batteries can be used for stationary-engine ignition in exactly the same manner as the storage batteries of nearly 100 years ago.

Dry-cell batteries are a great substitute for wet-cell batteries. Many manufacturers supplied dry cells straight from the factory with their engines. Being small and light in weight, they are easy to transport. These dry cells were constructed in a zinc-lined container with blotting paper, a carbon element (+), and an electrolyte made from sal ammoniac zinc oxide and zinc chloride. Dry cells can be checked with a volt and amp meter. A #6 ignition dry-cell battery should test at 1.4 volts and from 25 to 30 amps when new. The battery is almost exhausted when the meter reads 8 amps or less. Most early cylindrical dry-cell batteries were 1.5 volt. Today, dry-cell batteries are commonly found in 1.5, 6, and 12 volts. If you are using 1.5-volt batteries to supply electrical power, several batteries must be linked together to produce the necessary current output. Dry-cell batteries should operate an engine for a full year before they need to be replaced. An electrical short or an unfavorable condition will shorten battery life considerably. Protecting the batteries and coil from damage and a poor environment is important. Battery boxes were almost always supplied from the factory to house the battery(s) and coil.

Spark and Buzz Coils

There are two basic types of coils used for ignition purposes. The first type is a spark coil, used for low-tension make-and-break or hammer-break ignition. The buzz coil is used with jump-spark ignition and produces high-tension electrical current.

A spark coil is easy to identify. Visual inspection of this device will disclose that only two terminal posts are affixed to the unit. The positive wire lead from the

battery is connected to one of the terminals; another wire is run from the second terminal to the igniter's stationary electrode; and the ground cable completes the electrical circuit. The grounding wire passes through a knife switch and terminates at a grounding point on the engine. Spark coils can be found in many different sizes and shapes. The strongest coils have many wraps of copper wire around the iron core. Weight is sometimes a good identifying factor for a strong coil. A heavy coil would suggest that more copper wire was wound around the coil's core than on a light one. A simple check to perform on an old spark coil is a continuity test. If the coil checks out good with an electrical multi-tester, suggesting that there is no electrical short, chances are the coil is good.

Buzz coils are normally rectangular in shape and many have wooden cases. Terminals are usually found on the side or top of the coil. A vibrator or trembler usually is positioned on one end of the buzz coil. The purpose of the vibrator is to rapidly open and close the coil's primary circuit. This action causes the primary circuit to break and then demagnetize the coil's core. During the instant this all takes place, a spark is forced across the air gap between two stationary electrodes. This sparking sequence can be repeated by a buzz coil 60 to 100 times in less than a second. While it's operating, a buzz coil produces a steady stream of sparks that can be observed between the two stationary spark-plug electrodes. The vibrator is a good identification marking on the buzz coil. If a coil has a vibrator, then it is a buzz coil and is used for jump-spark ignition.

The vibrator is adjustable, and the thumb nut on the vibrator adjusts the distance between the coil points and the coil hammer core. As batteries become weak, this distance has to be closed. It is the action of the hammer being attracted to the core that separates the points. Buzz coils are designed with condensers that absorb the induced current in the coil's primary circuit, improving the action of the coil to a

A Sumter magneto can be seen just behind the engine's water hopper. A single wire is run from the magneto terminal to the engine's igniter electrode. The magneto is bolted directly to the engine's base, which provides a permanent circuit ground. The magneto is driven by a pinion gear, appearing just below the magneto's drive gear.

The Tritt Electric generator is flyball-governed and friction-driven. There are four permanent magnets attached to the sides of the pot metal armature housing. Lubrication is done through the cup greasers at each end of the armature shaft.

great extent. By preventing this flow of current, magnetism within the coil collapses rapidly and produces its greatest effect on the secondary winding. The condenser also stops the contact points from arcing, thus extending the useful life of the points.

The timing device completes the electrical circuit at the precise moment ignition is required. The duration time that the cam has with the contact point determines how long current from the buzz coil is drawn for spark. Timing is set by adjusting the moment of spark with the cam and contact point. Early contact advances the spark, while later contact retards it.

Magnetos, Generators, and Dynamos

Through the use of a magneto, generator, or dynamo, batteries can be eliminated or used sparingly. Numerous manufacturers made these extremely dependable electrical devices: Motsinger Device Manufacturing Co., Hendricks Novelty Co., Wizard Magnetos made by The Hercules Electric Co., Lemke Electric, Thordson Electric, Dayton Electrical Manufacturing, Chicago Coil, Splitdorf, Webster, and Pfanstiehl to name a few. They were made in various physical sizes and designed for many different applications. Magnetos, generators, and dynamos produce electrical current of either high or low tension. Low-tension magnetos and dynamos sometimes use the spark coil in the electrical system. The coil intensifies the spark much in the same way it does when used with batteries. Generators and dynamos connected to a buzz coil produce high-tension electrical current. High-tension magnetos are self contained and are usually directly wired to the jump-spark igniter.

The Accurate, Sumter, and Tritt Electric generators produce low-tension electrical current. A gear fitted to the generator shaft works off the crankshaft pinion gear. The Accurate, Elkhardt, and Sumter generators produce constant electrical current. They can be wired directly to the stationary electrode of the igniter. Rotary-style generators such as the Sumter can be timed for peak electrical output. This is accomplished by aligning gear teeth on the generator with corresponding teeth in the pinion gear.

The Wico high-tension jump spark magneto is one of the most durable magnetos ever built. The magneto is housed in a removable three-piece cover. The high-tension terminal is protruding from the left side of the outside cover. Lubrication is accomplished by dripping oil through the oil hole located on the front cover.

The Wizard generator is similar to the Tritt Electric generator. Notice that this unit uses two permanent magnets rather than four. The Wizard magneto has a brass body or armature housing. Magneto speed regulation is accomplished with the use of a flyball governor. The armature bearings are lubricated through two oil holes on the outer ends of its brass housing.

The Olds six-horsepower engine is equipped with a cast iron water hopper. Water hoppers provided portable engines with a convenient method of water cooling. Coolant is poured into the hopper from above and, once the hopper is filled, a cover is placed over the opening. The cover kept dirt out of the hopper and helped condense steam escaping from the hopper.

The Lobee positive-displacement water pump is gear driven. It's designed to circulate coolant continuously. There are many variations of this type pump, as gear-driven water pumps were widely used on stationary engines.

The Alamo tray cooling system is designed with several trays stacked on top of one another to chill the coolant. Coolant fell from one tray to the next and into the holding tank below. Tray cooling is a more efficient cooling process than the tank cooling method.

The Wizard low-tension constant-output generator uses a friction wheel to rotate its armature. Speed is regulated on friction-driven generators and dynamos with a centrifugal governor. As rpm increases, governor weights fly outward, causing the friction wheel to lose contact with its driving surface. As the generator or dynamo loses speed, the governor allows the friction wheel to once again make contact with the flywheel. Another method of rotating these units is by means of a belt. A leather belt placed around a flywheel or pulley connects the generator or dynamo with the engine and rotates the unit as the engine runs.

High-tension magnetos supply electrical current for jump-spark ignition systems. An example of a high-quality high-tension magneto is the Wico EK magneto manufactured by the Wico Electric Co. of West Springfield, Massachusetts. The Wico EK magneto is probably one of the most commonly found high-tension magnetos. Its design allows for at least three methods of "tripping" or cycling the magneto. A wire is run from the magneto's high-tension terminal directly to the spark plug. The magneto is grounded through its base or connecting points, completing the electrical circuit. All these characteristics make the Wico easy to use on a multitude of different engines.

Many engines have a dual electrical system wired into place. Battery power is used to start an engine, but after the engine has started, battery power is switched off, and a magneto, generator, or dynamo supplies continuous electrical power. A knife switch wired into the electrical circuit is used to change the electrical from one source to another. The knife switch allows only one source of power to be used at a time.

Strong batteries, coils, mags, generators, and dynamos are the key to success with an electric ignition

The Sure Go engine was manufactured by the Wogoman Manufacturing Co. It is designed with an external cooling tank. Coolant is circulated by a thermosyphon system or a water pump. A thermosyphon system relies on the natural propensity of hot coolant to rise for circulation, while water pumps circulate coolant continually from the engine's water jacket to the cooling tank.

system. Properly sized wire and good, tight, non-corroded connections are also important. Use only one supply of electrical current at a time. Feeding battery current through a magneto, dynamo, or generator may damage it. Follow these guidelines, and electrical problems will be few.

Cooling Systems

Stationary engines run most efficiently at engine temperatures from 160 to 210 degrees Fahrenheit. Excessive heat buildup can cause engine failures. Lubrication oils can even begin to burn if proper cooling is not provided. Water, oil, and air were commonly used to absorb and displace excess engine heat on the early stationary engines. Devices such as trays, tanks, and fins aided engine cooling.

Engines using air or oil for cooling do not suffer from temperature drops. Water-cooled engines, however, are very susceptible to damage from freezing. The best method to avoid damage from freezing is to drain the coolant completely out of the system. This should be done when the temperature drops below 40 degrees Fahrenheit. If draining can not be done easily, a mixture of antifreeze must be added. Modern antifreeze is the best coolant to use year-round. In the early years, antifreeze had to be mixed by the engine owner. Listed here are four of the most common recipes for an antifreeze mixture or solution:

1. Mix by weight 25 percent glycerin and 75 percent water plus 2 percent sodium carbonate.
2. Dissolve 4 pounds of calcium chloride in 1 gallon of hot water.
3. Dissolve 1-1/2 to 2 pounds of sodium chloride (salt) or magnesium chloride in 1 gallon of water.
4. Mix into solution 25 percent wood alcohol and 75 percent water (measure by volume).

Open-Jacket or Hopper Cooling System

The most common method of water cooling found on engines up to 15 horsepower is that of the "open-jacket" or "hopper" cooling system. There were many different shapes of water hoppers. The hopper holds engine coolant and forms part of the water jacket. Hoppers were sometimes cast in one piece with the engine cylinders. Passageways or chambers for coolant to flow around the cylinder form a water jacket. This produces a self-contained water-cooling system that is permanently affixed to the engine. When poured into the top of the hopper, coolant flows around the head and cylinder, absorbing engine heat. The engine operator's only real concern is to maintain a water level generally within several inches of the top of the hopper. As hopper water steams or boils off, coolant has to be added. The amount of water that boils off is directly proportional to the amount of work the engine is doing. Lighter loads generate less heat than do heavy loads, so heavier loads on the engine require more frequent water replacement.

Tank Cooling Systems

Tank cooling was widely used with stationary engines. There are two variations of tank cooling. The first method is called the "gravity" or "thermosyphon" system. The name thermosyphon came from the siphon action of the water caused by temperature differences in various parts of the system. It is also called a "gravity" system because heated water rises and then cold water flows to the lowest level in the system, to replace the water that has risen. Hot water moving upward causes colder water from the tank to flow into the engine's water jacket.

Location and proper piping of the system are all important in the overall success of this cooling system. The tank must be positioned as close to the engine as physically possible. The bottom of the tank should be positioned several inches below the lowest

The Hoosier engine made by Flint and Walling Manufacturing Co. was built with a screen cooling tank. Here, a thin layer of coolant adheres to the screen's large surface. Ambient air then works on the coolant to extract unwanted heat. Screen cooling is also more effective than tank cooling.

Air cooling can be found on many engines under five horsepower. A fan and cooling fins on this Galloway engine provide adequate air cooling.

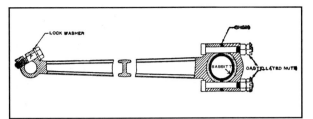

This is an I-beam connecting rod used on an International Harvester Co. Mogul engine. The bearings can be adjusted at both ends of the connecting rod to compensate for bearing wear.

Tindel - Morris Company
Eddystone, Penna.
Crank Shaft Makers

High Efficiency Crank Shafts for High Power Motors.
Hydraulic Forged Crank Shafts—Our Original Invention and Specialty.
Guaranteed Stronger than those made by any other Process.
Heat Treatment by the Latest Approved Methods and Appliances.

The Only Crank Shaft Thoroughly Forged ALL OVER—Wrist Pins as Well as Bearings.
All Varieties of Open Hearth and Special Alloy Steels.
Oldest Crank Shaft Makers in America.
Our Long Experience is at Your Service, and to Your Advantage.

The Tindel-Morris Co. made high-quality crankshafts for the single-cylinder stationary engine trade. Each crankshaft was forged, heat-treated, and machined before leaving the factory.

point in the engine's water jacket. Water piping should then be connected in the most direct path, with as few elbows or bends as possible. The pipe from the top of the tank must have a downward slope leading to the engine. Connecting the pipe in this fashion creates the action of a water siphon. Without a slope on the top pipe, no siphon action would occur. The top pipe must also be attached low enough on the side of the cooling tank so that the water level in the tank will always be maintained well above this connection. If the water level in the cooling tank falls below the top pipe connection, water circulation or the siphon action will stop. Cooling tanks using the thermosyphon method have to be large enough to properly cool the engine. The manufacturers recommended from 30 to 35 gallons of water per horsepower. An 8-horsepower engine would then require a 240- to 280-gallon cooling tank. The cooling tank must always be taller than its diameter to function properly.

Another tank cooling method for stationary engines used forced-coolant circulation. On these systems, a coolant pump is installed in the pipe leading to the engine from the lowest connection on the cooling tank. The pump can be gear- or belt-driven by the engine, and the amount of coolant forced through the engine varies with the engine's running speed. The best pumps for this system application are of the centrifugal or rotary design. This cooling system permits oil or water to be used as a coolant. With a forced-coolant circulation system, a smaller tank can be used compared to the siphon-feed method.

Tray cooling was another design used on stationary engines. Coolant flow in this system is similar to that of the tank-cooled system. Here, the coolant is forced through the engine and on to a series of metal trays. The coolant pump is belt driven by the engine. The pump provides constant circulation of the coolant through the engine. As water exits the pipe from the engine, it fills the top tray on the cooling tower. Cooling begins as the coolant makes contact with the ambient air and the trays. The coolant finds its way to holes in the trays and falls downward to the next tray in the tower. Breaking up the water from tray to tray aids cooling. This sequence continues until the water has traveled to the last tray, where it is then ready to be pumped back to the engine. The circulation of the coolant through the engine and down through the tray cooling tower is continuous as long as the pump remains in operation.

The force-feed-pump cooling system had another variation. In this system, a screen-cooled tank aids in the displacement of heat absorbed by the coolant. The method of piping is similar to the tank cooling system. The major difference is that the pipe leading to a tank first spills the coolant onto a screen. Several different variations of the screen cooling tank can be found in use. Rectangular tanks usually have a pipe running across the top of the entire tank screen. Holes are drilled at small intervals in the pipe so that coolant is forced to exit the pipe and distribute the coolant over the entire screen. By spreading the coolant over the screen's entire surface, a tremendous amount of cooling takes place. Screen cooling was efficient enough that smaller tanks and a smaller volume of coolant provided the same engine cooling as the tank cooling methods, in many cases reducing the cooling tanks size by more than half.

Another simple method of cooling was the use of a continuous flow of running water through the engine. Stationary engines that could be provided with a continuous supply of running water were directly piped to the supply. In these systems, water flow is controlled by opening or closing a water valve leading to the engine. Cooling water enters the lower water jacket and is forced through the engine. Water that circulates through the engine exits through the upper discharge pipe. As water exits the engine, it flows to a drain and is not recycled through the engine. If the flow rate is too high, the engine will not warm up. Insufficient water flow will cause the engine to overheat. Regulating engine heat using this method is normally by trial and error, until the proper flow rate is established. Installed on the continuous drain piping of the system is a funnel, put into the system so the operator could monitor the coolant flow rate. Temperature and flow rate can be monitored and adjusted to maintain exit-water temperature from 160 to 200 degrees Fahrenheit.

The radiator also arrived as a liquid-cooling device for stationary engines, and it became the most efficient and practical method of chilling engine coolants. It is a closed system, where coolant remains in constant circulation. Radiators were manufactured in various models, varying mainly in size and the number and thickness of cooling tubes that made up its interior. Most early radiators have an upper and lower tank. Between the tanks, cooling tubes made from different materials and in different shapes are fastened to connect the tanks. As the coolant passes through the tubes, it is exposed to a cooler that absorbed the heat and then displaced it.

Radiators extend engine running time by conserving coolant loss. Many radiators are found with fans installed to blow cool air across the radiator tubes and further enhance cooling efficiency. Coolant is usually circulated through the radiator by a pump, but radiators can also be used with thermosyphon systems. Using a pump provided better cooling than a thermosyphon system.

Air-Cooled Systems

Air cooling methods were developed early in the design and manufacturing of internal combustion engines. Large engines are never found with air cooling. It seems that stationary farm engines in sizes ranging up toward 6 to 10 horsepower were about the limit of air-cooled engines. Cooling fins or ribs cast radially around the cylinders make air-cooling identification positive. On many air-cooled engines, a fan is used to blow ambient air across the cylinder fins to aid cooling. Air-cooled engine heads also had fins cast into them to increase cooling efficiency. Attaching a series of tin or sheet metal fins to the cylinder created another variation of the cast-fin cooling method. The overall look was, however, almost identical at first glance. Cooling fins are very susceptible to breakage. Cast-iron fins are brittle, so fin damage is found on many engines. Some manufacturers covered the cooling fins with a metal shroud to protect them. The shroud helped the fan to force the air through the cooling fins, aiding cooling.

Short Block

The piston, crankshaft, and connecting rod make up the heart of a stationary engine. It is this assembly of three parts that converts the tremendous power released during combustion into rotary motion. Pistons transfer combustion energy to the connecting rod. The connecting rod delivers this energy to the crankshaft, where it sets the flywheels into motion. This rotary motion is then used to power hundreds of other devices. This power conversion was normally done

This is a new set of cast iron piston rings made for a 1 1/2-horsepower Hercules engine. The split ring design is used for all stationary engines.

with the use of pulleys and flat belts connected from the engine to the equipment. In many other permanent applications, engines were directly coupled to the units. The manufacturers designed pistons, connecting rods, and crankshafts in many different styles and sizes.

Pistons and Rings

With few exceptions, single-acting pistons in stationary gas engines were of the "trunk" style, which means that the head end of the piston is flat, and the back end of the piston is left open. Pistons were usually made from high-quality cast iron. On pistons over 8 inches in diameter, ribs were cast inside the hollow piston skirt near the head of the piston.

All trunk-style pistons were machined with ring grooves. Rings were then fitted into these grooves to seal in combustion gases and keep the piston centered in the cylinder. Pistons were designed with anywhere from three to seven ring grooves. Small engines with piston diameters of 5 inches or less normally had three ring grooves. Medium-size engines with piston diameter above 5 inches usually had four or five ring grooves. Seldom are more than five grooves found on a trunk-style piston.

Many times, an additional single ring groove is found on the piston behind the wrist-pin hole on the back end of the piston skirt. Rings behind the wrist pin serve several purposes. One is to help eliminate piston slap. Piston slap occurs when the piston pivots, causing the back end of the piston skirt to drag on the cylinder wall. As the engine cycles, the rear end of the piston skirt slaps the cylinder wall, causing the cylinder and piston to wear unevenly. This ring also collects lubricating oil from the cylinder drip oiler, which helps lubricate the piston and cylinder. In addition, it prevents escape of gases from the combustion chamber.

Piston rings were usually made from cast iron. The outside diameters of all rings were machined larger than the engine cylinder. The widths and inside diameters were machined to fit the grooves in the piston. The rings were designed to have some elasticity because they had to be compressed into the piston grooves to allow the piston and ring assembly to enter the cylinder. After being placed inside the cylinder, the rings expanded to form the seal around the piston.

There were three common styles of standard compression rings: straight cut, angle joint, and step joint. As the straight-cut ring is compressed, the face of the split ring butts together. The angle-joint ring is split on a 45-degree angle. The step-joint ring is cut forming a reverse "L" or step joint. As a general rule, angle- and step-joint rings formed a slightly better seal than the straight-cut ring. The selection of the proper piston ring is determined by its proportions. A

The front view of the Fairbanks Morse 1 1/2-horsepower Model Z Type D engine confirms that this is a headless engine. The cylinder bore was machined just short of the front of the engine casting. This allowed enough space in front of the piston for compressing the fuel charge and eliminated the need for a removable head.

straight-cut ring was used with narrow face widths. The angle-joint ring was used with average face widths, such as those commonly found on small stationary engines. Step-joint rings were commonly used on marine or large steam and large gas engines.

Another common ring used on stationary engines was the grooved compression ring. It is similar to the standard compression ring except that it has a continuous groove around the lower outer edge. Grooved compression rings were manufactured with angle, straight, or step joints. The ring groove was designed to help regulate cylinder oil and aid lubrication. These rings were normally found on the lower end of the piston, or as the ring furthest from the piston head.

Wrist Pins

Wrist pins on stationary gas engines were made from good-quality open-hearth steel. Many different designs of wrist pins were used. The straight wrist pin was commonly found on small stationary engines. The straight wrist pins, as well as others, were normally held in place with set screws. This design eliminates the tendency of the wrist pin to rotate within the wrist-pin bore. Tapered-style wrist pins fit the tapered bore through the piston from only one side. You must study the ends of the piston before trying to remove these type of wrist pins. Forcing the wrist pin in the wrong direction would crack or damage the piston. Another commonly used pin was made with a step in its length. On this pin, one end of the pin was smaller in diameter than the other. The bores or wrist-pin holes were of two different diameters as well. Pressure to remove this pin must always be applied from the small end, driving the pin toward the largest diameter.

Connecting Rods

Most connecting rods were made from forged open-hearth steel. Usually the carbon content of the steel was about 40 points. When manufacturers needed stronger steels for the connecting rod, nickel or vanadium steels were used. Some early connecting rods were made from cast iron that was malleablized. Brass connecting rods have also surfaced. Brass and cast-iron connecting rods, however, were not as durable as those made from forged steel. Many manufacturers of low-priced engines used cast-iron connecting rods. A few manufacturers used a phosphor bronze connecting rod, which was much more expensive than steel. The phosphor bronze connecting rod was durable and lasted as long as steel designs.

A number of connecting-rod designs are found on stationary engines. The "H" style or "H" beam was a very popular design. It was physically stronger than other common designs, and it required little machining. Only the ends of the rod required machining, which consisted of milling the ends true, boring the ends for bearings, drilling and tapping stud holes for the crankshaft bearing caps, and fitting the bearings.

The rectangular and round connecting-rod styles required several additional machining processes.

The most common way of fitting the wrist pin to the connecting rod was with a pressed-fit bearing. These bearings were generally made from bronze, brass, or high-carbon steel. Split wrist-pin bearings were found on many stationary-engine connecting rods. The split bearing is adjustable for wear by squeezing the bearing together with a take-up bolt. Other-style bearings were completely split in two. Shims on split-type bearings can be removed from in between bearing halves to compensate for wear. The bolts are tightened, and shims can be replaced or removed until the proper shim adjustment is made. A split bearing was always used on the crank pin end of the connecting rod. Babbitt, brass, and bronze were used for these bearings. Adjustment of the crank bearing is accomplished with the use of shims.

Wrist pins usually received oil by a splash lubrication method. Oil splashed onto the connecting rod and then traveled down the rod to lubricate the bushing and wrist pin. On the crank end of the connecting rod, a hole was drilled and tapped for a grease fitting. The crankshaft rotated 360 degrees inside the main bearings on every revolution of the flywheel, so the main or crankshaft bearings required liberal amounts of grease or oil during engine operation. Often on closed-crankcase engines, these bearings were lubricated with grease that entered through a passageway or hole machined in the crankshaft. The passageways permitted lubricant to be forced through the crankshaft and out into the bearings.

Crankshafts

Crankshafts were made from high-quality open-hearth steel. The connecting rod's lower split bearing connected to the center crankshaft journal. The distance from the center line of the crankshaft to the center line of the connecting-rod journal establishes the stroke length of the piston. The distance multiplied by two equaled the engine stroke. The journals of the crankshaft were machined smooth. The shaft was then set into the main bearings on the base of the engine. The bearing caps were then placed on top of the crankshaft journals and bolted together. Shims were added or removed until proper bearing fits were achieved. Flywheels, timing and magneto gears, and pulleys could then be fitted to the crankshaft.

Several manufacturers, such as the Foos Gas Engine Co. of Springfield, Ohio, used counterweights on the engine crankshaft. The weights were attached or cast onto the crankshafts in order to counterbalance other moving parts of the engine. Engines that are counterbalanced show tremendous smoothness while running because the vibration or tendency to jump on each combustion stroke of the engine is noticeably reduced. Due to increased production costs, counterbalanced crankshafts were only used on high-quality engines. Most manufacturers chose instead to cast additional weight into the flywheels to serve this purpose. While this method helped, the crankshaft-balanced engines were still superior in smoothness.

Engine Frames and Bases

The frame or base of a stationary engine is its cornerstone. The base carried the crankshaft bearings and supported the engine on its foundation or sub-base. Holes or openings were cast into frames to accommodate fuel piping, cam rods, valve rods, and other engine necessities. The frame or base later became known as the engine crankcase.

Engine bases were made from gray cast iron. The base design was affected by the engine's cylinder diameter, horsepower, and thrust pressure. In smaller farm-type engines, the wall thickness measured approximately 1/4 inch. As engine horsepower moved upward, huge bases were cast several inches thick that weighed several tons.

Most engine bases were built for a center-crank application. The crankshaft bearings were equally spaced on each side of the casting's center line. A few engines were built using the side-crank design. This design used one single crank arm. In the center-crank design, the lower crankshaft bearing halves were cast integral to the frame. Many manufacturers rotated the bearings 45 degrees toward the cylinder. By changing the bearing center line from horizontal, the pressures exerted by the piston on the connecting rod and crankshaft were better absorbed through the casting. The bearing center-line position also reduced bending tendencies that the piston exerted on the other moving parts.

There are many variations of the basic base design. Some bases were cast with heads, water hoppers, and cylinders in one piece. Other engines were built up from several castings. Some bases were cast with cylinder flanges so that the cylinder casting could be fastened to the base. This allowed the cylinder to be replaced if damaged, without scrapping the

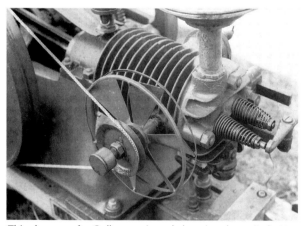

This close up of a Galloway air cooled engine shows its hot head and cooling fins. Valve stems and springs are also visible on the engines head.

The Sparta four-horsepower engine was designed with a valve locking device. The center stud screwed into a cast boss on the head which allowed the keeper plate to pivot, applying pressure to the intake valve. As pressure is applied to the intake valve, it is held closed.

One of the most identifiable features of all early stationary engines was their rotating flywheels. Flywheels smoothed out engine power by providing the momentum to keep the engine moving from one power cycle to the next. This four-horsepower International Harvester Co. Mogul engine flywheel had material removed from inside its rim until the flywheel was perfectly balanced. Its split hub can be tightened to the crankshaft with one bolt. Bolt holes were drilled and lugs were cast into the side of the flywheel to attach a power take-off pulley.

base. Studs were tightened into the base for mounting of the cylinder casting. Base castings were also designed with bolt holes for nut and bolt assembly. Additional casting holes allowed cooling pipes, fuel lines, valve rods, exhaust pipes, and cam rods to pass through the base.

Many bases were cast hollow to provide space for a fuel tank. Sheet-metal fuel tanks were then installed in the base. Some were secured with wood shims and metal rods. The rods were passed under the tank and shims through holes in the engine base. Peening the rods into holes in the base secured the rods and held the fuel tank in place. Other sheet-metal tanks were made with tabs on them and attached with bolts to the base casting. Bases were also cast with a hollow space that itself formed the fuel tank. Holes were drilled and tapped into this style base to fill the tank and to pipe fuel to the engine. Drain holes were tapped into the casting to clean or drain fuel from the tank.

The sub-base was in some cases an extension of the base. The engine base was secured to the sub-base with either studs or nuts and bolts. This sub-base served several purposes and proved to be very versatile. It provided additional height to the frame so that engine flywheels would clear the ground or foundation. Sub-bases were also used as fuel tanks on some engines. If an engine was mounted on a cart, the sub-base could be removed to lower the engine's center of gravity. Manufacturers designed engine bases and sub-bases to provide stability and reduce vibration. Bases and sub-bases were often very ornate, adding to their visual appeal. Elaborate painting schemes were developed to further enhance the overall effect.

Cylinder Heads

Engine manufacturers cast the head of every engine to accommodate specific design features. Two ba-

sic types of heads were commonly found: wet heads, which were water cooled, and hot heads. There also were engines that didn't have a removable head. These engines are commonly called "headless" engines. Understanding cylinder-head design is an important element in understanding different early engine designs.

The Fairbanks Morse Model Z Style D engine is an example of a headless engine that was cast in one piece. When the cast iron was poured into the mold, the cylinder was cast in one piece with the water hopper and base. When the master casting pattern was made, material needed for the piston cylinder and enough excess material to form an internal solid head also became part of the casting. No removable head was needed. In the casting, a chamber was formed that would allow fuel, ignition, and exhaust gases to enter and leave the engine without the use of a head.

Wet heads were cast with a water jacket and were removable. Not all water-cooled engines, however, used wet heads. Some engines used a hot head, and water cooling was only provided for the cylinder. Air-cooled engines always had hot heads. Hot heads were normally cast with fins to increase their cooling properties. The fins exposed more surface area to the cooler ambient air. Many air-cooled engines were designed with a fan to aid air cooling. The fan moves a large volume of air across the engine's cylinder and head. The additional flow of air increases the overall cooling effect. These fans are normally powered with a belt from the engine's flywheel.

Heads are held in place by a series of studs tapped into the cylinder casting, and a gasket is

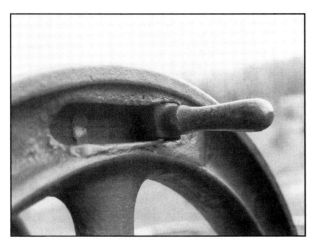

Many times hand cranks were cast into flywheels for rotating the engine during start-up. This hand crank is shown in the start position on the flywheel of a six-horsepower Olds engine. The crank handle pivots on a shaft and snaps back into the recess after the engine has reached running speed.

Sheet metal fuel tanks are commonly found on stationary engines. Shown here is a Stover fuel tank that has mounting tabs that allow the tank to be secured to the engines base, skid, or cart. Filling holes and fuel line connections are found on all fuel tanks.

placed between the head and the cylinder. Drawing up evenly on all the studs is important to maintain a proper compression and water seal. The gaskets are made with elongated holes or passages that allow coolant to flow into the head from the cylinder's water jacket to provide cooling for the cylinder head, igniter, and valves.

Cylinder heads were designed to accommodate valve guides for intake and exhaust valves and their porting. After the head was machined, both valves were seated on a beveled port on the inside of the head. The valves were installed from the inside, passing through the valve guide, and then secured. Valves were held in place with compression springs, which kept them firmly positioned against the beveled seat. Cotter pins, nuts, or retainers were used to hold the compression springs against the head and maintain tension on the valve stem. Arms or supports were cast into many heads so that an exhaust-lever could be pinned to the head. Casting the support directly into the head made a rigid fulcrum. The exhaust valve could then be actuated by the motion of the exhaust-valve lever and cam rod. Exhaust gases found their way out of the cylinder by way of the exhaust valve and a port in the head. The chamber or port was tapped and threaded to accept a pipe nipple that could be connected to a muffler. The intake valve and port functioned in a similar manner, the difference being that the intake port led to the combustion cylinder. Through this chamber the fuel mixture was drawn past the valve and into the combustion cylinder. Oil could be used to lubricate the stems with less chance of the oil burning or forming carbon.

Some heads were fitted with an intake- and exhaust-valve lock. This required an extra casting boss between the intake and exhaust valves. The boss was then tapped and a steel stud was threaded into it. A compression spring dropped over the stud and the intake and exhaust valve stems. A steel plate was cotter pinned to the stud and valve stems. As the exhaust valve operates, the action causes the plate to pivot, and the intake valve is held closed. Spring tension holds both valves closed when they are idle. Many different variations of this device are found in use.

A drilled and tapped hole normally found in the center of the head accommodated the spark plug. Larger passages were machined out for igniters. Gaskets and stud bolts fastened the igniter to the head. The head also supported the moving parts that operated the igniter during engine operation.

Many heads were drilled and tapped for drain cocks or cooling pipes. The plug or petcock was used to drain coolant from the engine. This provided a positive drain for the head separate from the cylinder's drain. On vertical engines, additional tapped holes served as a place to connect piping or prime the cooling system.

An examination of the cylinder head will allow you to determine its functions. A head that has cooling fins is probably used on an air-cooled engine or one that only has cylinder cooling. Nuts and stud bolts tell us that the head is removable. Thick, removable heads, as evidenced by the gasket position, are water cooled. Valve movement can be tested at the head. By pushing in on the stems, you can determine if they are stuck. If an engine has no visible head, then the piston works against the inside of the casting the same as it would if it had a removable head.

Flywheels

The flywheels of early stationary engines were their most outstanding and recognizable feature. Flywheels served to smooth out engine impulses and deliver power when the engine was coasting. Flywheels came

Novo vertical engines were built with a cast iron fuel tank that also supports the engine as its base. Fuel stored inside the base is pumped to the engine's carburetor. The fuel pump is designed with a foot valve and ball checks to maintain even fuel flow.

in hundreds of styles and sizes. Flywheels also could run magnetos and cool the engine they were attached to.

The appropriate physical size of a flywheel was calculated for each engine. Horsepower, engine rpm, outside rim diameter, and weight all had a part in the design formula. As a general rule of thumb, flywheels of small farm engines were normally four to five times the stroke of the piston in diameter. Lightweight flywheels measuring under 10 inches in diameter are as common as massive 6-foot-diameter flywheels weighing several tons each.

Flywheels were made from gray cast iron. A rim, hub, and spokes make up a flywheel. The rim is the outermost portion of the flywheel, and the spokes are the arms that hold the rim to the center hub. After casting, large lathes turned the outside face of the flywheel's rim until it was perfectly round. The hub was then bored to size, and a keyway was cut into the bore. The hub bore size was determined by the crankshaft diameter. Single and double split hubs were common.

The split hub allowed the flywheel to be tightened to the crankshaft. Bolts passing through the split hub were tightened to clamp the flywheel to the crankshaft. Keys were installed in the hub and crankshaft keyways to prevent the flywheel from turning on the crankshaft.

Flywheels were designed in many different styles including solid- and curved-spoke; five-, six-, and eight-spoke; single-row and double-row. The most common flywheel found is the six-spoke design. In the six-spoke design, spokes were cast every 60 degrees around the flywheel center. In large flywheels, those measuring approximately 15 inches across the rim face, it was common practice to use two rows of spokes. Spokes were most often cast with an oval cross section, but many other design shapes also exist. Lugs cast into the spokes were used to support pulleys that were bolted through the spokes and then tightened in place.

Some flywheel designs used an S-type pattern of spokes. Engineers felt that spokes of this configuration better absorbed the shock of combustion than the straight spoke. The S spokes also have a more pleasing appearance than those with straight spokes. Other flywheels were cast solid without spokes. They are sometimes referred to as dishpan or solid flywheels.

Some engines were designed with one flywheel, while others were designed with two. Single-flywheel engines tend to have much heavier flywheels than engines using two flywheels.

Split flywheels are not uncommon. Large flywheels were sometimes cast in segments, and flywheels made up of two halves are the most common. Very large engines or large portable engines often had flywheels made up of four or more segments. Bosses cast in the segments were matched for drilling and surface machining. After machining, the segments were assembled with nuts and bolts into a complete flywheel.

Engine balancing was one function of the flywheel. Balancing the flywheel to offset the weight of the engine's moving parts was done in two ways. The first method placed the counterweight opposite the moving parts on the flywheel, and this counterweight was normally cast into the rim between two of the spokes. The second method of counterweighting the flywheel was to remove the needed mass from the flywheel rim. This was accomplished in the casting process by coring out the wheel rim on the side of the flywheel next to the crankshaft. A flywheel that was cored out for balancing was considerably weaker at that point on the rim.

The main function of the flywheel is to store energy between the power impulses of the engine. On hit-and-miss-governed engines, the engine may have only one power stroke in several cycles of the engine. The flywheel's rotating mass keeps the engine cycling smoothly. While the engine coasts, flywheels deliver power to belted or attached equipment. Throttle-governed engines deliver power strokes more frequently, but they still require a rotating flywheel to store enough energy to keep the engine running smoothly in between power cycles.

Another common feature found on the flywheel was a groove cut into the circumference of the face. On many air-cooled engines, a belt was run in the groove to power the cooling fan. These grooves also powered belt-driven pumps for water cooling and ran dynamos and generators. Generators and dynamos were designed to run off of the outside of the flywheel rim. They were powered by making contact with the flywheel as it rotated. As flywheel speed increased, the magneto or dynamo relied on its governor to maintain the proper rpm. Most dynamo or genrator governors worked by making intermittent contact with the surface of the fast-moving flywheel.

Hand cranks for starting the engine were attached inside the rims of many flywheels. A hinged arrangement allowed the operator to pull the handle out of the flywheel for use. After turning the crank and engine start, the crank returned into a recess in the flywheel by centrifugal force.

Fuel Systems

The fuel system is responsible for supplying a continuous flow of properly mixed combustible gas to the engine. There are really very few elements that comprise the fuel system. Most engines were designed with a fuel system that consisted of a fuel tank, fuel lines, check valves, fuel pump, and carburetor or fuel mixer. Through a maze of piping and valves, liquid fuels are transported and mixed with ambient air into a combustible fuel gas. Many different fuels were used in stationary engines. Natural gas, gasoline, and kerosene are the most common. Producers gas, alcohol, naphtha, mineral spirits, coke-oven gas, blast-furnace gas, and crude oil were also used in specially equipped and designed engines. Gas engines that operated on natural gas were as common as those that ran on gasoline. Crude-oil engines used a heavy petroleum base oil.

Different fuel systems were designed to accommodate the various fuels. Understanding the methods and devices that make up an engine's fuel system will be necessary in the overall engine evaluation process. Being able to determine if a carburetor is of multifuel design or for an engine designed to run on natural gas or kerosene will become second nature.

Fuel Tanks

The fuel tank is the vessel that holds liquid or gaseous fuel until the engine requires it for combustion. Self-contained fuel tanks made from galvanized sheet metal are the most common on engines below 15 horsepower that run on gasoline or kerosene. When fabricating the tanks, the pieces were assembled using soldered joints.

All liquid fuel tanks need an access hole to fill the tank with fuel. The tank must also have a vent to elimi-

The Lunkenheimer Generator is shown attached to the intake pipe on a Sparta Economy engine. One of the best carburetors for stationary engine use, Lunkenheimer generators are cast from brass.

This is a Foos governor and bracket that has been removed from an engine. Visible here are the two governor flyballs and its drive gearing. The shaft is lubricated through two holes in the mounting bracket on either end of the governor shaft.

nate the possibility of a vacuum building when fuel is being drawn from the tank. To accomplish this, a simple air hole was drilled in the filler cap. In other designs, a small piece of pipe was soldered into the tank, extending well above the top of the fuel tank. Connections are also needed on the tank to attach fuel and drain lines for supplying fuel to the engine and returning fuel back to the tank. Drain holes are needed to flush or remove fuel from the tank. The drain hole is almost always found on the bottom or side of the tank. Some tanks have other additional pipe fittings so the same fuel tank could accommodate many different size engines and was therefore more versatile. Pipe plugs are installed to seal any other open fitting.

Fuel tanks were made in many different styles but round and rectangular sheet-metal tanks were predominant. The Sparta Economy engine used a rectangular sheet-metal tank that was housed inside the engine's base. The International Harvester Co. Mogul and the 5-horsepower Galloway engine used cylindrical external fuel tanks. On both these engines, the fuel tank was secured on the skid or cart behind the engine and fuel lines ran back to the engine's generator or mixer. Sheet-metal tanks were also found housed underneath the engine and inside the base. The tanks were secured there with metal rods and wood shims. Another means of fastening the fuel tank in place used metal tabs. Through holes in the tabs, the tank could be bolted to the engine base or skid. Two advantages the sheet-metal tank had over cast-iron models were that it could be replaced, and it was relatively inexpensive. Cleaning of the tank could be made easier by removing the tank and handling it separately.

Many manufacturers designed fuel tanks of cast iron as an integral part of the engine. These fuel tanks were made by enclosing a portion of the engine base to form the tank. In the casting process, the hollow space needed to hold a given amount of fuel became part of the overall engine design. A cast-iron base tank requires the same fittings as a sheet-metal tank. Filling, drain, vent, and fuel-line connections had to

be provided in the casting. The Novo 3-horsepower vertical gasoline engine is an example of an engine designed with the fuel tank in its cast-iron base. Notice the fuel lines leading to the fuel pump and up to the carburetor. An overflow fuel line from the carburetor returns excess fuel back to the tank. This tank has two filling holes, one on each side of the base casting. A pipe plug is used to close the hole after fuel has been poured into the tank. At least one plug was normally drilled with a small hole to act as the air vent for the tank.

Fuel Lines

Copper, brass, and steel fuel lines connected the fuel system together. Copper and brass piping or tubing have the advantage of being able to be bent into shape easily. Steel pipe and tubing have a tendency to rust and corrode. Bending pipe saved on fittings. It also left fewer connections in the fuel system that could develop a dangerous leak. Compression and threaded fittings are the most common methods of terminating piping. Flared tubing is used in many systems, so the flared ends must be checked for cracks if leaks develop.

There are some specialty fittings you should be aware of as you check an engine's fuel supply system or troubleshoot problems. A check valve is normally installed somewhere in the fuel line to prevent the fuel from draining back into the tank. This valve helps prevent the need to prime the fuel system between engine runnings. These devices can be troublesome. They have a tendency to stick or for the check ball to become covered with a residue that prevents it from moving freely. Check valves designed with tension springs are especially susceptible to these types of problems. Check valves were included in most of the plunger-type fuel pumps to prevent fuel from returning to the pump as it cycled.

The foot valve is a check valve found at the end of the fuel pickup line. These valves customarily have a screen on them where fuel is drawn into the valve. The screen prevents the valve from picking up dirt that would hold the check ball off its seat. The valve's main purpose is to prevent fuel from draining back into the tank once it has been pumped or drawn up from the fuel tank. Plugged foot-valve screens and defective operation of any check valve result in fuel supply problems.

Gasoline that is left in the system for long periods of time evaporates and leaves behind a sticky varnish. Varnish causes check balls to seize on their valve seats. This prevents the check valve from operating. Cleaning and polishing of the seat and check ball should correct any malfunction of the check valve.

Gravity-Fed Systems

In a gravity-fed fuel system, fuel flows to the carburetor, mixer, or generator due to the forces of gravity. In this system, the reserve fuel level must be higher

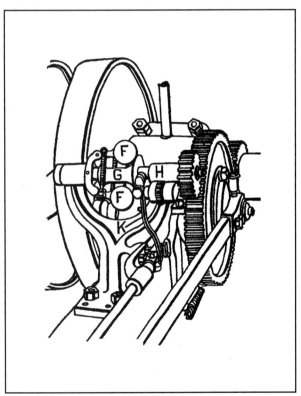

This illustration of the Foos governor shows the pinion gear governor drive. The governor bracket can be seen bolted to the engine's base. The governor is found on the working side of this Foos engine.

than the system's fuel-line intake, and the fuel lines must run level or slightly downhill to the carburetor. If a fuel line is installed that rises above the reserve fuel level, fuel flow stops. The Sparta Economy engine is a typical example of an engine that uses gravity fuel feed. The fuel tank is housed within the engine's base. Fuel flows to the Lunkenheimer generator through the fuel line, where the suction or vacuum created by the piston cycling activates the generator to mix gas and air in proper proportions on their way to the engine cylinder.

Pump-Fed Systems

Fuel pumps are the other method of supplying fuel to the engine's carburetor or fuel mixer. Fuel-pump systems have many advantages. With this system, fuel tanks could be placed underground or below the level of intake. This was a special advantage for engines that were going to run inside a building or on a permanent foundation. Refilling the tank could be done outside the building, eliminating fuel spills that could develop into fire hazards. Underground fuel storage tanks could be fabricated to store hundreds or thousands of gallons of fuel. This was important for applications that required continuously running engines, such as manufacturing shops and electrical generating facilities.

Fuel pumps for gas engines are commonly made from brass, bronze, cast iron, or pot metal. Most fuel pumps are of the plunger style. In this design, a metal shaft or plunger is cycled up and down inside the pump. Check valves working in unison with the pump control fuel flow by allowing the fuel to move in only one direction, toward the carburetor. The Novo and International Harvester Co. Famous fuel pumps are similar designs. The Novo pump is made from cast iron, while the International Harvester Co. pump is made from brass. A packing nut and bushing is used to compress a packing inside the pump. The packing is forced around the plunger and two beveled packing sealing surfaces. One bevel is formed inside the pump shaft, and the other is on the base of the packing bushing. The packing is compressed around the plunger by tightening the packing nut. Today, graphite- and wax-impregnated packing can be used for this purpose. Teflon packing also makes a good substitute.

Many ways were developed to convert rotary motion from the engine into a viable source of reciprocating power for the fuel pump. Most often this was accomplished with a cam or lever. Other pumps used a spring to force the plunger back to its starting position. Still other pumps used direct-coupled linkages, such as that on the International Harvester Co. Mogul fuel pump, which was connected directly to the eccentric cam located at the rear of the engine, and powered off of the engine's side shaft. In addition, many pumps were equipped so that the pump could be cycled by hand before the engine was started to prime the fuel system.

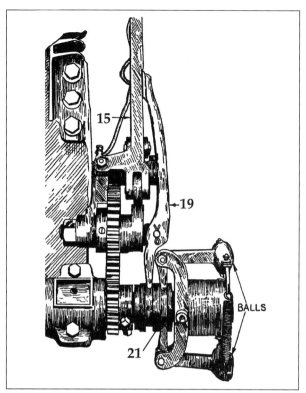

This illustration details a Gilson flyball governor. The parts of the governor are: 15 - pushrod and 19 - detent arm. The governor flyballs are seen located at 21.

Most fuel pumps can be rebuilt fairly easily; however, the pot-metal pumps are tough to rehabilitate because their bodies corrode. A good inspection of the fuel pump is worthwhile. If the plunger is loose and there are no visible breaks or cracks, chances are it's restorable.

Carburetors, Fuel Mixers, and Generators

Carburetors, fuel mixers, and generators are devices that atomize liquid fuels for internal combustion engines. This process turns the liquid fuel and air into a combustible gas mixture that can be exploded under compression within the engine's cylinder. Though there are hundreds of different-type fuel-mixing devices, the following detail describes the basics of how they all work. The air intake usually consists of an unfiltered intake tube or pipe. Brass, bronze, and cast iron are the dominant material from which the carburetors are made. All these units had a method of adjusting the fuel flow into the air stream. The needle valve served this purpose for many decades. Needle valves are adjusted by hand and are found on the body of the unit in the form of a thumb wheel or adjusting handle.

The Lunkenheimer vertical generator is an all-bronze fuel-mixing device found on numerous engines. The trade name given by the manufacturer was the Nonpareil generator valve. They were made in several different styles and in both left- and right-hand

This is a front view of an original International Harvester Company's Mogul engine governor. The side-shaft and governor spring can be seen protruding from the governor shroud. The drip oiler is used to lubricate the governor.

patterns. During the engine's intake stroke, a partial vacuum is created that causes an inlet disc (which looks like a poppet valve) to lift from its seat and air to be drawn into the generator. The needle valve allows a small amount of fuel to be drawn into the mixing chamber at the same time as the inlet-valve disc is held open. The needle-valve orifice is opened or covered as the inlet disc cycles with the engine. The inlet valve is spring loaded, so that as soon as the spring overcomes the suction of the piston, the valve is snapped back down on its seat. This makes the function of the valve automatic.

The valve (inlet disc) stem protrudes below the generator body. By pushing up on the stem, the generator can be primed. The gasoline inlet or fuel duct is positioned at a right angle to the inlet valve disc seat. This design provides extremely fast atomization of the fuel.

A tension spring is used to hold the needle-valve regulating wheel in place. The regulating wheel is numerically numbered, providing a method of predetermining the fuel adjustment, as vibration tends to rotate the needle valve out of adjustment. A pipe nipple attaches to a female thread at the top of the generator. The generator and nipple are then attached to the inlet-valve chamber on the engine's head.

Lunkenheimer made several variations of this same valve. The Type A was designed with a slide throttle to regulate the volume of fuel admitted into the engine. Type B generators are equipped with a regulating wheel that controls the lift of the inlet valve. Type C generators used all the features of Types A and B, but the Type C regulates fuel volume with a butterfly valve inside the mixing chamber. Type D generators were a horizontal design, functioning the same as the vertical Type generators described earlier. The generators came in five sizes. The 1/2 generator was used on engines with piston sizes up to 2-1/2 inches in diameter. The largest generator was used

with engines that had piston diameters up to 6-1/2 inches in diameter.

Governors

All internal combustion engines require a method to regulate and control engine rpm. A governor is a device used to limit maximum engine speed and provide automatic speed regulation on a continuous basis. Governors were manufactured in great numbers of different designs. The most common design was based on centrifugal force. This type of governor derives its action from engine speed. As engine rpm increases, centrifugal force acts on the governor weights, causing them to fly outward. This action mechanically moves other working parts of the governor causing all or a portion of the fuel supply to be cut off. On other governor designs this same action controls electric ignition. If the governor disconnects the electrical circuit, no ignition spark occurs. The engine is then forced to slow until the speed is reduced far enough to allow the governor to close the electrical circuit. With most governors, spring size and tension, along with the size of the fly-ball weights, control the engine speed. Heavy weights or strong springs require greater engine rpm to produce enough centrifugal force to actuate the governor. This suits fast-running engines. The opposite is true for engines that are running slow. Weak spring tension or light fly-ball weights are the key to slow-running engines. Throttle and hit-and-miss governing are the two most common methods of regulating speed on stationary engines.

Hit-and-Miss Governing

The hit-and-miss principle of governing regulates speed by causing the engine to miss power strokes. Hit-and-miss governing allows a constant volume of properly mixed fuel to be admitted to the cylinder at variable intervals. Hit-and-miss engines gain speed until the governor acts on a linkage, preventing any further increase in speed. The engine is then forced by the governor to coast or slow down. Engine speed continues to decrease until the governor once again allows the engine to cycle normally. Hit-and-miss engines require much heavier flywheels than throttle-governed engines. The heavy flywheels prevent excessive speed fluctuations between engine power strokes. Hit-and-miss governing is very economical, and ignition under light loads is more reliable than when using the throttle governing method.

There are several methods of hit-and-miss governing. One cuts off either the gas, gasoline, or oil supply to the engine. A slide gate or valve stops the passage of the mixed fuel into the engine's cylinder during the intake stroke.

The Foos hit-and-miss governor is typical of governors that control engine speed by shutting off fuel flow. As engine rpm increases above the governor set speed, the fly-balls begin to move outward, causing the spool to act on the roller, which is carried by a bracket or governor lever. This action moves the notch finger out of contact with the fuel lever blade. This prevents the fuel valve from opening and admitting a charge of fuel. Without fuel, the engine cannot fire. The engine loses rpm until the governor weights return to their normal position. When the governor weights fall back beyond their set point, the governor allows a charge of fuel to be once again drawn into the cylinder. Power cycles would continue normally until high speed once again causes the governor to act on the intake valve. Governor cycling continues as long as the engine is running, providing steady control of the engine running speed. This same type of design could also be affixed vertically to a longitudinal secondary shaft and driven with a bevel gear.

A second hit-and-miss governing method automatically opens and closes the exhaust valve to regulate engine speed. The governor linkage allows the exhaust valve to either cycle normally or be held open. If the governor holds the exhaust valve open, the engine cannot draw a fuel mixture into the cylinder because the intake valve works on a vacuum. If the vacuum is not developed inside the cylinder, the engine is unable to draw in fuel.

The Gilson hit-and-miss governor is typical of hit-and-miss governors that control engine speed by holding open the exhaust valve. The fly-balls are mounted around the crankshaft. As the fly-balls move outward they cause a collar to move, which pulls a detent lever outward, causing the opposite end of the lever to engage the catch on the push arm. The push arm is then held forward by the detent lever, effectively holding open the exhaust valve. With the exhaust valve open, the piston action inside the cylinder does not create a vacuum. Without the vacuum, the intake valve is unable to draw a charge of fuel into the engine. The engine then cycles, drawing in and pushing out charges of fresh air. This continues until the engine slows. As the speed is reduced, the governor relaxes, thus disengaging the lever from the push arm. The exhaust valve closes, and the intake valve once again cycles. The engine is able to fire with a fresh fuel charge, and engine speed is maintained or increased until the governor acts again.

The third hit-and-miss governing method regulates electrical ignition. In this method, the governor prevents the igniter from cycling. If the igniter trip is prevented from breaking the points apart, a spark will not be produced. Without a spark, the engine does not ignite its charge and the engine slows. Governors connected to commutators automatically shut the electrical current off before it reaches the sparking device. As the engine slows, a point is reached when the governor allows the commutator to close, and electrical current is once again delivered to the sparking device.

Throttle Governing

Throttle governing is accomplished by regulating the amount of explosive mixture allowed into the en-

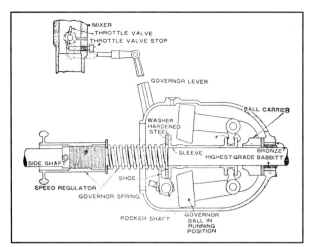

International Harvester Company's Mogul flyball governor is shown in sectional view. The governor is completely housed within a metal shroud. The governor works off of centrifugal force as the engines side-shaft rotates.

gine's cylinder. Quantitative governing varies or cuts off the charge by limiting the area or port size of the gas inlet to the engine. This throttling method was found to perform well for small engines using illuminating or natural gas. One disadvantage of this method is misfiring. Under light loads, weak fuel mixtures are admitted to the engine cylinder, and this fuel mixture is not strong enough to ignite properly, so the engine backfires when ignited. Under extremely heavy loads, excess fuel is not burned efficiently, so incomplete combustion results.

Stratification governing methods are used satisfactorily with large engines. In this method, air is admitted to the cylinder during the intake stroke until the governor allows the fuel mixture to begin to enter the cylinder. The charge then flows into the cylinder until the end of the intake stroke. By varying the duration of the intake fuel mixture, the volume of explosive mixture in the cylinder is controlled.

The International Harvester Co. Mogul fly-ball governor is located on the engine's side-shaft and is typical of throttle governors. International Harvester Co. Mogul side shaft engines are all throttle governed. When the engine reaches the governor's set speed, the governor moves the governor lever and adjusts the throttle valve automatically to regulate the fuel supply to the engine. Most of the moving parts of the governor were contained within a metal housing on the side shaft. The speed regulator was threaded to the side shaft. Adjusting the governor could vary engine rpm by as much as 20 percent. Rotating the regulator to the left or right changes governor spring tension. Light spring tension causes the governor to act on the fuel supply at low engine speeds. Heavy tension causes the engine to run faster.

Many different governor designs are found on stationary engines. Whether the governor is of the vertical or horizontal type, their basic functions remained the same. The key thing to remember is that governors are designed to act either on the fuel supply, ignition system, or exhaust-valve mechanism to regulate engine rpm. Other-style governors exist, but they make up an extremely small percentage of governors found on common engines. One such style governor functioned on principles of gravity and was called a pendulum governor. Another governor design was actuated by inertia.

Engine Lubrication

Engines require lubrication on a daily, hourly, and minute-by-minute basis. Pistons, cylinders, gears, and bearings must be serviced with lubricant regularly. Oil, grease, and kerosene are transported to lubrication points at predictive intervals through the use of mechanical lubricating devices. Gravity plays a large part in fluid flow in early oiling devices. Once oil is released or forced from a reservoir by gravity, it flows downward on its journey to the bearing surfaces. Many companies manufactured a multitude of differ-

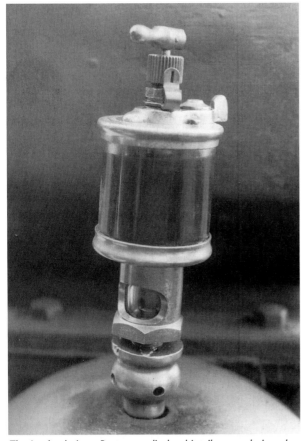

The Lunkenheimer Paragon cylinder drip oiler was designed with an internal vent pipe and check valve. These two devices prevented combustion gases and oil from blowing back into the oiler. They are among the best drip oilers ever designed for engine cylinder oiling. Expect to pay anywhere from $40 to $75 for a Lunkenheimer Paragon oiler today.

ent devices to aid in lubricating the engine. Drip oilers, cup greasers, mechanical oil pumps, oil gauges, oil cups, rod oilers, and site-feed manifolds all found their place on stationary internal combustion engines. Splash oiling of the main bearing, crankshaft, and wrist pins were common in many engine designs. However, other lubrication points of the engine had to be supplied lubricant through the use of accessory devices or the familiar oil hole. Lunkenheimer, Ohio Injector, Clarke, Powell, Essex, Wilkinson, Stahl's, National Brass, Michigan, and Detroit are a few of the many companies that manufactured engine lubricating devices.

All bearing surfaces must be kept lubricated. Bearings that are run without lubrication develop heat through friction. As heat builds, the bearing temperature rises until a point is reached where the bearings fail or are damaged. Lubricants act as a cushion between rotating and stationary surfaces, prevent wear, and carry heat away. Today, many grades of grease and oil are available to the gas-engine enthusiast. A good-quality 30-weight oil can be used for engine oiling or bearing lubrication. However, a multi-purpose grease is best suited for bearing-surface lubrication. Bearings maintained by oiling must be serviced more frequently than a bearing serviced with grease. Grease does not break down as fast as oil and provides longer surface contact. Grease should be used for all bearings where grease can be applied. Bearings made from brass, bronze, or babbitt can be lubricated with multi-purpose greases. All bearing surfaces should receive fresh grease every couple hours of running.

Manual lubricators must be adjusted each time a different volume of oil is desired from the oiler. Automatic oilers provide a constant discharge of oil at a set discharge rate. Spring-loaded lubricators apply steady pressure against grease volume within the unit. Grease is fed by this pressure as fast as the grease can exit the device. This action provides excellent lubrication. However, if bearing fits are loose, grease can be used up quickly. Care should be taken to monitor any unit that is automatic in operation. Once grease or oil reserves have been used, refill them immediately.

Drip Oilers

The most widely used lubricating device is called a drip or site-feed oiler. Drip oilers are simple in design. Various-size oilers are made to handle different oil volumes and discharge rates. Drip oilers were made in single- and multi-tube designs. Oiler sizes were numerically coded. The smaller the number (#00 to #8), the smaller the oil capacity of the unit. For instance, a #0 Lunkenheimer Sentinel oiler held 5/8 ounces of oil. A #8 oiler had a capacity of 34 ounces. Oil reservoirs are designed with an upper and lower flange. The flanges are normally made from metal, with a glass cylinder secured between the two flanges. The glass cylinder rests on a cork gasket top and bottom. The gaskets prevent oil from leaking out of the reservoir. The glass permits visual inspection of the oil level inside the oiler. Oilers are also made with metal or brass reservoir walls. This design does not permit the operator to view the oil level inside the reservoir.

On the top flange of the reservoir there is normally a filler hole. Oil is loaded into the reservoir through the hole. A swing cover slides back and forth over the oil filling hole to protect against oil splash. A control lever and regulating nut on top of the oiler are used to adjust the oil flow and turn it off and on by moving up and down a needle valve inside the central tube. The central supply tube passes through the reservoir and into a small compartment below the main body of the oiler. This compartment also has a glass cylinder that forms its sides. Here, oil can be viewed as it flows from the reservoir supply tube to a lubrication passageway. Holes in the central tube allow oil from the reservoir to flood the tube. When the needle valve is lifted from its seat, the oil then begins to drip into the compartment below. Visual inspection of the oil flow through the lower compartment determines if the oil rate has been properly set. Raising the valve stem further away from the seat allows the oil to flow faster. Closing this distance reduces the flow of oil. At the extreme bottom of the oiler, a pipe thread is cut into the base to accommodate fastening the oiler to a bearing or cylinder passageway. The oiler is then tightened to secure it in place and prevent oil from leaking. Oilers with check valves are an advantage. Check valves prevent combustion gases from blowing back into the oiler.

One problem with drip oilers is caused by severe weather conditions. As oil becomes colder, it becomes somewhat thicker and flows more slowly. The operator must remember to readjust the oiler when weather conditions change. Different viscosity oils warrant adjustments as well. A good rule of thumb is to always check the oil flow at each start-up of the engine. Another rule to remember is that an engine cylinder requires at least several drops of oil per minute when in operation. Of course, bearings need to be kept well lubricated, whether automatically or by manual wetting.

Cup Greasers

Cup greasers are designed to be automatic or manual in their operation. Spring-loaded or automatic greasers with a regulating screw will supply grease to bearings at a constant rate. By removing its cap or base, hand loading the cup can be accomplished. The cap is then put back on the greaser and the plunger is released. This causes grease to begin to flow out of the greaser and toward the lubrication point. An operator does not have to constantly force grease out of the automatic oiler, but operators must remember to make sure that a greaser has an adequate amount of grease in its reservoir.

Manually operated cup greasers feature a threaded cap and body. Grease is loaded into its cap. After filling, the cap is threaded back onto the body. The base of the greaser has a hole that permits grease to pass. By turning the cap down onto the body one turn at a time, grease is forced from the reservoir and into the lubrication point. The base is made with an integral nut for tightening. Pipe threads are cut into the greaser's base so that it can be tightened into a tapped or threaded lubrication passageway. Engine operators must remember to adjust or turn this type of greaser occasionally to supply fresh grease to the bearing surfaces.

Mechanical Oilers

A mechanical oiler, such as the Madison Kipp, provides a method of lubricating various points on the engine automatically. This oiler is powered with an internal ratchet, that is belt or lever driven. As the oiler cycles, internal pumps push the oil to any number of lubrication points. Once oil is delivered from the pump to the flow tube, gravity takes over, causing the oil to travel down the tube to its lubrication point. These oilers were made in various sizes. The most common units used on stationary engines service two to six lubrication points. Physical size of the oiler is controlled by the overall number of points it was designed to lubricate, so a two-station oiler is physically smaller than one designed for six. The size of the

Many companies such as Powell, Essex, Lunkenheimer and Detroit manufactured quality drip oilers. Here are a few examples of original oilers made shortly after 1900

Grease cups> are use to force grease into lubrication points. Many companies manufactured brass or steel greasers in various sizes and thread diameters. Greasers are commonly either manually operated or spring loaded for automatic operation. The manually operated greasers shown are the most common greasers used on stationary engines.

The Madison Kipp 30 mechanical oil pump supplies oil to three lubrication points automatically. Three feed tubes can been seen through the oiler's site window at the top of the unit. The oiler's filling hole is directly to the left. The pump can be manually operated with a hand crank seen at the right of the oiler. After the engine is running, the pump is automatically cycled from its left side off of an eccentric cam. The cam causes the pump lever to cycle up and down, thus pumping oil. This oiler is attached to an International Harvester Co. Mogul engine.

reservoir also adds to its physical size. The Madison Kipp oiler is adjustable. By increasing or decreasing oiler cycles, the flow of oil is regulated. Faster cycle times force more oil from the oil pump to the lubrication tubes. Engine speed also affects oiler cycle time. As the engine rpm increases, a larger volume of oil is forced to the lubrication points.

The Oil Hole

While not exactly a device for oiling an engine, the oil hole requires discussion. An oil hole is simply a drilled or cast hole in the engine, parts, or guards that allows lubricant to flow to its moving parts. As you look over an engine, many of these points for lubrication become apparent. The igniter and pinion gear shafts often used this method of lubrication. Oil from

a hand-operated oil can is used to fill these holes. Oil runs down the hole to the lubrication point. It's important to look over an engine and locate every lubrication point. Oil should then be applied at regular intervals to all of these points on the engine.

Lubrication is an important preventative maintenance procedure for all stationary engines. Drip oilers and other lubrication devices aid the operator in maintaining proper engine lubrication. Oilers and their flow adjustments must be monitored frequently. These devices require refilling and must be checked to ensure that the device will be able to provide lubricant while the engine is in operation. Note that during engine examination prior to purchase, the presence of these devices and their condition can make a difference in the overall purchase price. Oilers can cost from as little as $1 to several hundred dollars each.

Chapter Three

Common Engines

This gives a general overview of several popular stationary engines. Each listing gives some basic information and then explains how to start and shut down the engine. Despite the fact that there were thousands of stationary engines, most of them used a few basic systems. Even if your particular engine is not listed, you should be able to find one that uses similar systems.

Mogul Side-Shaft Engine

International Harvester Co. manufactured the Mogul side-shaft engines from 1913 to 1919. They were available in sizes from 4 to 50 horsepower. The engine could be ordered in stationary, portable, or skidded models. During the years that this engine was manufactured by IHC it won many notable awards. The Department of Agriculture awarded IHC's Mogul engine its Best Engine Award at the 1915 and 1916 San Diego Expositions. IHC's Mogul engines were truly an outstanding engine of the time.

The Mogul's unique carburetor system made this engine very economical. The engine also featured side-shaft control of the governor, intake and exhaust valves, cam pressure release, and engine ignition timing. The Mogul's carburetor was designed to use kerosene and had a separate gasoline bowl used for start-up.

The Mogul side-shaft engines were designed with a hammer-break igniter and magneto ignition. The points were made from nickel alloy, which is highly corrosion resistant. The igniter points are held together until the side shaft and linkage engages the igniter. Mogul side-shaft engines were shipped with a high-grade, low-tension oscillating magneto. The magneto is mechanically tripped. The engine is timed by adjusting the linkage between the magneto lever and the igniter, which adjusts the magneto trip upward or

A 1913 International Harvester Co. Mogul four-horsepower hopper-cooled side-shaft engine.

downward. Longer contact results in later ignition. The opposite is true of shortening contact. An ignition wire runs from the magneto terminal to the stationary electrode of the igniter. The engine frequently used the Accurate Type O magneto.

A fuel-saving throttle governor controls engine speed. As engine power is demanded, the governor automatically opens the throttle. The governor connects to a butterfly valve in the carburetor and regulates the fuel mixture by opening and closing the butterfly valve. The fuel pump is piped from an external fuel tank to the mixer. The fuel pump is driven off of the back end of the side shaft. The pump is connected to an eccentric, which oscillates the pump plunger up and down, forcing fuel into the fuel line. The pump was designed with check valves

Mogul showing head end of engine and Accurate Type O magneto, fuel mixer, side shaft, cam, valve arm, and igniter trip eccentric.

This is another 1913 International Harvester Co. Mogul side-shaft engine. This one uses screen cooling with an external cooling tank.

inside the pump fuel passageways. They prevent the gas from backing up into the pump as it cycles. A packing was used around the shaft with a compression nut to tighten the packing around the plunger, sealing the fuel inside the pump. The plunger can be hand operated to prime the system and fill the kerosene side of the fuel mixer prior to starting the engine. The spring under the hand plunger knob acts on the plunger to return the plunger to the top of the pumping stroke.

The engine's single piston has five cast-iron rings, making it very durable. The extra long length of the piston reduces piston slap. The five rings hold the piston centered in the cylinder far better than would three rings. The fifth ring is attached near the end of the piston and on the outboard side of the wrist-pin hole.

The engine's side shaft controls the intake and exhaust valves, magneto trip, magneto timing, compression release, governor, and fuel pump. It is fitted with a compression-release cam.

Mogul engines ranging from 4 to 10 horsepower were built with hopper or external-tank cooling systems. The water-hopper method of cooling was not adequate for engines over 12 horsepower. All engines from 12 to 50 horsepower were tank cooled. Tank-cooled models have circulating pumps that move the coolant from the tank into the engine and back.

The closed crankcase seals out dirt and keeps the oil contained. Hand holes and covers were provided for access to the crankcase for servicing the gears, bearings, and moving parts. By opening the proper hole, the bearings can be checked for wear. By moving the crank to the vertical position and putting the flywheel under a bind, the operator can reach inside and feel for excessive movement in the bearings.

Mogul engines are equipped with a crankcase breather valve that equalizes the pressures caused by rapid piston motion inside the closed crankcase. Excess oil is also purged out the breather valve.

Preparations to Start the Mogul Engine
Pre-Start Checklist
1. Fill the engine's fuel tank.
2. Fill the coolant tank to within a couple inches of the overflow outlet. On hopper-cooled engines, fill the hopper with water to within about 3 inches of the top.
3. Make a visual inspection of all connecting or moving linkages. Tighten any loose nuts, bolts, or leaking connections. Make sure electrical wires and connections are in the clear of moving parts.
4. Prime the fuel mixer bowl. Remove the plug in the mixer cover and fill with gasoline.
5. Fill all the mechanical oilers with oil. A good synthetic or mineral oil is preferred. Adjust all the mechanical and drip oilers. Fill all the greasers with a good-grade grease. Make sure that all moving parts are well lubricated.
6. Adjust the fuel mixer for start-up.
7. Position the mixer butterfly valves in the start position.

Pre-Start Detail

The Mogul engines are designed to use any of the following fuels for combustion: gasoline, naphtha, motor spirits, kerosene, gas oil, solar oil, or power distillate. Before starting the engine, the gasoline bowl must be filled externally by the operator because the fuel pump does not supply fuel to the gas bowl. Gasoline is poured through a tapped access hole in the gasoline bowl cover. The gas bowl holds about 8 ounces of fuel. The engine can run for about 20 minutes on the gasoline in the mixer bowl. This serves to preheat the engine prior to changing over to another fuel, such as kerosene. A gasoline needle valve located on the mixer is used to regulate the amount of gasoline drawn into the fuel mixer.

The two lower valves on the mixer are used for running the engine after the warm-up period. The lower fuel needle valve regulates the fuel that is pumped to the fuel mixer from the fuel tank. The water needle valve is used to add water to the fuel mixture when burning kerosene. By mixing the kerosene with water, pre-ignition and cylinder hammer or knock are eliminated. At start-up, both the lower valves have to be in the off position when warming the engine with gasoline.

Adjust the oilers to emit about two to three drops of oil per minute. The Madison Kipp automatic oiler located on top of the crankcase needs to be turned many revolutions by hand to prime the oil pump and supply oil to the cylinder and bearings before the engine is started. All moving parts on the engine should be oiled. The following lubrication points require two to four drops of oil: magneto bearings (only a couple drops per week), igniter, spark advance lever and linkage, magneto trip and eccentric, valve arms, side shaft, fuel-pump linkage, governor and governor linkage, water pump, cylinder, and bearings. This oiling is best done with the use of an oil can, so oil can be regulated to a couple drops at a time.

Next, set up the mixer's lower fuel bowl. The hand pump on the fuel pump should be cycled many times to fill the mixer with kerosene. After warm-up, the lower fuel bowl is filled with kerosene. The fuel pump supplies an excess amount of fuel to the fuel mixer while running. The mixer has a weir on the inside of the bowl that allows excess kerosene to dump over. As the excess fuel is pumped into the bowl, it travels over the cast weir and returns to the tank through the drain line. The drain line is attached to the bottom of the mixer and terminates at the fuel tank. This system is not pressurized, but the pipe plug cap on the gas tank is drilled with a small hole to allow air into the tank, so the fuel pump does not have to overcome the vacuum that is created as fuel is pumped from the tank.

Move the butterfly valves inside the mixer to the start position. The upper valve is moved to the right and the lower valve to the left. Both valve positions are indicated on the casting of the mixer. The first position reads "start," and the second "run." There are also

The Mogul's engine governor and throttle linkage as well as the governor and side-shaft drip oilers.

graduated stops, allowing adjustment in between the start and run positions. With all these areas attended to, the operator is now ready to start the engine.

Starting the Mogul Side-Shaft Engine

Follow these steps when starting the Mogul engine:

1. Move the compression-release cam on the side shaft toward the head of the engine to engage it.
2. Open the gasoline needle valve 3/4 of a turn.
3. Move the spark advance lever to the retard position.
4. Cycle the fuel pump manually until the mixer cup is full. Visually check by removing the cover on the mixer.
5. Slowly begin turning the flywheels to start engine. Rotate the flywheels away from the engine's cylinder.
6. Move the butterfly damper to the run position.
7. After the engine has fired, disengage the compression-release cam.
8. Move the spark advance lever to the run position.
9. After a 10-minute warm-up, change over to the tank fuel. Adjust the two lower needle valves on the mixer.

A Mogul fuel pump with a hand plunger.

This view of the Mogul side shaft shows the trip eccentric, shaft oiler, intake valve control arm, and exhaust relief cam.

Starting Detail

The first thing the operator has to do is engage the compression-release cam. Located on the engine's side shaft, this cam moves forward and backward on the shaft. By moving the cam forward toward the magneto, it slides into the start position. While engaged on the side shaft, the cam allows a portion of the compressed fuel mixture to escape out the exhaust valve until the engine fires. This is accomplished by holding the exhaust valve open mechanically for a period of the compression stroke. As the piston moves further into the compression stroke, it has less stroke in which to compress the fuel mixture. This compression reduction in the starting cycle allows the engine to be turned over easily by hand. If the cam is not engaged, the operator will have difficulty overcoming engine compression.

After the engine fires, pull the cam backward toward the flywheels. This disengages the compression-release cam, allowing the engine to come up to full compression.

Adjust the upper gas needle valve open about 3/4 turn. This valve controls the fuel mixture as long as fuel remains in the gasoline bowl. Remember, this bowl was filled manually with gasoline prior to engine start-up.

Push the spark advance lever downward to the retard position for starting. If the weather is very cold, squirt a small amount of gas into the mixer's inlet air pipe. Gas is then directly in contact with the air coming into the fuel mixer. Saturating the air mixture with gas vapor aids the initial start-up. The operator is then ready to turn the flywheels and begin rotation of the engine for starting. The flywheels are always rotated opposite the cylinder end of the engine.

Move the spark advance lever upward to the advanced position. Then, move the fuel mixer dampers to the run positions. The spark advance lever should be adjusted to advance the spark as far as possible without causing engine knock. As soon as the engine begins to fire under its own power, disengage the compression-release cam.

After an approximate warm-up period of 10 minutes, open the lower fuel valve about 3/4 turn, turn off the upper gas needle valve, and open the water needle valve about 3/4 turn, mixing water with the kerosene to prevent pre-ignition or knocking.

Fine tuning of the fuel mixture requires adjustment of the needle valves. By closing the fuel valve down, less fuel is delivered to the cylinder. Closing off too much of the fuel to the engine will result in the engine not being able to maintain ignition. The engine will stall and shut down. If the engine is emitting black smoke from the muffler, it is running too "rich." By reducing the amount of fuel to the engine, mixture enrichment is corrected and normal combustion results. If smoke coming from the engine is blue in color, then too much oil is getting to the cylinder and past the rings. Adjusting the oiler will normally correct this condition. If the smoke cannot be cleared up, possible ring problems may exist.

Shutting Down the Mogul Engine

Follow these steps when shutting down the Mogul engine:
1. Close off the water needle valve.
2. Close off the fuel valve.
3. Drain the cooling system.
4. Turn off the oilers.

In cold weather the engine requires draining so it will not freeze. Freezing causes engines to burst, doing damage that few owners or operators can repair. Back when this engine was built, just as today, there were additives to use in the engine cooling water to prevent freezing. However, I prefer to drain the engine and leave nothing to chance.

Have you ever heard a Mogul run? Well, once you have heard a Mogul run, you will never forget the sound that one makes! It is distinctly Mogul.

IHC Famous Vertical Engine

The International Harvester Co. (IHC) began building the Famous vertical engine line in 1905, and production continued until 1917. IHC sold many of their engines through trade dealers, including McCormick dealers. These vertical engines were made in 2, 3, and 5 horsepower. International Harvester Co. also used the Famous trade name for its horizontal line of gas engines during this time. I will, however, limit our inspection of the Famous engine to the vertical style.

The Famous vertical uses a hammer-break igniter with a battery and coil for ignition. Hit-and-miss governing is used with a manual speed control called a detent shifter. The battery box is attached to the skid, and holds a series of dry-cell batteries, and a coil. A single knife switch is normally wired into the ignition circuit for disconnecting the electrical supply to the igniter. The Famous could also be ordered with a magneto or dynamo. The Motsinger Auto-Sparker was one such device that was commonly used as an ignition alternative. Elkhart, Bosch, and Sumter magnetos would work as well.

The Famous was designed to use vaporized gas, gasoline, or alcohol. The fuel tank is built into the base on the skidded model. The tank is piped up to the carburetor with a return line for the drain back to the tank. External tanks were also sold for stationary applications, and tanks could be buried if the engines

This rear view of the Mogul shows the breather valve, fuel pump, and hand hole cover.

were to operate inside a building. Check valves are used on the fuel supply line to keep the gasoline from draining back to the tank. The fuel pump is operated by a rocker arm that works off the cam-gear eccentric. The fuel pump is a plunger type and is spring loaded. The fuel pump was cast from brass, making them very durable. The pump plunger is made of 1/2-inch steel and is pinned to the gasoline pump lever. The pump operates continuously as the engine runs, supplying fuel to the carburetor.

The up-draft carburetor has only one needle valve. The carburetor was cast with two inside weirs. One is used as an overflow for the gasoline to return back to the tank. The second weir forms a center gas reservoir inside the carburetor. Gas is pumped from the fuel pump up and over this weir until it fills the center reservoir. After the fuel fills the center reservoir, the excess gas flows over the second weir and into the return line draining back to the gas tank. This system maintains a constant fuel level within the carburetor at all times.

Two counterweights can be seen on one flywheel. The weights are connected to the governor. The centrifugal governor controls the engine running speed. As engine speed increases, the weights move outward and the governor begins to work against the detent arm, forcing it over and holding the exhaust valve open until the engine slows. As engine speed decreases, the detent arm disengages and the engine is able to complete another firing cycle.

The crankcase is accessed from two hand holes. On one side of the crank chamber, a hand-hole cover is cast with a relief opening in it. During the engine's operation, oil splash can be observed through this opening. Viewing a small amount of oil splashing on the drain surface indicates that the proper oil level has been achieved. The oil splash provides adequate oiling of the connecting rod, wrist pin, and cylinder wall. Through the hand hole, the connecting rod bearings can be adjusted. As the bearing wears, shims can be removed from between the split bearings to maintain proper fit. If the bearing becomes too loose, an audible knock develops. The second hand-hole cover has identification markings cast into the plate. After 1906, the word Famous was cast on the outside surface of the cover plate. Earlier covers were smooth, without casting marks.

The wrist-pin bearing can be tightened to adjust for wear. To adjust the wrist-pin bearing, the connecting rod and piston has to be removed from the cylinder. The piston is machined to accommodate a set of three piston rings. They provide a compression seal against the cylinder wall and piston. If the rings become worn enough, compression would decrease to the point where the engine would not run under load. Piston rings are easily replaced and today can be found in sizes from 1 inch to 10 inches.

Mounted to the ends of the crankshaft are two flywheels. Standard flywheels are 26.5 inches in diameter for the 3-horsepower model. Pulleys ranging in diameter from 5 inches to 14 inches are bolted to the flywheels for belting to equipment. The 9-inch pulley

was favored for this engine. The speed of the belt can also be controlled by engine rpm.

The valves are located in the head on the top of the engine. The intake valve is spring loaded and has a lock-out valve catch that prevents any fuel from being drawn into the cylinder when the engine is coasting or slowing down. As the piston moves downward on the intake stroke, the valve-spring tension is overcome by vacuum. The fuel mixture is then drawn into the cylinder. As soon as the intake-valve spring overcomes the vacuum, the valve again closes.

The exhaust valve is actuated by cycling the valve lever and valve rod. This keeps the exhaust valve operation in time with the engine. The igniter is bolted through the side of the cylinder head and can be removed by loosening two bolts. A gasket is placed between the igniter and the cylinder head to prevent compression leaks. The igniter is operated by an igniter trip mounted to the valve rod. By moving the rod clamp up or down, ignition timing can be adjusted. Moving the clamp upward advances engine timing. Moving the clamp downward retards the timing.

Front view of the Mogul showing the fuel mixer, upper gasoline bowl and needle valve, lower fuel bowl with water control needle valve (left) and kerosene needle valve (right), igniter and trip linkage, and exhaust piping.

Needle control valves on the Mogul engine.

The two main crankshaft bearings are fitted with grease cups for lubrication. The wrist pin and cylinder receive lubrication as the oil lifter splashes oil around in the crankcase during operation. A drip oiler is used to supply oil to the cylinder wall. The oiler is located on the opposite side of the igniter. Adjust the drip oiler to supply from three to five drops of oil per minute.

The external coolant tank is fitted with a screen to provide cooling for the skidded model. Screen cooling is an early form of the modern radiator. Water running down over the screen cools faster than if it were just pumped back into the tank. This method of cooling requires smaller amounts of water than a holding-tank system, while providing the same measure of cooling. Water from the tank is pumped into the lower end of the cylinder jacket. At the top of the cylinder, the hot water is pushed out of the water jacket and drains back to the screen cooling tank. The water pump works on the plunger method. It is packed to prevent leaks and is driven off an eccentric. Rotation of the eccentric provides the back-and-forth motion to work the pump. The engine can also be cooled by hooking it up directly to a constant water supply, like a water hose. Using this method requires a drain, as the cooling water is not generally circulated through the engine again.

Preparations for Starting the International Harvester Co. Famous Engine
Pre-Start Checklist
1. Lubricate all moving parts of the engine.
2. Fill all oilers and the greaser.
3. Make sure that the oilers are adjusted to supply five drops per minute.
4. Check the crankcase oil level.
5. Rotate the grease cups on the main bearings to lubricate them.
6. Prime the water system and pump.
7. Check electrical wiring connections. Make sure that the wires do not come in contact with any of the moving parts of the engine.
8. Rotate flywheels back and forth slightly to ensure that the engine is free.
9. Check the battery, coil, and electrical switch connections.
10. Fill the fuel tank with gasoline, and prime the carburetor.

Pre-Start Checklist Detail
The pre-start check is as important as the starting procedure. Manual oiling of all engine parts must be done first. Starting at the top of the engine, give the igniter, valves, exhaust-valve lever, and igniter trip a drop of oil. Fill up the cylinder sight-feed oiler with enough oil for the anticipated running time. Adjust the oiler to feed from three to five drops of oil per minute. Oil the eccentric through the open slot. This can normally be filled with several drops of oil. Lightly oil the exposed gearing and other eccentric straps.

Lubricate the fuel-pump rocker arm and lever. Locate the drill holes in the castings and apply the oil through these holes. The water pump requires a small amount of oil to be applied to the brass plunger that works in and out of the pump. Several drops of oil must be put on the top of the fuel pump to keep the plunger and packing lubricated.

Check the level of the oil in the crankcase. The oil dipper must be able to pick up enough oil from the crankcase to splash on the bearings, wrist pin, and cylinder when the engine is running. After the engine is started, you can determine if there is enough oil by viewing the cover drain. A small amount of oil should splash on the cover while the engine is running.

Rotate the grease cups enough to fill the crankshaft bearings with grease. If a small amount of grease can be seen working out of the ends of the bearing, that is enough lubricant. Regular greasing keeps the contaminants flowing out of the bearing and extends bearing life. I recommend that you use too much grease rather than not enough. A good wiping rag can usually take care of any excess grease, but if the

Madison Kipp oiler typically found on Mogul engines.

The fuel tank of the Mogul engine.

bearings are damaged, all the grease in the world won't repair them.

If you have run the engine before, the water pump should not need to be primed. If you have not primed the pump, this can be done in several ways. Open one of the plugs in the cylinder-head water jacket, and fill up the system with coolant. When the system is full, replace the plug. You may also have a valve installed in the water line that will allow you to add coolant. If so, use this method. Make sure that the pump valve is in the on position to allow the water to flow. Check the water in the screen cooling tank. Make sure that at least 5 gallons of coolant is present in the cooling tank. The outlet pipe leading to the pump must be covered with coolant at all times. Water will not be pumped to the engine if the water level should drop below this point. As soon as the engine is finally started, you should make sure that water is flowing properly in and out of the engine, with coolant running down over the tank screen. If the pump fails, shut the engine down and correct the problem.

Look over the engine and make sure all wires are clear from moving parts. Make sure loose tools are not left on the engine to become entangled and cause damage to the working parts. Move the flywheels back and forth to ensure that nothing is binding. If the engine binds, do not force the flywheels. Locate the cause of the bind and take measures to free up the engine.

Check the battery box. If you're using a 6-volt or 12-volt automobile battery, the two terminal wires should be secured to the two terminals. Check the position of the knife switch. It should be in the open position. If it is closed, there is a possibility that the battery may have been shorted. If the engine does not start immediately, check the battery. If you're using 1-1/2-volt dry-cell batteries, they must be wired in series. The modern square 6-volt lantern battery will also provide hours of electrical power for running an engine. Normally a minimum of 6 volts is necessary to maintain proper engine ignition. Check the coil to ensure that the wires are properly connected and are tight. Look at the wires connected to the igniter and make sure there are no loose connections.

Remove the plug on the pipe to the fuel tank and fill the fuel tank. Remove the carburetor fill cap and pour enough gas into the carburetor to fill the reservoir and prime the fuel line down to the fuel pump. Another method of priming the system requires the

A Mogul fuel mixer air intake with butterfly control valves.

Front view of Mogul head showing spark advance/retard control, igniter, magneto, and side-shaft eccentric.

use of the fuel pump. First, hook up the cam lever so the pump can be manually cycled. Begin pumping the handle and cycling the fuel pump. Watch for the fuel to enter the reservoir, and continue pumping fuel until it is full.

You have now completed the pre-start check procedure. The engine should be prepared for starting.

Starting the 3-Horsepower International Harvester Co. Famous

Follow these steps when starting the Famous engine:
1. Adjust the carburetor needle valve.
2. Place the starting crank on the crankshaft.
3. Close the knife switch.
4. With your left hand, depress the intake valve.
5. Using your right hand, begin turning the engine over with the crank.
6. Release the intake valve and lift the choke plate.
7. As the engine fires, release the choke damper.
8. Allow the engine to come up to speed.
9. Adjust the speed control. Moving the lever forward or backward increases or decreases the engine's normal running speed.
10. Adjust the fuel needle valve for proper fuel mixture.

Famous Starting Detail

Open the carburetor needle valve until the number "2" that is scribed in the face of the valve is at the 12 o'clock position. This should be a little more than one turn open. Slip the starting crank in place on the crankshaft. Close the electrical knife switch. This should energize the electrical system. With your left hand, hold the intake valve open and begin to roll the engine over with the crank. Holding the intake valve in at this point helps you overcome the engine compression until you have some momentum behind the flywheels. Now, release the intake valve and push the air damper on the carburetor air pipe upward. This will cause less air to enter the cylinder, effectively "choking" the engine. As soon as the engine fires, release the air damper. The engine should then continue to run until it attains normal running speed.

After the engine has warmed up, the carburetor needle valve should be adjusted. The number "1" scribed in the valve can now be turned to the 12 o'clock position. This is the factory-set running position. However, the carburetor valve setting may not be totally accurate. Adjusting the valve to clear up smoke from the exhaust may be required. Black smoke from the muffler generally indicates too much fuel is getting in

International Harvester Co. Famous three-horsepower vertical engine.

The hammer-break igniter and trip assembly found on the Famous engine.

the engine cylinder. If the engine backfires, there may be a problem with too little fuel getting to the cylinder. Blue smoke from the exhaust is an indication the engine is getting too much oil. Slowing down the site-feed oiler should clear the problem up. If not, check the oil in the crankcase. If the oil level is high, too much oil is being splashed on the cylinder wall from below. Drain excess oil out of the crankcase to eliminate this problem. If you're still unable to eliminate the blue smoke, check for piston-ring wear or damage.

Another method of starting is done without the use of the hand crank. Begin by checking the fuel in the carburetor and opening the needle valve to the start position. Make sure that the electrical switch is not engaged or closed because you do not want the igniter to spark during this operation. Lift up on the air damper while rotating the flywheel and drawing in a charge of fuel. You will be able to hear and see the intake valve working as the fuel is drawn into the cylinder. After the fuel mixture has been drawn into the cylinder, close the electrical switch and prepare to start the engine. Begin rotating the flywheels backward against compression until the igniter trips. If the engine draws in the proper charge of fuel, it should fire. This method of starting the engine can be implemented on many engines. It generally takes less effort to start a well-tuned engine using this method.

Shutting Down the International Harvester Co. Famous Engine

Follow these steps when shutting down the Famous engine:
1. Close off the fuel valve.
2. Open electrical switch.
3. Drain the cooling system.
4. Turn off the oilers.

Sears and Roebuck Sparta Economy Engine

The Sparta Economy engines were sold by the early mail-order giant Sears Roebuck and Co. Sears began selling engines built by Otto and Stickney. In 1909, Sears purchased the first Sparta Economy engines from the Holm's Machine Manufacturing Co. in Sparta, Michigan. The Sparta Economy engines were manufactured in Sparta from 1909 to 1912.

In 1912, the Holm's Machine Manufacturing Co. was sold and moved to Evansville, Indiana. The company was renamed The Hercules Gas Engine Co. Hercules assembled many of the Sparta engines in Evansville, Indiana, from parts left from the Holm's Co. in Sparta. The newly designed engines built in Evansville were named "Hercules." Thousands of the late-model Hercules engines are still found today, but fewer than 600 Sparta Economy engines are known to exist today. There were five models of the Sparta Economy engine: A, B, C, CA, and CX. The engines were built in 1, 1-1/2, 2, 4, 6, 8, and 10 horsepower.

All Sparta Economy engines were painted red with black pin striping. The engines were designed with a hammer-break igniter, but the engines were shipped with the Standby Multiple Battery and a spark coil. The Standby Multiple Battery was made of six 1-1/2-volt dry-cell batteries with a coil mounted on top of the wood battery box. Two wires connect the igniter to

Famous engines used this Motsinger Auto-Sparker.

The plunger-type fuel pump of the Famous.

the battery and coil. One is connected to the insulated pole, the second to the noninsulated pole of the igniter. The igniter is actuated mechanically by the igniter trip blade. The igniter trip blade is secured to the igniter trip bracket and works back and forth on the cam rod. As the igniter trip blade moves toward the front of the engine, it engages the igniter pawl, and closes the points. This completes the electrical circuit. As the cam rod and igniter trip bracket cycles forward on the power stroke, the igniter trip blade snaps off the igniter pawl and the reverse spring action opens the points on the igniter. The cam rod operates the exhaust valve and is spring loaded. The spring on the front end of the rod holds it in contact with the eccentric on the crankshaft pinion gear. This eccentric and cam-rod action keeps the engine timing and valve operation synchronized. As the points open, a spark occurs. The engine has to be timed closely with this one spark from the igniter to fire properly.

An Elkhart magneto came as standard equipment on the 8- and 10-horsepower engines. An Elkhart magneto could also be purchased separately for $12.95 from Sears. When using the magneto, the need for a battery and coil is eliminated. The magneto connects directly to the insulated igniter terminal with one wire. A bevel gear runs the magneto at twice the engine speed and meshes with the crankshaft gear. Having a 2:1 ratio on the gearing provides the magneto with enough rpm to supply a steady electrical current, even at start-up speeds. As the flywheels rotate, the crankshaft gear powers the magneto. When the magneto starts rotating, electric current is immediately produced by the magneto. The magneto is secured to the magneto bracket with two bolts to the base casting.

Engine timing is adjusted by moving the igniter trip blade. Moving the blade forward causes the igniter to trip earlier and advances the spark. Adjusting the blade in the opposite direction retards the spark. The igniter trip blade is adjusted by rotating a screw at the rear of the igniter trip bracket.

A fly-ball governor is used to control engine speed. As the engine picks up speed, the governor balls begin to move outward. As the engine climbs over the pre-set speed, a spring-loaded rod on the inside of the governor moves toward the detent blade. This continues until the detent blade is held against the catch on the cam rod. This causes the engine to hold the exhaust valve open so fuel will not be drawn into the cylinder. The trip blade is also far enough forward that the igniter won't be tripped. As engine speed drops back down, the governor balls begin to collapse and the detent disengages from the catch. The exhaust valve closes, and a fresh charge is drawn into the cylinder. Ignition once again occurs, and the engine fires. By repeating this action, the hit-and-miss method of governing is accomplished.

The flywheels were designed with a split hub. The split in the flywheel hub allows the hub to be drawn to-

Famous updraft carburetor with fuel control needle valve. The cylinder drip oiler is shown at left.

gether with one or two bolts. By tightening up on the hub, the flywheel is held to the crankshaft. The crankshaft is also keyed to the flywheel hub. Flywheel diameters range from 20 inches on the 1-1/2-horsepower engine to 42 inches on the 10-horsepower engine.

Sparta Economy engines use hopper cooling. The water hopper, water jacket, cylinder, and head are separate castings that are gasketed and bolted together. The square water hopper, with its removable top ring, was only used on Sparta engines. Later models used solid, cast hoppers. Coolant fills the entire area around the cylinder, cylinder head, and up into the water hopper. Heads on the 1-1/2- and 2-horsepower models are not water cooled. Coolant is poured in the top of the water hopper to a level within about 3 inches of the top. Cooling water is drained by opening a valve or drain cock located at the bottom of the cylinder casting.

Five bolts fasten the water-cooled, cast-iron heads to the cylinders. The inside face of the head was machined to fit slightly inside the cylinder. An asbestos packing was used for a gasket between the head and cylinder. The valves are spring loaded and positioned one on top of the other. A valve lock is used to keep

The Famous engine's screen cooling tank.

Famous engine head showing the intake and exhaust valves and exhaust valve control arm.

the intake valve shut when the exhaust valve is open. This prevents the engine from drawing in a charge of fuel and wasting it when the engine is coasting.

The engine's base is cast iron and supports the main bearings at 45 degrees. This seat design positions the base casting to better absorb the impact of crankshaft cycling. The cylinder casting is bolted in four places to the base. The base is also fitted with four holes on the corners for fastening the engine securely to a foundation, skid, or cart.

The crankshaft is made from drop-forged steel. The extended crankshaft on the pulley side is unusual. This long stub shaft can accommodate pulleys up to 12 inches wide. This unique feature found on the Sparta helps to quickly identify this engine. The connecting rod is made of malleable iron. The connecting rod is of the cast I-beam type. On one end, it has a split Babbitt bearing that connects it to the crankshaft. A solid steel bearing is fitted to the other end where the wrist pin attaches the piston to the connecting rod.

Gasoline is used to fuel all Economys. The fuel tank is housed inside the base and is secured with two 1/4-inch rods and two wooden shims. The fuel tank filler comes up through the base at the back of the cylinder. The fuel line to the generator passes through the lower front corner of the base casting. A drain plug on the bottom of the fuel tank is used to drain contaminated fuel.

A Lunkenheimer solid-brass Type E generator was supplied straight from the factory on Sparta engines. This generator is actually nothing more than a carburetor. A gravity-fed fuel line from the gas tank is connected to the union on the generator. The needle valve controls the amount of gas that is allowed to be drawn into the cylinder. A spring-loaded intake valve on the generator works on the suction of the engine piston. As the valve is forced open by piston suction, combustion air rushes by the needle valve and atomizes the gas on its way to the cylinder.

Sparta engines are very heavy engines. The little 1-horsepower engine with a 3-1/4-inch bore and 5-inch stroke ran at 500 rpm and weighed 215 pounds. On the other end of the scale was the largest Sparta at 10 horsepower. Its 7-1/2-inch bore with a 13-inch stroke ran 300 rpm, and the engine weighed 2,175 pounds.

In their catalog, Sears advertised the engines in many different configurations. They could be bought as sawing and feed-grinding outfits, as portable units mounted on trucks, as stationary engines that were simply bolted through the base to a foundation, and as pumping outfits. Sears even advertised them belted up to wash machines and cream separators. The advertising slant indicated that these engines could do almost everything.

Now, let's take a closer look at an original 4-horsepower Sparta Economy engine belonging to the author. It has a 4-1/2-inch bore and 6-inch stroke. It weighs in at 650 pounds, and its normal running speed is 400 rpm. I purchased the engine from a very good friend in the fall of 1993. The piston was stuck inside the cylinder and nothing moved; the engine was locked up tight. I did, however, see considerable potential. It was fitted with an original Elkhart magneto. The magneto looked like it could be refurbished and continue to service its engine for years to come. Most of the original parts were still on the engine. The only missing part was the hammer-break igniter.

Famous plunger-type water pump.

Sears and Roebuck four-horsepower Sparta Economy Engine.

Eighteen months of soaking, wire-wheel brushing, scraping, oiling, and cleaning turned the engine around. The piston was soaked in Gibbs oil for months. I used a homemade jig to press the piston out. The piston broke loose rather easily after steady pressure was applied, but one of the piston rings cracked during the removal of the frozen piston. New piston rings were purchased and installed. The original gas tank was used as a pattern for the new fuel tank. I had to purchase an igniter. Replacement of the wrist pin was necessary due to excessive wear. The wrist-pin bearing was worn, and a new one was machined and installed. The cylinder was in repairable shape and did not need to be sleeved. I spent hours honing the cylinder with my trusty cylinder hone and a bucket of kerosene. I think this engine is destined to remain in my collection for the duration. It has become one of my favorites.

Side view of the Sears and Roebuck engine showing the igniter, igniter trip, water hopper, cam rod, cylinder drip oiler, head, and muffler.

Preparing to Start the Sparta Economy
Pre-Start Checklist
1. Make sure the drain cock is closed.
2. Fill the water hopper with coolant.
3. Fill the fuel tank.
4. Fill drip oiler.
5. Load the grease cups.
6. Oil gears and moving parts.
7. Check electrical connections.

Pre-Start Checklist Detail
Check the cylinder drain cock and make sure it is closed. Now, fill the water hopper to within 3 inches of the top with water. If you're running the engine in cold weather, warm water is preferred.

Fill the gas tank through the filler pipe located behind the cylinder in the engine base.

Fill the cylinder sight-feed oiler. Adjust it to emit about five drops of oil per minute. The connecting rod and both main bearings are fitted with grease cups. Fill the three grease cups with a multipurpose grease made for Babbitt. Rotate the caps on all three grease cups until the bearings are lubricated. Oil the exposed gears on the crankshaft, magneto (if present), and fly-ball governor. A couple drops of oil should also be used on the governor, valves, cam rod, exhaust lever, igniter trip, and movable electrode prior to starting. Rotate the flywheels enough that the piston skirt is exposed at the back of the cylinder and add a few drops of oil to the piston skirt before starting the engine.

Check the batteries', coil's, and igniter's electrical connections. Make sure that all the connections are tight. Leave the electrical knife switch in the open position. If a magneto is installed, check the wire connections at the magneto and igniter. Make sure that they are tight. Lubricate the magneto bearings with a couple drops of light oil. Magneto lubrication is not required every time the engine is started as over oiling the magneto is harmful. Try only to keep the magneto bearings wet. That requires a little oil for every 20 hours or so of running time.

Cycle the engine a couple times and make sure that nothing is binding. The last act in the pre-start process is to push up on the generator valve and hold it open until a small amount of gasoline drips down into the elbow.

The Sears and Roebuck engine's gear-driven Elkhart magneto. The main bearing cap is under the grease cup.

Starting the Sparta Engine

When starting the Sparta engine, follow these steps:
1. Check the battery and coil wire connections.
2. Close the knife switch.
3. Adjust the generator needle valve.
4. Place the starting crank on the crankshaft.
5. Depress the detent blade with the left hand.
6. With your right hand, begin turning the engine over with the crank.
7. Choke the engine.
8. As the engine fires, discontinue choking.
9. Allow the engine to come up to speed.
10. Adjust the speed control. Moving the lever forward or backward increases and decreases the engine's normal running speed.
11. Adjust the fuel needle valve for proper fuel mixture.

Starting Detail

All 1- to 4-horsepower engines were furnished with hand cranks for starting. The 6-, 8-, and 10-horsepower engines are started by rotating the flywheels by hand. Place your hand on one of the flywheels to roll the engine over. Always rotate the flywheels toward the back of the engine.

Begin the starting sequence by closing the knife switch to the battery and coil. Engines equipped with a magneto are direct wired to the igniter and remain ready to run. Adjust the generator valve to the left and open it about 1/2 turn. The factory-recommended setting was 7 for starting. Hold the detent blade in against the cam rod with your left hand. Slowly begin cranking the engine over with the hand crank. Increase the speed of the flywheel rotation and release the detent blade. The engine should draw in a charge of fuel and fire on the next compression stroke. As soon as the engine fires, remove the crank from the crankshaft. Be careful that you don't let go of the handle while removing the crank, or the crank could catch on the crankshaft and fly off and hit you. After the engine is running, readjust the generator valve to

about 4 or 4-1/2 for sustained running. Once again, this was the factory-recommended setting for a new engine. The best setting for your engine may vary somewhat from the factory's recommendation.

Stopping the Sparta Engine

When shutting down the Sparta engine, follow these steps:
1. Close off the fuel valve.
2. Open electrical switch if equipped with one.
3. Drain the coolant.
4. Turn off the oilers.

To stop this engine, the Lunkenheimer generator valve must first be closed. This will stop the flow of gasoline to the cylinder. Next open the electrical knife switch, if it is a battery-and-coil ignition system. Turn the cylinder sight-feed oiler off. Open the drain cock on the water hopper and drain the engine coolant.

Fuller & Johnson Model N

The history of the Fuller & Johnson Co. in Madison, Wisconsin, is a long one. It begins in the 1840s and ends in 1954. Prior to the production of stationary engines, the company manufactured many types of farm implements, including cultivators, rakes, plows, and other horse-drawn equipment. Because stationary engines were gaining popularity in the late 1890s, Fuller & Johnson began developing an engine of their own. Shortly after the turn of the century, Fuller & Johnson introduced an oil-cooled stationary engine. They were built in sizes from 1-1/2 to 6 horsepower. The oil-cooled engines were very short lived. By 1905, Fuller & Johnson had developed a new hopper-cooled engine that replaced the oil-cooled engine line. Both horizontal and vertical hopper-cooled engines filled the production lines at Madison. Fuller & Johnson made many different models of hopper- and air-cooled engines including, the DE (double efficiency), Peoples Priced, N, K, NA, NB, NC, ND, KA, NK, and farm pump.

Fuller & Johnson sold the N engines to many companies around the world. They could be found on everything from pump and saw rigs to power supplies for thousands of cement mixers. Many direct-coupled power-spraying outfits were also made. The engines could be ordered as portables, mounted on a truck. Stationary models with extended bases could be bolted in place or set on a foundation for permanent-type installations.

The most successful flywheel hopper-cooled engine Fuller & Johnson produced was the Model N. Model N engines were manufactured from 1913 to 1925, in seven sizes from 1-1/2 to 12 horsepower. Many small changes can be noticed on the Ns during their years of production. Later N bases and castings were cast shorter and required the use of a skid or truck so that the flywheels would not be obstructed. Early engines were shipped with battery-and-coil ignition. Late-model Ns were developed with low-tension magnetos, and even high-tension magnetos with spark-plug ignition would become available. Basic engine design, however, was not altered. The N engines were heavy. The 2-1/2-horsepower engine with its 22-inch-diameter flywheels shipped from the factory at 500 pounds. The 10-horsepower engine with 40-inch flywheels tipped the scale at a ton. Engine rpm ratings were fairly close. The small 1-1/2 horsepower engine ran at 500 rpm, while the 10-horsepower engine turned 350 rpm. The 4-horsepower engine was rated at 400 rpm.

On the N engine, the site-feed oiler pipe passes through a hole in the water hopper. Oil is fed down the pipe and into the cylinder. The cylinder casting was tapped and threaded to accommodate the pipe. These connections must seal properly, or water that surrounds the pipe will be drawn into the cylinder. The hole at the top of the water-hopper casting supports the oil pipe to minimize jarring while the engine is running.

The water hopper and cylinder were cast as one unit. The coolant stored in the hopper floods around the cylinder and into the water-cooled head. The cylinder head is ported in several spots, and the gasket between the head and cylinder is open to allow the coolant to pass freely.

One of the interesting features of this engine is the hopper cover that closes off most of the open area at the top of the hopper. The casting was made with about a 2-inch vent to allow steam to escape. This cap conserves coolant because the steam condenses on the cover, and the coolant drips back into the hopper. In addition, the cover keeps out contaminants and keeps water from splashing out of the hopper. The water-hopper casting is flat on top to allow the cap to fit properly. Most other manufacturers used a casting lip, rather than a cover, to restrict water splash.

The cylinder head was cast with passages for water cooling. Two poppet valves are positioned side by side in the head. The wet head provides direct cooling for the valves during operation. The head is fastened to the cylinder with five studs that were tapped into the cylinder casting. A tapped port in the head allows exhaust gases to escape through a pipe nipple to the muffler. On the opposite side of the head, the vaporizer attaches to the intake port. The valves are held in place and operated by compression springs. The springs are held in place by a cotter-pinned retainer.

Hit-and-miss governing is used to control engine speed. The governor is of the fly-ball type. The detent is forced into contact with the cam catch as the en-

This Sparta gear-driven flyball governor and detent control was used on Sears and Roebuck engines.

A two-bolt flywheel hub on a Sears and Roebuck engine.

gine rpm increases past the set speed. This action opens the exhaust valve and prevents the igniter from tripping. Engine cycling does not begin again until the engine speed falls below the set point. A thumb screw, attached between the governor and detent, is used to control engine speed. By increasing or de-

creasing the tension on the detent, the speed of the engine can be changed. The governor allows engine speed to be set at from half the rated rpm to 110 percent of the rated speed.

The cam rod is actuated off the eccentric on the crankshaft pinion gear. The igniter trip is attached to the top side of the cam rod. The igniter trip can be moved on the cam or adjusted to trip the igniter at the proper timing point. This unit is an under-pick trip. That means that the trip blade works the igniter pawl from the bottom rather than from the top. (This hammer-break igniter was featured in Chapter 2.)

The cam rod controls the action of the exhaust valve. The exhaust lever is pinned through the exhaust-lever bracket. A valve lock is used on the bracket to hold the intake valve open when the exhaust valve is open. This prevents the engine from drawing any fuel into the cylinder while the engine is coasting. The valve lock is provided on all engines from 2-1/2 to 12 horsepower.

A galvanized fuel tank is held in the engine base with steel straps. The base is held to the cylinder cast-

A Sears and Roebuck engine's water hopper with a square top ring.

This rear view of a Sears and Roebuck engine shows the crankshaft, connecting rod, piston skirt, fuel tank filling pipe, main bearings and grease cups, magneto, and flyball governor.

A Sears and Roebuck engine's five-bolt cylinder head, valves, and exhaust control arm.

ing with four bolts. Fuel tanks were sized by the factory to hold enough gasoline to run the engine 8–10 hours, depending on engine load. The fuel tank is connected to the mixer with pipe or tubing. A check valve is installed on the fuel supply line to prevent gas from draining back to the fuel tank. There was no return line on this fuel system back to the tank. Only the exact amount of fuel needed to run the engine was drawn up to the mixer on each intake stroke. Gas tanks were sometimes mounted on engine trucks. These external tanks could be piped to the engine if it was used in a stationary application.

The mixer or vaporizer, as Fuller & Johnson called it, works on the Venturi principle. Fuel enters the mixer about halfway between the damper and the throttle-valve control knob. Fuel is sucked into the mixer in the form of a spray. As the air rushes into the lower end of the vaporizer, it is lifted upward into the spray of fuel, and a single throttle valve controls the amount of gas that is able to pass into the mixer on each intake stroke of the engine. The damper lever on the mixer is used as a choke. By closing it at start-up, more fuel is drawn into the cylinder. After the engine starts, the damper is opened so that the fuel can be better regulated. The damper is located inside the suction tube above the suction-tube trap. Most of these engines have no fuel pump and rely on the sucking action of the piston to move the fuel from the fuel tank to the mixer. A fuel pump was supplied for engines where the fuel tank was to be below ground or some distance from the engine.

The fuel mixture is ignited by an electrical spark. The hammer-break igniter is connected with a battery and coil, or a gear-driven low-tension magneto could be installed. In the later years of production, spark-plug ignition could be ordered. This requires a battery and buzz coil or a high-tension magneto. Accurate, Esselman, Splitdorf, and Wico magnetos were often used on these engines.

Fuller & Johnson took extra pains in manufacturing the pistons for this engine. Special oil grooves were cut into the piston skirt to aid cylinder oiling. Cast-iron piston rings were split and pinned in place to keep them from rotating. The connecting rod is of the I-beam type and has a split Babbitt bearing connecting it to the crankshaft. A bronze bushing is press fit into the other end of the connecting rod for the wrist pin. The main bearings were also made from Babbitt. The bearings were set in the base casting and offset 30 degrees. That forces the thrust of the connecting rod directly into the bottom of the bearings.

Safety guards on the Model N engines are worthy of note. The connecting rod is covered with a rolled-tin guard, fastened with two steel support straps and bolted to the base casting. The guard prevents hands and fingers from coming in contact with the connecting rod as the engine runs. A cast-iron gear guard also covers the crankshaft and pinion gears.

The factory furnished many extras that they called regular equipment with these engines. The gasoline tank, a plain pulley, cylinder site-feed oiler, three grease cups, battery box, batteries, spark coil, funnel, cylinder oil, wrenches, a measure, muffler, oil

This Lunkenheimer Type E generator was used on Sears and Roebuck engines.

A 1918 Fuller and Johnson (F&J) three-horsepower Model N engine.

F&J water-cooled cylinder head, fuel mixer and fuel needle control valve, cam arm, igniter, valves, and valve control arms.

An F&J Model N flyball governor, detent control, and gear guard.

A Model N igniter and trip.

can, and an instruction book was packed with every engine that left the Fuller & Johnson plant.

Preparing to Start the Model N Engine
Pre-Start Checklist
1. Lubricate all the moving engine parts.
2. Fill all the drip oilers and greasers.
3. Fill the engine's cooling system with water or coolant.
4. Fill the fuel tank with gasoline.
5. Check the electrical wiring for loose connections.
6. Lubricate the magneto bearing if the engine is so equipped.

Pre-Start Checklist Detail
Prepare to start the engine by lubricating all the working parts. Fill the site-feed oiler with a good-grade mineral oil. Adjust the oiler to feed six to 10 drops of oil per minute. Oil the cam rod, valves, and igniter with a drop or two of oil. Roll the engine over slowly and lubricate all open gearing. Place a few drops of oil on the exhaust-valve bracket and lever. The fly-ball governor and detent should also be lightly oiled. The grease cups must be filled for the main and connecting-rod bearings. (Give each grease cup a

turn every 5 hours of running time to lubricate the bearings.)

Fill the water hopper with coolant. Maintain a coolant level within a couple inches of the top of the water hopper. Place the cover back over the water hopper.

Filling the gasoline tank is next. If a fuel pump is used, you may want to prime the system. This is done by hand-operating the pump lever on the fuel pump several times. After the engine is running, the fuel pump operates automatically off the cam rod.

Check the batteries, coil, and igniter electrical wire connections. Make sure all connections are tight. The knife switch should be in the open position. If the igniter is excessively dirty, use kerosene to clean off excess oil and grime. Keeping the igniter clean will prevent the igniter from grounding out.

If a magneto is installed on the engine, you should lubricate the bevel gear. Add a drop or two of light bearing oil to the magneto bearings once a week. The magneto should be kept as clean as possible to prevent electrical shorts.

Finally, rotate the engine over slowly and make sure that the engine doesn't bind. You should now be ready to start the engine.

Starting the Three-horsepower Fuller & Johnson Model N

Follow these steps to start the Model N:
1. Open the throttle valve to "S" position.
2. Close the damper.
3. Slide the hand crank into position on the crankshaft.
4. Prime the engine.
5. Close the electrical knife switch.
6. Rotate the engine over to start.
7. After the engine has started, remove crank handle.
8. Open the damper.
9. Adjust the throttle valve for running.

Starting Detail

Begin by opening the throttle valve to the "S" position. Close the damper on the vaporizer to choke the engine on start-up. Place the hand crank on the crankshaft in position for starting. Open the priming cup located on the engine's head. Opening the priming cup will relieve engine compression, making the engine turn over easier. Start rotating the engine in the direction it runs. If you're positioned on the igniter side, this is clockwise. Continue to turn the engine over until the igniter just snaps. Rotate the engine slightly more until the piston is on the intake stroke and stop. Fill the priming cup with gasoline. Use less gasoline if the engine is warm, more gasoline in the winter when the engine is cold. Now, slowly rotate the flywheel until the fuel is taken into the cylinder. Close the priming cup. Close the knife switch to the battery. With the crank handle, turn the engine over several times rapidly. As soon as the engine starts, remove the crank handle. Then open up the damper. The vaporizer throttle valve will need to be adjusted back somewhere close to the "R" position. As the engine warms up, a slight adjustment of the throttle valve may be needed. The throttle valve can continue to be closed until the engine running speed is attained or the engine backfires. If either occurs, open the throttle valve slightly. As you become more familiar with your engine, these adjustments and fine tuning of the engine will become almost automatic.

An F&J Model N fuel vaporizer with needle control valve and butterfly damper control lever.

Shutting Down the Fuller & Johnson N Engine

Follow these steps to shut down the Model N engine:
1. Close the throttle valve.
2. Open the electrical knife switch.
3. Turn off the oil feed from drip oiler.
4. Drain the engine coolant. Make a habit of draining the coolant. You will never forgive yourself if the coolant should freeze and you find your engine damaged from cracking.

Chapter Four

Maintenance and Troubleshooting

At times, stationary gas engines may be difficult to start, or may not run properly. In previous chapters, engine parts and the workings of several specific engines have been explained. The operator should now be able to begin to understand the problems associated with stationary gas engines. The following troubleshooting information should be used as a guideline to diagnose gas engine troubles, symptoms and possible remedies.

Troubleshooting

Engine does not start
Fuel Trouble; Lack of Fuel
Carburetor needle valve closed
Fuel-line check valve stuck, improperly seated or
    installed backwards
Fuel line frozen
Fuel not atomizing
Fuel pump is not functioning
Fuel supply line leaks
Fuel tank is empty
Plugged carburetor
Plugged carburetor orifice
Plugged fuel lines from tank to carburetor
Water in the fuel

Fuel-Mixture Troubles
Choking device not properly adjusted
Compression release left open
Engine flooded
Engine intake or cylinder not primed
Engine is too cold or hot
Fuel mixture too rich
Fuel mixture too weak

Fuel not atomizing
Priming cup left open

Defective Make-and-Break Low-Tension Igniter System
Battery is weak or dead
Carbon buildup on igniter causing electrical short
Coil defective
Coil, battery, or engine terminals loose
Dead coil
Defective dynamo, generator, or magneto
Electrical system has been grounded
Electrical system has been wired incorrectly
Engine timer not making proper contact
Igniter fouled
Igniter has been grounded
Igniter is out of adjustment
Igniter not tripping
Igniter points loose, not making contact, or missing
Igniter points not separating
Igniter trip is out of time
Ignition switch or knife switch is not closed
Incomplete electrical circuit
Knife switch not closed
No electrical spark
Point separation too slow—weak springs
Wiring is not complete

Defective Jump-Spark High-Tension Ignition System
Battery is weak or dead
Buzz coil defective
Buzz coil trembler not making contact
Coil, battery, or engine terminals loose
Defective dynamo, generator, or magneto

Electrical system has been grounded
Electrical system has been wired incorrectly
Engine timer not making proper contact
Ignition switch or knife switch not closed
Incomplete electrical circuit
Knife switch not closed
No electrical spark
Spark-plug gap incorrect
Spark plug shorted out or damaged
Wiring is not complete

Cold Engine and Fuel
Air intake pipe cold
Choking device inoperable
Extremely cold fuel when temperatures are below 25
    degrees Fahrenheit
Poor atomizing or fuel mixture
Water-jacket coolant cold

Water in Fuel or Cylinder
Cracked head or cylinder
Frozen fuel line or carburetor
Fuel pump frozen
Head gasket blown or leaks
Igniter gasket blown or leaks
Water in fuel lines
Water in fuel tank

Incorrect Engine Settings
Exhaust valve does not close
Exhaust valve does not open
Exhaust valve not timed
Governor out of adjustment
Spark out of time

Other Causes
Cam gear installed improperly
Engine's moving parts are bound
Excessive compression leaks
Exhaust rod not making contact with exhaust valve
Fuel pump not cycling
Intake valve sticks or will not open
No compression

Engine Runs But Lacks Power
Lack of Fuel
Carburetor needle valve might be adjusted
    improperly
Fuel-line check valve problems—stuck
Fuel pump is not supplying enough fuel
Fuel supply line leaks
Fuel tank is almost empty
Partially plugged carburetor
Partially plugged fuel lines from tank to carburetor

Incorrect Fuel Mixture
Carburetor adjustment incorrect
Choke set improperly

Engine is being flooded
Fuel-line air leak
Fuel mixture too rich
Fuel mixture too weak
Improper fuel used
Partially clogged fuel line
Partially plugged carburetor
Water in fuel

Defective Ignition
Battery is weak
Carbon buildup on igniter causing uneven firing
Electrical terminal loose
Engine timer is making intermittent contact
Igniter is out of adjustment
Igniter trip is out of time or loose
Point separation too slow—weak springs
Points not making contact

Overheating
Bearings are tight
Broken rings
Engine timing not set properly
Engine working too long under heavy load
Fan on air-cooled engine not operating
Insufficient lubrication
Lack of coolant in cooling system
Overheated piston
Poor-quality lubricants
Pre-ignition
Rings not properly lubricated
Rings not sealing in piston cylinder
Too many broken cooling fins or ribs on air-cooled
engine

Compression Leaks
Broken piston ring
Cracked cylinder or head
Head or cylinder gasket leak
Igniter or igniter gasket leak
Intake and exhaust valves not properly seated
Piston has developed a pin-hole leak
Piston rings do not seal against cylinder wall
Rings are not properly lubricated
All the piston-ring joints are in a line on the piston
Rings stuck in piston grooves
Spark plug itself leaks
Spark plug not tightened in the head properly
Valve cage not properly packed
Valve springs weak, loose, or broken
Valve stems bent, worn, or binding in valve guides

Valve and Air Passages Constricted
Air intake plugged with debris
Carburetor plugged with debris
Carburetor plugged with frost or ice
Improper length or size exhaust pipe
Intake valve spring too strong
Valve stems or levers binding, bent, or loose

Engine is Overloaded
Engine not sized properly for machinery being powered
Friction of working parts overcoming engine power

Pounding Noise as Engine is Running
Pre-Ignition
Carbon builds up inside cylinder—red-hot carbon causes ignition
Metal points inside cylinder—metal glowing, causing ignition
Overheated piston or cylinder
Poor ignition timing
Spark ignition is too late

Cylinder Compression Leaks
Broken piston ring
Cracked cylinder or head
Head or cylinder gasket leak
Igniter or igniter-gasket leak
Intake and exhaust valves not properly seated
Piston has developed a pin-hole leak
Piston rings do not seal against cylinder wall
Rings are not properly lubricated
Rings are set in piston with all breaks in line
Rings stuck in piston grooves
Spark plug leaks
Spark plug not tightened in the head properly
Valve cage not properly packed
Valve springs weak, loose, or broken
Valve stems bent, worn, or binding in valve guides

Loose Engine Parts
Connecting-rod bearing caps
Connecting-rod bearing not properly adjusted
Main-bearing caps loose
Main bearings not adjusted properly
Flywheel loose on crankshaft
Flywheel hub cracked
Flywheel spoke broken or cracked
Flywheel rim cracked or broken
Flywheel sections loose
Governor parts clash
Gears not meshing properly

Moving Parts of Engine Hitting Some Obstruction
Inspect by slowly rotating engine over by hand to determine cause

Speed Regulation Not Consistent
Defective Ignition
Battery is weak
Belt powering dynamo or generator slipping
Carbon buildup on igniter causing electrical short
Coil defective
Coil, battery, or engine terminals loose or broken
Defective wire—cracked insulation or broken
Dynamo needs adjustment
Electrical system has intermittent ground
Electrical wire problem

Engine timer not making proper contact
Generator needs adjustment
Igniter has been grounded
Igniter is out of adjustment
Igniter trip is out of time
Ignition points loose or missing
Ignition switch or knife switch is not closed
Magneto needs adjustment
Point separation too slow—weak springs
Points not making contact
Spark-plug fouling
Spark-plug insulator cracked

Governor is Out of Adjustment
Detent lever has excess clearance
Governor not properly lubricated
Governor-spring tension incorrect
Governor springs cracked or broken
Governor weights too heavy or light
Moving parts binding
Moving parts out of adjustment
Weak or broken governor spring

Incorrect Fuel Mixture
Choking device not working properly
Fuel mixture too rich or too lean
Water in fuel
Wrong fuel

Excess Fuel Consumption
Leaks
Carburetor or mixer leaks
Check valve leaks
Cylinder leaks
Fuel line leaks
Fuel pump leaks
Gas tank leaks

Other Causes of Excess Fuel Consumption
Choke is closed or not adjusted properly
Defective ignition—improperly set
Engine parts binding, causing additional friction
Engine running too cold
Engine runs too fast on light loads
Incorrect fuel mixture—too rich
Poor fuel quality

Backfiring
Delayed Ignition of Previous Fuel Charge
Fuel mixture is too weak
Spark timing too late

Other Causes
Glowing carbon inside combustion chamber
Glowing metal inside combustion chamber

Explosions Inside Muffler or Exhaust Pipe
Defective Make-and-Break Low-Tension Igniter System
Battery is weak or dead

Carbon buildup on igniter causing electrical short
Coil defective
Coil, battery, or engine terminals loose
Electrical system has been wired incorrectly
Engine timer not making proper contact
Igniter has been grounded
Igniter is out of adjustment
Igniter tripping is out of time
Ignition points loose or missing
Ignition switch or knife switch is not closed
Magneto is defective or needs repair or adjustment
Point separation too slow—weak springs
Points not making contact
System has been grounded improperly
Wiring is not complete

Defective Jump-Spark High-Tension Ignition System
Battery is weak or dead
Buzz coil defective or out of adjustment
Buzz coil trembler not making contact
Coil, battery, or engine terminals loose
Electrical system has been wired incorrectly
Engine timer not making proper contact
Ignition switch or knife switch is not closed
Magneto is defective—needs repair or adjustment
Spark-plug gap incorrect
Spark plug shorted out or damaged
System has been grounded improperly
Wiring is not complete

Other Causes
Choke is closed or not adjusted properly.
Fuel mixture too rich

Engine Smoke
Smoke at Exhaust Pipe
Excessive lubrication of the cylinder—too much oil—causing blue smoke at the muffler
Fuel mixture too rich causing black smoke at muffler

Smoke at Open End of the Piston Cylinder
Connecting-rod bearing lubricant burning
Hole in piston
Piston rings leak

Carburetor and Fuel Mixture Adjustment

An engine may smoke while running. Any smoke that is noticeable from the exhaust or the open end of the cylinder must be corrected. Smoke may be a sign of an improper fuel adjustment or a compression loss. Observing the smoke color of an engine's exhaust will help diagnose its cause. By adjusting the engine's fuel mixture or lubrication, most smoke problems will disappear.

If black-colored smoke is observed coming from the exhaust, it indicates an excess amount of fuel. To correct black exhaust smoking, adjust the fuel-supply needle valve and close off some of the fuel supplied to the engine cylinder. If the cylinder has been loaded with an excessive amount of fuel, it may take

several moments of running before the smoke clears. If the black smoke continues, close off the fuel supply some more. Do this until the engine runs without any sign of black smoke. Should the engine begin to backfire, open the needle valve back up just slightly to prevent backfiring.

Blue smoke at the exhaust is generally created when too much lubricating oil enters the cylinder. The engine tries to burn this oil, thus producing blue smoke. There are several causes of this problem. An engine that has been inactive for some period of time may have accumulated oil in the cylinder. This will cause blue smoke for several minutes, but only at engine start up. If the engine continues to emit blue smoke after the engine has been running for several minutes, close off the supply of lubricating oil going to the piston. It normally takes several minutes to see any visual oil-smoke correction after the adjustment has been made. This is because oil burns slowly and takes time to clear out of the cylinder. If the engine starts up without any smoke but starts to smoke after the engine has been running, close off some of the oil supply going to the cylinder. Again, allow several minutes for the problem to clear up. Another cause might be an oiler or lubricator that needs readjustment.

Smoke that exits at the open end of the cylinder is often caused by a compression leak letting exhaust gases escape past the piston and rings. Begin by inspecting the piston rings, piston, and cylinder for wear or damage. Honing the cylinder, ring replacement, or a new piston may be needed to correct the compression leak.

Engine Timing

Improper timing leads to many engine running difficulties. Engine timing must be set correctly no matter which ignition system is used. A general understanding of ignition timing will enable the operator to make timing adjustments.

Ignition must take place slightly before the piston reaches top dead center of the compression stroke. The slower the engine runs, the closer to top dead center the ignition can be set. As engine speed increases, the spark must come earlier. This is due to the fact that combustion is not instantaneous. The spark must be generated inside the cylinder a moment before combustion is desired. If the timing is too early, the engine will want to kick backwards. If the timing is too late, power is lost or the charge may not ignite. It is the adjustment of the firing or sparking of the ignition device that changes engine timing.

Ignition timing of hot-tube-equipped engines relies on the adjustment of an open flame on the hollow tube. The hot tube is heated inside a chimney by the external flame. As heat is applied to the outside of the tube, it shortly becomes red hot. On the compression stroke, the fuel mixture is compressed into the tube. It continues to travel up the tube until it reaches a point at which the tube is hot enough to ignite the fuel mixture. At the moment the fuel mixture reaches this point in the tube, combustion occurs.

Adjusting this ignition point on the hot tube changes the engine timing. The higher up into the tube that the fuel mixture is compressed before ignition occurs, the later in the engine's cycle combustion takes place. If the tube is heated too far up from the engine, the fuel mixture will not ignite. Heating the tube closer to the engine or the base of the tube creates a hot spot that will ignite the fuel mixture earlier in the engine cycle. Remember, the faster the engine runs, the earlier the fuel must be ignited. The slower the engine runs, the later ignition can occur.

Hot-bulb ignition is very similar to hot-tube ignition. A cast-iron bulb is placed in the end of the cylinder or on the cylinder head. The bulb is then externally heated with a blow torch prior to engine start-up. As the bulb is heated, it begins to gain temperature and glow. When the bulb is hot enough to ignite the fuel mixture, the engine can be started. The heat from ignition normally is enough to maintain bulb heat during operation. After the engine is brought up to running speed, the blow torch is turned off. This ignition method was commonly used on Mietz & Weiss semi-diesel engines.

Jump-spark-equipped engines require adjustment of the timer or cam contact to change ignition timing. Many engines use a rotating cam that makes contact with a spring finger. As contact is maintained, the electrical circuit is completed. Electrical current flows through the buzz coil, and a high-tension electric current is developed. The making and breaking of this circuit by the buzz coil trembler during the contact period creates hundreds of individual sparks between the stationary electrodes. By adjusting the spring finger, contact with the cam can be made earlier or later during the engine cycle. This adjustment advances or retards engine timing.

Jump-spark ignition produced with a high-tension oscillating magneto, as described on the International Harvester Co. Mogul engine, requires adjustment of the magneto trip and connecting linkage. By adjusting length of the trip lever and connecting linkage, ignition timing is made earlier or later during the engine cycle.

There are many different timing arrangements found on stationary engines. The important thing to remember is that proper engine timing can be accomplished by correctly setting or adjusting the moment that ignition is forced to occur. Study the tripping of the igniter or the sparking of the plug in relationship to the piston cycle. If the spark occurs after the piston has passed top dead center of the compression stroke, it is occurring too late. If the spark occurs too many degrees before top dead center of the compression stroke, chances are it is too early. Many original owner's manuals detail engine timing settings. If you don't have an owner's manual, you must experiment with these adjustments until the engine runs properly.

Igniter Maintenance

The number of engine-igniter designs is almost as vast as the number of engines manufactured. Their sizes and shapes differ tremendously; however, principal workings and basic parts are all about the same. Many maintenance activities are common to all igniter designs. Igniters occasionally need electrical and mechanical maintenance. Igniters are timed and tripped mechanically during engine operation, so igniter points and electrodes had to be insulated from one another or the electric circuit would short out. The igniter is an excellent place to start engine troubleshooting. More times than not, electrical problems cause engine performance and running difficulties.

The first check to make on an igniter is a compression test. Roll the engine over and make sure that no compression is being lost through the igniter gasket or blowing back through the electrodes. If the gasket between the engine and igniter is leaking, tighten the bolts. If this fails to seal the leak, then replace the gasket. Start by removing and cleaning the rust and stuck gasket materials from the engine casting and igniter. A light film of grease or a gasket sealer applied to both sides of the gasket will also help seal any leaks.

Electrode leaks can be caused by worn insulating washers or packing. If the hole through the igniter flange has been worn oversize, it can be filled with weld and redrilled to size. It can also be drilled oversize and a new electrode made to fit. Mica washers or packing are used to insulate the electrode from the igniter flange. If either have deteriorated, replace with new material. Adjusting or re-tightening the electrode should correct any compression leaks. Wear and carbon buildup may cause the electrode to develop leaks. Repair these electrodes by removing them and re-seating the electrode using the same methods you would in grinding a valve. After grinding, replace the electrode.

Igniters must work freely and extremely fast. After the igniter has been removed from the engine, work the points open and closed several times to ensure the igniter isn't binding. If it binds, disassemble it and clean all the working parts. Steel wool or fine sand-paper can be use to shine all the moving parts. Clean the holes through the flange with a drill of the right size.

After cleaning, lightly oil the moving parts and reassemble the igniter. Check the coil springs on the igniter. Many igniters have a small hole that allows lubrication of the igniter's moving parts. Remove any rust or fouling from inside this oiling passageway. If the igniter has a weak or broken spring, replace it. An igniter that doesn't snap back with enough force will not open the points. If the spring is too weak, the igniter will not respond quickly enough to ignite the fuel at the proper moment needed for ignition.

While inspecting the igniter, make sure the points are not loose or missing. Replace missing points with new ones. New points can be purchased easily for all types of igniters. The best replacement points are made from a platinum alloy. Loose points can be re-peened to tighten them up. Some points were threaded into the igniter, so care should be taken to identify your course of action on loose points. Points become fouled with carbon during combustion. Clean the igniter points thoroughly with a wire brush if they're fouled. If the points do not address each other squarely, file the points until the two point surfaces come in complete contact with one another. Never over-file the points. Always try cleaning the points first. Points will last longer if filed only when absolutely necessary.

Magnetos, Dynamos, and Generator Maintenance

Magnetos, dynamos, and generators supply low- or high-tension electrical current for many stationary engines. They are very durable and generally have a long life, but lubrication, maintenance, and timing adjustments are needed from time to time, and many of the moving parts will eventually need repair or replacement. Proper care and adjustment of these units result in dependable spark ignition.

Every unit requires some degree of lubrication. Bearings and bushings must be frequently oiled. Check the unit by looking for oil access holes to the bearings. A few drops of light electric-motor bearing oil should be applied to the bearings at least once a week, if the engine is run daily. In the case of seasonal operation, a drop or two each time the engine is run becomes necessary. On rotary units with gear drive, apply several drops of oil to the gears prior to each start-up. Oscillating-type magnetos have springs, and their attachment points should have a light film of oil to reduce friction during oscillations. Apply oil at both ends of each spring prior to engine start-up. High-tension magnetos such as the Wico EKs are sometimes driven by a bearing off a cam. Always apply a few drops of oil to the bearing and cam surfaces on this type of magneto setup.

Dynamos and generators that use a friction drive require governor adjustment. If the unit is equipped with a fly-ball governor, the governor's spring tension controls the operation rpm of the device. Weak spring tension allows the unit to run slower. Strong tension on the governor spring increases the unit's rpm. A good rule of thumb is to run them no faster than 900 to 1200 rpm. Higher rpm can cause damage to the unit.

Dynamos and generators are sometimes belted to pulleys and flywheels. Here rpm adjustment can only be changed by altering the diameter of the pulleys or flywheel or changing engine speed. The flywheels obviously are not easily changed. Use a tachometer to check the unit's operating speed. A jack shaft could also be used between the unit and its source of rotary power to increase or decrease rpm.

Check for loose wire leads before starting the engine. Loose leads can cause irregular ignition. Make sure the wire does not come in contact with any mov-ing engine parts. Cycle the engine to confirm free movement. Thumb nuts or spring-tension wire-attachment devices also need to be checked. Make sure they grip the wire firmly.

For many of the common units, reproduction instruction manuals are available. These manuals detail each unit's construction and adjustment procedures. Parts are identified, and in many cases replacement parts can be purchased.

If the unit is not producing any spark and you are not able to repair these units yourself, send them to a competent repair shop for service.

Valve Grinding or Replacement

Leaking valves cause fuel mixture and compression problems that result in a loss of engine power. Overheated or burnt exhaust valves may warp or deteriorate. Corrosion is another cause of valve leakage. If the valves seat properly, engine compression, fuel mixing, and horsepower will improve. Problems associated with leaky valves normally can be remedied by replacing the valves or grinding the old valves and their seats.

Intake and exhaust valves are normally found in the cylinder head. Cages and special chambers that are cast into headless-type engines also house valves. To grind a valve, it must first be removed from the engine. If the valves are found in the head, remove the head. The springs that hold the valves in place must then be released. Compress the spring and remove the spring retaining device. Spring retainers come in many different configurations. Two common retainers used a nut and cotter pin or a washer and cotter pin. The cotter pin pushes through a hole in the end of the valve stem in front of the nut or washer. Some valve stems are threaded for the retaining nut, allowing spring tension adjustment. Remove the nut, and the valve should push out of the valve guide to remove it from the head. Inspect the valve and seat for wear. If the valve has serious damage or has warped, a new valve is preferable. The seat should also be inspected. Many engines have removable valve seats. These can be replaced if damaged or worn. The valve must have enough stock at its edge to allow some material to be removed during the grinding process. A razor-edged valve will only burn up or warp if used in that condition. Valves or seats that have extremely deep grooves may need to be taken to a shop that can machine or grind them. If the grooves cannot be trued with enough stock left for seating, replace the valve.

There are many tools available for grinding valves, from suction-cup hand-held tools to electric-powered oscillating units. Select one of these tools to begin the grinding of the valves.

Grinding a Valve
1. Secure the head or valve cage in a vise.
2. Place a small amount of valve-grinding paste on

the seat and valve edge.

3. Drop the valve back into the valve guide and onto its seat.

4. Attach the valve-grinding tool to the valve head.

5. Start to rotate the valve back and forth with a slight amount of downward pressure on the valve and seat.

6. While continually rotating the valve, occasionally lift it from the seat and then drop the valve back down. This varies the contact surface and ensures that the seating surfaces are being lapped equally.

7. Remove the valve from the seat and inspect them both.

8. Repeat the grinding process as many times as necessary until a uniform seat has been made completely around the valve and seat. When properly lapped or ground, a small shiny circular rim from 3/32- to 1/8-inch wide should be visible completely around the valve and seat. This seat should occur at about the center of the beveled edge of the valve, starting no less than 3/32 inch from the top of the valve head. If less stock is left than that, the valve will burn quickly and be damaged. If grinding causes the edge to become thin, replace the valve.

9. After grinding is complete, remove all residue from the valve seat and valve. Flush them with kerosene, if necessary. Valve stems that are gummed up or have excessive carbon buildup must be cleaned with kerosene or a light sanding. Do not leave any grinding compound on the valves, seats, or any engine parts prior to reassembly.

10. Reassemble the engine.

New valves should be treated the same as old, leaking valves. Always lap or grind new valves onto the seats. If the grinding of the valve and seat has been done properly, no leaks should be found. Check valves and seats by rotating the engine over on the compression stroke and listening for air passing through the valve ports or out of the valve guides. If no compression is lost, your repair has been done successfully.

Honing the Engine Cylinder

When the cylinder is lightly pitted or worn, the bore can sometimes be renewed by honing it. Honing of the cylinder creates a smooth bore and allows the rings to seal against the cylinder wall. Maintaining a smooth bore is critical in maximizing engine power and performance. A good opportunity to hone the cylinder is during the installation of new piston rings.

To begin the honing process, remove the piston and connecting rod from the engine. Make sure that shims, bearings, and caps are match-marked for re-assembly. Headless engines must be honed from the rear cylinder opening. Remove the engine head on all other engines. The cylinder can now be accessed for honing.

Begin the honing process by removing all heavy carbon deposits from the cylinder and head with a scraper. Fine sand-paper can be used to further clean the bore and head. After completion of hand cleaning, remove all residues with kerosene. Clean all carbon deposits from the valves and valve seats. Adjust the hone to the proper cylinder diameter, and lubricate it with kerosene or light honing oil. Splash the cylinder with kerosene and insert the hone. Slowly start rotation of the hone. Slide the hone all the way in to the end of the cylinder. At this point, begin to pull the hone back toward the starting position. Care should be taken not to extend the hone too far past the cylinder end because the hone will jump out of the cylinder and be damaged. Always try to hold the hone in the center of the cylinder as you repeat the forward and backward motion. Maintain a steady speed while moving the hone forward and backward. This guarantees all cylinder surfaces are being dressed equally. To keep the hone stones clean, apply liberal amounts of oil or kerosene during honing. Continue this process until the cylinder bore has been cleaned up. The cylinder should have the same clean, polished appearance from end to end and completely around the circumference of the bore. Once cylinder honing is completed, flush away all remaining sediments left behind from the honing process. Prior to assembling the engine, coat the cylinder walls, rings, and piston with a liberal film of lubricating oil. This will protect these components until the engine oiling device is able to provide adequate lubrication.

If the cylinder has a ridge, a ridge cutter will be needed to remove the ridge before the honing process starts. Extremely bad bores will require machine boring. If boring opens the cylinder beyond the limits of over-sized piston rings, a cylinder sleeve will have to be made and installed.

A good bore coupled with properly seated rings will ensure optimum engine horsepower. Do the best cylinder honing job possible. The reward is increased engine compression and fuel efficiency.

Chapter Five

Powered Equipment

The rotating motion produced by gas engines powered a multitude of equipment and machinery for farms, small businesses, and industries across America. Gas engines could power equipment that was driven by a belt, by friction, or by gears. In addition, one engine could be moved around, as needed, to supply power to countless different machines.

Stationary engine applications best suited everyday tasks that were continuous in nature. By belting a stationary engine to an overhead line shaft, many machines could be powered at once. Line shafts held in place with bearing blocks could have several pulleys attached along their lengths. These pulleys were aligned with shop equipment such as drill presses, grinders, lathes, boring machines, and saws. When the engine was started, the line shaft was set in motion and provided power to every machine belted to it.

Portable engines mounted on a skid or cart could be moved from job to job and used for many different tasks. Prospective engine owners evaluated machinery and equipment needs to determine what horsepower engine to buy. If the engine was to be used as a portable, it had to be powerful enough to run the equipment demanding the most horsepower. Therefore, these engines were often oversized for some of their intended uses.

Water Pumps

Hand-dug wells equipped with winches and buckets provided water for thousands of years. Later, windmills and steam power would be developed to aid the pumping of water. But not until the gas engine was developed were individuals able to provide their own homes and farms with a continuous water supply at a price that was affordable. Existing wells could be con-verted with pump jacks and powered with a gas engine. The Aermotor Co. designed a complete line of pumps and engines for water wells. These small eight-cycle engines could easily pump thousands of gallons of water each week for livestock. The Aermotor engine and pump could also be used to fill water tanks that worked on gravity. These tanks would be built on the upper floors of a structure, and pipe was run throughout the building to supply running water.

F. E. Myers and Brothers of Ashland, Ohio, was a Co. that devoted itself to the manufacture of pumping equipment. The Myers Co. pump jacks were designed to upgrade a hand pump to use gas engine power. Each manufacturer claimed that their design was absolutely the best of all, but the truth is they all worked about the same, raising and lowering the pump plunger arm as the pump jack was cycled. Slightly dif-

The 1909 Aermotor pumping engine.

ferent gear ratios made some cycle faster or slower than others. Normally, one jack could be adapted to many different well pumps. The gas engine was belted to the pump jack pulley to supply its power.

Rotary and centrifugal pumps were also used to move water. The rotary pump could be belted or di-

rectly connected to the gas engine. As the engine turned the pump, water was transported through pipes to the field or a storage reservoir. Pump sizes varied greatly. Small pumps might be used to keep water in a trough for livestock. In this application, an engine could run for a period of time and then shut off, or an overflow pipe could be provided to return excess water back to the well. The Gould centrifugal used an impeller inside the housing to move the liquid as the pump was rotated. Mud pumps were designed to drain water from swamps or flooded fields. These large diaphragm pumps were slow acting but displaced a large volume of water with each stroke. The diaphragm pump reciprocated up and down, sucking in water and then pushing it out. The well was not the only source of water. Water could also be pumped directly from a river or lake using the same methods that have been discussed. From our rivers and lakes, fields were irrigated and livestock watered. Huge pumps and even larger gas engines would eventually supply cities with water.

Spray rigs were built to pump water mixed with chemicals. Both centrifugal and piston pumps were manufactured for this task. Either pump was easily connected to a gas engine with belts or gears. Early portable spraying outfits provided a method of protecting fruit, vegetables, and grain from insects and disease. Fluid tanks, pumps, carts, skids, and hoses were the major components that made up spray rigs. Horses, tractors, or manpower were used to move the sprayers to the job.

Sawmills and cut-off saws powered by gas engines changed lumber processing dramatically. Gas-engine-powered units became affordable for many individuals. Gas engines belted up to saws were designed to be portable. They weighed much less than the portable steam engines or steam traction engines that had powered saws for many years. Gas engines were much safer to operate than steam engines, eliminating boiler explosions and the fire hazards associated with steam engines. The gasoline engine didn't require as much warm-up time as did the steam engine. Boilers had to be fired to generate steam. Not until the boiler's water had been converted into

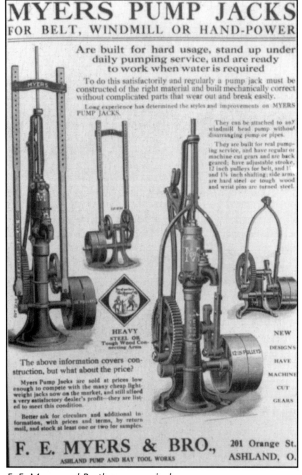

F. E. Myers and Brothers pump jacks.

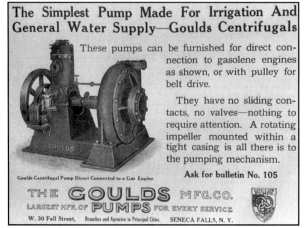

Gould Manufacturing Co., gasoline engine and centrifugal pump.

Maxwell and Fitch Co. spraying outfit.

steam could the steam engine provide power to run any type of machinery. This made the gas engine a tremendous time-saver. As soon as a gas engine develops its running speed it can be put to work. Portable, gas-powered saws could be pulled right to the job site. Once there, wood could then be processed as soon as it was harvested. Sawmills were easily set up in the field, and firewood for heating was cut in a fraction of the time that had once been spent with handsaws.

Cement Mixers

Badger Concrete mixing machines with small rotating barrels were engineered to batch materials using the stationary gas engine as its power source. Cement is formed by mixing sand, cement, rock aggregate, and water together. Mortar for bricklaying was batched the same way only without limestone or an aggregate. Small quantities of cement and mortar had been mixed by hand before these small, 1/4-yard machines made their appearance. Cement mixers came in many different sizes and designs, but they all rotated, turned, or oscillated, using power produced from a gas engine.

Air Compressors

Air compressors that operated off gasoline engines were used for a variety of purposes. Service stations used compressed air for car and truck lifts. Compressors supplied air for filling tires and starting gas engines. There were even pneumatic water-supply plants. Air compressors were manufactured in inverted vertical, vertical, and horizontal models. As the compressor cycles, air is compressed and stored at high pressure inside a storage tank. The compressor is designed similar to a gas engine. Its piston is used to compress ambient air. The compressor piston recipro-

cates in a manner similar to an internal combustion engine's piston, but the piston is only compressing air that has been drawn into the cylinder. The air is then forced out of the cylinder and into the storage tank. The compressor piston has a set of rings that prevent

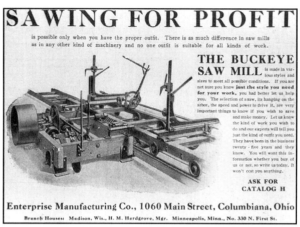

Enterprise Manufacturing Co. Buckeye Sawmill.

Hertzler and Zook cut-off saw built in models requiring 1 1/2 to 10 horsepower engines.

The gasoline engine powered Badger Concrete Mixer.

71

The Jacobson Machine Manufacturing Co. air compressor.

The Coles Co. "no-flicker" electric dynamo.

the air from passing by the piston. When air is compressed, heat is generated, and this heat must be absorbed and then transferred away from the compressor's moving parts. Extreme heat buildup will cause binding or, worse yet, damage to the moving parts of the compressor. Air cooling generally provided the compressor with adequate heat transfer.

Generators and Dynamos

Gas engines didn't power electric motors, but the engine could rotate an electrical dynamo or generator to produce electrical current. This use of the gas engine—powering a generator—may have been the most significant use of all. Rural towns and mining camps used them to power machinery and illuminate buildings and shops. Electric motors and fans were operated using the current produced from the generator. Single-family homes were illuminated with the aid of an engine and dynamo. This brought electricity to homes and families decades before utility companies would electrify America. Engines used with electrical generating equipment had to maintain a steady speed under many different loading parameters. Engine rpm variance had to be kept to a minimum. Spe-

cial engines were designed to meet this demanding use. One noticeable feature used on these engines was extremely large or wide flywheels. The added inertia of these oversized flywheels helped the engine maintain its rpm.

Farm Equipment

On every farm across America, the chores of everyday life were nearly endless. Nowhere could the help of the internal combustion engine have been more welcome. Many laborious tasks could now be accomplished with gas power. The needs of the animals were as demanding as those of the family. Corn and grain had to be ground to feed the animals. A gas engine needed only to be belted up to a mill, and grain could be ground into feed.

Gas-powered grinding or feed mills such as the Spartan Corn Belt were plentiful. These gasoline-powered feed mills normally required engines with horsepower ratings from 1-1/2 to 25 horsepower. Farm demand was so great that many companies manufactured and marketed mills of a variety of different designs. The manufacturer of the Superior #1 Feed Mill guaranteed that a 2-horsepower gas engine belted to the #1 mill and run at 550 rpm would grind 10 bushels of grain per hour. The same machine running with a 5-horsepower engine running at 1,150 rpm would grind 30 bushels. What they had forgotten to mention was how fast you had to load the grain into

The Corn Belt feed mill manufactured by the Spartan Manufacturing Co.

The Adams Husker Co. corn husker

the mill hopper to achieve these production capacities. These machines were commonly used to grind corn, cotton seed, oats, and wheat.

The hay baler is another farm machine that was converted to use gas power. Early balers were powered with horses. Hay that had been cut in the field was moved and stacked loosely with pitch forks. Hay was fed into the baler, and horses applied pressure through the use of an arm or lever to compress the hay. Bailers compressed loose hay and straw into convenient manageable bundles. The bundles could then be stacked, stored, moved, and lifted with ease. Hay balers such as the Ann Arbor were powered with internal combustion engines that eliminated the need for horses. Gas-powered balers mounted on trucks could be moved easily from one work site to another.

The corn husker was another specialized machine used to process grain. Small units like the Adams Husker made in Marysville, Ohio, were powered with small gas engines. Corn was hand fed into the husker. The husk was then removed automatically from the ear of corn. After processing, the corn was ready for a corn crib or drying and grinding.

Hoists

In boat yards and in industry, the need to lift heavy loads was ever present. What had once been done with steam power could now be done with gas, thus the development of small, more compact, portable hoists such as the Little Giant. Gas engines provided economical power to turn the winch hoist. The farmer used hoists to operate equipment such as the hay fork, which lifted stacks or bales of hay into the lofts of barns. Industry used hoists to operate gravel and soil loaders. Clamshell buckets dredged and dug while operating by cable hoist. Pile drivers used hoists to lift their hammers. Hoists were also used on railroad cars and barges to load and unload materials. Hoists mounted on carts or skids could be pulled directly to the work site. Once the hoist was belted up to a gas engine, the rigged load could be moved.

Washing Machines

Laundry is a chore in every household. Many manufacturers envisioned placing a washing machine equipped with a gas engine in every home in America. Competition for that market became fierce, and advertising campaigns stressed the labor and time savings of their wonderful machines. Maytag has al-

Crestline Manufacturing Co. grinder.

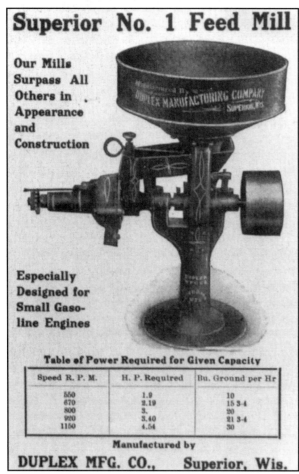
The Superior No. 1 Feed Mill

ways been a giant in the washing-machine industry. Maytag developed an engine to power its many washing-machine designs. Maytag's two-cycle, kick-start engines are now gaining popularity as a collectible engine. This small, lightweight engine was made in many different models throughout its production run. The engine was manufactured in vertical and horizontal models. Spark plugs located in the air-cooled cylinder head, magneto ignition, and a single flywheel were basic design elements found on all Maytag engines.

Portable and stationary internal combustion engines powered hundreds of thousands of machines in this country during their heyday. Machines that had been designed a hundred years before the gas engine were now modified to use the power it could provide. Gas-engine technology was changing the world. New machines developed to satisfy the needs of ever-expanding markets, and the internal combustion engine met that challenge.

The Little Giant hoist marketed by the Brown Clutch Co.

The Ann Arbor Baler was built by the Ann Arbor Machine Co.

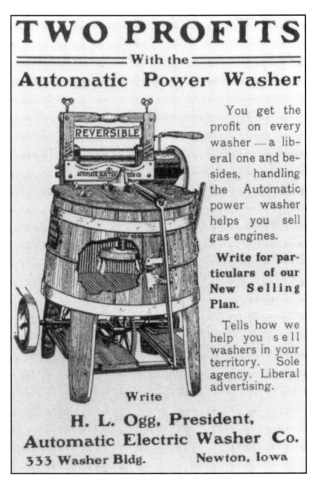
Automatic Electric Washer Companies built this Automatic Power Washer.

A 1917 Maytag vertical two-cycle engine.

The Queen City Power Washer made by John Dietz Manufacturing Co.

Chapter Six

Engine Evaluation

You've decided to purchase a stationary engine and have found one that is appealing. You begin to ask yourself questions. Are all the parts there? Are they original? Can I fix that? What color was the original? Will it run? How do I check an engine that's running? How will I move it? How much does it weight? Is it worth the price? Can I afford the cost of the engine and any additional costs for restoration? How badly do I want it? Making these decisions will become easier when you have developed a method or checklist for engine evaluation.

If the engine is running, a good portion of your inspection will be made easier. If the engine does not run, you should be prepared to spend as much time as required to evaluate all the individual components of the engine and its accessories. Proceed from one part to the next until you have examined every part

Lobee positive-displacement gear-driven water pump.

or every system of that particular engine. Assess the type of repairs you are able to do for yourself. Be familiar with the basic costs of parts and machining. You will need to figure in these costs when deciding if the engine is a good buy.

Non-running Engines

Let's assume first that you're inspecting an engine that is not in running condition and needs restoration. The first thing to do is make sure that the flywheels are free to turn. This ensures that the engine is loose. Never force the flywheels into motion, as doing so may bend or break engine parts. If the flywheel can be spun on the crankshaft, observe how true the flywheel rotates. If the flywheels wobble or hop, the crankshaft, bearings, or flywheels may be damaged, thus causing this unsafe condition. If the flywheels do not move, the piston or piston rings are likely to be rusted to the cylinder wall. Freeing a piston can be as easy as spraying oil into the cylinder, or as hard as flame burning the piston out of the cylinder. The cylinder walls must be inspected for pitting, cracks, and scoring. Deep pitting or cylinder damage will require boring, resleeving, or honing to restore the cylinder. Cracked cylinders can sometimes be repaired by welding the cracked or damaged area. The cylinder will then require reboring.

Next, look over the engine for damaged or missing components. Igniters, hot tubes, and magnetos are often missing, as evidenced by the hole left in the cylinder wall on the working side of the engine or in the cylinder head. Many times, the studs that held the igniter in place are still attached to the engine. In some cases, the engine may have been an igniter engine that was converted for spark-plug ignition. A plate was generally cut to fit the igniter hole and bolted to the original igniter studs. It was then drilled and tapped for a spark plug. This type of setup was normally a conversion and not original equipment. Igniters can cost from $20 to several hundreds dollars to replace. Magnetos normally are attached to a base or mounting bracket. Empty mounting brackets located close to pinion gears are a dead giveaway for a missing magneto, but many of the Wico high-tension magnetos were mounted on engine water hoppers above the igniter or exhaust rod, so look there, too. Missing magnetos can cost from $15 to $250 to replace. Hot tubes consisted of some sort of chimney and a hollow tube. If the chimney and tube are missing, new chimneys can be cast. Hot tubes can be purchased or made. If you have to purchase these parts, expect to spend from $50 to $100 on the hot tube.

Search the entire engine for cracks and breaks. Flywheel cracks or breaks can be dangerous. Only professionals should attempt repairs to any flywheel. Improper repairs may lead to serious accidents if the flywheel should separate during engine operation. I recommend that damaged flywheels be replaced. Water hoppers and cylinder heads are the most common areas where cracks are found. Always inspect the undersides of heads extremely well, as many times damage will be found lurking there. Water-jacket cracks can be repaired fairly easily. Checking for cylinder-wall cracks or breaks requires removing the head. If you're able to look from behind, that portion of the cylinder can be checked. Another method of checking for cylinder cracks is with the use of water. If the engine is loose, fill the cooling system with water. If water enters the cylinder, it will work its way out behind the piston. This check takes time. A defective gasket can also cause the same visual effect. Remove the piston or head for a positive check.

Water pumps, fuel pumps, carburetors, gas tanks, exhaust-valve levers, and all the other moving parts must be inspected. Inspect each individual part on the engine. Note any parts that already appear to be repaired. Replacement carburetors and fuel pumps can be hard to find, as well as expensive. If you find damaged parts, ask yourself if you are able to make the necessary repair. If the condition of the original is extremely poor, a replacement part may be the only solution. Are you willing to pay someone for a replacement part? Paying to have old parts repaired or replaced can be expensive.

Overall gear wear or damage must be accessed. Look over all exposed gears. Pointed or sharp gear teeth suggest that the gear is near the end of its life. On many engines, the small pinion gears that supply rotary power to the governor will appear to be worn the most. This type of wear is acceptable and is normal due to their size, as small gears make many more revolutions than the larger gears. If the gearing is enclosed in a crankcase, open the inspection-cover plate

Fairbanks Morse 1 1/2 horsepower headless engine in as found condition.

and inspect the gearing through this hole. If the gears in general are badly worn, they must be replaced.

Testing shafts and bearings for wear is fairly simple on engines up to 10 or 12 horsepower. Main and connecting-rod bearings are normally found inside a split bearing. The bearing cap is removable, providing access to the Babbitt bearing liners. Generally it will be these Babbitt liners that require adjustment or replacement. The crankshaft can be lifted with a bar to see how much movement the bearing has. If the shaft moves up and down or side to side, bearing adjustment or liner replacement will be needed. A small amount of clearance is always needed so that the shaft will turn freely in the bearings, but this clearance should be at the most a few thousandths of an inch. Most split bearings have shims between the two bearing halves that can be removed. Split bearings that have been worn beyond the limits of the shims must be replaced. Pouring your own bearings can be a tricky job. Several engine parts suppliers offer a bearing pouring service. Many even stock Babbitt bearings for the more common engines.

Cam and pinion gears rotate on steel shafts. Typically, the gear slid over the shaft, and a washer and cotter pin secured it in place. If the gears are loose, the bore on the gear or the shaft may be worn. These are simple things to fix. A new shaft can be made or the gear can be bored and rebushed.

Wrist pins are hard to check without loosening the connecting rod from the crankshaft. If you're able, pull back and forth on the connecting rod to test the free play in the bushing or wrist pin. Also, try to twist the connecting rod to the right and then to the left to check for side-to-side wear.

Side shafts must also be checked for bearing wear. This shaft rotates as the engine runs and is

Fairbanks Morse 1 1/2 horsepower headless engine after cleaning and lubrication.

found on the working side of the engine. Lightly pry on the side shaft to test for excessive movement.

Exhaust valve rods constantly move forward and backward during engine operation. Check for wear in the holes where the rod passes in castings and brackets. This fit does not need to be perfect; just check that a fair amount of stock remains around the holes where the rod passes. Some exhaust valve levers attach to support-bracket arms cast into the cylinder head. The pin that allows the lever to move and holds it in place must be loose. The arm supports must have enough material around the hole for future wear. This is not a critical fit, since a new pin can be installed here with ease. Check wear at the end of governor shafts and cam-rod shafts. Many of these rods have a circular bearing that rotates on a steel pin. Pins must be checked for wear. If the pin is broken or worn, a new pin can be made and installed. Take your time inspecting shafts, bearings, and guide holes where a shaft worked in and out. Sloppy fits and worn-out castings will also need to be repaired. It is important that you know approximately how much rod and bearing work needs to be done before buying an engine.

Valve guides can be checked by holding the valve and spring assembly with your hand and applying pressure up and down on the valve. If the valve wiggles or rocks inside the valve guide, there is a good chance that compression will leak through. All valves have some clearance for movement within the guide, however, because heat would bind them if they did not. Valve movement should not exceed 3/32 inch. Valve guides can be repaired by boring and resleeving. Look at the condition of the valve springs and retainers. Weak or deteriorated springs will need to be replaced.

The fuel tank is always of great concern on old engines. All too often, old gas or kerosene was left in

the tank to gum up the fuel lines or leave residue inside the tank. The first test is to open the filler cap. Look inside with a flash light to assess the tank's condition. A foul smell from inside tells you that old fuel remains inside the tank. Cleaning will restore the tank for use. If the tank has visible holes or rust deterioration, the tank must be repaired. A commercial tank sealer may be used to restore the fuel tank. If the tank is beyond repair, a new tank can be made or purchased. A galvanized fuel tank made exactly like your original can cost anywhere from $15 to $200, depending on its size, shape, and the number of fittings required during fabrication. If the engine's fuel tank was cast in its base, you must inspect them the same way you did the sheet-metal tank. Compressed air can be used successfully to remove dry material and rust from inside the tanks or castings. Blow air into one opening while allowing the materials to exit from one or several other openings in the tank. If the casting is leaking, use a commercial epoxy sealer to restore and seal the inside. The preferred repair method is to weld or braze the casting to seal the leak.

Fuel pumps are notorious for being in need of repair. Check balls, pump shafts, and seats almost always require restoration. Pumps are made from brass, cast iron, and pot metal. Each pump material has its own special properties. Cast-iron pumps are known for rusting and being frozen tight. Pot-metal pumps will not take any forcing of the parts without breaking. Brass pumps are very durable and are about the easiest to restore. Look over the fuel pump for cracks or breaks. If possible, make sure that the fuel pump will cycle. Some pumps can be cycled by hand. Check the fuel-pump shaft or plunger to see if it's loose in the pump. Check balls, shafts, packing nuts, packing, and springs can't be checked without disassembling the pump. Plan on inspecting, cleaning, and repacking the fuel pump, at minimum.

Water pumps are similar in construction to fuel pumps. Proceed with this inspection the same as you did with the fuel-pump inspection. Look for cracks or breaks first. Plunger-type pumps must be loose and cycle freely. If not, they will need to be rebuilt. Pump packing may leak when put in service. Many times, as the material is compressed or swells, it will self seal, preventing any further water from leaking. If leaking persists, new packing must be installed. Rotary pumps that are belted to the flywheels or driven from a jack shaft need to be inspected as well.

A common pump is that of the positive-displacement type. Inside the pump, gears are used to force water through the cooling system. Inspect the water pump for cracks and make sure that the shaft can be rotated. Move the shaft up and down to determine if the bearings are loose or worn out. Inspect the condition of the internal gears for wear. Sharp gear teeth are a sure sign of a well-worn pump. If the pump is badly frozen up or worn, rebuilding will be necessary.

Carburetors must be inspected for breaks and cracks. Turn all the needle valves on the carburetor to make sure that they move freely. Removing them will allow you to determine their condition. Many times, they are found to be deteriorated or bent. If the end of the needle does not come to a fine point, the needle valve and its seat could be damaged. Throttle shafts should be moved to make sure everything is loose. Linkages to the throttle or governors should also move freely. If the carburetor has a fuel bowl, sediment and rust often will be found inside. Bead blasting and a good cleaning will restore most of these units.

Magnetos and generators are hard to assess with only a visual inspection. Oscillating mags can be mechanically cycled, assuring that the electrodes are free. However, this tells little about the condition of the electrical generating components. If you are able to remove the magneto, cycle the magneto and take readings with an electrical multi-tester. If the magneto is attached to an igniter, it can be removed and cycled to see if the points spark. High-tension magnetos such as the Wico EK can be tested by pulling the magnets apart as quickly as possible. As the magneto's magnetic field collapses, you should be able to get a reading with a multi-tester. Generators and dynamos can be checked a little easier. By rotating these devices, an output reading can be checked with the multi-tester. Another little tip for testing generators with permanent magnets is to rotate the unit's armature around slowly. You should be able to feel a slight resistance twice during each 360-degree rotation of the armature. This resistance is produced as the magnetic fields inside the unit are broken. If the resistance is felt, chances are that there is not much wrong with the unit. Examine moving parts and gears carefully for excessive wear. Always check bearings for excessive motion or wear. Shafts should have little play in them and must move freely in the bearings. A couple drops of oil will sometimes free up a dry bearing and shaft.

After your inspection has been made, review what is broken or missing and needs to be rebuilt or replaced. Determine what will require professional restoration and what you can do yourself. Then assess the cost to complete the restoration. Many engines have been brought back to life from scrap piles. Your individual abilities and resources will determine if acquiring this engine is right for you.

Running Engines

You must evaluate an engine that runs, the same way as you did the engine that does not run. If you are told that the engine runs, make your static inspection first; then ask for it to be started. Checking an engine while it's running should answer a lot of the basic questions.

Observe the flywheels while the engine is running. Flywheels that tend to hop or cycle back and forth are either damaged or bent. Flywheels that do not run true can also be the cause of a bent crankshaft or extremely loose main bearings. Flywheels must always run smoothly, regardless of whether the engine is running or they are being turned over by hand.

While the engine is running, look for fuel and water leaks. A leak's origination can be a clue to the repairs that might be needed. If the fuel pump is leaking, it may need to be packed or the shaft may be in bad repair. If the leaks are at a connection, chances are that tightening or the use of a pipe sealer will correct the problem.

Check for compression leaks while the engine is in operation. If smoke is visible from the rear of the piston, you can assume that the rings are passing combustion gases. New rings, honing of the cylinder, or ring seating may be required. The piston wall should have an even coat of oil on the piston skirt. Pistons that are not lubricated properly will have compression problems. Check the drip oiler or mechanical oiling device and make sure it is delivering oil to the cylinder. The igniter is another place to check for compression leaks. Many igniters have a seat on the electrode that is similar to a valve. If this surface is not clean and properly lapped in, leaks will occur through the igniter. Insulation washers will eventually deteriorate and leak compression around the electrode. New insulation washers are easy to come by and can be replaced in minutes. Listen for knocking noises. A knock that remains constant might be caused by a journal working back and forth in a loose bearing. A wrist pin that has become worn will begin to knock if not adjusted right.

Engine accessories can add up to a lot of money on any restoration project. Always make sure you know exactly what you're getting. Ask if the engine comes with a battery and coil. If not, you can figure that a 6-volt wet-cell battery and buzz coil will cost around $75. Induction coils used with igniters can run from $15 to $40 apiece. Find out if the hand starting crank is there. Cranks can cost from $5 to $50, if you are able to find one. Carts and original skids add value to the overall purchase. Original skids or carts can cost hundreds of dollars. Pulleys, gears, and flat belts that drove equipment will bring $5 to $200, each. Drip oilers are increasing in price. A drip oiler can cost from $5 to $100, depending on the size, manufacturer, and condition. Mechanical oilers such as the Madison Kipp can cost from $20 to $250 to replace. Again, condition and size play a big part in the overall price. Original factory owner's manuals will often come with an engine. Manuals may cost from $2 to $100 each. Any original factory item such as tool kits, oil cans, batteries, funnels, toolboxes, greasers, and grease guns enhance the overall worth of the engine. Always try to acquire these original items along with the engine, if possible.

Remember that a good inspection pays off in the end. Poor inspections can leave you with deep disappointment. Take your time with every engine inspection. There is no need to be in a hurry. Ask the owner questions. He may shed light on things about the engine you have missed. Talk about problems you see with the engine. If the engine is in good shape, then just talk price.

A checklist can help during the inspection process. Here is a sample of the check sheet for your next engine evaluation.

Stationary Engine Check Sheet

Date:
Owner Name:
Address:
Phone Number:
Price:
Engine Manufacturer:
Model:
Serial Number:
Cooling System:
Flywheel Diameter:
Fuel:
Horsepower:
Ignition:
Piston Diameter:
Piston Stroke:

Engine Part: Broke/Cracked
               Worn/Missing/ Froze
               Other
Accessories
Base or Frame
Battery
Bearings
     Caps
     Liners
Buzz Coil
Carburetor
Cart
Connecting Rod
Cooling Fins
Cooling Screen
Cooling Tank
Crankshaft
Cylinder
Detent
Dynamo
Exhaust Valve
Exhaust-Valve Lever
Fan
Flywheels
Fuel Pump
Fuel Tank
Gaskets
Gears
Generator
Governor
Greasers
Guards
Hot Tube
Igniter

Igniter Trip
Induction Coil
Intake Valve
Magneto
Manual
Oilers
Piping
Piston
Side Shaft
Skid
Spark Plug
Springs
Starting Crank
Water Hopper
Water Pump
Wiring
Wrist Pin

The Fairbanks Morse Engine Purchase

The purchase of my Fairbanks Morse 1-1/2-hp headless engine is an example of how the careful evaluation of an engine can lead to a successful restoration. When the engine was found, it was dirty and showing its age. It had an abundance of grease visible over many of its working parts. Grease should not scare you away. In fact grease preserves parts from deterioration by insulating them from the elements. Grease can be removed with a steam cleaner or with commercial solvents. After inspection, the engine was found to have no cracks, breaks, or broken parts. The engine's flywheels were loose, and turned true by hand. The engine even produced some resistance on the compression stroke, suggesting that it had some compression. The under-pick igniter and original Sumter low-tension magneto were free to cycle. All the open gearing was in very good condition. The carburetor and its parts were intact. The needle valve was loose on its seat, and the needle was in good shape. Both valves were fairly tight in the valve guides and moved in and out. The fuel tank and fuel line were in place and properly connected. The engine showed some original paint, and the original factory identification plate was in nice shape on the face of the water hopper. The engine's serial number was visible and stamped into the casting boss on the top of the water hopper. The inside of the water hopper was dirty and needed cleaning. At the bottom of the hopper casting, this engine has two freeze plugs. Both plugs were solid and undamaged. The water drain cock located at the side of the engine was in place and operable. The governor and detent control needed cleaning and freeing up, but were in good condition. The crank guard was attached, and the original bolts were holding it in place. All the engine greasers and the one drip oiler were visible. The engine was mounted on its original factory skid. The original Fairbanks Morse starting crank was also with the engine.

This positive evaluation of the engine suggested that this was a good engine for restoration, if the price was favorable. This engine was purchased in May 1995 for $500. A copy of the original owner's manual was purchased for about $6, so the engine could be set up properly after the restoration process was completed.

After transporting the engine to the shop, a more detailed inspection and cleaning was needed. The engine was steam cleaned, removing all dirt and grease. The carburetor was removed and cleaned. The needle valve required wire brushing, lubrication, and a new tension spring. The valves were inspected, and the intake and exhaust valves were lapped in. The governor and detent were freed up and lubricated. The governor was adjusted. The mag was cleaned with electrical solvent, and the bearings were lubricated. The pickup point was corroded and required cleaning. A new ignition wire was made up to connect the igniter with the mag. The piston was removed, and the ring grooves, piston, and rings were cleaned. They were then lubricated and reinstalled. The bearings were adjusted, cleaned, and lubricated. One shim was removed from between each of the main-bearing halves. The water hopper came clean with the steam-cleaning process. The drain cock was removed and unclogged. The skid handle was bent back into shape with a body hammer. Tank sealer was used on the inside of the fuel tank, after all the loose dirt was removed. All the pipe fittings were cleaned and coated with pipe-thread sealant before being replaced. Thread sealant and proper tightening prevented any leaks. The foot valve located on the bottom of the fuel pickup line was cleaned. New gaskets were purchased and installed for the head and igniter. The cost of all this rehabilitation amounted to less than $50.

This engine did not require a high level of engine knowledge or mechanical expertise to restore. A cleaning brush, solvent, screwdrivers, wrenches, spark plug, wire, electrical fasteners, owner's manual, file, scraper, and wire brush were the only tools used in

The Fairbanks Morse 1 1/2 horsepower headless engine after a total restoration.

the restoration process. The steam cleaning was done by a local garage for about $15. A good deal of time was spent reading the owner's manual to understand engine timing and the running requirements of this engine. After timing the engine according to the instruction in the manual, I filled the fuel tank with gas, filled the hopper with water, opened the needle valve, lubricated the bearings with grease, adjusted the drip oiler to a flow of about six drops per minute and positioned the crank on the crankshaft. After about three chokes of the carburetor, and about 20 cranks of the flywheel, this engine once again came back to life.

The final touches to complete the restoration included paint that matched the original factory green. The engine was then detailed out, and all the brass was polished or replaced. The restoration process was a satisfying experience that began with thoughtful evaluation prior to purchase.

Chapter Seven

Price Guide

The Price Guide provides a suggested retail price range based on overall engine condition. A numerical scale of 1 through 5 defines engine condition, with #1 being an engine in mint condition and #5 being a "parts" engine. Pictures and descriptions of each engine are listed in alphabetical order by manufacturer and may be used for positive engine identification. When using the guide to evaluate an engine prior to purchase, study the descriptions and pictures carefully. One missing part, such as a magneto, can affect the cost of an engine considerably.

The engine prices were developed by monitoring selling prices at antique engine shows, auctions, and individual sales. Pricing was also gathered from current advertising found in hobby and trade magazines. Many engine collectors were also interviewed for their input and comments on engine prices and value. Pricing throughout the guide is rounded off in $25 increments. A listing of "rare" means that these engines are rare and pricing is not available. It's a seller's market on most rare engines, with prices starting at a few thousand dollars and rising.

Gas engines are frequently sold at farm and estate sales. Auctions usually generate higher overall prices for engines. All auction items are sold "as is," and most times all sales are final. Antique power shows and individual hobbyists provide some of the best opportunities to purchase an engine at a fair price because, generally, you are able to take your time evaluating each engine, and price can be discussed directly with the owner. Many engines are also sold through individual ads in engine hobby and trade magazines. Here again, the buyer has the opportunity for inspection and to negotiate the terms of sale.

The best deals are made by educated buyers. Read all available books and materials, keep a notebook, and use a checklist to aid you in evaluating an engine's condition. Most of all, take your time and have fun.

Rating Guide
Condition Description

#1	Mint or as new—in running condition; all original; includes factory accessories (e.g., carts, skids, tanks, tools, pulleys, cranks, toolbox, battery box, and so on).
#2	Very good condition—in running condition; 90 percent of the original parts visible; may have been repainted; some wear is visible; minor mechanical repairs needed (e.g., gaskets or oil leak); minor cleaning needed; includes some factory accessories.
#3	Good to fair overall restorable engine—85 percent of the original parts on engine, may or may not be running or may need some repairs; needs paint restoration; rust showing; very minor damage; minor parts missing (e.g., oilers, grease cups, pipe plugs, springs, and so on); complete cleaning required; few factory accessories.
#4	Damaged engine (e.g., cylinder cracked or rusted tight)—some parts missing (e.g., magneto, igniter, or governor); not running; needs total restoration; visible wear, with heavy rusting; each part needs sand or bead blasting and painting.
#5	Parts engine—an engine that is not restorable but may have several usable parts that can be used or reconditioned.

The Aermotor general-purpose engine.

The Aermotor eight-cycle one-horsepower engine.

A stationary engine built by the Associated Manufacturers Co.

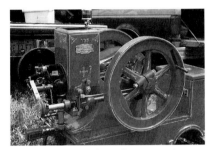

A Domestic Type A stationary engine.

This is a Domestic Type F stationary engine. It is hopper-cooled and hit-and-miss governed.

The Fairbanks Morse Type Z "headless" engine.

Aermotor General-Purpose Engine

General-purpose engine, hammer-break igniter, oscillating low-tension magneto or battery-and-coil ignition, hit-and-miss governed, hopper cooled, gasoline fueled.

Horsepower	Condition/Price ($)				
	#1	#2	#3	#4	#5
2-1/2	4,000	3,000	2,000	700	400
5	4,500	3,200	2,200	725	425

Aermotor Pumping Engine

Pumping engine, eight cycle, hammer-break igniter, magneto or battery-and-coil ignition, hit-and-miss fly-ball governed, air cooled, gasoline fueled.

Horsepower	Condition/Price ($)				
	#1	#2	#3	#4	#5
1	1,500	1,100	700	500	250

Associated Manufacturers Co. Engines

Chore Boy (1-3/4 horsepower), Hired Man (2-1/4 horsepower), Farm Hand (4 horsepower), Six Mule Team (6 horsepower), Foreman (8 horsepower), and Twelve Mule Team (12 horsepower) stationary engines; hammer-break igniter; low-tension rotary magneto or battery-and-coil ignition; hit-and-miss fly-ball governed; hopper cooled; gasoline fueled.

Horsepower	Condition/Price ($)				
	#1	#2	#3	#4	#5
1-3/4	700	650	400	275	125
2-1/4	650	575	375	250	125
4	750	600	500	250	125
6	800	650	525	250	125
8	1,000	850	600	275	175
12	1,200	900	775	275	175

Domestic Engine & Pump Co. Type A Engine

Type A stationary engine, hammer-break igniter, battery-and-coil ignition, hit-and-miss governed, hopper cooled, gasoline fueled.

Horsepower	Condition/Price ($)				
	#1	#2	#3	#4	#5
1-1/2	2,900	2,175	1,000	525	250
2	2,800	2,000	950	525	250

Horsepower	Condition/Price ($)				
3	2,500	1,800	900	500	250
4	2,500	1,800	900	500	250
6	2,800	2,000	950	525	250
8	3,250	2,400	1,500	650	300
10	4,000	3,250	2,250	650	300
12	5,000	4,250	3,000	700	400

Domestic Engine & Pump Co. Type F Engine

Type F stationary engine, spark-plug ignition with battery and buzz coil, hit-and-miss governed, hopper cooled, gasoline fueled.

Horsepower	Condition/Price ($)				
	#1	#2	#3	#4	#5
1-1/2	2,500	1,800	1,150	500	325
2	2,400	1,600	1,100	550	325
2-1/2	2,400	1,600	1,100	550	300
3-1/2	2,500	1,500	1,000	500	300
5	2,500	1,500	1,000	500	300
7	2,800	1,700	1,100	550	375
9	2,900	1,825	1,125	575	375
11	3,200	2,000	1,200	600	475
13	3,450	2,200	1,650	700	475
15	3,800	2,500	1,850	800	500

Fuller & Johnson Pump Engine

Stationary pump engine, spark-plug ignition with high-tension magneto or battery and buzz coil, hit-and-miss governed, air cooled, gasoline fueled.

Horsepower	Condition/Price ($)				
	#1	#2	#3	#4	#5
1-1/2	1,000	700	450	350	200

Fuller & Johnson Model N Engine

Model N stationary engine, hammer-break igniter, low-tension rotary magneto or battery-and-coil ignition, hit-and-miss fly-ball governed, hopper cooled, gasoline fueled.

Horsepower	Condition/Price ($)				
	#1	#2	#3	#4	#5
3	700	600	450	225	175
5	850	650	550	250	175
7	900	775	600	250	200

The Fairbanks Morse Type T engine.

The Fuller and Johnson Farm Pump stationary engine.

The International Harvester Co. Famous engine.

Horsepower	Condition/Price ($)				
9	1,450	1,200	950	375	250
12	1,800	1,500	1,100	425	275

Fairbanks Morse Type Z Engine

Type Z headless stationary engine, hammer-break igniter, low-tension magneto ignition, hit-and-miss governed, hopper cooled, gasoline fueled.

Horsepower	Condition/Price ($)				
	#1	#2	#3	#4	#5
1-1/2	700	600	475	250	150

Fairbanks Morse Type T Engine

Type T Jack of all Trades vertical stationary engine, hammer-break igniter, battery-and-coil ignition, hit-and-miss governed, tank cooled, gasoline or kerosene fueled.

Horsepower	Condition/Price ($)				
	#1	#2	#3	#4	#5
2	2,400	1,500	1,050	500	300
3	2,400	1,500	1,050	500	300
4	2,600	1,600	1,150	575	300
6	2,700	1,700	1,175	575	300
9	3,200	1,850	1,500	600	350
12	3,450	2,200	1,650	700	400

William Galloway Boss of the Farm Engine

Boss of the Farm stationary engine, hammer-break igniter, low-tension magneto or battery-and-coil ignition, hit-and-miss governed, air cooled, gasoline fueled.

Horsepower	Condition/Price ($)				
	#1	#2	#3	#4	#5
1-3/4	850	775	650	400	250

Galloway Stationary Engines

Galloway stationary engines, hammer-break igniter, low-tension magneto or battery-and-coil ignition, hit-and-miss fly-ball governed, hopper cooled, gasoline fueled.

Horsepower	Condition/Price ($)				
	#1	#2	#3	#4	#5
2	850	775	650	400	250

The Fuller and Johnson Model N engine.

A Hercules Jaeger engine.

A Hercules engine.

This International Harvester Co. Mogul kerosene engine is throttle-governed and screen tank-cooled.

This is another International Harvester Co. Mogul kerosene engine, this one hopper-cooled.

International Harvester Co. Model M stationary engine (IHC built McCormick-Deering machines).

The Novo Model S stationary engine.

A Sandwich Manufacturing Co. engine.

This 1 1/2-horsepower Cub engine was manufactured by the Sandwich Manufacturing Co.

Horsepower	Condition/Price ($)				
2-1/2	850	775	650	400	250
5	1,500	1,200	850	500	275
7-1/2	1,800	1,400	950	550	275
10	2,500	1,800	1,000	650	350
15	2,700	2,000	1,200	700	425
18	rare				
22	rare				
28	rare				

Hercules Gas Engines with Low-Tension Ignition

Hercules Economy, Jaeger, and Arco stationary engines; hammer-break igniter; low-tension oscillating magneto ignition; hit-and-miss fly-ball governed; hopper cooled; gasoline fueled.

Horsepower	Condition/Price ($)				
	#1	#2	#3	#4	#5
1-1/2	700	550	475	250	100
2-1/2	650	525	450	225	100
3	675	550	475	225	100
5	750	550	475	275	150
7	850	600	525	275	150
9	1,000	875	675	300	200
12	1,200	950	775	325	200

Hercules Gas Engines with High-Tension Ignition

Hercules Economy, Jaeger, and Arco stationary engines; spark-plug ignition with high-tension magneto; hit-and-miss fly-ball governed; hopper cooled; gasoline fueled.

Horsepower	Condition/Price ($)				
	#1	#2	#3	#4	#5
1-1/2	625	525	375	200	125
2-1/2	600	500	375	200	125
3	600	500	375	200	125
5	650	550	400	300	250
7	700	600	450	300	250
9	900	825	575	350	225
12	1,050	900	675	400	250

International Harvester Co. Famous Engine

Famous vertical stationary engine, hammer-break igniter, battery-and-coil ignition, hit-and-miss governed, screen cooled, gasoline fueled.

Horsepower	Condition/Price ($)				
	#1	#2	#3	#4	#5
2	2,500	1,600	1,000	550	275
3	2,250	1,400	900	500	275
6	2,700	1,850	1,250	650	375

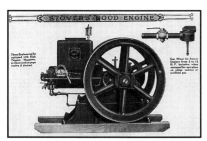
The Stover hopper-cooled engine.

The Stover hand portable engine.

A Stickney engine.

International Harvester Co. Model M Engine

Model M stationary engine, spark plug ignition with high-tension magneto, throttle governed, hopper cooled, kerosene and gasoline fueled.

Horsepower	Condition/Price ($)				
	#1	#2	#3	#4	#5
1-1/2	675	600	475	300	150
3	650	575	450	300	150
6	750	600	475	325	175
10	950	800	650	375	225

International Harvester Co. Hopper-Cooled Mogul Engine

Mogul kerosene stationary engine, side-shaft valve and ignition control, hammer-break igniter, low-tension magneto ignition, throttle governed, hopper cooled, kerosene and gasoline fueled.

Horsepower	Condition/Price ($)				
	#1	#2	#3	#4	#5
4	7,500	6,500	4,000	2,000	950
6	7,700	6,600	4,100	2,100	950
8	8,000	6,750	4,300	2,200	1,000

International Harvester Co. Tank- or Screen-Cooled Mogul Engine

Mogul kerosene stationary engine, side-shaft valve and ignition control, hammer-break igniter, low-tension magneto ignition, throttle governed, tank or screen cooled, kerosene and gasoline fueled.

Horsepower	Condition/Price ($)				
	#1	#2	#3	#4	#5
4	7,300	5,300	3,100	2,000	900
6	7,500	5,400	3,200	2,000	900
8	7,800	5,550	3,800	2,100	950
10	8,000	6,000	4,750	2,700	1,100
12	8,500	6,500	5,000	2,800	1,125
15	9,000	7,000	5,800	3,000	1,200
20	rare				
25	rare				
50	rare				

Novo Engine Co. Model S

Model S vertical stationary engine, spark-plug ignition with high-tension magneto or battery and buzz coil, hit-and-miss governed, hopper cooled, gasoline fueled.

Horsepower	Condition/Price ($)				
	#1	#2	#3	#4	#5
Junior	1,400	900	750	375	150
1-1/2	1,100	800	600	375	150
2	900	600	450	275	150
3	900	600	450	275	150
4	900	600	450	275	150
6	1,000	700	500	275	175
8	1,000	700	500	275	175
10	1,800	1,000	800	425	200
15	2,000	1,200	925	450	200

Sandwich Manufacturing Co. Big Engines

Light Six, Big, Big Six, and similar design stationary engines; hammer-break igniter; oscillating low-tension magneto or battery-and-coil ignition; hopper cooled; gasoline fueled.

Horsepower	Condition/Price ($)				
	#1	#2	#3	#4	#5
3	850	700	650	350	150
4-1/2	950	750	675	375	175
6	1,050	850	725	425	200
8	1,800	1,400	1,000	700	325
10	2,500	1,850	1,250	950	450

Sandwich Manufacturing Co. Cub Engine

Cub stationary engine, hammer-break igniter, oscillating low-tension magneto or battery-and-coil ignition, hopper cooled, gasoline fueled.

Horsepower	Condition/Price ($)				
	#1	#2	#3	#4	#5
1-1/2	775	650	550	275	150

Sears, Roebuck and Co. Economy Engine

Economy stationary engine, hammer-break igniter, low-tension magneto or battery-and-coil ignition, hit-and-miss fly-ball governed, hopper cooled, gasoline fueled.

Horsepower	Condition/Price ($)				
	#1	#2	#3	#4	#5
1	875	650	450	350	250
1-1/2	875	650	450	350	250
2	950	800	575	375	275
4	1,200	900	675	475	275
6	1,375	1,000	700	500	300
8	1,500	1,100	775	550	325
10	rare				

Charles A. Stickney Co. Engines

Stickney stationary engine, hammer-break igniter, battery-and-coil ignition, hit-and-miss governed, hopper cooled, gasoline fueled.

Horsepower	Condition/Price ($)				
	#1	#2	#3	#4	#5
1-1/2	3,500	2,750	1,500	900	500
1-3/4	3,250	2,650	1,300	800	500
3	3,500	2,700	1,850	500	500
5	3,800	2,800	1,950	500	650
7	5,000	4,000	3,000	1,100	650
10	6,000	5,000	4,000	1,800	750
13	7,750	6,500	4,650	1,800	750
16	8,500	6,000	5,500	1,850	1,000
20	9,500	7,000	6,500	1,900	1,000

A Galloway engine.

The Galloway "Boss of the Farm" engine.

Stover Engine Works Hand-Portable Engine

Stover hand-portable engine, hammer-break igniter, oscillating low-tension magneto, hit-and-miss fly-ball governed, hopper cooled, gasoline fueled.

Horsepower	Condition/Price ($)				
	#1	#2	#3	#4	#5
1	750	675	550	300	225
1-1/2	700	600	450	250	175
2	700	600	450	250	175

Stover Engine Works Stationary Engine

Stover stationary engine, hammer-break igniter, oscillating low-tension magneto, hit-and-miss fly-ball governed, hopper cooled, gasoline fueled.

Horsepower	Condition/Price ($)				
	#1	#2	#3	#4	#5
3	750	600	550	275	200
4	750	600	550	275	200
6	850	675	575	300	225
8	950	750	600	325	250
10	1,800	1,050	850	450	300
12	1,800	1,050	850	450	300

Chapter Eight

Reference Guide

This guide is arranged in alphabetical order by manufacturer. The photo captions begin with the manufacturer's name and address and include prominent features of each engine. Many pictures and illustrations were taken from original factory advertising, while others are pictures of engines found today. Use this section as a field guide to quickly identify an engine and its major features.

Where Trade Names and Dates are unable to be verified the abbreviation na (not available) is used. However, many times part of the engine manufacturer's name is commonly used as its engine trade name. A typical example might be: Cushnoc Motor Works, Augusta, ME., engine trade name "Cushnoc" or the Davis Motor Works, Waterloo, Iowa, engine trade name "Davis".

Engine Manufacturer	Factory Location	Trade Name	Dates
A & L Mtr. Corp.	Albany, OR	na	1922
A. C. Elect. Co.	Dayton, OH	Dayton Light	na
Abbe Engnrg. Co.	New York, NY	na	1906
Abenaque Mach. Works	West Minster Station, VT	Abenaque	1895–1916
Acme Eng. Co.	Lansing, MI	Acme	1913
Acme Eng. Co.	Lansing, MI	Banner	1913
Acme Eng. Co.	Lansing, MI	Peerless	1913
Acme Engnrg. Co.	Louisville, KY	Farm-O-Lite	na
Acme Gasoline Eng. Co.	St. Louis, MO	na	1898
Acme Mfg. Co.	Bradford, PA	Acme	na
Acme Oil Eng. Co.	Bridgeport, CT	Acme	1903
Acme Pump Co.	Ligonier/Shakespeare, IN	Acme	1907
Acme Pump Co.	Ligonier/Shakespeare, IN	Haney	1907
Acme Road Machry. Co.	Frankfort, NY	na	na
Acme Sucker Rod Co.	Toledo, OH	Acme	na
Adam Kale	Corcentre, NY	Adam Kale	na
Adams & Richards Mach. Co.	New Brunswick, NJ	Adams & Richards	1889
Adams & Richards Mach. Co.	New Brunswick, NJ	Richards	1889
Adams-McCoy Elect. Co.	Muscatine, IA	Adams	na
Adams Co.	Dubuque , IA	Adams	1905–1913
Adams Co.	Dubuque, IA	Farwell	1905–1913
Adco Mfg. Co.	Columbus, OH	Adco Oil Eng.	1915–1920
Advance-Pohl Co.	Vernon, NJ	Farmers Favorite	na
Advanced Elect. Co.	Indianapolis, IN	Advanced	na
Advanced Eng. Co.	Veron, NY	Pohl	1905
Advanced Machry. Co.	New York, NY	Advanced	1907
Advanced Mfg. Co.	Hamilton, OH	Advanced	1898
Advanced Mfg. Co.	Hamilton, OH	Hamilton	1898
Advanced Mfg. Co.	Hamilton, OH	Hamilton/Advanced	1898
Advanced Mfg. Co.	Hamilton, OH	Oil Turn	1898
Advanced Mfg. Co.	Hamilton, OH	Richie	1898
Advanced Mfg. Co.	Hamilton, OH	Standard	1898
Advanced Road Machry. Co.	Frankport, NY	Advanced	1907
Advanced-Rumely Thresher Co.	La Porte, IN	Oil Turn	na

Engine Manufacturer	Factory Location	Trade Name	Dates
Advanced-Rumely Thresher Co.	La Porte, IN	Rumely	na
Aermotor Co.	Chicago, IL	Aermotor	1909
Aermotor Co.	Chicago, IL	Apacs	1909
Aero & Marine Mtr. Co.	Boston, MA	Marine Engines	1907
Aerolite Eng. Co.	Bayonne, NJ	Ultimotor	1948
Aerothrust Eng. Co.	La Porte, IN	Aerothrust	1916–1917
Aerothrust Eng. Co.	La Porte, IN	Pormo	na
Aetna Mfg. Co.	Ellwood, PA	Aetna	na
Aetna Mfg. Co.	Menomonie, WI	Aetna	na
Affiliated Mach. Co.	Bloomer, WI	Keller	na
Affiliated Manufacturers Co.	Milwaukee, WI	Affiliated	1911–1914
Affiliated Manufacturers Co.	Milwaukee, WI	Cream City	1911–1914
Affiliated Manufacturers Co.	Milwaukee, WI	Keller	1911–1914
Agricultural Mach. Imp. Co.	New York, NY	na	na
Air Cooled Mtr. Co.	Lansing, MI	Air Cooled	1906–1911
Air Cooling Mtr. Co.	Minneapolis, MN	na	1919
Ajax Iron Works	Corry, PA	Ajax	1892
Ajax Iron Works	Corry, PA	All In One	1892
Ajax Iron Works	Corry, PA	California Special	1892

Abenaque engines were first built around 1895 by the Abenaque Machine Works in West Minster Station, Vermont. This 1894 Abenaque pan hopper-cooled engine was manufactured in 3- to 18 horsepower. Low-tension wipe spark ignition was commonly used to ignite its gasoline fuel mixture.

This 1903 Abenaque side-shaft engine used pan hopper cooling. The pans are about three inches wide and run the length of the engine. This type of cooling system was unique to engines manufactured by the Abenaque Machine Works.

The Acme Engine Co. was located in Lansing, Michigan. A 2 1/2-horsepower hit-and-miss-governed engine is shown. Low-tension ignition with a hammer-break igniter lights the fuel mixture.

The Aermotor Co. of Chicago, Illinois only produced a 2 1/2- or 5-horsepower fluted hopper-cooled gasoline engine. Hit-and-miss governing regulated engine speed. The Webster low-tension magneto can be seen attached to its hammer-break igniter bracket.

The one-horsepower Aermotor Pump Engine was used to power windmills. This air-cooled engine used back gearing to develop tremendous torque. Commonly referred to as an eight-cycle engine, they fired only once in every four revolutions of the crankshaft.

Right
Acme engines were first manufactured in the early 1910s. Engine sizes ranged from 2 1/2 to 15-horsepower. Hopper cooling was a standard feature on this line of engine.

Engine Manufacturer	Factory Location	Trade Name	Dates
Akron Engnrg. Co.	Akron, OH	Akron	na
Alamo Farm Light Co.	Chicago, IL	Silent Alamo	na
Alamo Mfg. Co.	Hillsdale, MI	Alamo	1903
Alamo Mfg. Co.	Hillsdale, MI	Alamo Blue Line	1913
Alamo Mfg. Co.	Hillsdale, MI	Alamo D Light	na
Alamo Mfg. Co.	Hillsdale, MI	Alamo Jr.	na
Alamo Mfg. Co.	Hillsdale, MI	Alamo Oil	na
Alamo Mfg. Co.	Hillsdale, MI	B.F. Avery	na
Alamo Mfg. Co.	Hillsdale, MI	Bloomfield	na
Alamo Mfg. Co.	Hillsdale, MI	Blue Line	na
Alamo Mfg. Co.	Hillsdale, MI	Dairy King	na
Alamo Mfg. Co.	Hillsdale, MI	De Laval	na
Alamo Mfg. Co.	Hillsdale, MI	Eagle	na
Alamo Mfg. Co.	Hillsdale, MI	Empire	na
Alamo Mfg. Co.	Hillsdale, MI	Flying Dutchman	na
Alamo Mfg. Co.	Hillsdale, MI	H. Brewer & Co.	na
Alamo Mfg. Co.	Hillsdale, MI	Hoosier	na
Alamo Mfg. Co.	Hillsdale, MI	Lansing	na
Alamo Mfg. Co.	Hillsdale, MI	Lindsay	na
Alamo Mfg. Co.	Hillsdale, MI	Lindsay—Alamo	1920
Alamo Mfg. Co.	Hillsdale, MI	Magnolia	na
Alamo Mfg. Co.	Hillsdale, MI	McVickers	na
Alamo Mfg. Co.	Hillsdale, MI	Moline	na
Alamo Mfg. Co.	Hillsdale, MI	Moody	na
Alamo Mfg. Co.	Hillsdale, MI	Rock Island	na
Alamo Mfg. Co.	Hillsdale, MI	Royal	na
Alamo Mfg. Co.	Hillsdale, MI	Silent Alamo	na
Alamo Mfg. Co.	Hillsdale, MI	Standard	na
Alamo Mfg. Co.	Hillsdale, MI	Style M	na
Alamo Mfg. Co.	Hillsdale, MI	Victor	na
Alberger Gas Eng. Co.	Buffalo, NY	Alberger	1900
Alberger Gas Eng. Co.	Buffalo, NY	Buffalo	1900
Albion Eng. & Mtr. Co.	Albion, MI	Miller	1903
Albion Windmill & Imp. Co.	Detroit, MI	Cook	na
Alexander & Crough	Chicago, IL	Alexander & Crough	1904–1906
Alexander-James	Chicago, IL	Humming Bird	na
Alford Mtr. & Mach. Co.	Goshen, IN	na	1913
Algoma Fdry. & Mach. Co.	Algoma, WI	Algoma	na
Algoma Fdry. & Mach. Co.	Algoma, WI	O.K.	na
Allfree Mfg. Co.	Indianapolis, IN	Allfree	na
Allis-Chalmers Co.	Milwaukee, WI	Allis	1903
Allis-Chalmers Co.	Milwaukee, WI	Allis-Chalmers Light Plight	na
Allis-Chalmers Co.	Milwaukee, WI	Allis-Chalmers	1907
Allis-Chalmers Co.	Milwaukee, WI	Nurnberg	na
Allis-Chalmers Co.	Milwaukee, WI	Oil Pull	na
Allman & Thompson	New York, NY	Allman & Thompson	1889
Allman Gas & Mach. Co.	New York, NY	Allman	1897
Alma Mfg. Co.	Alma, MI	Alma	1903–1929
Alma Mfg. Co.	Alma, MI	Alma Jr.	1903–1929
Alma Mfg. Co.	Alma, MI	Automatic	1903–1929
Alma Mfg. Co.	Alma, MI	Clipper	1903–1929
Alma Mfg. Co.	Alma, MI	Farmers Friend	1903–1929
Alma Mfg. Co.	Alma, MI	Little Marvel	1903–1929
Alma Mfg. Co.	Alma, MI	McVickers	1885–1929
Alma Mfg. Co.	Alma, MI	McVickers Automatic	1903–1929
Almen-Crosby Mtr. Co.	Seattle, WA	Almen-Crosby	1916
Althouse & Ewing	Bluffton, OH	Althouse & Ewing	1910
Alto Mfg. Co.	Chicago, IL	Alto Light Plant	na
Altoona Mfg. Co.	Altoona, IA	Iowa	na
Amalgamated Sales & Serv. Corp.	Chicago, IL	Seaman Uniflow	na
Am. Clay Making Machry. Co.	Bucyrus, OH	na	na
Am. Krupp Sys. Diesel Eng. Co.	New York, NY	na	1913
Am. Mtr. Vehicle Mfg. Co.	New Haven, CT	na	1902
Am. Steel & Iron Co.	Norwalk, OH	American	1908

Engine Manufacturer	Factory Location	Trade Name	Dates
Am. & British Mfg. Co.	Bridgeport, CT	American O.K. Odorless	1895
Am. Bicycle Co.	New York, NY	na	1902
Am. Car Wheel Co.	St. Louis, MO	na	na
Am. Cement Mach. Co.	Kerokuk, OH	Boss	na
Am. Diesel Eng. Co.	New York, NY	American Diesel	1901
Am. Eng. & Fdry. Co.	Charles City, IA	Americo Light Plant	na
Am. Eng. Co.	Detroit, MI	American-Marine	1914
Am. Eng. Co.	Detroit, MI	American Jr.	1914
Am. Engnrg. Co.	Springfield, OH	American	1901
Am. Fdry. & Mach. Co.	Anderson, IN	Globe	na
Am. Fire Eng. Co.	Seneca Falls, NY	Shepherd	na
Am. Gas Eng. Co.	New York, NY	American	na
Am. Gas Eng. Co.	Philadelphia, PA	American	1897–1901
Am. Gas Eng. Co.	Sheboygan, WI	American	na
Am. Gas Eng. Co.	Portland, ME	Dirigo	1902
Am. Gas Eng. Co.	Sheboygan, WI	Griffin	na
Am. Gas Eng. Co.	Kansas City, MO	Weber	na
Am. Gas Eng. Co.	Cincinnati, OH	na	1901
Am. Gasoline Mtr. Co.	Baldwinsville, NY	American (Marine)	1908
Am. Harrow Co.	Detroit, MI	American	na
Am. Harrow Co.	Detroit, MI	Detroit-American	na
Am. Katalite Corp.	Brooklyn, NY	na	1927
Am. Mach. Co.	Wilmington, DE	American	na
Am. Mtr. Co.	New York, NY	American	1898
Am. Mtr. Co.	Brockton, MA	American	na
Am. Mtr. Co.	Eau Claire, WI	American—Marine	1908
Am. Mtr. Parts Co.	E. Moline, IL	Reindeer	na
Am. Mtr. Parts Co.	E. Moline, IL	Triumph	na
Am. Oil Eng. Co.	New York, NY	American Oil	1900–1911
Am. Oil Mtr. Co.	Milwaukee, WI	na	1918
Am. Railroad Appliance Co.	Oil City, PA	Araco	1897
Am. Rotary Eng. Co.	Boston, MA	na	1906
Am. Steel & Iron Co.	Norwalk, OH	Davis	1908
Am. Steel Export Co.	New York, NY	na	1916
Am. Steel Products Co.	Macomb, IL	Silent High	na
Am. Well Works	Aurora, IL	American	1903
Am. Well Works	Aurora, IL	Deepwell	1903
Am. Whaley Eng. Co.	Boston, MA	na	1921
Amet Eng. Co.	Waukegan, IL	Amet	1903
Anderson Automatic Eng. Co.	Fairfield, IA	na	na
Anderson Co., Carl	Chicago, IL	Gus	1902
Anderson Co., Carl	Chicago, IL	Special	1902
Anderson Eng. Co.	Chicago, IL	Anderson	na
Anderson Eng. Co.	Shelbyville, IL	Anderson	1913
Anderson Fdry. & Mach. Co.	Anderson, IN	Anderson	1913
Anderson Fdry. & Mach. Works	Anderson, IN	Anderson Oil	1907
Anderson Mtr. Co.	Anderson, IN	Anderson	1913
Anderson Mtr. Co.	Anderson, IN	BP	na
Anderson Mtr. Co.	Anderson, IN	Dice	1909–1913
Anderson Mtr. Co.	Anderson, IN	EB	na
Anderson Mtr. Co.	Anderson, IN	Power Space	na
Anderson Tool Co.	Anderson, IN	Anderson	1903–1904
Anglo-Am. Rapid Vehicle Co.	Racine, WI	Regan	1896
Angola Eng. & Fdry. Co.	Angola, IN	Angola	1904–1911
Apple Elect. Co.	Dayton, OH	Apple	na
Appleton Mfg. Co.	Batavia, IL	Appleton	1897–1917
Appleton Mfg. Co.	Batavia, IL	Chanticleer	1901–1917
Appleton Mfg. Co.	Batavia, IL	Haish	1901–1917
Appleton Mfg. Co.	Batavia, IL	Western	1901–1917
Armac Mtr. Co.	Chicago, IL	1902	na
Armstrong Mfg. Co.	Waterloo, IA	Armstrong	1909
Armstrong Mfg. Co.	Waterloo, IA	Simple Simon	1909
Arnold's & Son, G. W.	Ionia, MI	Arnold	1905–1909
Arnold's & Son, G. W.	Ionia, MI	Little Baker	1905–1909

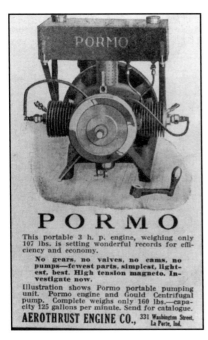

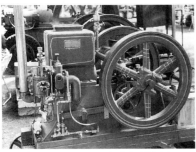

The Alamo engines were built in Hillsdale, Michigan by the Alamo Manufacturing Co. Engines from 3 to 50 horsepower used low-tension magnetos and a hammer-break igniter for ignition. The fuel pump is cycled by the engine's exhaust lever. A cast iron water hopper cools this gasoline engine.

In 1913, Associate Manufacturers Co. from Waterloo, Iowa marketed several engines that ranged in size from 1 1/2 to 12-horsepower. The Busy Boy shown here was a 1 1/2-horsepower engine. A hammer-break igniter and a low-tension rotary magneto were used for ignition. This hit-and-miss-governed engine is air-cooled and runs on gasoline.

This Aermotor engine used a flywheel governor to regulate engine rpm. The sausage-shaped hopper is rather unique and is often referred to as the sausage hopper Aermotor.

Left
Aerothrust Engine Co. built their engines at 331 Washington Street in La Porte, Indiana. The Pormo three-horsepower air-cooled engine used high-tension spark plug ignition. The two-cycle engine is air-cooled.

A 1 1/2-horsepower engine was the smallest engine that Appleton Manufacturing Co. made. Appleton engines were manufactured in Batavia, Illinois with sizes ranging from 1 1/2 to 18-horsepower. Hit-and-miss governing and low-tension ignition were standard equipment for these hopper-cooled engines.

This illustration of the Air-Cooled Motor Company's 1 1/2-horsepower air-cooled engine appeared in a trade magazine in 1909. The company built two-cylinder air-cooled opposed engines up to 10 horsepower in Lansing Michigan.

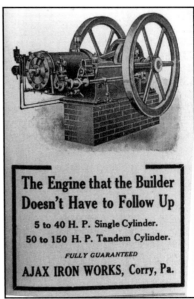

The Ajax Iron Works started designing engines in Corry, Pennsylvania during the 1870s. This 1910 model Ajax engine was built in 5- to 40-horsepower models. The engine is equipped with a rotary magneto that is driven off of the side-shaft. Tandem cylinder engines in sizes from 50 to 150 horsepower were also manufactured.

Left
Angola Engine and Foundry Co. marketed several side-shaft engines in horsepowers from 2 1/2 to 20. A hammer-break igniter connected to a battery and coil formed its low-tension ignition system. A vertical flyball governor regulates the speed of this external tank-cooled engine. The company was located in Angola, Indiana.

Engine Manufacturer	Factory Location	Trade Name	Dates
Aurora Automatic Mach. Co.	Aurora, IL	Aurora	na
Arrow Mtr. & Mach. Co.	New York, NY	Arrow Marine	1917
Arthur Mach. Co.	Richwood, OH	na	1911
Ash-Harper & Co.	Lyons, MI	na	1901
Ashbrook Elect. Co.	Chicago, IL	Ashbrook Light Plant	na
Ashurst Press Drill Co.	Havana, IL	Havana	1902–1904
Ashurst Press Drill Co.	Havana, IL	Red & Ready	1902–1904
Associated Mfr.'s Co.	Waterloo, IA	Amanco	1909–1946
Associated Mfr.'s Co.	Waterloo, IA	Assoc. Kerosene	na
Associated Mfr.'s Co.	Waterloo, IA	Associated	1912
Associated Mfr.'s Co.	Waterloo, IA	Baker	na
Associated Mfr.'s Co.	Waterloo, IA	Banner	na
Associated Mfr.'s Co.	Waterloo, IA	Battery	na
Associated Mfr.'s Co.	Waterloo, IA	Bluffton	na
Associated Mfr.'s Co.	Waterloo, IA	Busy Boy	na
Associated Mfr.'s Co.	Waterloo, IA	Chore Boy	na
Associated Mfr.'s Co.	Waterloo, IA	Colt	na
Associated Mfr.'s Co.	Waterloo, IA	Enterprise	na
Associated Mfr.'s Co.	Waterloo, IA	Farm Hand	na
Associated Mfr.'s Co.	Waterloo, IA	Foreman	na
Associated Mfr.'s Co.	Waterloo, IA	Freedom	na
Associated Mfr.'s Co.	Waterloo, IA	Iowa	na
Associated Mfr.'s Co.	Waterloo, IA	Johnny Boy	na
Associated Mfr.'s Co.	Waterloo, IA	Milwaukee	na
Associated Mfr.'s Co.	Waterloo, IA	Ottawa	na
Associated Mfr.'s Co.	Waterloo, IA	Twin Cylinder	na
Associated Mfr.'s Co.	Waterloo, IA	United	na
Associated Mfr.'s Co.	Waterloo, IA	Wonder	na
Associated Mfr.'s Co.	Waterloo, IA	Hired Man	na
Associated Mfr.'s Co.	Waterloo, IA	Hired Hand	na
Associated Mfr.'s Co.	Waterloo, IA	Iowa Oversized	na
Associated Mfr.'s Co.	Waterloo, IA	Jack Boy	na
Associated Mfr.'s Co.	Waterloo, IA	Jack Jr.	na
Associated Mfr.'s Co.	Waterloo, IA	Jerry Boy	na
Associated Mfr.'s Co.	Waterloo, IA	Mule Team	na
Atlantic Eng. Co.	Meadville, PA	Atlantic	1912
Atlantic Mtr. Co.	Portland, ME	na	1905
Atlas Eng. Works	Indianapolis, IN	Atlas Diesel	na
Atlas Eng. Works	Indianapolis, IN	Atlas	1906–1912
Atlas Eng. Works	Indianapolis, IN	King Bee	1906–1912
Atlas Gas Eng. & Truck Co.	Pittsburgh, PA	na	1903
Atlas Gas Eng. Co.	Oakland, CA	Marine Engines	na
Atlas-Imp. Diesel Eng. Co.	Oakland, CA	Atlas-Imperial	na
Atlas-Imp. Diesel Eng. Co.	Oakland, CA	Atlas-Thornberg	na
Atlas Mach. Co.	Fort Worth, TX	Ajax	na
Atlas Mfg. Co.	Milwaukee, WI	Christensen	na
Atlas-Thornberg Co.	Mattoon, IL	Atlas-Thornberg	na
Auglaize Mach. Co.	St. Marys, OH	na	1901
Augustine Automatic Rotary Eng. Co.	Buffalo, NY	Augustine	1918
Aultman Co.	Canton, OH	Priestman	1886
Aultman Co.	Canton, IL	Aultman	1898–1905
Aurora Automatic Machry. Co.	Aurora, IL	Thor	1909
Aurora Mfg. Co.	Aurora, IA	Augustine	1906
Austin & Son	Grand Rapids, MI	Austin	1901–1921
Austin Mfg. Co.	Chicago, IL	Austin	1906
Austin Mfg. Co.	Chicago, IL	Charter	1906
Auten Machry. Co.	Chicago, IL	Auten	1910
Auten Machry. Co.	Chicago, IL	Elgin	na
Auten Machry. Co.	Chicago, IL	Elgin Comet	1909
Auten Machry. Co.	Chicago, IL	The Comet	na
Automatic Bearing Mach. Co.	San Jose, CA	na	1925
Automatic Gas Eng. Co.	Oil City, PA	na	1899
Automatic Light Co.	Port Clinton, OH	Alco	na
Automatic Light Co.	Ludington, MI	Automatic	na

Engine Manufacturer	Factory Location	Trade Name	Dates
Automatic Light Co.	Ludington, MI	Holt Farm Light	na
Automatic Light Co.	Ludington, MI	Power Light	na
Automatic Mach. Co.	Bridgeport, CT	Automatic	na
Automobile Co. of Am.	New York, NY	American	1900
Automotive Valves Co.	Los Angeles, CA	na	1921
Averill, F.E.	Buffalo, NY	na	na
Avery Co.	Peoria, IL	Avery	na
Avery Co.	Peoria, IL	Monitor	na
Avery Power Machry. Co.	Peoria, IL	Avery	na
Ayers Gasoline Eng. Works	Rochester, MI	Ayers	na
Ayers Gasoline Eng. Works	Saginaw, MI	Ayers	1904–1907
B-S Supply Co.	St. Louis , MO	Garlock	na
B. F. Avery & Sons	Atlanta, GA	Alamo	na
B. F. Avery & Sons Plow Co.	Kansas City, MO	Fairfield	na
Backus Water Mtr. Co.	Newark, NJ	Backus	1890–1901
Bacon & Donovan Eng. Co.	Springfield, MA	B & D	na
Badger Concrete Mixer Co.	Milwaukee, WI	Sexton Jr.	1913
Badger Eng. Co.	Milwaukee, WI	Badger Jr.	1923
Badger Eng. Co.	Milwaukee, WI	Farmers Friend	na
Badger Eng. Co.	Milwaukee, WI	Lauson	na
Badger Mfg. Co.	Oshkosh, WI	na	na
Badger Mtr. Co.	Milwaukee, WI	Badger	1906
Badger Mtr. Co.	Milwaukee, WI	Badger Jr.	1906
Badker Gas Eng. Co.	Omaha, NE	na	1901
Baier Bros. Mfg. Co.	Cissna Park, IL	Baier	1915
Baird Mach. & Mfg. Co.	Detroit, MI	Yale-Marine	1910
Baker, Jackson H.	Ottumwa, IA	Baker	1916
Baker Co., C. L.	Norwalk, CT	Baker	na
Baker Co., C. L.	Norwalk, CT	New Baker	na
Baker Co., C. L.	Norwalk, CT	Type "X"	na
Baker Mfg. Co.	Evansville, WI	Baker	1904–1944
Baker Mfg. Co.	Evansville, WI	Baker Monitor	1901
Baker Mfg. Co.	Evansville, WI	Little Baker	na
Baker Mfg. Co.	Evansville, WI	Little Monitor	na
Baker Mfg. Co.	Evansville, WI	Sterling Monitor	na
Baldwin Mach. Works	New Haven, CT	Baldwin	1907
Baldwin Mtr. Co.	Baldwin, NY	Baldwin	1902
Ballou Mfg. Co.	Belding, MI	Brown Marvel	na
Baltimore Oil Eng. Co.	Baltimore, MD	Baltimore	1921
Balzer Co.	Bronx, NY	Balzer	1893–1907
Banner Eng. Co.	Lansing, MI	Banner	na
Barber Bros.	Syracuse, NY	Barber-Marine	1885–1907
Barker, C. L.	Norwalk, CT	Barker	1909
Barnes Co., Charles	Cincinnati, OH	Barnes	1903
Barnhart-Davis Co.	Warren, PA	Bullseye	na
Barrett, Mora M.	San Francisco, CA	na	1883
Bates & Edmonds Mtr. Co.	Lansing, MI	Baker & Hamilton	1900–1923
Bates & Edmonds Mtr. Co.	Lansing, MI	Bates	1900–1923
Bates & Edmonds Mtr. Co.	Lansing , MI	Bates & Edmonds	1900–1923
Bates & Edmonds Mtr. Co.	Lansing, MI	Bull Dog	1900–1923
Bates & Edmonds Mtr. Co.	Lansing, MI	Callahan	1900–1923
Bates & Edmonds Mtr. Co.	Lansing, MI	Columbia	1900–1923
Bates & Edmonds Mtr. Co.	Lansing, MI	Columbiana	1900–1923
Bates & Edmonds Mtr. Co.	Lansing, MI	Fairbanks	1900–1923
Bates Thermic Eng. Co.	Philadelphia, PA	na	1896
Batterman Reversible Gasoline Co.	Biglerville, PA	na	1909
Battery Co.	Milwaukee, WI	Battery	na
Bauer Bros. Co.	Springfield, OH	Scientific	na
Bauer Eng. Co.	Kansas City, MO	Bauer	1894–1920
Bauer Mach. Works Co.	Kansas City, MO	Bauer	1894–1920
Bauer Mach. Works Co.	Kansas City, MO	Ever-Ready	1894–1920
Bauer Mach. Works Co.	Kansas City, MO	Rex	1894–1920
Bauroth Bros.	Springfield, OH	Bauroth	1899
Bauroth Bros.	Springfield, OH	Handy Andy	na

Engine Manufacturer	Factory Location	Trade Name	Dates
Bay State Mach. Co.	Erie, PA	Baystate	1906
Bay State Mtr. Works	Holyoke, MA	Perfect Simplicity	na
Bay State Mtr. Works	Holyoke, MA	Simple Perfection	na
Baylis Co.	New York, NY	na	na
Baystate Gas Eng. Co.	Boston, MA	na	1903
Beach, O. B.	Stony Point, CT	na	na
Bean Mfg. Co.	Lansing, MI	Bean	na
Bean Spray Pump Co.	San Jose, CA	Bean-Collis-Ostenberg	1914
Bean Spray Pump Co.	Lansing, MI	Bean-Collis-Ostenberg	na
Beaudette/Graham Eng. Co.	Boston, MA	Syco-Lite	1918
Beaver Mach. Co.	Cincinnati, OH	Beaver	na
Beaver Mfg. Co.	Milwaukee, WI	Beaver	1904–1912
Beaver Mfg. Co.	Milwaukee, WI	Reliance	1904–1912
Beaver Mfg. Co.	Milwaukee, WI	Unit Plan Motor	1904–1912
Beeler Slide Valve Mtr. Co.	Chicago, IL	na	1913
Beers Bros. Eng. Co.	Rochester, NY	na	1904
Beilfuss Mtr. Co.	Lansing, MI	Beilfuss	1904
Beilfuss Mtr. Co.	Lansing, MI	Never Miss	1904
Belcomer Mach. Co.	Bloomer, WI	Keller	na
Belcomer Mach. Works	Milwaukee, WI	Ketter	na
Belden Engnrg. Co.	Pittsburgh, PA	na	1911
Bell, George C.	LaCrosse, WI	na	1902
Belle City Mfg. Co.	Racine Jct., WI	Belle City-Marine	1904
Belle Island Mtr. Co.	Detroit, MI	Little Hummer	1907–1911
Belle Island Mtr. Co.	Detroit, MI	Skiddo	1907–1911
Beloit Gas Eng. Co.	Beloit, WI	Beloit	1892
Benedict Mfg. Co.	Salamanca, NY	na	1905
Benninghofen & Sons	Hamilton, OH	Benninghofen	1915
Benninghofen & Sons	Hamilton, OH	Big Ben	1910–1922
Benton & Son	LaCrosse, WI	Benton Marine	1903
Benton Harbor Mach. Co.	Benton Harbor, MI	Benton	1902–1905
Benton Harbor Mach. Co.	Benton Harbor, MI	Upton	1903
Berry Co.	Petrolia, PA	Berry	na
Bessemer Gas Eng. Co.	Grove City, PA	Bessemer	1899–1929
Bessemer Gas Eng. Co.	Grove City, PA	Gasolene/Kerosene	na
Best Mfg. Co.	San Leondra, CA	Best	1872
Bethlehem Shipbuilding Corp.	Bethlehem, PA	na	na
Bethlehem Steel Co.	Bethlehem, PA	na	na
Bettendorf Axle Co.	Davenport, IA	Bettendorf	na
Bettendorf Axle Co.	Davenport, IA	Brown-Cochran	na
Bettendorf Co.	Bettendorf, IA	Thermoil	na
Beverly Eng. & Mach. Co.	Beverly, MA	na	na
Bevier Gas Eng. Co.	Kalamazoo, MI	na	1910
Bicknell Mfg. & Supply Co.	Janesville, WI	Bicknell	1911
Bicknell Mfg. & Supply Co.	Janesville, WI	Perfection	na
Bieder Mfg. Co.	Ashtabula, OH	Bieder	1908–1912
Bieder Mfg. Co.	Ashtabula, OH	Home Power	1912
Binghamden Hyd. Power Co.	Binghamden, NY	Adams & Richards	1889–1893
Binghamden Hyd. Power Co.	Binghamden, NY	Richards	na
Binghampton Gas Eng. Co.	Binghampton, NY	na	1898
Bingo Eng. Works	Flora, IN	Bingo	1914–1916
Binns Mach. & Tool Works	San Francisco, CA	na	na
Birch & Birch	Crawfordville, IN	Little Liz	1907
Bishop & Son Co.	Fargo, ND	Gate City	na
Bit Co.	Chicago, IL	Super Diesel	na
Black Swan Co.	Minneapolis, MN	Swanlite	na
Blackrock Mfg. Co.	Bridgeport, CT	Aristox	na
Blacksmith Supply Co.	St. Louis, MO	Garlock	na
Blaisdell Machry. Co.	Bradford, PA	Blaisdell	1893
Blakeslee Mfg. Co.	Birmingham, AL	Blakeslee	1901
Blakeslee Mfg. Co.	Birmingham, AL	Junior	na
Blanchard Mach. Co.	Cambridge, MA	na	1911
Blandy Fdry.	Zanesville, OH	Blandy	na
Blatchley	Philadelphia, PA	Blatchley	1905

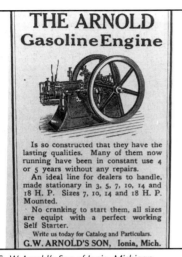

G. W Arnold's Son of Ionia, Michigan manufactured 3-, 5-, 7-, 10-, 14- and 18-horsepower engines. The Arnold engines were designed with side shafts, vertical flyball governing and were equipped with external tank cooling. All Arnold engines sold for under $600 new.

Bauroth Brothers of Springfield, Ohio began building engines just prior to 1900. This Bauroth vertical engine uses hit-and-miss governing to control its rpm. A low-tension electrical system was installed with a hammer-break igniter to provide ignition. The engine is cooled with water circulated from an external cooling tank. Bauroth vertical engines burned gasoline.

Right
Bauer Machine Works Co. located at 119-23 West 18th Street, Kansas City, Missouri built engines in sizes from 1 1/2 to 40 horsepower in this side-shaft design. A battery, coil and hammer-break igniter are used to fire this engine. Bauer claimed in their advertising that this engine could be maintained for less than sixty cents per year.

This Associate Manufacturers' engine is fired by a hammer-break igniter and low-tension rotary magneto. Hit-and-miss governing controls the engine's speed. A round gasoline fuel tank can be seen just below the engine's head and valves, attached to its skid.

Early in the 1890s, Backus Water Motor Co. of Newark, NJ. entered the gasoline engine manufacturing business. Their Backus engine of 1895 uses hot tube ignition. This style engine was produced in sizes from 1 to 75 horsepower.

The Bloomer Machine Works of Bloomer, Wisconsin manufactured the Keller engine. Hit-and-miss governing is used with high-tension spark plug ignition to drive this four-cycle engine. The unusually shaped water hopper is a unique feature of the Keller gasoline engine.

Atlas Engine Works of Indianapolis, Indiana manufactured this King Bee engine. The King Bee was fitted with a vertical flyball governor to control engine speed. An external tank is used for cooling this gasoline engine.

The Baker Manufacturing Co. located in Evansville, Wisconsin manufactured the Monitor horizontal engine. This engine was made in 3-, 5-, and 8-horsepower models. A battery box can be seen mounted to the front of the water hopper.

The Bluffton Cream Separator Co. manufactured their engines in the town of Bluffton, Ohio. Water- and air-cooled models could be ordered. The engine weighed 275 pounds and ran at 450 rpm. The flywheels were 17 inches in diameter and weight 46 pound each. A hammer-break igniter, battery, and coil supplied ignition. Bluffton sold this engine for $38.00.

Two and four-horsepower hot tube vertical engines were manufactured in Bradford, Pennsylvania by Bovaird and Co. This engine was advertised by Bovaird and Co. in Gas Review *magazine in 1908.*

The Brown-Cochran Co. was located in Lorain, Ohio. Brown-Cochran began manufacturing stationary engines in 1901. Their portable engines ranged from 4 to 25-horsepower. Hammer-break igniters and vertical flyball governors are common features found on these Ohio engines. Cast iron melted at the blast furnaces of the Johnson Steel Co. was used at the Brown-Cochran Co. to manufacture their engines.

Brownwall Engine and Pulley Co. was located first in Lansing and later in Holland, Michigan. Brownwall engines used high-tension spark plug ignition and ran on gasoline.

Burnoil engines were manufactured by the Burnoil Engine Co. located in South Bend, Indiana. The Dynoil shown here was a 4 1/2-horsepower engine that used compression ignition. Dynoil engines were built in many sizes from 2 1/2 to 40 horsepower. They can be run on oil or kerosene.

Charles Brunner engines were manufactured in Peru, Illinois. Their 1 1/2-horsepower air-cooled engine uses high-tension spark plug ignition. A battery box, battery, buzz coil, and cooling fan were supplied direct from the factory with this gasoline engine.

Right
This ornate, two-horsepower, Burtt Manufacturing Co. horizontal engine was manufactured in Kalamazoo, Michigan in 1909. Spark plug ignition using a battery and buzz coil came as standard equipment. A flyball governor controls the engines speed. It is hopper-cooled and runs on gasoline.

This original six-horsepower Brown engine was built by the Brown-Cochran Co. of Lorain, Ohio. A side-shaft, low-tension ignition, hammer-break igniter and vertical flyball governor were standard features on this very high quality engine. The Co. also built marine engines which they called the Lacy Marine line.

The Buckeye Machine Co. in Lima, Ohio built this style engine in sizes from 1 to 25 horsepower. A Lunkenheimer generator, high-tension spark plug ignition, and hopper cooling are standard features for this stationary gasoline engine.

Engine Manufacturer	Factory Location	Trade Name	Dates
Blissfield Mtr. Works	Blissfield, MI	Blissfield	na
Blomstrom Mtr. Co.	Detroit, MI	Blomstrom	1906–1909
Bloomer Mach. Works	Milwaukee, WI	Bloomer	1904–1920
Bloomer Mach. Works	Milwaukee, WI	Eau Claire	na
Bloomer Mach. Works	Milwaukee, WI	Keller	na
Bluffton Cream Separator Co.	Bluffton, OH	Bluffton	na
Bluffton Cream Separator Co.	Bluffton, OH	Boss	na
Bluffton Mfg. Co.	Bluffton, OH	Bluffton	na
Bluffton Mfg. Co.	Bluffton, OH	Boss	na
Bluffton Mfg. Co.	Bluffton, OH	Ideal	na
Blum Bros. Co.	Chicago, IL	na	1907
Boardman Co.	Oil City, PA	Boardman	na
Bock & Co.	Antioch, IL	Advance	na
Bogart Gas Eng. Co.	Covington, KY	Bogart	1892
Bogart Gas Eng. Co.	Buffalo, NY	na	1911
Bohan Co.	Harrodsburg, KY	Bohan Dixie King/Nelson	na
Bohan Co.	Harrodsburg, KY	Bohan/Nelson Bros.	na
Boisselet Auto. & Sp. Gaso. Mt. Co.	New York, NY	Boisselet	na
Bolens Mfg. Co.	Port Washington, WI	Gilson	1914–1920
Bolinders Co.	New York, NY	Bolinders	na
Booher Mach. Works	Dayton, OH	Booher	na
Boos Oil Eng. Co.	St. Marys, OH	Boos	1916
Borden & Selleck Co.	Chicago, IL	Borden/Selleck	na
Bosh Chemical Co.	Louisville, KY	Delco	1916
Boston Gasoline Eng. Co.	Boston, MA	Boston	1903–1911
Bovaird & Co.	Bradford, PA	Araco	na
Bovaird & Co.	Bradford, PA	Bovaird	na
Bovaird & Seyfang Mfg. Co.	Boston, MA	Bovaird	na
Bovaird & Seyfang Mfg. Co.	Bradford, PA	Bovaird	1895–1936
Bowen & Co.	Buffalo, NY	Bowen	1901
Bowen & Quick	Auburn, NY	na	1909
Bowen Elect. Co.	Providence, RI	na	na
Bowers Co., F. E.	New Haven, CT	na	1907
Brackett-Shaw & Lunt Co.	Boston, MA	Reliance-Jobbed Eng.	na
Brackett-Shaw & Lunt Co.	Somersworth, NH	Reliance-Jobbed Eng.	na
Brackett-Shaw & Lunt Co.	Boston, MA	Saxon-Jobbed Eng.	na
Brackett-Shaw & Lunt Co.	Somersworth, NH	Saxon-Jobbed Eng.	na
Braden Co.	Parkersburg, WV	Braden	na
Braden Gas Eng. Co.	Butler, PA	Braden	1901
Braden Mfg. Co.	Hanford, CA	Braden	1895
Bradford Gas Eng. Co.	Camden, NJ	na	1902
Bramwell Mtr. Co.	Boston, MA	Bramwell	1901
Brass Fdry. & Heating Co.	Peoria, IL	na	na
Brayton Pet. Eng. Co.	Boston, MA	Brayton	1872–1892
Brayton Pet. Eng. Co.	Boston, MA	Ready Motor	1872–1892
Brazelle Mtr.	St. Louis, MO	Brazelle	1912
Brazier	Philadelphia, PA	Brazier	1902
Breeze Mtr. Co.	Newark, NJ	Breeze Automatic	1909
Brennan Mtr. Co.	Syracuse, NY	Brennan	1903–1908
Bridge City Const. Co.	Logansport, IN	na	na
Bridgeport Mtr. Co.	Bridgeport, CT	Bridgeport	na
Briggs & Stratton Corp.	Milwaukee, WI	Basco	na
Briggs & Stratton Corp.	Milwaukee, WI	Briggs & Stratton	1908
Briggs & Stratton Corp.	Milwaukee, WI	Motor Wheel	na
Brill Eng. Works	Appleton, WI	na	1912
Brillion Iron Works	Brillion, WI	Brillion	1912
Brinker Rotary Gas Eng. Co.	Centerville, MI	na	1913
Brisco Consolidated Iron Works	Hanford, CA	na	na
Brombacher, Max	Buffalo, NY	Climax-Jobbed	1897–1903
Brombacher's & Sons	Brooklyn, NY	Climax-Jobbed	1897
Brooklyn Gas Eng. Co.	Brooklyn, NY	Brooklyn	1900
Brooklyn Railway Supply Co.	Stamford, CT	Brooklyn	1900
Brooks Mtr. Co.	Detroit, MI	na	1907
Brown-Cochran Co.	Lorain, OH	Bettendorf	1900–1913

C.H. and E. Manufacturing Co. was located in Milwaukee, Wisconsin. The C.H. and E. engine shown here has a centrifugal flywheel flyball governor and is hopper-cooled. The gasoline fuel tank is hidden under the engines base.

The Challenge 1 1/2-horsepower horizontal engine is easily identified by its hourglass-shaped water hopper. The engines use high-tension spark plug ignition and run on gasoline.

Right
Christensen Engineering Co. was located at 105 Badger Street in Milwaukee, Wisconsin and manufactured the Farmer's Friend gasoline engines. They were made in 2 1/2 to 30 horsepower. The Co. backed this engine with a five-year guarantee.

W.P. Callahan and Co. made high-quality engines in Dayton, Ohio. This 1896 style side-shaft engine is equipped with a low-tension hammer-break ignition system. These engines are water-cooled and were manufactured in sizes from 4 to 100 horsepower.

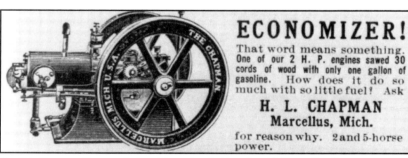

The H.L. Chapman Co. manufactured its engines in Marcellus, Michigan. The Chapman two- or five-horsepower horizontal engine is shown here. Low-tension ignition and a hammer-break igniter are standard equipment on these tank-cooled gasoline engines.

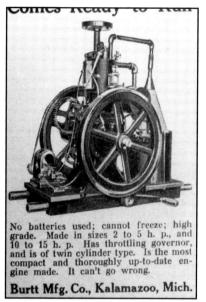

The Burtt Manufacturing Company's vertical engine was equipped with a rotary magneto that ran off of the engine flywheel. This engine was built in two and five-horsepower models. The engine is throttle-governed and tank screen-cooled.

Batavia, Illinois was home to the Challenge Co. The company was located at 60 River Street. These vertical air-cooled engines were manufactured in sizes ranging from 2 1/2 to 15-horsepower. The engines were equipped with a hammer-break igniter and low-tension ignition and run on gasoline.

Engine Manufacturer	Factory Location	Trade Name	Dates
Brown-Cochran Co.	Lorain, OH	Brown	1900–1913
Brown-Cochran Co.	Lorain, OH	Brown-Cochran	1900–1913
Brown-Cochran Co.	Lorain, OH	Lacy-Marine	1900–1913
Brown Eng. Co.	Fitchburg, MA	Beco	na
Brown Eng. Co.	Fitchburg, MA	Brown	na
Brown Gas Eng. Co.	Columbus, OH	Brown	1897–1900
Brown Mtr. Works	Rock Island, IL	na	1917
Brown-Loftus Co.	Cedar Rapids, IA	Perfection	1916
Brownell-Trebert Co.	Rochester, NY	na	1900
Browning Ind. Equip. Co.	Dallas, TX	Browning	na
Brownwall Co.	Holland, MI	Canuck	na
Brownwall Eng. & Pulley Co.	Lansing, MI	Brownwall	1912–1920
Brownwall Eng. & Pulley Co.	Lansing, MI	Jaeger	1912–1920
Brownwall Eng. & Pulley Co.	Lansing, MI	United States	1912–1920
Bruce, Albert W.	Bloomfield, IA	na	1916
Bruce-Meriam-Abbott Co.	Cleveland, OH	na	1909
Bruce-Macbeth Eng. Co.	Cleveland, OH	Bruce-Macbeth	1909
Bruce-Macbeth Eng. Co.	Cleveland, OH	Meriam	na
Brunner, Charles	Peru, IL	Brunner	na
Brunner Fdry. & Machry. Co.	Peru, IL	Winner	na
Brunner Fdry. & Machry. Co.	Peru, IN	Brunner	1911
Brush & Hudson	Brooklyn, NY	na	1906
Brutt Mfg. Co.	Vicksburg, MI	Bronson	na
Bry-Son Gas Eng. Co.	Princeton, IL	na	1910
Bryan Mfg. Co.	Baltimore, MD	Bryan	na
Bryant, C. R.	Manistee, MI	na	1907
Buck, J. W.	Davenport, IA	na	na
Buckeye Eng. & Fdry. Co.	Joliet, IL	Buckeye	1904
Buckeye Eng. & Fdry. Co.	Joliet, IL	B & B	na
Buckeye Eng. & Fdry. Co.	Joliet, IL	Honest Abe	1906
Buckeye Eng. Co.	Salem, OH	Buckeye	1897
Buckeye Gasoline Eng. Co.	Aurora, IL	Buckeye	1904–1912
Buckeye Gasoline Eng. Co.	Aurora, IL	Little Giant	1904–1912
Buckeye Mach. Co.	Lima, OH	Buckeye	na
Buckeye Mach. Co.	Lima, OH	Buckeye Barret	na
Buckeye Mfg. Co.	Anderson, IN	Buckeye	1895–1904
Buckeye Mfg. Co.	Anderson, IN	Lambert	1897
Buckeye Mtr. Co.	Columbus, OH	Buckeye	1903
Bucklen & Co.	Elkhart, IN	Herbes	na
Bucksport Launch & Eng. Works	Bucksport, ME	Marine Eng.	1909
Buda Mfg. Co.	Harvey , IL	na	1891
Budd, L. M.	Saginaw, MI	na	1907
Budd-Ranney Co.	Columbus, OH	Reeves	na
Buffalo Drilling Co.	Sheffield, PA	Snow	na
Buffalo Eng. Co.	Buffalo, NY	Buffalo	1903
Buffalo Gasolene Mtr. Co.	Buffalo, NY	Buffalo-Marine	1909
Buffalo Gasolene Mtr. Co.	Buffalo, NY	Buffalo Reputation	na
Buick Mfg. Co.	Detroit, MI	Buick	1901–1903
Burger Co.	Dayton, OH	Van Horne	1896–1899
Burger Gas Eng. Co.	Fort Wayne, IN	Burger	na
Burger Gas Eng. Co.	Fort Wayne, IN	Burger	na
Burgess-Norton Mfg. Co.	Geneva, IL	na	1921
Burgett	Middlebough, NY	Burgett	na
Burke Bros.	Chattanooga, TN	na	1904
Burke Engnrg. Co.	Holland, MI	Holland	1948
Burkett Mfg. Co.	Columbus, OH	Burkett	1913
Burlingame & Co.	Providence, RI	na	na
Burnett-Larsh Mfg. Co.	Dayton, OH	Duro	1919
Burnoil Eng. Co.	South Bend, IN	Burnoil	1916
Burnoil Eng. Co.	South Bend, IN	Dynoil	na
Burrill & Co.	Chicago, IL	Burrill	na
Burton Mach. Works	San Francisco, CA	na	na
Burtt Mfg. Co.	Chicago, IL	Always Ready	na
Burtt Mfg. Co.	Kalamazoo, MI	Burtt	1902–1912

Engine Manufacturer	Factory Location	Trade Name	Dates
Burtt Mfg. Co.	Kalamazoo, MI	Kalamazoo	1909
Busch-Sulzer Bros. Diesel Eng. Co.	St. Louis, MO	Busch-Sulzer	1898
Butler Eng. & Fdry. Co.	Butler, PA	Ball	na
Butler Engnrg. Co.	East Butler, PA	na	1904
Butterworth, Wm. H.	Trenton, NJ	Butterworth	na
C. H. & E. Mfg. Co.	Milwaukee, WI	C. H. & E.	na
C. P. Power Co.	Newark, NJ	na	1910
Cal. Hyd. Eng. & Supply Co.	San Francisco, CA	Little Giant	na
Cal. Hyd. Eng. & Supply Co.	San Francisco, CA	Rawleigh	1912
Cady Co.	Danartoto, NY	Cady-Marine	na
Cady Co. Inc.	Canastota, NY	Cady	na
Cage Eng. Syndicate Inc.	New York, NY	na	1921
Caille Perfection Mtr. Co.	Detroit, MI	Caille Perfection	na
Caille Perfection Mtr. Co.	Detroit, MI	Liberty Drive	na
Caille Perfection Mtr. Co.	Detroit, MI	Perfection	na
Caille Perfection Mtr. Co.	Detroit, MI	Perfection Special	na
Caldwell & Sons	Waterloo, IA	Caldwell	na
Caldwell & Sons	Chicago, IL	Caldwell	na
Caldwell & Sons	Waterloo, IA	Charter	na
Caldwell & Sons	Chicago, IL	Charter	na
Caldwell & Watson Mtr. Co.	Portage, OH	Caldwell & Watson	1901
Caldwell Co.	Bradford, PA	Caldwell	1907
Caldwell-Hollowell Mfg.	Waterloo, IA	Pennsylvania Boy	1906
Caldwell-Charter Eng. Co.	Sterling, IL	Caldwell	1891
Caldwell-Howell Mfg.	Waterloo, IA	Caldwell	1906
Caldwell-Howell Mfg.	Waterloo, IA	Caldwell, Howell	1906
Caldwell-Howell Mfg.	Waterloo, IA	Caldwell Special	1906
Callhan & Co., W. P.	Dayton, OH	Callahan	1896–1926
Callhan & Co., W. P.	Dayton, OH	Coffield	1896
Callhan & Co., W. P.	Dayton, OH	Fairbanks	1896
Camden-Anchor-Rockland Mach. Co.	Rockland, ME	Camden	1900–1912
Camden-Anchor-Rockland Mach. Co.	Rockland, ME	Camden Anchor	1907
Camden-Anchor-Rockland Mach. Co.	Rockland, ME	Knox	na
Campbell Iron Works	St. Louis, MO	Campbell	na
Campbell Machry. Co.	San Diego, CA	West Coast	na
Campbell Mtr. Co.	Wayzata, MN	Campbell	1907
Canedy	Chicago, IL	Canedy	1907
Canfield Gas Eng. Works	Binghamton, NY	Canfield	1906
Capital Gas Eng. Co.	Indianapolis, IN	Capital	1904
Capital Gas Eng. Co.	Indianapolis, IN	Gem	na
Capital Gas Eng. Co.	Rochester, NY	Gem	na
Capital Gas Eng. Co.	Indianapolis, IN	Hoosier	na
Capital Gas Eng. Co.	Indianapolis, IN	Knickerbocker	na
Capital Gas Eng. Co.	Indianapolis, IN	Osborne Household Hustler	na
Carbon-Oxygen Gas Eng. Co.	Boston, MA	na	1913
Carlin Mach. & Supply Co.	Allegheny, PA	na	na
Carlisle & Finch Co.	Cincinnati, OH	Carlisle & Finch	1898
Carr & Sprague	Fowlerville, MI	na	na
Carr Co.	Chicago, IL	Carr	na
Carroll Iron Works	Chicago, IL	Our Winner	na
Carroll Iron Works	Chicago, IL	Winner	na
Carse Bros. & Co.	Chicago, IL	na	na
Carson Mtr. Co.	Detroit, MI	Aristocrat	na
Carter Co.	New York, NY	Stover	na
Casaday Mfg. Co.	South Bend, IN	Casady	1905
Cascaden Mfg. Co.	Waterloo, IA	Cascaden	na
Cascaden Mfg. Co.	Waterloo, IA	Davis	na
Cascaden Mfg. Co.	Waterloo, IA	Davis Frost Proof	na
Cascaden Mfg. Co.	Waterloo, IA	Davis Jr.	1915
Cascaden-Vaughan Co.	Waterloo, IA	na	na
Case Threshing Mach. Co.	Racine, WI	Case	na
Case Threshing Mach. Co.	Racine, WI	Raymond	1892
Case Threshing Mach. Co.	Racine, WI	Raymond Improved	na
Castle Engnrg. Co., A.M.	LaCrosse, WI	Castle	1913

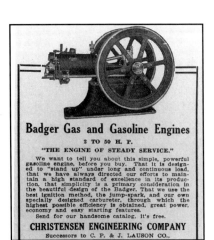

Columbus engines were manufactured by the Columbus Machine Co. in Columbus, Ohio. This 1895 side-shaft engine sports a vertical flyball governor and low-tension ignition. An external tank provides adequate cooling for these high-quality stationary engines.

The Badger engine was made by the Christensen Engineering Co. of Milwaukee, Wisconsin. These engines were manufactured in 2- to 50-horsepower models and featured jump spark ignition. They were tank-cooled and could be ordered equipped to run on natural gas or gasoline.

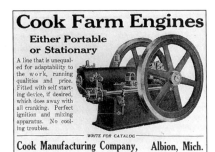

The Clark Machine Co. of St. Johnsville, New York built the Clark tank-cooled vertical engine. Four models were manufactured in 3-, 5-, 8-, and 12-horsepower models. The flyball governor can be seen attached to the center of the flywheel. A battery box, battery, coil, and cooling tank pump were supplied direct from the factory with every engine.

Albion, Michigan was home to the Cook Manufacturing Co. Two-and-a-half to 50-horsepower engines were manufactured that used a vertical flyball governor, hammer-break igniter, and low-tension ignition. A rotary magneto could be supplied with the engine in place of batteries and a coil.

This 1893 Dayton vertical engine was displayed at the Coolsprings Power Museum during the 1995 summer expo. The water-cooled engine was manufactured by the Dayton Gas Engine Co. of Dayton, Ohio.

This Columbus engine advertisement found in Gas Review magazine claimed that their engines could be ordered in sizes from 3 to 600 horsepower. Not all of the engines were designed as the one shown. The single-cylinder models were probably made up to 50 or 60 horsepower, while their tandem, double-acting engines produced 500 to 600 horsepower.

Right
Pictured here is an eight-horsepower Dayton horizontal engine. This engine was manufactured in 1893. The Dayton Gas Engine Co. manufactured engines from 1893 to 1904.

Pictured here is an eight-horsepower Dayton horizontal engine. This engine was manufactured in 1893. The Dayton Gas Engine Co. manufactured engines from 1893 to 1904.

During the 1920s, Deere and Co. of Moline, Illinois, ventured into the gasoline engine business. John Deere engines were manufactured in 1 1/2-, 3-, and 6-horsepower. The engine pictured here used hit-and-miss governing and low-tension ignition. A hammer-break igniter, enclosed crankcase, and water-cooled head were part of this engine's design.

Engine Manufacturer	Factory Location	Trade Name	Dates
Caterpillar Tractor	Peoria, IL	na	1925
Caton's Fdry. & Mach. Co.	San Jose, CA	na	1902
Cavannaugh & Darley Gas Eng. Co.	Chicago, IL	Little Giant	1908
Cavannaugh & Darley Gas Eng. Co.	Chicago, IL	Red Devil	na
Cedar Rapids Fdry. & Mach. Co.	Cedar Rapids, IA	Cedar Rapids	1911
Cedar Rapids Fdry. & Mach. Co.	Cedar Rapids, IA	Governor	1910–1932
Central Cal. Mach. Works	Fresno, CA	na	1904
Central City Iron Works	Quincy, IL	Central	1907
Central City Iron Works	Stevens Point, WI	Central	1907
Central City Iron Works	Stevens Point, WI	Mitchell	na
Central City Iron Works	Stevens Point, WI	Model	1904–1910
Central Mach. & Tool Co.	Battle Creek, MI	Central	na
Central Mach. & Tool Co.	Battle Creek, MI	Dickinson	1904
Challenge Co.	Batavia, IL	Challenge	1905
Challenge Co.	Batavia, IL	Handy Andy	na
Challenge Co.	Batavia, IL	Muncie	na
Challenge Co.	Batavia, IL	Taylor Vacuum Eng.	na
Challenge Windmill & Feed Mill Co.	Batavia, IL	Challenge	1898
Challenge Windmill & Feed Mill Co.	Batavia, IL	Dandy	na
Chamberlin Mach. Works	Waterloo, IA	Chamberlin	na
Chamberlin Mach. Works	Waterloo, IA	Honest John	1912
Chamberlin Mach. Works	Waterloo, IA	Ideal	na
Chamberlin Mach. Works	Waterloo, IA	Miss Simplicity	na
Chambers & Co.	Des Moines, IA	Chambers	na
Champion Gas Eng. Co.	Beaver Falls, PA	Champion	1893
Champion Gas Eng. Co.	Chicago, IL	na	na
Champion Thresher Co.	Orrville, OH	Champion	1901
Chapman Co., H. L.	Marcellus, MI	Good	na
Chapman Co., H. L.	Marcellus, MI	Chapman	1904–1911
Chapman Co., H. L.	Marcellus, MI	Economizer	1923
Chapman Co., H. L.	Marcellus, MI	Scat	na
Chapman Forge & Eng. Works	Marcellus, MI	Chapman	1903–1904
Charles City Eng. Service	Charles City, IA	Armstrong	na
Charter Gas Eng. Co.	Sterling, IL	Charter	1883
Charter Gas Eng. Co.	Sterling, IL	Mietz	1926
Charter Gas Eng. Co.	Sterling, IL	Mietz & Weiss	na
Charter Gas Eng. Co.	Sterling, IL	Sterling	1907
Chase Gas Eng. Co.	Mason City, IA	Chase	1916
Chase Mach. Co.	Cleveland, OH	Wooters	na
Chase Mfg. Co.	Mason City, IA	Chase	na
Chase-Hayes & Edwards Mfg. Co.	Milwaukee, WI	Chase-Hayes & Edwards	na
Chicago Flexible Shaft Co.	Chicago, IL	Chicago	1915
Chicago Flexible Shaft Co.	Chicago, IL	Little Major	na
Chicago Flexible Shaft Co.	Chicago, IL	Little Wonder	na
Chicago Flexible Shaft Co.	Chicago, IL	Stevens	na
Chicago Flexible Shaft Co.	Chicago, IL	Stewards	1910
Chicago Flexible Shaft Co.	Chicago, IL	Stewards Little Major	na
Chicago Flexible Shaft Co.	Chicago, IL	Stewards Little Wonder	na
Chicago Flexible Shaft Co.	Chicago, IL	Stover-Lanova	na
Chicago Gasoline Eng. Co.	Chicago, IL	Chicago	1906
Chicago Pneumatic Tool Co.	Chicago, IL	Chicago	1916
Chicago Pneumatic Tool Co.	Chicago, IL	Duntley	na
Chicago Pneumatic Tool Co.	Chicago, IL	Giant	na
Chicago Pneumatic Tool Co.	Chicago, IL	Little Giant	na
Chicago Water Mtr. & Fan Co.	Chicago, IL	Backus	1903
Chicago Wheel & Mfg. Co.	Chicago, IL	Chicago	na
Chriss Schramm & Son	Philadelphia, PA	Dean	na
Christensen	Brooklyn, NY	Christensen	na
Christensen Engnrg. Co.	Milwaukee, WI	Badger	na
Christensen Engnrg. Co.	Milwaukee, WI	Christensen	na
Christensen Engnrg. Co.	Milwaukee, WI	Farm Hand	na
Christensen Engnrg. Co.	Milwaukee, WI	Farmers Friend	na
Christensen Engnrg. Co.	Milwaukee, WI	Renfrew	na
Christensen Engnrg. Co.	Milwaukee, WI	Renfrew Standard	na

Engine Manufacturer	Factory Location	Trade Name	Dates
Christensen Engnrg. Co.	Milwaukee, WI	Standard	na
Christphen	Wichita, KS	Christphen	na
Church	Boston, MA	Church	1902–1905
Church, S. B.	Seymour, CT	Joy	na
Church, S. B.	Seymour, CT	Church	na
Church Mfg. Co.	Adrain, MI	Church	na
Chuse & Co., J. F.	Mattoon, IL	na	1900
Clark & Norton Mfg. Co.	Wellsville, NY	Clark	na
Clark Bros.	Olean, NY	Clark	na
Clark Eng. Co.	Jackson, MI	na	1906
Clark Mach. Co.	St. Johnsville, NY	Clark	1909–1911
Clark Mach. Co.	St. Johnsville, NY	Farmers Friend	1909–1911
Clark Mfg. Co.	Fond du Lac, WI	na	1903
Clarke Gas Eng. Co.	Evansville, IN	na	na
Clarkmobile Co.	Lansing, MI	na	na
Clay Center Windmill & Fdry. Co.	Clay Center, KS	na	na
Clay Eng. Co.	Chagrin Falls, OH	Clay	1904
Clay Eng. Co.	Chagrin Falls, OH	Honest Clay	1904
Clay Eng. Co.	Cleveland, OH	na	1913
Clay-Christie Co.	Cedar Falls, IA	na	na
Cleveland Gas Eng. Co.	Cleveland, OH	na	1895
Clift Mtr. Co.	Bellingham, WA	Clift	1913
Clifton Mtr. Works	Cincinnati, OH	Clifton	1904
Clifton Mtr. Works	Cincinnati, OH	Clifton-Marine	na
Climax Eng. Mfg. Co.	Clinton, IA	Climax	1920
Climax Elect. Works	New Salem, MA	Climax	1907
Climax Gas Eng. Co.	Brooklyn, NY	Climax	1898
Climax Tag Co.	Dayton, OH	na	1904
Clinton Iron & Novelty Works	Cincinnati, OH	Clinton	na
Clinton Mach. Co.	Maquoketa, IA	Clinton	na
Clinton Motorcycle & Power Co.	Clinton, IA	na	1896
Clinton Novelty Iron Works	Clinton, IA	Clinton	na
Clinton Separator & Eng. Co.	Clinton, IA	na	1901
Clipper Gas Eng. Co.	Brooklyn, NY	Clipper	1897
Clipper Lawn Mower Co.	Dixon, IL	Clipper	1907
Clizbe Bros. Mfg. Co.	Plymouth, IN	Clizbe	na
Clizbe Bros. Mfg. Co.	Plymouth, IN	Crown	na
Clot & Co.	San Francisco, CA	na	na
Coey Co., C. A.	Chicago, IL	Coey-Jobbed	1905
Coey Co., C. A.	Chicago, IL	Little Surprise	1905
Coffee & Son, R. W.	Richmond, VA	na	na
Coffey Eng. Works	Riverside, CA	Coffey	na
Colbert Machry. Co.	St. Joseph, MO	American Boy-Jobbed	na
Colbert Machry. Co.	St. Joseph, MO	Colborne-Jobbed	na
Colbert Machry. Co.	St. Joseph, MO	Davis-Jobbed	na
Colborne Mfg. Co.	Chicago, IL	Chicago	1901
Colborne Mfg. Co.	Chicago, IL	Colborne	1901
Coldwell Lawn Mower Co.	Newburgh, NY	Coldwell	1901
Colean Imp. Co.	East Peoria, IL	na	1902
Coleman Co., O. L.	St. Louis, MO	Sinning	na
Collins Co., O. L.	St. Louis, MO	Sinning	na
Collins Mfg. Co.	San Antonio, TX	na	na
Collis Co.	Clinton, IA	Bean	na
Collis Co.	Clinton, IA	Collis	na
Collis Co.	Clinton, IA	Pierson	na
Collis Co.	Clinton, IA	Superior Pierson	na
Collis Co.	Clinton, IA	Tangley	1920
Collis Plow Co.	Quincy, IL	Eli	na
Colo Diesel Co.	San Francisco, CA	na	na
Colton Co., A.	Detroit, MI	Colton	na
Colton Co., A.	Detroit, MI	Colton Modern	na
Colton Co., A.	Detroit, MI	Columbia	na
Colton Co., A.	Detroit, MI	Columbiana	na
Columbia Eng. Co.	Detroit, MI	Coal Oil Johnny	na

Engine Manufacturer	Factory Location	Trade Name	Dates
Columbia Eng. Co.	Detroit, MI	Columbia-Kero	1909
Columbia Eng. Co.	San Francisco, CA	na	na
Columbia Engnrg. Co.	Detroit, MI	Braddock Jr.	na
Columbus Gas Eng. & Mach. Co.	Columbus, OH	na	na
Columbus Mach. & Tool Co.	Columbus, OH	Columbus	na
Columbus Mach. Co.	Columbus, OH	Columbus	1899–1913
Columbus Mach. Co.	Columbus, OH	Duplex	na
Columbus Mach. Co.	Columbus, OH	Jaeger-Jobbed	na
Columbus Pump Co.	Columbus, OH	Franklin-Jobbed Nelson	na
Columbus Pump Co.	Columbus, OH	Slave-Jobbed Nelson	na
Comings Mfg. Co.	Upper Sandusky, OH	Underwood	na
Commercial Eng. Co.	Los Angeles, CA	Commercial	1905
Commet Eng. Co.	Berkeley, CA	na	na
Comstock Motor Co.	Topeka, KS	na	1897
Concrete Form & Eng. Co.	Detroit, MI	Little Hummer-Marine	1911
Concrete Form & Eng. Co.	Detroit, MI	Skiddo-Marine	1911
Connecticut Valley Mfg. Co.	Center Brook, CT	na	na
Consol. Gas & Gasoline Eng. Co.	New York, NY	Excelsior	na
Consolidated Gas Eng. Co.	New York, NY	Heavi-Duti	na
Consolidated Gas Eng. Co.	New York, NY	Consolidated	na
Consolidated Gas Eng. Co.	New York, NY	Ever Ready	na
Consolidated Gas Eng. Co.	New York, NY	Excelsior	na
Consolidated Gas Eng. Co.	New York, NY	Ohio	na
Consolidated Mfg. Co.	Toledo, OH	Yale	na
Consolidated Utilities Corp.	Chicago, IL	Matthews Light Plant	1920
Continental Eng. Co.	Chicago, IL	Continental	na
Continental Engnrg. Co.	Augusta, ME	na	1914
Continental Gas Eng. Co.	New York, NY	na	na
Continental Gin Co.	Birmingham, AL	Continental	na
Continental Mtr. Corp.	Muskegon, MI	Continental	1901
Continental Mtr. Corp.	Muskegon, MI	Red Seal	1901
Cook Eng. Co.	Cambridge, IL	na	1914
Cook Mfg. Co.	Albion, MI	Cook	1902
Cook Mtr. Co.	Delaware, OH	Cook	1902
Cook Mtr. Co.	Delaware, OH	Dennison	1902
Cook Mtr. Co.	Delaware, OH	Dennison Power Maker	1902
Cook Mtr. Co.	LaCrosse, WI	Standard	1909
Cook-Stoddard Mfg. Co.	Dayton, OH	Natl.	na
Cook-Stoddard Mfg. Co.	Dayton, OH	Natl. Jr.	na
Cooley Mfg. Co.	Waterbury, VT	na	na
Cooper Co., C. & G.	Mt. Vernon, OH	Cooper	1910–1929
Cooper Mach. Co.	Saltburg, PA	Cooper	na
Cooper-Bessemer Corp.	Mt. Vernon, OH	Cooper-Bessemer	na
Corliss Gas Eng. Co.	San Francisco, CA	Corliss	na
Corliss Gas Eng. Co.	San Francisco, CA	Oriental	1899–1902
Cormack & Co.	Rockford, IL	na	na
Corn Belt Mtr. Co.	Waterloo, IA	Gold Band/Galloway	1915–1920
Cornell Mach. Co.	Chicago, IL	Cornell	1897
Cornell Mtrs. Corp.	Petersburg, IL	na	1919
Cornwell Co., R. M.	Syracuse, NY	Wonder	1905
Cornwell Co., R. M.	Syracuse, NY	Wonder Light Plant	1905
Crabb Gas Eng. Co.	West Union, IA	Crabb	1910–1918
Crane Gas Eng. Co.	Boston, MA	na	1903
Crankless Eng. Co.	Jacksonville, FL	na	1922
Crankshaft Valve Movement Corp.	Green Bay, WI	na	1917
Crary Co.	Detroit, MI	na	1913
Crawford, J. B.	Lemars, IA	na	na
Crawford-Cummings Co.	Erie, PA	Crawford	na
Cray Bros.	Cleveland, OH	Cray-Jobbed	1918
Crescent Mach. & Tool Co.	Indianapolis, IN	Crescent	1903
Crescent Mfg. Co.	Titusville, PA	na	na
Crest Mfg. Co.	Cambridgeport, MA	Crest	1901
Crimer Co., H. J.	Burlington, IA	Crimer	1910
Cross Eng. Co., M. O.	Detroit, MI	Cross-Marine	na

Engine Manufacturer	Factory Location	Trade Name	Dates
Crough Co., C. P.	Chicago, IL	Crough Jr.	1906
Crown Mach. Works	Dayton, OH	Crown	1901
Cummings Mach. Co.	Minster, OH	na	1916
Cummins Eng. Co.	Columbus, OH	Cummins	1919–199?
Cummins Eng. Co.	Columbus, OH	Thermoil	na
Cunningham Sons & Co., J.	Rochester, NY	Cunningham	1909
Curtis Mfg. Co.	Hammondsport, NY	na	na
Cushman Mtr. Works	Lincoln, NE	Bean	1903
Cushman Mtr. Works	Lincoln, NE	Bean Special Cub	1903
Cushman Mtr. Works	Lincoln, NE	Bob-A-Lawn	1903
Cushman Mtr. Works	Lincoln, NE	Cub	1903
Cushman Mtr. Works	Lincoln, NE	Cushman-Marine	1903
Cushman Mtr. Works	Lincoln, NE	Cushman	1903
Cushman Mtr. Works	Lincoln, NE	Cushman All Purpose	1903
Cushman Mtr. Works	Lincoln, NE	Cushman Cub	1903
Cushman Mtr. Works	Lincoln, NE	Cushman Does More Light	1903
Cushman Mtr. Works	Lincoln, NE	Cushman Husky	1903
Cushman Mtr. Works	Lincoln, NE	Economy-Jobbed Sears	1942–1946
Cushman Mtr. Works	Lincoln, NE	Farm Master	1903
Cushman Mtr. Works	Lincoln, NE	Farm Cushman	1903
Cushman Mtr. Works	Lincoln, NE	Fifield	1903
Cushman Mtr. Works	Lincoln, NE	Husky	1903
Cushman Mtr. Works	Lincoln, NE	Massey-Harris	1903
Cushnoc Mtr. Co.	Augusta, ME	na	1910
Custer Mfg. Co.	Mation, IN	na	na
Cutler-Hammer Mfg. Co.	Milwaukee, WI	na	1918
Cyclone Iron Works	Stockton, CA	Cyclone	na
D. C. & U. Gas Eng. Co.	McDonald, PA	D. C. & U.	1902
Daellenbach Gas Eng. Co.	Pittsburgh, PA	na	1905
Daimler Mtr. Co.	Log Island, NY	Daimler	1895
Daimler Mtr. Launches	New York, NY	Daimler Marine	na
Dake Eng. Co.	Grand Haven, MI	na	1888
Dart Mfg. Co.	Waterloo, IA	Dart	na
Davenport Gasoline Eng. Co.	Davenport, IA	na	1898
Davenport Ice Chipping Mach. Co.	Davenport, IA	na	1909
Davenport Mach. & Fdry. Co.	Davenport, IA	Kulmer	1905
Davenport Mfg. Co.	Davenport, IA	Davenport	1900–1910
Davis Gasoline Eng. Co.	Waterloo, IA	Davis	1896
Davis Mfg. Co.	Milwaukee, WI	Avery	na
Davis Mfg. Co.	Milwaukee, WI	Davis	na
Davis Mtr. Co.	Brigham, UT	na	1921
Davis Mtr. Works	Waterloo, NY	na	1903
Davis-Colbert Co.	St. Joseph, MO	American Boy	na
Day & Co., L. P.	Cincinnati, OH	Day	1908
Dayton Elect. Mfg. Co.	Dayton, OH	Dayton Light Plant	na
Dayton Gas Eng. Co.	Dayton, OH	Dayton	1894
Dayton Globe Iron Works	Dayton, OH	Dayton	1890
Dayton Mtr. Works	Dayton, OH	Stoddard-Dayton	na
De La Vergne Mach. Co.	New York, NY	De La Vergne	1890
De La Vergne Mach. Co.	New York, NY	Hornsby-Akroyd	1890
De La Vergne Mach. Co.	New York, NY	Koerting	1890
De Laval Separator Co.	Chicago, IL	Alpha/Lauson	na
De Laval Separator Co.	New York, NY	Alpha/Lauson	na
De Laval Separator Co.	Chicago, IL	De Laval	na
De Laval Separator Co.	New York, NY	De Laval	na
De Loach Mill Mfg. Co.	Bridgeport, AL	De Loach	na
De Tamble Mtr. Co.	Anderson, IN	Carrico	1908
De Tamble Mtr. Co.	Anderson, IN	De Tamble	na
Dean Elect.	Elyria, OH	Dean Elect.	na
Dean Elect.	Elyria, OH	Elyria-Dean	na
Dean Elect.	Elyria, OH	Homelite	na
Dean Gas Eng. & Fdry. Co.	Newport, KY	Dean	1904
Dean Gas Eng. & Fdry. Co.	Newport, KY	Honest Injun	1904
Dean Mfg. Co.	Newport, KY	Fox	1910

Delray Motor Works was built in Detroit, Michigan. High-tension spark plug ignition was used on this tank-cooled gasoline engine. Six dry-cell batteries can be seen mounted in the skid connected to the buzz coil and an electrical switch.

Another Dempster engine is pictured here. This engine was fitted with a low-tension Webster oscillating magneto that is mounted to the hammer-break igniter bracket. It is hopper-cooled and burns gasoline. Notice that the working side of this engine is the left side and it uses a hot head that does not have an internal water jacket.

Detroit Motor Car Supply Co. was located in Detroit, Michigan. The Sandow 2 1/2-horsepower vertical engine used hopper cooling and sold for $45.00 new.

The DeMooy Brothers of Cleveland, Ohio were known for their line of marine engines. The two-cycle engines were built in one-, two-, three-, and four-cylinder models. The eight-horsepower DeMooy Marine is shown here. Marine engines circulated lake, sea, or river water throughout the engine water jacket for cooling.

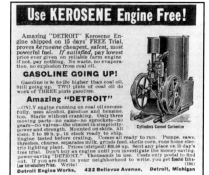

The Detroit Engine Works of Detroit, Michigan manufactured the Detroit line of two-cycle engines from 2 to 20 horsepower. Using high-tension spark plug ignition and tank cooling, the engines were designed to burn kerosene, coal oil, benzene, or alcohol. Prices for the two-horsepower model started at $29.50.

Right
The Domestic side-shaft engine was manufactured in Shippensburg, Pennsylvania by the Domestic Engine and Pump Co. The low-tension ignition, hit-and-miss governing, and a hammer-break igniter were fitted to this model from the factory.

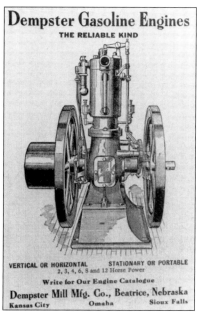

The Dempster Mill Manufacturing Co. in Beatrice, Nebraska sold this style vertical engine in sizes from 2- to 12-horsepower models. Low-tension ignition and a tank cooling system were standard equipment on these gasoline-powered engines. The engine's sub-base mounted to the floor also doubled as the fuel tank.

In Minneapolis, Minnesota, the Diamond Iron Works manufactured several four-cylinder stationary engines for hoists, tractors, dredges, light plants, and pumps. These large engines were designed with cylinder bores from 5 1/2 to 7 1/2 inches and 8- and 9-inch strokes. They could be fueled with kerosene or gasoline.

The Master Power engine was built by the W.E. Dunn Manufacturing Co. located in Holland, Michigan. Heavy oil could be used as fuel for this hopper-cooled engine.

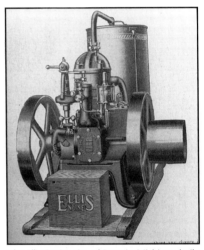

The Ellis Engine Co. of Detroit, Michigan built Ellis two-cycle vertical engines in one- and two-cylinder models. Engine speed could be adjusted from 250 to 1,000 rpm. High-tension spark plug ignition and tank cooling were standard equipment. The engines could be reversed and were designed to run on kerosene, distillate, or gasoline.

Pictured here is a six-horsepower, two-cycle, two-cylinder marine engine manufactured by the Elbridge Motor and Tool Co. of Elbridge, New York. This engine was called the Elbridge Marine and was sold in June of 1907 for $175, ready to install.

A 1915 Model

The Ellis Engine Co. built their Ellis horizontal engines in Detroit, Michigan. This 1915 model was mounted on a fuel tank. The filling plug can be seen at the rear on the engine base.

The Hercules crude oil engine was manufactured in Terre Haute, Indiana by the Engine Co. of Indiana. In the June 1914 issue of Gas Power magazine, the engine is described as able to run on crude oil, fuel oil, or distillate.

Enterprise Machine Co. of Minneapolis, Minnesota manufactured one-, two- and four-cylinder marine engines. The 1907 Westman engines were built in sizes ranging from 3 to 70 horsepower.

Erie Pump and Engine Co. located in Erie, Pennsylvania built the Erie Electric Light 12-horsepower two-cylinder engine. These four-cycle engines were built in sizes from 3 to 80 horsepower and could be purchased equipped to run on natural gas or gasoline.

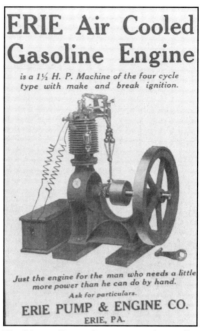

ERIE Air Cooled Gasoline Engine

is a 1½ H. P. Machine of the four cycle type with make and break ignition.

Just the engine for the man who needs a little more power than he can do by hand.

Ask for particulars

ERIE PUMP & ENGINE CO.
ERIE, PA.

The Erie gasoline engine was manufactured by the Erie Pump and Engine Co. in Erie, Pennsylvania. The Erie 1 1/2-horsepower vertical flyball-governed engine used high-tension spark plug ignition, air cooling, and ran on gasoline. This four-cycle engine's hammer-break igniter and valves are actuated by the vertical side shaft which is run off of the crankshaft spiral gear.

The Fairbanks Morse Model Z engine uses high-tension spark plug ignition. The engine's water hopper can be seen steaming as the engine runs on gasoline. Thousands of Z engines were built and are still commonly found yet today.

One of the giants in stationary engine manufacture was the Fairbanks Morse and Co. of Beloit, Wisconsin. Fairbanks Morse and Co. is still manufacturing some of the world's largest and most powerful engines yet today. This early 1892 vertical engine is equipped with hot-tube ignition and is externally tank water-cooled. The engine runs on gasoline. The round hand hole cover on the engines crankcase is a very early design; later models were rectangular or square.

THE FAIRBANKS-CHARTER
Gas and Gasoline Engine.

Unexcelled for any duty for which such Engines are appropriate. Can be used with Natural Gas, Manufactured Gas or Gasoline.

FAIRBANKS, MORSE & CO.,
Sole Manufacturers.

CHICAGO, ST. PAUL, MINNEAPOLIS, ST. LOUIS, DENVER, KANSAS CITY, OMAHA, INDIANAPOLIS, LOUISVILLE, CINCINNATI and CLEVELAND.

This 1896 illustration of a The Fairbanks-Charter engine was built by Fairbanks Morse and Co. in Beloit, Wisconsin. The engine is equipped with hot tube flame ignition and an external cooling tank. The engine was designed to run on either natural gas or gasoline.

Left
Falk engines were manufactured by the Falk Co., in Milwaukee Wisconsin. This volume-governed side-shaft engine uses low-tension ignition and tank cooling and runs on kerosene.

Right
The Faultless Engine Co. located in Kansas City, Missouri built the Faultless engine. This three-horsepower engine used a hammer-break igniter, hit-and-miss governing, and low-tension ignition. Engine cooling was accomplished with a water hopper. These engines were manufactured in sizes from 3 to 15 horsepower and ran on gasoline.

This Eclipse Number One engine was manufactured by the Fairbanks Morse and Co. The 1 1/2-horsepower vertical engine was first produced in 1911 and used high-tension spark plug ignition and hopper cooling. The round fuel tank was supported from the engine's carburetor casting.

The Fairbanks Morse Jack Junior headless one-horsepower engine was designed with low-tension ignition. It is hit-and-miss-governed and equipped with a hammer-break igniter. This engine runs on gasoline and is hopper-cooled.

111

Engine Manufacturer	Factory Location	Trade Name	Dates
Dean-Waterman Co.	Covington, KY	Dean	na
Dean-Waterman Co.	Greenfield, IN	Hancock	na
Deere & Co.	Moline, IL	Big Chief	1918
Deere & Co.	Moline, IL	Deere	1918
Deere & Co.	Moline, IL	Harris	1918
Deere & Co.	Moline, IL	Hustler	1918
Deere & Co.	Moline, IL	Imperial	1918
Deere & Co.	Moline, IL	Jackson	1918
Deere & Co.	Moline, IL	Jacobson	1918
Deere & Co.	Moline, IL	John Deere	1918
Deere & Co.	Moline, IL	Lester	1918
Deere & Co.	Moline, IL	Majestic	1918
Deere & Co.	Moline, IL	Overtime	1918
Deere & Co.	Moline, IL	Parks Ball Bearing	1918
Deere & Co.	Moline, IL	Pennsylvania Boy	1918
Deere & Co.	Moline, IL	Reindeer	1918
Deere & Co.	Moline, IL	Waterloo Boy	1918
Deere Plow Co., John	Kansas City, MO	Dean Elect.-Jobbed Dean	na
Deere Plow Co., John	Kansas City, MO	Eli	na
Deering Harvester Co.	Chicago, IL	na	1897
DeFrees Thermotor Co.	Indianapolis, IN	na	1898
Delamater Iron Works	New York, NY	Ericsson Hot Air	na
Delano, E. A.	Chicago, IL	na	1907
Delaware Mach. Works	Wilington, DE	na	na
Delco Light Co.	Dayton, OH	Delco Light	na
Delco Light Co.	Dayton, OH	Little Joe	na
Delco Light Co.	Dayton, OH	Red Line	na
Delong, G. E.	Elbridge, NY	Elbridge	1907
Delray Mtr. Works	Detroit, MI	Delray-Marine	na
Deltamater Iron Works	Chicago, IL	Ericsson Hot Air	na
Demooy Bros. Co.	Cleveland, OH	Demooy-Marine	1889
Dempsey Cycle Co.	Philadelphia, PA	na	1918
Dempsey Mill Mfg. Co.	Beatrice, NE	na	na
Dempster Mill Mfg. Co.	Beatrice, NE	Dempster	1902
Dempster Mill Mfg. Co.	Beatrice, NE	Dempster Master Stroke	1902
Dempster Mill Mfg. Co.	Beatrice, NE	Master Stroke	1902
Dennison, J. F.	New Haven, CT	Dennison	na
Dennison Elect. Engnrg. Co.	Detroit, MI	na	na
Des Moines City Gas Eng. Works	Des Moines, IA	Des Moines	1899
Des Moines Gas Eng. & Elect. Co.	Des Moines, IA	Standard	na
Des Moines Gas Eng. & Elect. Co.	Des Moines, IA	Demoin	na
Des Moines Gas Eng. & Elect. Co.	Des Moines, IA	Des Moines	1907
Detroit Aeronautic Const. Co.	Detroit, MI	Aermotor	na
Detroit Auto-Marine Co.	Detroit, MI	Detroit	na
Detroit Brass & Novelty Co.	Detroit, MI	na	na
Detroit Eng. Works	Detroit, MI	Amazing Detroit	1896
Detroit Eng. Works	Detroit, MI	Detroit	1896
Detroit Eng. Works	Detroit, MI	Sandow	1896
Detroit Gas Corp.	Detroit, MI	Hicks	1897
Detroit Gas Eng. & Mach. Co.	Detroit, MI	Major	na
Detroit Mtr. Car Supply Co.	Detroit, MI	Detroit	1913
Detroit Mtr. Car Supply Co.	Detroit, MI	Sandow	1913
Detroit Mtr. Car Supply Co.	Detroit, MI	Sandow-Kero	1913
Detroit Mtr. Parts Co.	Detroit, MI	Detroit	1907
Detroit Mtr. Works	Detroit, MI	na	1900–1902
Detroit River Gas Eng. Co.	Detroit, MI	Detroit	1907
Device Improvement Co.	Hanover, PA	Device	na
Device Improvement Co.	Hanover, PA	Hilite	1910
Deyo-Macey Eng. Co.	Binghamton, NY	Davis	1901–1916
Deyo-Macey Eng. Co.	Binghamton, NY	Deyo	1902
Deyo-Macey Eng. Co.	Binghamton, NY	Deyo-Macey	na
Diamond Eng. Co.	Des Moines, IA	Diamond	1909
Diamond Eng. Co.	Des Moines, IA	Diamond Jr.	1909
Diamond Eng. Co.	Des Moines, IA	Junior	1909

Engine Manufacturer	Factory Location	Trade Name	Dates
Diamond Iron Works	Milwaukee, WI	Diamond	1885
Diamond Iron Works	Milwaukee, WI	Sorg Oil Eng.	na
Dice Eng. Co.	Anderson, IN	Dice	1910
Dickson Mfg. Co.	Scraton, PA	Dickson	1885
Dickson Mfg. Co.	Scraton, PA	Stockport	1885
Diesel Mtr. Co.	New York, NY	na	1895
Dieter Fdry.	Cherryville, PA	Dieter	na
Diets & Co.	Marinette, WI	Silberzahn	na
Dimmer Mach. Works	Detroit, MI	na	na
Dingfelder Mtr. Co.	Detroit, MI	na	1902
Dirigo Eng. & Mach. Works	Portland, ME	Dirigo	1902
Dissinger & Bros. Co.	Wrightsville, PA	Capital	1890–1914
Dissinger & Bros. Co.	Wrightsville, PA	Dissinger	1904
Do It All Tractor Corp.	Broadway, NY	Do It All	na
Doack Eng. Co.	San Francisco, CA	Doack	1900–1907
Doak Gas Eng. Co.	Oakland, CA	Doak	1907
Dock Gas Eng. Co.	New York, NY	na	na
Dodd Mtr. Co.	Des Moines, IA	Dodd	1907
Dodge Inc., H. C.	Boston, MA	Dodge Light Plant	na
Dodge Tool Co.	Grinnell, IA	na	1919
Doman, H. C.	Oshkosh, WI	Doman-Marine	1902
Domestic Eng. & Pump Co.	Shippenburg, PA	Atlantic	1902
Domestic Eng. & Pump Co.	Shippenburg, PA	Bond	na
Domestic Eng. & Pump Co.	Shippenburg, PA	Domestic	1903
Domestic Eng. & Pump Co.	Shippenburg, PA	Domestic Jr.	na
Domestic Eng. & Pump Co.	Shippenburg, PA	Fisherman	na
Domestic Eng. & Pump Co.	Shippenburg, PA	Leader	na
Domestic Eng. & Pump Co.	Shippenburg, PA	Leader Domestic	na
Domestic Eng. & Pump Co.	Shippenburg, PA	Reeco	na
Domestic Eng. & Pump Co.	Shippenburg, PA	Regular	na
Domestic Eng. & Pump Co.	Shippenburg, PA	Rider-Erricsson	na
Domestic Eng. & Pump Co.	Shippenburg, PA	Schramm	na
Domestic Eng. & Pump Co.	Shippenburg, PA	Shippenburg	na
Domestic Eng. Co.	Hagerstown, MD	Domestic	1903
Domestic Engnrg. Co.	Dayton, OH	Delco Light Plant	na
Donegan & Swift Co.	New York, NY	na	na
Dow Pump & Eng. Works	Alameda, CA	na	1919
Downes Co., P. J.	Minneapolis, MN	Downes Special-Jobbed	na
Downie Pump Co.	Downieville, PA	Downie	na
Downing Eng. Works	Des Plaines, IL	Bill	na
Downing Eng. Works	Des Plaines, IL	Downing	na
Downing Eng. Works	Des Moines, IA	Downing	1907
Downing Eng. Works	Des Plaines, IL	Little Marvel	na
Doyle Mfg. Co.	Syracuse, NY	Doyle	na
Drahanousky Mtr. Co.	Chicago, IL	na	na
Drewline Co.	Elmira, NY	Drew	na
Drewline Co.	Fort Atkinson, WI	Drew	na
Drury Engnrg. Co.	Evansville, IN	Duralite	1920
Du Brie Mtr. Co.	Detroit, MI	Du Brie-Marine	1911
Dubois Iron Works	Dubois, PA	Dubois	1890
Dubuque Gasoline Eng. Co.	Dubuque, IA	Dubuque	1911
Ducro Mfg. Co.	Buffalo, NY	Niagara	1906
Duesenberg Mtrs., Inc.	Indianapolis, IN	na	
Duncan, Q. M.	Green Bay, WI	Olsen	1906
Dunham Mtr. Co., H. E.	Seattle, WA	na	1920
Dunn Mfg. Co., W. E.	Holland, MI	Dunn	1915
Dunn Mtr. Works	Ogdensburg, NY	Dunn (Marine)	1900
Dunton-Chenery Co.	Portland, ME	na	na
Duplex Elect.-Gas Mtr. Co.	Edwardsville, IL	na	1889
Duplex Mfg. Co.	Superior, WI	Duplex-Jobbed	1909
Duplex Truck Co.	Lansing, MI	na	na
Duro Pump & Mfg. Co.	Dayton, OH	Duro-Jobbed	na
Dyersville Gasoline Eng. Mfg. Co.	Dyersville, IA	Lucky Star	1909
Dykes, A. L.	St. Louis, MO	Dykes	na

Engine Manufacturer	Factory Location	Trade Name	Dates
Dyneto Elect. Co.	Syracuse, NY	Dyneto Light Plant	na
E. Davenport Mach. & Nov. Works	Davenport, IA	Kuhner	1899
Eagle Bicycle Co.	Torrington, CT	Eagle	1907
Eagle Co.	Newark, NJ	Eagle	1900
Eagle Eng. Co.	San Francisco, CA	Eagle	1903
Eagle Mfg. Co.	Appleton, WI	Eagle	1904
Eagle Sawing Mach. Co.	Kansas City, MO	Eagle	na
Earl Mach. Works	Burlington, NJ	Earl	1907
Eason Eng. Co.	New York, NY	Eason	1908
Eaton Gas Eng. C.	Eaton, OH	Eaton	na
Eau Claire Mfg. Co.	Eau Claire, WI	Eau Claire	na
Eau Claire Mfg. Co.	Eau Claire, WI	Keller	1914
Eckhard Mtr. Co.	Brighton, NY	Eckhard	1899
Eclipse Mtr. Co.	Mancelona, MI	Eclipse	1907
Economic Eng. Co.	Utica, NY	Economic	1904
Economic Mtr. Co.	New York, NY	Economic	1885
Economist Gas Eng. Co.	San Francisco, CA	Economist	1901
Economizer Eng. Works	Marcellus, MI	Chapman	1903
Economizer Eng. Works	Marcellus, MI	Economizer	1903
Edison Storage Battery Co.	Orange, NJ	Edison	na
Edson Mfg. Co.	Boston, MA	Edson	na
Edwards, Ellis & Cornell Co.	Rochester, MN	na	1908
Edwards Mtr. Co.	Springfield, OH	Edwards	1920
Edwards Mtr. Co.	Sandusky, OH	Edwards	na
Elbridge Eng. Co.	Rochester, NY	Elbridge-Marine	1909
Elbridge Mtr. & Tool Co.	Elbridge, NY	Elbridge-Marine	1907
Elbridge Mtr. & Tool Co.	Rochester, NY	Elbridge	1907
Elbridge Mtr. & Tool Co.	Rochester, NY	Gem	1907
Elect. Auto-Lite Corp.	Toledo, OH	Willys Jr. Light Plant	1920
Elect. Boat Co.	Bayonne, NJ	na	1907
Elect. Light & Power Co.	Denver, CO	American Automatic	na
Elect. Mfg. & Gas Eng. Co.	New York, NY	Redemotor	1914
Elect. Mfg. & Gas Eng. Co.	New York, NY	Rollason-Jobbed Out	na
Elect. Mfg. & Gas Eng. Co.	Greenbrush, NY	Safety Vapor	na
Elect. Vapor Eng. Co.	San Francisco, CA	na	1890
Elect. Wheel Co.	Quincy, IL	E.W.C.	na
Electro-Carbon Mtr. Co.	Chicago, IL	na	1890
Elgin Gas Eng. Co.	Elgin, IL	Comet	na
Elgin Gas Eng. Co.	Elgin, IL	Elgin Comet	na
Elgin Gas Eng. Co.	Elgin, IL	Little King	na
Elgin Gas Eng. Co.	Elgin, IL	Little Pet	na
Elgin Gas Mtr. Works	Elgin, IL	Haf A Hors	1920
Elgin Gas Mtr. Works	Elgin, IL	Little Pet	1919
Elgin Wheel & Eng. Co.	Elgin, IL	Baby	1911
Elgin Wheel & Eng. Co.	Elgin, IL	Elgin	1911
Elgin Wheel & Eng. Co.	Elgin, IL	Elgin Comet	1911
Elgin Wheel & Eng. Co.	Elgin, IL	Elgin Wheel	1911
Elgin Wheel & Eng. Co.	Elgin, IL	Haf A Hors	1911
Elgin Wheel & Eng. Co.	Elgin, IL	Little Hummer	1911
Elgin Wheel & Eng. Co.	Elgin, IL	Little King	1911
Elgin Wheel & Eng. Co.	Elgin, IL	Little Pet	1911
Elgin Wheel & Eng. Co.	Elgin, IL	Red E Mtr.	1911
Ellington Mfg. Co.	Quincy, IL	Cornell	1904
Ellington Mfg. Co.	Quincy, IL	Ellington	1904
Ellis Eng. Co.	Detroit, MI	Ellis	1910
Ellsworth Fdry. & Mach. Works	Ellsworth, ME	Ellsworth	na
Ellsworth Iron Works	Ellsworth, WI	Ellsworth	na
Ellwood City Gas Eng. Co.	Ellwood City, PA	Ellwood	1899–1901
Elto Outboard Mtr. Co.	Milwaukee, WI	na	1921
Elwood Iron Works	Elwood, IN	na	1913
Elyria Gas Power Co.	Elyria, OH	Elyria	1907
Elyria Gas Power Co.	Elyria, OH	Elyria-Tandem	na
Elyria Gas Power Co.	Elyria, OH	Little Big Eng.	na
Elyria Gas Power Co.	Elyria, OH	Producers Gas Eng.	na

Fernyak Machinery Co. located in Mansfield, Ohio, built the Little Gem vertical engine. This four-horsepower engine was equipped with high-tension spark plug ignition. The open crankcase design is visible, and an external tank was used for cooling. The four-cycle engine could burn either natural gas or gasoline. Four dry-cell batteries and a buzz coil were supplied direct from the factory with every engine.

The Field-Brundage Company's Type W engine is pictured here. These engines were made in sizes from 1 1/2 to 15-horsepower. A hammer-break igniter was used with the low-tension battery and coil ignition system. The engine's fuel tank is housed inside the skid. The battery box can be seen mounted behind the engine. This hopper-cooled engine was designed to run on kerosene or gasoline.

Right
The Bradford Improved Flickinger Iron Works engine was manufactured in Bradford, Pennsylvania. The engines were built in 10- to 200-horsepower models that were designed with cross heads. These engines were designed to run on natural gas.

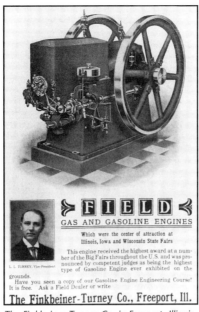

The Finkbeiner-Turney Co. in Freeport, Illinois manufactured this Field four-horsepower side-shaft engine. The headless engine uses a hammer-break igniter with low-tension ignition. The vertical flyball governor regulates the engine's speed. This hopper-cooled engine could be run on natural gas or gasoline.

The 1910 Field Junior vertical engine line was manufactured by the Field-Brundage Co. This three-horsepower engine used high-tension spark plug ignition and came equipped with a battery and buzz coil. It is hit-and-miss governed and fitted with hopper cooling. These engines run on gasoline.

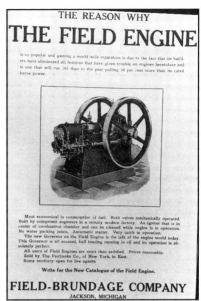

The Field 30-horsepower engine was manufactured by the Field-Brundage Co. in Jackson, Michigan. This side-shaft engine uses low-tension ignition with a hammer-break igniter. Its governor was totally encased, and external tank cooling was standard. The company guaranteed the engine would pull at least 10 percent more than its rated horsepower.

This is a picture of a restored Flickinger engine. This engine is equipped with an oscillating magneto which is cycled off of a pinion gear. The engine is on display at the Coolspring Power Museum located in Coolspring, Pennsylvania.

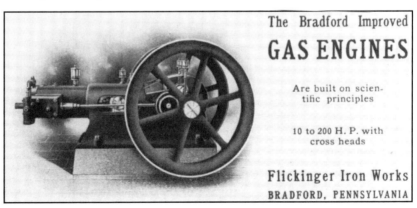

Engine Manufacturer	Factory Location	Trade Name	Dates
Emeny Co., G. J.	Fulton, NY	New Parker	na
Emerson Eng. Co.	Alexandria, VA	na	1909
Emerson-Brantingham Co.	Rockford, IL	Arnet	1912
Emerson-Brantingham Co.	Rockford, IL	E-B	1912
Emerson-Brantingham Co.	Rockford, IL	Emerson-Brantingham	1907
Emerson-Brantingham Co.	Rockford, IL	Rockford	1912
Emerson-Brantingham Co.	Rockford, IL	Rockford	1912
Empire Cream Separator Co.	Bloomfield, NJ	Empire-Jobbed	1907
Empire Eng. & Mtr. Co.	Orangeburgh, NY	Empire	1901
Empire Mach. Works	Pittsburgh, PA	Empire	na
Empire Novelty Co.	Waterloo, IA	Empire	na
Empire Spec. Milking Mach. Co.	Rochester, NY	Empire Special-Jobbed	na
Engberg Elect. & Mech. Works	St. Joseph, MO	Engberg	1908
Eng. Co. Of Indiana	Terre Haute, IN	Hercules	1914
Ensco Diesel Eng. Co.	Seattle, WA	na	na
Enterprise Co.	Columbiana, OH	Enterprise	1914
Enterprise Eng. Co.	San Francisco, CA	Enterprise	na
Enterprise Eng. Works	Independence, IA	Associated	na
Enterprise Mach. Co.	Minneapolis, MN	Busy Bee	1901
Enterprise Mach. Co.	Minneapolis, MN	Enterprise	1901
Enterprise Mach. Co.	Minneapolis, MN	Westman	1901
Enterprise Mach. Co.	Minneapolis, MN	Westman Busy Boy	1901
Enterprise Mach. Co.	Minneapolis, MN	Westman Heavy Duty	na
Enterprise Mach. Works	Richmond, VA	Enterprise	1899
Equipment Co.	Kansas City, MO	Equipment Co.	na
Erd Mtr. Co.	Saginaw, MI	Erd	na
Ericsson & Moon Mfg. Co.	Detroit, MI	Ericsson	1906
Erie City Iron Works	Erie, PA	Erie	na
Erie Gas Eng. Co.	Erie, PA	Climax	1896
Erie Pump & Eng. Co.	Erie, PA	Elect. Lighting	na
Erie Pump & Eng. Co.	Erie, PA	Erie-Air Cooled	na
Erie Pump & Eng. Co.	Erie, PA	Erie-Marine	1902
Eska Mo Co.	Dubuque, IA	Eska Mo	na
Essandee Corp.	Chicago, IL	Essandee Light Plant	na
Essex Eng. Co.	Lynn, MA	Essex-Marine	1903
Eureka Mfg. Co.	Chariton, IA	Eureka	1906
Evans Eng. Co.	Westport, CT	na	1917
Evans Mfg. Co.	Butler, PA	Evans	1891
Evansville Mfg. Co.	Evansville, IN	Evansville	1929
Evansville Mfg. Co.	Evansville, IN	Hustler	1929
Evansville Mfg. Co.	Evansville, WI	Evansville	1911
Evarts Mach. Co.	Hartford, CT	Evarts	na
Everlite Co.	Minneapolis, MN	Everlite	na
Evinrude Mtr. Co.	Milwaukee, WI	Evinrude	1917
Ewald Die & Mach. Co.	Chicago, IL	na	na
Excelsior Motorcycle Co.	Chicago, IL	Excelsior	na
Explosive Vapor Mtr. Co.	East Orange, NJ	na	1899
Fairbanks Co.	New York, NY	Bull Dog	na
Fairbanks Co.	Pittsburgh, PA	Bull Dog	na
Fairbanks Co.	New York, NY	Bull Pup	na
Fairbanks Co.	New York, NY	Callahan	na
Fairbanks Co.	New York, NY	Fairbanks	na
Fairbanks Co.	New York, NY	Super Diesel	na
Fairbanks Co.	Pittsburgh, PA	Super Diesel	na
Fairbanks Gasoline Eng. & Mtr. Co.	Chicago, IL	Fairbanks	1905
Fairbanks-Grant Mfg. Co.	Ithaca, NY	Fairbanks-Grant-Marine	1905
Fairbanks-Morse & Co.	Beloit, WI	Double Duty Light Plant	na
Fairbanks-Morse & Co.	Beloit, WI	Eclipse	na
Fairbanks-Morse & Co.	Beloit, WI	Empire	na
Fairbanks-Morse & Co.	Beloit, WI	Empire Special	na
Fairbanks-Morse & Co.	Beloit, WI	Fairbanks Morse	1893
Fairbanks-Morse & Co.	Beloit, WI	Fairmor	na
Fairbanks-Morse & Co.	Chicago, IL	Frost King	na
Fairbanks-Morse & Co.	Beloit, WI	Home Lite	na

Engine Manufacturer	Factory Location	Trade Name	Dates
Fairbanks-Morse & Co.	Beloit, WI	Jack Jr.	1911
Fairbanks-Morse & Co.	Beloit, WI	Jack Of All Trades	1904
Fairbanks-Morse & Co.	Beloit, WI	Monitor	na
Fairbanks-Morse & Co.	Beloit, WI	Mor-Lite	na
Fairbanks-Morse & Co.	Beloit, WI	Quick Start	na
Fairbanks-Morse & Co.	Beloit, WI	Ransome Special	na
Fairchilds & Betts Co.	Warren, PA	na	na
Fairfield Eng. Co.	Fairfield, IA	Fairfield	1907
Fairfield Mtr. Co.	Bridgeport, CT	Fairfield	1901–1920
Fairmont Engnrg. Co.	Philadelphia, PA	Chadwick	na
Fairmont Gas & Railway Mtr. Car Co.	Fairmont, MN	Fairmont	na
Fairmont Railway Mtrs. Inc.	Fairmont, MN	Chadwick	1909
Fairmont Railway Mtrs. Inc.	Fairmont, MN	Fairmont	1909
Fairmont Railway Mtrs. Inc.	Fairmont, MN	Hy Load	1909
Fairmount Eng. Works	Philadelphia, PA	Fairmount	1907
Falk Co.	Milwaukee, WI	Falk	1910
Falk Co.	Milwaukee, WI	Falkon	1910
Falk Co.	Milwaukee, WI	Oil Turn	1910
Famous Mfg. Co.	Chicago, IL	Champion	1909
Fargo Co., F. B.	St. Paul, MN	Favorite	na
Fargo Co., F. B.	St. Paul, MN	Lewis	na
Farguhar Co., A. R.	York, PA	Farguhar	na
Faribault Mfg. Co.	Faribault, MN	Faribault	na-1904
Farm Elect. Utilities Corp.	Baltimore, MD	Farmelectric	1922
Farmers Gasoline Eng. Co.	Milwaukee, WI	na	1912
Farmers Mfg. Co.	Detroit, MI	Farmers	na
Farquhar Co., A. B.	York, PA	Farquhar	1915
Farrar & Trefts	Buffalo, NY	Bogart	1902–1907
Farrar & Trefts	Buffalo, NY	Farrar & Trefts	1907
Faultless Eng. Co.	Kansas City, MO	Ever Ready	na
Faultless Eng. Co.	Kansas City, MO	Faultless	na
Faultless Eng. Co.	Kansas City, MO	Monarch	na
Faultless Gasoline Eng. Co.	Waterloo, IA	Faultless-Jobbed	na
Fay & Bowen Eng. Co.	Geneva, NY	Fay & Bowen Eng.	1903
Federal Gas Eng. Co.	Los Angeles, CA	Federal	1908
Fenwyck Galloway Mfg. Co.	Newark, NJ	Ajax	na
Ferman Mtr. Works	Grand Rapids, MI	Ferman	1909
Fernyak Mach. Co.	Mansfield, OH	Little Gem	na
Fernyake & Stavenik Mach. Co.	Mansfield, OH	Fernyake & Stavenik	na
Ferro Mach. & Fdry. Co.	Cleveland, OH	Ferro-Marine	1908
Ferro Mach. & Fdry. Co.	Cleveland, OH	Ferro-Farm	na
Fey Co., L. H.	Northfield, MN	Lincoln-Marine	na
Fidelity Mach. Works	Santo Paulo, CA	na	na
Field Brundage Co.	Jackson, MI	Field Brundage	1905
Field Force Pump Co.	Elmira, NY	Elmira	1909
Field Force Pump Co.	Elmira, NY	Leader	1909
Field Force Pump Co.	Elmira, NY	Ospraymo	1909
Field Force Pump Co.	Elmira, NY	Tayoco	na
Field Mach. Co.	Grand Rapids, MI	Field	1916
Field Mtr. Co.	Grand Rapids, MI	Field	na
Field-Brundage Co.	Jackson, MI	Atlanta	1926
Field-Brundage Co.	Jackson, MI	Atlantic	na
Field-Brundage Co.	Jackson, MI	Champion	na
Field-Brundage Co.	Jackson, MI	Downes	na
Field-Brundage Co.	Jackson, MI	Downes Special	na
Field-Brundage Co.	Jackson, MI	Fairbanks	na
Field-Brundage Co.	Jackson, MI	Field	na
Field-Brundage Co.	Jackson, MI	Field Jr.	1910
Field-Brundage Co.	Jackson, MI	Field Special	na
Field-Brundage Co.	Jackson, MI	Hisco	1926
Field-Brundage Co.	Jackson, MI	Hummer	na
Field-Brundage Co.	Jackson, MI	Macleod	1925
Field-Brundage Co.	Jackson, MI	Miller	na
Field-Brundage Co.	Jackson, MI	Racine-Sattley	na

Flinchbaugh Manufacturing Co. in York, Pennsylvania manufactured the York line of engines. The 1 1/2-horsepower Our Pet engine is shown powering an early tractor.

This Foos natural gas engine was built by the Foos Gas Engine Co. in Springfield, Ohio. The engines could be made in sizes from 2 to 30 horsepower. This engine was equipped with low-tension wipe spark ignition, a magneto, and an external tank for cooling.

Wayne natural gas and gasoline engines were manufactured by the Fort Wayne Foundry and Machine Co. in Fort Wayne, Indiana. These engines were built in sizes from 10 to 18 horsepower. Low-tension ignition and hammer-break igniters are standard equipment. These engines are flyball-governed and require an external tank for cooling.

The Flint and Walling Manufacturing Co. of Kendallville, Indiana, built the Hoosier vertical engine line. A water pump and screen cooling tank came as standard equipment. The engine was designed to use gasoline.

This eight-horsepower portable Foos engine is equipped with a magneto and low-tension wipe spark ignition. The engines crankshaft is counter-balanced and a water hopper provides engine cooling. The gasoline fuel tank is seen mounted to the water hopper between the flywheels.

The Friend Manufacturing Co. was located in Gasport, New York. Friend spraying engines were built in several models: the 2 1/2 horsepower CX, the three-horsepower EX, the four-horsepower BX and the five-horsepower DX. A high-tension Wico magneto and spark plug ignition is used on these hopper-cooled gasoline engine.

This is a picture of a restored York engine. The engine is equipped with a hammer-break igniter for low-tension ignition. A battery box can be seen at the rear of the engine, attached to the engine's cart. A water hopper coolant level can be monitored externally with the site tube that is attached to the front of the hopper. The fuel tank is housed in the engine's base.

The Foos Jr. four-horsepower engine used low-tension wipe spark ignition. This engine does not have crankshaft balancing weights, found on each side of the connecting rod journal, that the early hopper-cooled engines did. Hopper cooling and a battery box can be seen mounted to the engine's cart behind the engine.

This Double Efficiency natural gas engine was manufactured by the Fuller and Johnson Manufacturing Co. located in Madison, Wisconsin. They were first built in sizes ranging from three to nine horsepower. These were very heavy engines compared to others of the same horsepower.

The Frontier Iron Works was incorporated in Detroit, Michigan. Vertical engines were built in sizes from 1 to 10 horsepower. The Frontier natural gas or gasoline horizontal engine shown here was manufactured in sizes ranging from 10 to 100 horsepower. The horizontal engines were tandem-designed engines.

Engine Manufacturer	Factory Location	Trade Name	Dates
Field-Brundage Co.	Jackson, MI	Rayner-Fields	na
Field-Brundage Co.	Jackson, MI	Sattley	1916
Field-Brundage Co.	Jackson, MI	Sheffield	na
Field-Brundage Co.	Jackson, MI	Special	na
Field-Brundage Co.	Jackson, MI	Wolverine	na
Fifield Bros. Builders	Fairfield, IA	Fifield	na
Fifield Bros. Builders	Augusta, ME	Fifield	na
Findlay Mtr. Co.	Findlay, OH	na	1912
Finkbeiner-Turney Co.	Freeport, IL	Bull Dog	na
Finkbeiner-Turney Co.	Freeport, IL	Field	na
Fischbach Mfg. Co.	Peoria, IL	na	na
Fischer Mtr. Corp.	New York, NY	Fischer	1915
Flack & Shaffer Co.	Latrobe, PA	Fasco Light Plant	na
Flexible Eng./Threshing Mach. Co.	Rock County, WI	na	1890
Flickinger Iron Works	Bradford, PA	Bradford	na
Flickinger Iron Works	Bradford, PA	Flickinger	1912
Flinchbaugh Mfg. Co.	York, PA	Flinchbaugh	1898
Flinchbaugh Mfg. Co.	York, PA	Our Pet	1898
Flinchbaugh Mfg. Co.	York, PA	York	1898
Flint & Walling Mfg. Co.	Kendallville, IN	F & W	na
Flint & Walling Mfg. Co.	Kendallville, IN	Flint & Walling	1910
Flint & Walling Mfg. Co.	Kendallville, IN	Hoosier	na
Foos Gas Eng. Co.	Springfield, OH	Bauroth	na
Foos Gas Eng. Co.	Springfield, OH	Foos	1887
Foos Gas Eng. Co.	Springfield, OH	Foos Jr.	1887
Foos Gas Eng. Co.	Springfield, OH	Junior	1894
Foos Gas Eng. Co.	Springfield, OH	Scientific	1894
Fopay & Co.	Dieterich, IL	na	na
Force & Briggs	Pittsburgh, PA	Kowalsky	1907
Fort Dearborn Mfg. Co.	Sterling, IL	Ft. Dearborn Light Plant	1919
Fort Madison Gas Eng. Co.	Fort Madison, IA	Criner	1910
Fort Madison Gas Eng. Co.	Fort Madison, IA	Fort Madison	1910
Fort Scott Mfg. Co.	Fort Scott, KS	Fort Scott	1906
Fort Wayne Engnrg. & Mfg. Co.	Fort Wayne, IA	Paul	na
Fort Wayne Fdry. & Mach. Co.	Fort Wayne, IN	Fort Wayne	1906
Fort Wayne Fdry. & Mach. Co.	Fort Wayne, IN	Wayne	1904
Foss Gasoline Eng. Co.	Kalamazoo, MI	Foss	1906
Foster & Hosier	Chicago, IL	Granite	na
Foster Mtr. Co.	New Haven, CT	na	na
Fostoria Fdry. & Mach. Co.	Fostoria, OH	na	na
Fox & Sons, J. W.	La Porte City, IA	Fox	1898
Fox Reversible Gasoline Eng. Co.	Covington, KY	Fox-Marine	na
Franklin Model Shop	New York, NY	Franklin	1900
Franklin Supply Co.	Franklin, PA	Franklin	na
Franklin Valveless Eng. Co.	Franklin, PA	Franklin Valveless	1907
Free-Piston Gas Eng. Co.	Detroit, MI	na	1905
Freeport Wind Mill & Gas Eng. Co.	Freeport, IL	Freeport	1909
Fremont Fdry. & Mach. Co.	Fremont, NE	na	na
Frey-Scheckler Co.	Bucyrus, OH	na	1899
Frick Co.	Waynesboro, PA	Frick	na
Friend Mfg. Co.	Gasport, NY	Friend	na
Friend Pump Co.	Gasport, NY	Pony Friend	na
Frisbee-Heft Mtr. Co.	Middletown, CT	Frisbee	na
Froehlich, John	Froehlich, IA	na	na
Frontier Gasoline Mtr. Co.	Buffalo, NY	Frontier	na
Frontier Iron Works	Detroit, MI	Frontier	na
Frost Eng. Co.	Evansville, WI	Frost	1912
Frost Eng. Co.	Evansville, WI	Hustler	na
Fruehling Iron Works	Los Angeles, CA	Zenith	1895
Fuel Gas & Mfg. Co.	Pittsburgh, PA	Pittsburgh	na
Fuel Oil Eng. Co.	Providence, RI	na	1911
Fuel Oil Power Co.	New York, NY	na	1903
Fuller & Johnson Mfg. Co.	Madison, WI	Big 4 Pumper	na
Fuller & Johnson Mfg. Co.	Madison, WI	Coldwell	na

Engine Manufacturer	Factory Location	Trade Name	Dates
Fuller & Johnson Mfg. Co.	Madison, WI	Double Efficiency	na
Fuller & Johnson Mfg. Co.	Madison, WI	Edmonds	na
Fuller & Johnson Mfg. Co.	Madison, WI	Famous	na
Fuller & Johnson Mfg. Co.	Madison, WI	Farm Pump	1909
Fuller & Johnson Mfg. Co.	Madison, WI	Fuller & Johnson	1901–1952
Fuller & Johnson Mfg. Co.	Madison, WI	Manitoba	na
Fuller & Johnson Mfg. Co.	Madison, WI	Multimotor	na
Fuller & Johnson Mfg. Co.	Madison, WI	Peoples Price	na
Fuller & Johnson Mfg. Co.	Madison, WI	Popular Price	na
Fulton Iron Works	St. Louis, MO	Fulton	1915
Fulton Mfg. Co.	Erie, PA	Fulton	na
Funk & Hoctritt	Medford, WI	Cyclone	1903
Funk & Hoctritt	Medford, WI	Medford	1903
Furgason Mtr. Co.	Lansing, MI	Furgason	na
Gade Bros. Mfg. Co.	Iowa Falls, IA	Dual Cooled	1904
Gade Bros. Mfg. Co.	Iowa Falls, IA	Gade	1904
Gade Bros. Mfg. Co.	Iowa Falls, IA	Hawkeye	1904
Gallie Eng. Co.	Detroit, MI	Gallie	na
Galloway Co., Wm. A.	Waterloo, IA	Boss	na
Galloway Co., Wm. A.	Waterloo, IA	Boss Of The Farm	1910
Galloway Co., Wm. A.	Waterloo, IA	Bull Dog	na
Galloway Co., Wm. A.	Waterloo, IA	Bull Pup	na
Galloway Co., Wm. A.	Waterloo, IA	Captain	na
Galloway Co., Wm. A.	Waterloo, IA	Davis	na
Galloway Co., Wm. A.	Waterloo, IA	Drednaut	na
Galloway Co., Wm. A.	Waterloo, IA	Galloway	na
Galloway Co., Wm. A.	Waterloo, IA	Gold Band	na
Galloway Co., Wm. A.	Waterloo, IA	Handy Andy	na
Galloway Co., Wm. A.	Waterloo, IA	Masterpiece 6	na
Galloway Co., Wm. A.	Waterloo, IA	Success	1906–1910
Galloway Co., Wm. A.	Waterloo, IA	Sylvestor	na
Galloway Co., Wm. A.	Waterloo, IA	Wonder	na
Gardner Conv. Steam & Gas Eng. Co.	Washington, PA	Gardner	1907
Gardner Elevator Co.	Detroit, MI	Gade	na
Gardner Elevator Co.	Detroit, MI	Gardner	na
Gardner Mtr. Co.	St. Louis, MO	Gardner	na
Garfield, Richardson & Co.	Algona, IA	na	na
Garratt & Co.	San Francisco, CA	Garratt	na
Garretson Eng. Co.	Buffalo, NY	na	1900
Garrett Mach. Works	Garrett, IN	Garrett	1903
Gas & Gasoline Eng. & Mtr. Co.	Chicago, IL	na	1890
Gas Corliss Co.	Minneapolis, MN	na	na
Gas Eng. & Machry. Co.	Cincinnati, OH	O.K.	na
Gas Eng. & Power Co.	New York, NY	Seabury	na
Gas Eng. & Supply Co.	Newport, KY	Diamond	na
Gas Eng. Pneumatic Co.	Plainfield, NJ	na	
Gas Machry. Co.	Cleveland, OH	na	1908
Gas Producers & Engnrg. Corp.	NJ	Leissner	na
Gas Producers & Engnrg. Corp.	NJ	Gas Producer	1923
Gasoline Eng. Works	Lansing, MI	na	1894
Gasport Mtr. Co.	Gasport, NY	Gasport	1910
Gates Mfg. Co., E. L.	Chicago, IL	Columbia	na
Gates Mfg. Co., E. L.	Chicago, IL	Gates	na
Gates Mfg. Co., E. L.	Chicago, IL	Gates Columbia	1904
Gates Vapor Eng. Co.	Kalamazoo, MI	Spaulding	na
Gault & Co.	Chicago, IL	Gault	na
Gearless Gas Eng. Co.	Springfield, OH	Gearless	1910–1911
Gebhardt Mtr. Co.	Philadelphia, PA	Gebhardt	1911
Geiser Mfg. Co.	Havana, IL	Baby	na
Geiser Mfg. Co.	Waynesboro, PA	Geiser	1908
Geiser Mfg. Co.	Waynesboro, PA	Geiser Baby	na
Geiser Mfg. Co.	Waynesboro, PA	Metcalf	na
Geiser Mfg. Co.	Waynesboro, PA	Peerless	na
Gem City Mfg. Co.	Dayton, OH	Champion	na

Engine Manufacturer	Factory Location	Trade Name	Dates
Gem City Mfg. Co.	Dayton, OH	Gem	1903–1905
Gemmer Eng. & Mfg. Co.	St. Marion, IN	Gemmer	1900
Gemmer Eng. & Mfg. Co.	St. Marion, IN	All Day Digger	1906
General Elect. Co.	Schenectady, NY	na	1905
General Eng. Co.	Franklin Park, IL	GE	na
General Eng. Co.	Franklin Park, IL	General	na
General Gas & Elect. Co.	Hanover, PA	Genco Light	na
General Mfg. Co.	Elkhart, IN	General	na
General Mfg. Co.	Elkhart, IN	New Polo	na
General Merchandising Co.	Omaha, NE	Windsor	na
General Mtrs. Corp.	Detroit, MI	na	na
General Power Co.	New York, NY	General	1907
General Power Co.	New York, NY	Secor	na
Gere Yacht & Launch Works	Grand Rapids, MI	na	na
Gerling Mfg. Co.	Pierre, SD	na	na
Gernandt Mtr. Corp.	Chicago, IL	na	1917
Ghormley Gas & Gasoline Eng. Co.	Kansas City, MO	Ghromley	na
Gibbs Gas Eng. Co.	Atlanta, GA	Gibbs	1910
Gibson, A. T.	West Winfield, NY	Gibson	na
Gibson Mfg. Co.	Washington, WI	Gibson	na
Giddings, C. M.	Rockford, IL	na	1901
Gifford Eng. Co.	Lansing, MI	Gifford	1912–1918
Gilbert & Barker Mfg.	Springfield, MA	Gilbert & Barker	na
Gile Boat & Eng. Co.	Ludington, MI	Gile	na
Gile Marine Eng. Co.	Boston, MA	Gile-Marine	1917
Gillespie & Co., L. W.	Marion, IN	Gillespie	na
Gilmore Mtr. Co.	Detroit, MI	Farmers Friend	1915
Gilmore Mtr. Co.	Detroit, MI	Gilmore	1915
Gilson Mfg. Co.	Port Washington, WI	Gilson Air Cooled	1905–1914
Gilson Mfg. Co.	Port Washington, WI	Gilson	1905–1914
Gilson Mfg. Co.	Port Washington, WI	New Gilson	1905–1914
Gilson Mfg. Co.	Port Washington, WI	Goes Like 60	1905
Gilson Mfg. Co.	Port Washington, WI	Johnny On The Spot	1926
Gisholt Mach. Co.	Madison, WI	na	na
Gladden Products Corp.	Glendale, CA	Busy Bee	na
Gladden Products Corp.	Glendale, CA	Gladden	na
Gleason, Bailey, & Sciple Mfg. Co.	Seneca Falls, NY	Sciple	na
Globe Elect. Co.	Milwaukee, WI	Globe Light Plant	na
Globe Fdry. & Mach. Co.	Sheboygan, WI	Climax	na
Globe Fdry. & Mach. Co.	Sheboygan, WI	Globe	1913
Globe Gas Eng. Co.	Philadelphia, PA	Globe	1895
Globe Gas Eng. Co.	Philadelphia, PA	Pacific	1895
Globe Gas Eng. Co.	Philadelphia, PA	Regan	1895
Globe Gas Eng. Co.	Philadelphia, PA	Union	1895
Globe Iron Works	Sacramento, CA	na	1915
Globe Iron Works Co.	Stockton, CA	Globe	1907
Globe Iron Works Co.	Menomonie, WI	Globe	na
Globe Iron Works Co.	Minneapolis, MN	Globe	na
Globe Iron Works Co.	Menomonie, WI	White	na
Globe Iron Works Co.	Minneapolis, WI	White	1898
Globe Machry. & Supply Co.	Des Moines, IA	Globe	na
Globe Mfg. Co.	Macomb, IL	Globe	na
Globe Mfg. Co.	Perry, IA	Midget	na
Goby Eng. Co.	Cleveland, OH	na	1916
Godschalk & Co., E. H.	Philadelphia, PA	Giant	na
Godschalk & Co., E. H.	Philadelphia, PA	Godschalk	1907
Goetz-Coleman Mfg. Co.	New Albany, IN	na	1901
Golden, Belknap & Swartz Co.	Detroit, MI	na	1910
Golden Gate Gas Eng. Co.	San Francisco, CA	Golden Gate	1893
Golden State/Miners Iron Works	San Francisco, CA	na	1907
Good Gas Eng. Co.	Dayton, OH	Good	1901–1905
Good Inventions Co.	Brooklyn, NY	na	1912
Goodman, W. A.	Waterloo, IA	na	na
Goodwin & Co.	Norfolk, VA	na	na

The Model N engine shown here was built by the Fuller and Johnson Manufacturing Co. Hit-and-miss governing and low-tension hammer-break ignition were standard features. This hopper-cooled engine runs on gasoline.

The William Galloway Co. built engines in Waterloo, Iowa. Galloway's Boss of the Farm engine is rated at 1 3/4-horsepower. Air cooling was aided with a fan driven from the flywheel. A hammer-break igniter and low-tension ignition is used on this gasoline engine.

This 18-horsepower Galloway engine works with hit-and-miss governing. The low-tension ignition and hammer-break igniter provided spark to fire this gasoline engine. Fuel is atomized by a Lunkenheimer up-draft generator. A large clutch pulley is attached to the engine's crankshaft.

Gardner Convertible Steam and Gas Engine Co. manufactured engines in Washington, Pennsylvania. The Gardner single-cylinder engines pictured here were built in sizes from 15 to 30 horsepower. The engine is of two-cycle design and uses hot tube ignition.

The Gilson Goes Like Sixty engine was manufactured by the Gilson Manufacturing Co. of Port Washington, Wisconsin. This portable truck-mounted engine is hopper-cooled and runs on gasoline.

In the December 1912 issue of Gas Power magazine, the Gifford Engine Co. of Lansing, Michigan advertised their Gifford 1 1/2-horsepower engine. The engine uses high-tension jump spark ignition and is hopper-cooled. The Gifford used no gearing and could be adjusted to run from 300 to 600 rpm. The gasoline is stored in the engine's base fuel tank.

The Gray Motor Co. located in Detroit, Michigan manufactured marine and stationary engines. Pictured here is a stationary engine designed for either use. These two-cycle engines were fired with high-tension spark plug ignition. The base could easily be removed and the engine mounted in a boat. Multicylinder models were built from 2 1/2 to 40 horsepower.

Left

Pictured here is a restored Gray engine. This gasoline engine was designed with high-tension spark plug ignition and hopper cooling. The main bearings and journals receive lubrication by filling the oil reservoirs in the crankshaft bearing caps.

Engine Manufacturer	Factory Location	Trade Name	Dates
Goshen Mtr. Works	Goshen, IN	Goshen-Marine	na
Gould Mfg. Co.	Seneca Falls, NY	Gould	na
Gove Mtr. Co.	Biddeford, ME	na	1921
Grand Rapids Gas Eng. & Yacht Co.	Grand Rapids, MI	Grand Rapids	na
Grand Rapids Gas Eng. & Yacht Co.	Grand Rapids, MI	Monarch	na
Grant Mfg. & Mach. Co.	Bridgeport, CT	na	na
Grant-Ferris Co.	Troy, MI	Howard	na
Grant-Ferris Co.	Troy, NY	na	na
Grasser Mtr. Co.	Toledo, OH	Grasser	1910
Gray & Co.	Poultney, VT	Gray	na
Gray & Prior Mach. Co.	Hartford, CT	Brush	na
Gray & Prior Mach. Co.	Hartford, CT	Hartford	1904–1930
Gray Aldrich Co.	Boston, MA	Gray-Aldrich-Jobbed	na
Gray Bros.	Plainfield, IL	na	1901
Gray Bros. Gas Eng. Corp.	Cleveland, OH	Gray	1900
Gray Mtr. Co.	Detroit, MI	777	na
Gray Mtr. Co.	Detroit, MI	Big 6	na
Gray Mtr. Co.	Detroit, MI	Big Reliable	na
Gray Mtr. Co.	Detroit, MI	Gray-Lectric Light	na
Gray Mtr. Co.	Detroit, MI	Gray	na
Gray Mtr. Co.	Detroit, MI	Gray Gearless-Marine	na
Gray Mtr. Co.	Detroit, MI	Gray Jr.	na
Gray Mtr. Co.	Detroit, MI	Honest John	na
Gray Mtr. Co.	Detroit, MI	Marvel	na
Gray Mtr. Co.	Detroit, MI	Monarch	na
Gray Mtr. Co.	Detroit, MI	Throughbred	na
Gray Mtr. Co.	Detroit, MI	Wizard	na
Gray's & Sons, A. W.	Middletown Springs, VT	Gray	1913
Gray-Hawley Mfg. Co.	Detroit, MI	Little Skipper-Marine	na
Gray-Hawley Mfg. Co.	Detroit, MI	Skipper-Marine	na
Green & Lycon	Ligonier, IN	Haney Self Ignition	na
Green, G.	Lambertsville, NJ	Green	1902
Green Bay Mach. Co.	Green Bay, WI	na	na
Greendale Gas Eng. Co.	Worchester, MA	Greendale	na
Greenfield Gas Eng. Co.	East Newark, NJ	Greenfield	na
Gregory & Son, Wm.	Los Angeles, CA	Gregory	na
Griffith Mtr. Co.	Flint, MI	Griffith	na
Gulf Iron Works	Tampa, Fl	na	1914
Gulf Mtr. Works	New Orleans, LA	Gulf	1901
Gyro Mtr. Co.	Washington, D.C.	Gyro	1912
H.I.S. Mtr. Corp.	Pomeroy, WA	na	1920
Haberkorn Eng. Co.	Fort Wayne, IN	na	1904
Hadfield-Penford Steel Co.	Bucyrus, OH	Hadfield	1923
Hadwein Swain	San Francisco, CA	Hadwein	na
Hagan Gas Eng. Mfg. Co.	Winchester, KY	Hagan	1897–1917
Hagan Gas Eng. Mfg. Co.	Winchester, KY	Vaugh	na
Hainline Mtrs. Corp.	Portland, OR	na	1927
Haish, Jacob	Dekalb, IL	Appleton	1905
Haish, Jacob	Dekalb, IL	Chanticleer	1915
Haish, Jacob	Dekalb, IL	Haish	1905
Haish, Jacob	Dekalb, IL	Rock Island	1905
Hale, William	Chicago, IL	na	na
Hall Bros. Gas Eng. Works	Philadelphia, PA	Hall	1907
Hall Gas Eng. Co.	Byeville, OH	Hall	na
Hall Gas Eng. Co.	Byeville, OH	Hallett	na
Hall Gasolene Eng. Co.	Portland, ME	na	1904
Hall-Holmes Mfg. Co.	Jackson, MI	Hall-Holmes	1913
Hall-Scott Mtr. Car Co.	Oakland, CA	na	na
Hallett Mfg. Co.	Inglewood, CA	Hallett	na
Hallin Gas Eng. & Boat Co.	Tacoma, WA	Hall-Scott	1910
Hancock Eng. Co.	Greenfield, IN	Hancock	1903
Haney Gas Eng. Co.	Ligonier, IN	na	1909
Hannebaum, Wm.	Billings, MO	Hannebaum	na
Hansen Mach. Co.	Eureka, CA	Eureka	na

The Gray 777 horizontal engine was rated at seven horsepower. The hopper-cooled engine weighed 777 pounds. A rotary magneto is gear-driven from the engine's crankshaft. Gray stationary engines were built in sizes from 1 1/2 to 25 horsepower.

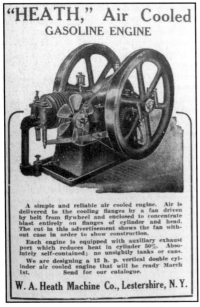

The Heath air-cooled engine was built in Lestershire, New York by the Heath Machine Co. This enclosed crankcase engine is equipped with a centrifugal-governed and flywheel driven cooling fan. The Co. also built a vertical 12-horsepower twin-cylinder engine.

The Griffith vertical engine was manufactured by the Griffith Motor Co. of Flint, Michigan. High-tension spark plug ignition fired the engine's fuel charge. The Griffith was designed with a compressing cylinder that filled the working cylinder with a fresh charge of fuel on every revolution.

Many of the most common engines found today were manufactured in Evansville, Indiana by the Hercules Gas Engine Co. Pictured here is a restored Hercules hit-and-miss-governed engine. A high-tension Wico EK magneto provides the electrical current for the spark plug ignition. The fuel-filling spout can be seen just ahead of the flywheel and below the detent arm. There are thousands of these engines still running today.

Right
Thermoil engines were manufactured by the Hercules Gas Engine Co. of Evansville, Indiana. This Thermoil engine is rated for seven horsepower. Notice that the pushrod comes through the center of the base casting to actuate the valves. Thermoil engines were designed to run on oil or kerosene.

Winchester, Kentucky was the home of the Hagan Gas Engine Manufacturing Co. The engine was manufactured in sizes from 2 to 20 horsepower. Pictured here is a restored Hagan engine equipped with low-tension ignition, a hammer-break igniter, an eternal cooling tank, and a pulley-driven carburetor.

The Heer Engine Co. in Portsmouth, Ohio manufactured the Heer double-opposed six-horsepower engine. The Heer is equipped with high-tension spark plug ignition and is throttle-governed. Dual water hoppers are used for cooling. A rotary magneto can be seen above the flywheel and driven off of a pinion gear.

Pictured here is another Hercules hit-and-miss-governed engine. Notice that this engine uses a Webster low-tension oscillating magneto for ignition. The engine's flywheel spokes are not visible because this engine is running at about 600 rpm.

The Hildreth Manufacturing Co. in Lansing, Michigan built the Novo engines. This three-horsepower engine is equipped with spark plug ignition and is hit-and-miss-governed. This engine was designed with valve cages that made maintenance quick and easy.

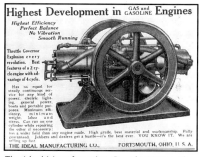

The Ideal Manufacturing Co. of Portsmouth, Ohio manufactured this throttle-governed two-cycle engine.

Indiana Gas Engine Co. manufactured this two cylinder opposed self starting engine in Indianapolis, Indiana. The illustration of their Model 79 35-horsepower shows that a flyball governor was used to control engine speed.

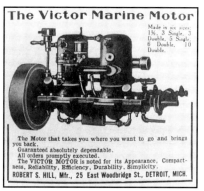

Robert S. Hill Manufacturing Co. built two-cycle marine engines in Detroit, Michigan. The Victor six-horsepower engine is pictured here. The engines were built in single- and twin-cylinder models from 1 1/2 to 10 horsepower.

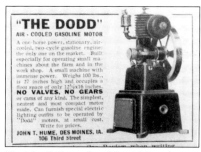

The John T. Hume Co. of Des Moines, Iowa manufactured the Dodd air-cooled engine. This one-horsepower two-cycle engine was designed with one flywheel. The engine weighed a mere 100 pounds.

Ideal Motor Co. of Lansing, Michigan built the Ideal hit-and-miss-governed engine pictured here. This engine uses a high-tension spark plug ignition system and is fitted with a gasoline fuel pump. This engine is hopper-cooled and has an enclosed crankcase.

Holm's Machine Manufacturing Co. developed and manufactured Sparta Economy engines in Sparta, Michigan. This restored four-horsepower hit-and-miss-governed engine is one of the few Holms engines that still exist. The Sparta Economy engine used a hammer-break igniter with low-tension ignition. A removable splash ring was used on the inside of the engine's water hopper. The fuel tank was secured under the engine's base.

The Home Power Co. in Ashtabula, Ohio manufactured washing machine engines. This restored Housewife engine is rare. It produced one horsepower and was air-cooled. High-tension spark plug ignition with a battery and buzz coil kept this engine running smoothly.

The Ingeco crude oil two-cycle engine was produced by the International Gas Engine Co. in Cudahy, Wisconsin. These huge engines have flywheels over six feet in diameter. The engine's weight is well over five tons.

Engine Manufacturer	Factory Location	Trade Name	Dates
Hansen Mach. Co.	Eureka, CA	Eureka Drag Saw	na
Hanson Mfg. Co., H. D.	Chicago, IL	Davis-Hanson	na
Hapgood Plow Co.	Alton, IL	Hapgood-Jobbed	na
Hardie Mfg. Co.	Hudson, MI	Arco	na
Hardy Mtr. Works	Port Huron, MI	Har-D-Motor	na
Hardy Mtr. Works	Port Huron, MI	Har-De	na
Hardy Mtr. Works	Port Huron, MI	Hardy	1902
Hares Mtrs., Inc.	New York, NY	na	na
Harmon, Gibbs & Co.	Corry, PA	Ajax	1877–1904
Harris Bros. Co.	Chicago, IL	Rumely-Olds	na
Harris Bros. Co.	Chicago, IL	Wearwell	na
Harris Patents Co.	Philadelphia, PA	na	na
Harrison, H. K.	St. Paul, MN	na	1907
Harsh Mfg. Co.	Portland, OR	Vaughn	na
Hart, H. E.	Beaver Dam, WI	na	1904
Hart Mfg. Co.	Detroit, MI	na	na
Hart-Carter Co.	Peoria, IL	na	na
Hart-Parr Co.	Charles City, IA	Hart-Parr	na
Harter, H. J.	Beaver Dam, WI	Harter	na
Hartford Plow Co.	Hartford, WI	na	na
Hartig Standard Gas Eng. Co.	Newark, NJ	Hartig	1897
Hartman Co.	Chicago, IL	Famous Majestic	na
Hartman Co.	Chicago, IL	Hartman	na
Hartman Co.	Chicago, IL	Majestic	na
Hasbrouck Mtr. Co.	New York, NY	Hasbrouck	na
Hasbrouck Mtr. Works	Yonkers, NY	na	na
Havana Mfg. Co.	Havana, IL	Automatic	1905–1916
Havana Mfg. Co.	Havana, IL	Baby Red	1905–1916
Havana Mfg. Co.	Havana, IL	Havana	1905–1916
Havana Mfg. Co.	Havana, IL	Havana Jr.	1905–1916
Havana Mfg. Co.	Havana, IL	Junior	1905–1916
Havana Mfg. Co.	Havana, IL	Red & Ready	1905–1916
Hawkeye Mfg. Co.	Tama, IA	na	na
Hawkins & Barnett Mach. Co.	Trinidad, CO	Hawkins	1913
Hawkins & Barnett Mach. Co.	Trinidad, CO	Simple	na
Hawkins Mfg. Co.	San Francisco, CA	Hawkins	na
Hayes Pump & Planter Co.	Galva, IL	Hayes	na
Haynes-Apperson Co.	Kokomo, IN	na	na
Hayton Pump Co.	Quincy, IL	na	1911
Hazard Mtr. Mfg. Co.	Rochester, NY	na	1911
Heath Mach. Co.	Lestershire, NY	Heath	1909
Heer Eng. Co.	Portsmouth, OH	Heer Oil Eng.	1901–1915
Heffernan Eng. Works	Seattle, WA	na	1905
Heinel & Co.	Wilmington, DE	na	na
Heller-Aller Co.	Napoleon, OH	Heller-Aller	na
Hendee Mfg. Co.	Springfield, MA	Hedstrom	na
Hendricks Mfg. Co.	Waynesboro, PA	na	1904
Hendricks Novelty Co.	Indianapolis, IN	Indian Comet	na
Hendy Iron Works	San Francisco, CA	Hendy	1903–1947
Hendy Mach. Works, J.	San Francisco, CA	Model	1903
Henry, Millard & Henry Co.	York, PA	Advance	na
Henry, Millard & Henry Co.	York, PA	Henry, Millard & Henry	1910
Henry, Millard & Henry Co.	York, PA	Royal	na
Henshaw, Buckley & Co.	San Francisco, CA	Doack	na
Henshaw, Buckley & Co.	San Francisco, CA	Henshaw	na
Hepworth & Co.	Yonkers, NY	Parker	na
Hercules Buggy Co.	Sparta, MI	Sparta-Economy	na
Hercules Gas Eng. Co.	Evansville, IN	Ajax	1912–1947
Hercules Gas Eng. Co.	Evansville, IN	Arco	na
Hercules Gas Eng. Co.	Evansville, IN	Atlas	na
Hercules Gas Eng. Co.	Evansville, IN	Atlas-Mixer	na
Hercules Gas Eng. Co.	Evansville, IN	Barnwall	na
Hercules Gas Eng. Co.	Evansville, IN	Champion	na
Hercules Gas Eng. Co.	Evansville, IN	Economy	na

Engine Manufacturer	Factory Location	Trade Name	Dates
Hercules Gas Eng. Co.	Evansville, IN	Economy King	na
Hercules Gas Eng. Co.	Evansville, IN	Enen	na
Hercules Gas Eng. Co.	Evansville, IN	Hardie	na
Hercules Gas Eng. Co.	Evansville, IN	Hercules Hoag	na
Hercules Gas Eng. Co.	Evansville, IN	Hvid	na
Hercules Gas Eng. Co.	Evansville, IN	Jaeger	na
Hercules Gas Eng. Co.	Evansville, IN	Keystone	na
Hercules Gas Eng. Co.	Evansville, IN	Loane	na
Hercules Gas Eng. Co.	Evansville, IN	Reeco	na
Hercules Gas Eng. Co.	Evansville, IN	Rohaco	na
Hercules Gas Eng. Co.	Evansville, IN	Saxon	na
Hercules Gas Eng. Co.	Evansville, IN	Servel	na
Hercules Gas Eng. Co.	Evansville, IN	Taylor Vacuum	na
Hercules Gas Eng. Co.	Evansville, IN	Thermoil	na
Hercules Gas Eng. Co.	Evansville, IN	Williams	na
Hercules Gas Eng. Works	San Francisco, CA	Hercules	1893
Hercules Gas Eng. Works	San Francisco, CA	Hercules Special	na
Hercules Mtr. Corp.	Canton, OH	Hercules	na
Herrmann Engnrg. Co.	Detroit, MI	Aristocrat	1916
Herschell-Spillman Co.	North Tonawanda, NY	na	na
Herschell-Spillman Co.	Tonawanda, NY	Hershell-Spillman	1913
Hertzler & Zook Co.	Belleville, PA	H & Z	na
Hess Mono Marine	Algonac, MI	Hess Mono-Marine	na
Hettinger, H. A.	Bridgeton, NJ	Hettinger	na
Hick's Gasoline Eng. Co.	Minneapolis, MN	Hicks	na
Hick's Gasoline Eng. Co.	Minneapolis, MN	Little Wonder	na
Hickey, H.	Fort Dodge, IA	na	1918
Hicks Eng. Co.	San Francisco, CA	Hicks	na
Hicks Gas Eng. Co.	Cleveland, OH	Hicks	na
Hicks Gas Eng. Co.	Buffalo, NY	na	1900
Hicks Gas Mtr. Co.	Waycross, GA	na	1906
Higginsbottom, S. H.	Saginaw, MI	na	na
High Efficiency Mtr. Corp.	Brooklyn, NY	na	1917
Hildreth Mfg. Co.	Lansing, MI	Hildreth	na
Hildreth Mfg. Co.	Lansing, MI	Hildreth-Marine	na
Hildreth Mfg. Co.	Lansing, MI	Novo	na
Hildreth Mfg. Co.	Lansing, MI	Novo Jr.	na
Hildreth Mtr. Pump Co.	Lansing, MI	Hildreth	na
Hill, R. S	Detroit, MI	Victor-Marine	na
Hill Diesel Eng. Co.	Lansing, MI	Bates	na
Hill Diesel Eng. Co.	Lansing, MI	Hill	na
Hill Mach. Co.	Anderson, IN	na	na
Hinds, T.	Malone, NY	na	na
Hinrichs Globe Iron Works	Menomonie, WI	Koehler	na
Hipp-Steiner Co.	Chilton, WI	Hipp-Steiner	1915
Hiscox, A. K.	New York, NY	na	na
Hitchcock Gas Eng. Co.	Bridgeport, CT	na	1907
Hoch Bros.	Grand Rapids, MI	All Go-Marine	na
Hoff, J. B.	Lakewood, NJ	na	na
Hoffman Mtr. Works	Chicago, IL	na	na
Hogan Mtr. Power Co.	New Haven, CT	na	1904
Hoggson, Pettis & Co.	New Haven, CT	na	na
Holbrook & Armstrong Iron Co.	Racine, WI	Holbrook	1907
Holbrook, C. D.	Minneapolis, MN	Holbrook	na
Holderman Mach. Co.	Toledo, OH	Holderman-Marine	na
Holiday Mfg. & Engnrg. Co.	Chicago, IL	Holiday	1908
Holland Eng. Co.	Holland, MI	Brownwall	1919–1924
Holland Eng. Co.	Holland, MI	Holland	na
Holland Eng. Co.	Holland, MI	Kemp	na
Holland Eng. Co.	Holland, MI	Leader	1923
Holland Eng. Co.	Holland, MI	Mandt	na
Holland Eng. Co.	Holland, MI	Pine Tree	na
Holley Mtr. Co.	Bradford, PA	Holley	na
Holloway, George	Sandusky, OH	Holloway	1910

This Ingeco six-horsepower side-shaft engine was manufactured by the International Gas Engine Co. The engine is hopper-cooled and uses a magneto for hammer-break low-tension ignition. The company advertised engines from 1 1/2 to 350 horsepower in both vertical and horizontal models.

This 1911 Famous horizontal six-horsepower engine has been restored. The picture illustrates that the engine is in running condition by the blur of the engine's flywheel spokes. Hit-and-miss governing and a speed control lever allows the operator to regulate the engine's rpm. A Webster low-tension oscillating magneto provides the electrical current to the engine's hammer-break igniter.

McCormick-Deering engines were manufactured by the International Harvester Co. in Chicago, Illinois. The Model M shown here is one of the most plentiful stationary engines today. Thousands of these 1 1/2-, 3-, 6-, and 10-horsepower engines were made. The Model M engines are throttle-governed and are equipped with high-tension spark plug ignition. The fuel tank is housed inside the engine base.

The International Gas Engine Co. was located in Cudahy, Wisconsin. Pictured here is their Ingeco 60-horsepower throttle-governed side-shaft engine that operates on kerosene. The Ingeco Standard is equipped with a hammer-break igniter and low-tension magneto ignition.

In 1914, the Jackson Gas Engine Co. of Jackson, Michigan sold their 1 1/2-horsepower Jackson engine for $31. Jackson engines were manufactured in several sizes from 1 1/2 to 12-horsepower. These engines used a hammer-break igniter with low-tension ignition. They are hit-and-miss-governed and hopper-cooled.

The notable International Harvester Co. of Chicago, Illinois produced the Famous engine line. This three-horsepower hit-and-miss-governed engine uses low-tension ignition. A hammer-break igniter is bolted to the removable water-cooled head. The engine's subbase served as the fuel tank and a brass fuel pump was installed to pump gas to the overflow carburetor. External tank- and screen-cooled models are commonly seen at antique power shows.

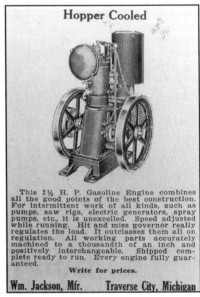

The William Jackson Manufacturing Co. built engines in Traverse City, Michigan. Pictured here is their 2 1/2 horsepower vertical engine. The manufacturer equipped these gasoline engines with hit-and-miss governing and hopper cooling.

Engine Manufacturer	Factory Location	Trade Name	Dates
Holm's Mach. Mfg. Co.	Sparta, MI	Sparta-Economy	1910–1912
Holmes & Blanchard Co.	Boston, MA	H & B-Jobbed	na
Holmes & Blanchard Co.	Boston, MA	na	na
Holmes, I. A.	Philadelphia, PA	Facile	na
Holt Co., S. L.	Boston, MA	Holt	na
Holub Mach. Shop	San Antonio, TX	Holub	na
Homan Co.	New York, NY	Star	na
Homan Co.	New Lexington, OH	Star	na
Home Elect. Lighting Co.	East Orange, NJ	Home Light	1919
Home Power Co.	Ashtabula, OH	Bieder	na
Home Power Co.	Ashtabula, OH	Home Power	na
Home Power Co.	Sandusky, OH	Home Power	na
Home Power Co.	Ashtabula, OH	Housewife	na
Homer Gas Eng. Co.	Homer, MI	Homer	1909–1910
Hoopeston Gas Eng. Co.	Hoopeston, IL	Hoopeston	na
Hoopeston Gas Eng. Co.	Homer, MI	na	na
Hoosier Storage Battery Co.	Evansville, IN	Hoosier Elect.	na
Hooven-Ownes-Rentschler Co.	Hamilton, OH	Hamilton-Gray	na
Hooven-Ownes-Rentschler Co.	Hamilton, OH	Hooven	na
Hope Forge & Mach. Co.	Mount Vernon, OH	Reeves	na
Horton, E.	Saginaw, MI	Horton	na
Houle Mtr. Works	Holyoke, MA	Houle-Marine	1907
How F.	New York, NY	Spiel	na
Howard Gasoline Eng. Co.	Chicago, IL	Howard	na
Howe, F. H.	Los Angeles, CA	Coffield	na
Howe Co., A. D.	Wheeling, WV	na	na
Howe Eng. Works	Indianapolis, IN	Howe	na
Howe Scale Agency	Chicago, IL	Champion	na
Howe Scale Agency	Chicago, IL	Chicago	na
Howe Scale Agency	Chicago, IL	Howie	na
Howell & Co.	Minneapolis, MN	Howell-Jobbed	na
Howell & Co.	Minneapolis, MN	Monarch-Jobbed	na
Hubbard Mtr. Co.	Middletown, CT	Baby	na
Hubbard Mtr. Co.	Middletown, OH	Hubbard	1907
Huber Mfg. Co.	Marion, OH	Huber	1894
Hudson Mtr. Car Co.	Hudson, NY	Hudson	na
Hudson Mtr. Eng. Co.	New York, NY	Hudson	na
Hukle Gas Eng. Mfg. Co.	Lexington, KY	Hukle	1908
Hume, John	Des Moines, IA	Diamond Jr.	na
Hume, John	Des Moines, IA	Dodd	1908
Hummer Mfg. Co.	Springfield, IL	Hummer	na
Hummer Mfg. Co.	Springfield, IL	Racine-Sattley	na
Hummer Mfg. Co.	Springfield, IL	Sattley	na
Humphreys, F. J.	Skaneateles, NY	na	na
Humphreys Mfg. Co.	Mansfield, OH	Humphreys	na
Hunt & Cornell Co.	Scranton, PA	na	na
Huntington, A.	Ripley, NY	Huntington	na
Huntington Eng. & Mach. Co.	Huntington, WV	Huntington	1904
Huntsville Fdry. & Mach. Works	Huntsville, AL	Huntsville	1913
Huron Steel & Iron Co.	Norwalk, OH	American	na
Huron Steel & Iron Co.	Norwalk, OH	Davis	1909
Hurst Mfg. Co.	Canton, OH	Hurst-Greyhound	na
Hustler-LaCrosse Imp. Co.	Minneapolis, MN	Hustler	na
Hutchinson Mach. & Fdry. Co.	Hutchinson, MN	na	na
Hutsell Mtr. Co.	Spokane, WA	Hutsell	1920
Hvid Co.	Chicago, IL	Hvid	na
Hydraulic Press Mfg. Co.	New York, NY	Hydraulic Press	na
Ideal Gas Eng. Co.	Independence, IA	Chamberlain	na
Ideal Gas Eng. Co.	San Francisco, CA	Ideal	na
Ideal Gas Eng. Co.	Independence, IA	Ideal	na
Ideal Gas Eng. Co.	Lansing, MI	Ideal	na
Ideal Gas Eng. Co.	Independence, IA	Miss Simplicity	na
Ideal Gas Eng. Co.	Lansing, MI	Original	na
Ideal Gas Eng. Co.	Beaver Falls, PA	na	1899

Engine Manufacturer	Factory Location	Trade Name	Dates
Ideal Gas Eng. Co.	Pittsburgh, PA	na	1899
Ideal Lawn Mower Co.	Lansing, MI	Iron Age	na
Ideal Mfg. Co.	Portsmouth, OH	Ideal	1907–1910
Ideal Mtr. Co.	Lansing, MI	Hardie	na
Ideal Mtr. Co.	Lansing, MI	Ideal	na
Ideal Mtr. Co.	Lansing, MI	Junior	na
Ideal Mtr. Co.	Lansing, MI	Original	na
Ideal Mtr. Co.	Lansing, MI	S.S.S.	na
Ideal Mtr. Co.	Lansing, MI	Standard	na
Ideal Power Lawn Mower Co.	Kalamazoo, MI	Ideal Jr.	na
Ideal Power Lawn Mower Co.	Kalamazoo, MI	Ideal-Mower	na
Il. Gas Eng. & Machry. Co.	Chicago, IL	na	1899
Illinois Mtr. Co.	Chicago, IL	na	1917
Ilmer Gas Eng. Co.	Reading , PA	na	1904–1916
Imperial Eng. Works	Painted Post, NY	na	1905
Imperial Gas Eng. Co.	San Francisco, CA	Imperial	na
Independent Harvester Co.	Plano, IL	Independent	1905–1910
Independent Light & Power Co.	Oelwein, IA	Independent Light Plant	na
Indiana Gas Eng. Co.	Indianapolis, IN	Model 79	na
Industrial Development Co.	New York, NY	na	na
Industrial Iron Works	Clinton, MO	Clinton	1905–1912
Industrial Iron Works	Clinton, MO	Industrial	1905–1912
Industrial Iron Works	Clinton, MO	Missouri	1905–1912
Industrial Research Corp.	Toledo, OH	na	1919
Ingersoll-Rand Co.	New York, NY	Ingersoll	na
Ingersoll-Rand Co.	New York, NY	Price-Rathbun	na
Ingram-Hatch Mtr. Corp.	New York, NY	Hatch	na
Int. Crude Oil Eng. Co.	New York, NY	na	na
Int. Engnrg. & Mfg. Co.	Kokomo, IN	Elect. Farmer Light Plant	na
Int. Process & Engnrg. Corp.	New York, NY	na	na
Intl. Gas Eng. Co.	Cudahy, WI	Ingeco	na
Intl. Gas Eng. Co.	Cudahy, WI	Ingeco Light	na
Intl. Gas Eng. Co.	Milwaukee, WI	International	na
Intl. Harvester Co.	Chicago, IL	Booster	na
Intl. Harvester Co.	Chicago, IL	Famous	1906–1917
Intl. Harvester Co.	Chicago, IL	Giant	na
Intl. Harvester Co.	Chicago, IL	International Harvester Co.	1904
Intl. Harvester Co.	Chicago, IL	International	na
Intl. Harvester Co.	Chicago, IL	Invincible	na
Intl. Harvester Co.	Chicago, IL	McCormick-Deering	na
Intl. Harvester Co.	Chicago, IL	Mogul	1913
Intl. Harvester Co.	Chicago, IL	Mogul Jr.	na
Intl. Harvester Co.	Chicago, IL	Nonpareil	na
Intl. Harvester Co.	Chicago, IL	Ready Power Generator	na
Intl. Harvester Co.	Chicago, IL	Titan	1904–1918
Intl. Harvester Co.	Chicago, IL	Titan Jr.	na
Intl. Harvester Co.	Chicago, IL	Tom Thumb	1905
Intl. Harvester Co.	Chicago, IL	Victor	1914
Intl. Gas Eng. Co.	New York, NY	na	1902–1916
Intl. Hoist Co.	Antigo, WI	na	1912
Intl. Mtr. Co.	Detroit, MI	Claus	1909
Intl. Mtr. Co.	St. Louis, MO	International	na
Intl. Oil Eng. Co.	New York, NY	Kero-Oil-Marine	na
Intl. Oil Eng. Co.	New York, NY	Kerosene Oil	na
Intl. Power Vehicle Co.	Stamford, CT	International	1902
Intl. Steam Pump Co.	New York, NY	Snow	na
Iowa Dairy Separator Co.	Waterloo, IA	Chore-Boy	1909
Iowa Gas Eng. Co.	Waterloo, IA	na	1909
Iowa Gasoline Eng. Co.	Waterloo, IA	Iowa	1909
Iowa Mach. Works	Clinton, IA	Lamb	na
Iowa Marine Eng. & Launch Works	Bellevue, IA	Red Top	na
Iowa Marine Eng. & Launch Works	Bellevue, IA	Red Top-Marine	na
Iowa Spreader & Eng. Co.	Waterloo, IA	Ever Ready	na
Ironton Eng. Co.	Ironton, OH	Ironton	1903–1917

Engine Manufacturer	Factory Location	Trade Name	Dates
Jackson Eng. & Mtr. Co.	Jackson, MI	Miller	na
Jackson Gas Eng. Co.	Jackson, MI	Jackson	1913
Jackson Mach. Works	San Francisco, CA	Jackson	1907
Jackson Mfg. Co., Wm.	Traverse City, MI	A Little Wonder	na
Jackson Mfg. Co., Wm.	Traverse City, MI	Jackson	na
Jackson Mtr. Works	Traverse City, MI	Jackson	na
Jackson Petroleum Mtr. Co.	Augusta, ME	na	1912
Jackson Works	Jackson, MI	Queen City	na
Jacobson Eng. Co.	Chester, PA	Jacobson	na
Jacobson Eng. Works	Titusville, PA	Jacobson	na
Jacobson Engnrg. Co.	Saratoga Springs, NY	Jacobson	1911
Jacobson Engnrg. Co.	Saratoga Springs, NY	Maynard	na
Jacobson Gas Eng. Co.	Jamestown, NY	Jacobson	1903
Jacobson Mach. Co.	Warren, PA	Invincible	na
Jacobson Mach. Mfg. Co.	Warren, PA	Bullseye	na
Jacobson Mach. Mfg. Co.	Warren, PA	Jacobson	na
Jacobson Mach. Mfg. Co.	Warren, PA	Mascot	na
Jacobson Mach. Mfg. Co.	Warren, PA	Newark	na
Jacobson Mach. Mfg. Co.	Warren, PA	Sturdy Jack	na
Jacobson Mach. Mfg. Co.	Warren, PA	Sturdy Jack Jr.	na
Jacobson Mach. Mfg. Co.	Warren, PA	Sturdy Jack Pumper	na
Jacobson Mach. Mfg. Co.	Warren, PA	Wards	na
Jaeger Mach. Co.	Columbus, OH	Jaeger-Jobbed	na
Jager Co., C. J.	Boston, MA	Brownwall	na
Jager Co., C. J.	Boston, MA	Jaeger	1907
Jamieson & Co.	Warren, PA	Jamieson	na
Jefferson Gas Eng. Co.	Jefferson, IA	Jefferson	na
Jeffery & Co.	Kenosha, WI	na	na
Jencick Mtr. Corp.	Port Chester, NY	na	na
Jensen, J.	Minneapolis, MN	Jensen	na
Joerns-Mohr	St. Paul, MN	Northlite Light Plant	na
Johnson Co.	Lorain, OH	Brown	1913
Johnson & Fortnum Mach. Works	Berlin, WI	Johnson	na
Johnson-Bevington Co.	Chicago, IL	Jebeco-Jobbed	na
Johnson Eng. Co.	Lansing, MI	Iron Horse	na
Johnson Eng. Co.	Lansing, MI	Johnson	na
Johnson Eng. Co.	Manchester, NH	Johnson	1907
Johnson Fdry. & Mach. Co.	Reading, PA	Johnson	na
Johnson Mtr. Co.	Waukegan, IL	Iron Horse	na
Johnson Mtr. Co.	Waukegan, IL	Iron Horse Generator	na
Johnson Mtr. Co.	Waukegan, IL	Johnson	na
Johnson Mtr. Co.	Port Washington, WI	Johnson	na
Johnson Mtr. Co.	Waukegan, IL	Utlimotor	na
Joliet Mfg. Co.	Joliet, IL	Faultless-Jobbed	na
Jones Bros. Mercantile Co.	Kansas City, MO	Sampson	na
Jones Co., S. M.	Toledo, OH	Acme-Jones	na
Jones Co., S. M.	Toledo, OH	Jones	1917
Jones Co., S. M.	Toledo, OH	Rathbun	1910
Jones Oil Eng. Co.	Syracuse, NY	Jones Oil	na
Joy Engnrg. Co.	Chicago, IL	Joy Motor	na
Kaestner Mfg. Co.	South Bend, IN	na	na
Kahlenberg Bros. Co.	Two Rivers, WI	Kahlenberg-Marine	na
Kalamazoo Gas Eng. Co.	Kalamazoo, MI	Diamond	na
Kalamazoo Gas Eng. Co.	Kalamazoo, MI	Kalamazoo	na
Kalamazoo Railway Supply Co.	Kalamazoo, MI	Kalamazoo	na
Kander Mach. Co.	Reading, PA	Ever-Ready	na
Kane & Co., T.	Chicago, IL	Electro Vapor	na
Kane & Co., T.	Chicago, IL	Regan Vapor	na
Kane & Co., T.	Chicago, IL	Victor Vapor	na
Kansas City Eng. Hay Press Co.	Kansas City, MO	Lightening	1900
Kansas City Eng. Hay Press Co.	Kansas City, MO	Lightening Jr.	1900
Kansas City Eng. Hay Press Co.	Kansas City, MO	K. C. Jr.	na
Kansas City Eng. Hay Press Co.	Kansas City, MO	Kansas City	na
Kansas City Eng. Works	Kansas City, MO	Elliott	na

The Mogul 2 1/2-horsepower throttle-governed engine is pictured here. It was manufactured by International Harvester. The Mogul engine used low-tension ignition and is fitted with a rotary magneto. Hopper cooling was provided for this gasoline powered engine. An engine like this could cost $700 to $900 today.

The Jacobson Machine Manufacturing Co. in Warren, Pennsylvania manufactured this side-shaft engine. It is currently run at the Coolspring Power Museum in Coolspring, Pennsylvania. The engine is fitted with a hammer-break igniter and a gear-driven low-tension rotary magneto.

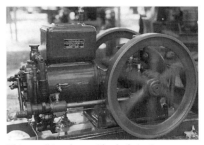

This small Jacobson side-shaft engine uses a battery, coil, and hammer-break igniter to fire the fuel mixture. A vertical flyball governs the engine and the water hopper cools it. A restored engine in this condition might sell for as much as $3,000.

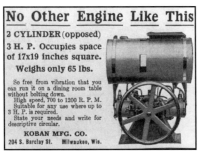

The Koban Manufacturing Co. in Milwaukee, Wisconsin, built a two-cylinder opposed engine. This three-horsepower engine was equipped with high-tension spark plug ignition. The cooling tank is attached to the top of the unit. This engine was a space-saver requiring only 17x19-inches of floor space. Weighing 65 pounds, the engine was easy to transport. Normal running speed for the Koban was 700 to 1,200 rpm.

Here is another Jacobson side-shaft engine that is equipped with low-tension ignition. A Webster magneto is attached to the hammer-break igniter bracket on the engine's head. The vertical flyball governor can be seen just over the near flywheel.

Right
Inverted vertical engines are generally rare. Pictured here is an engine manufactured by the Kenton Gas Engine Co. in Kenton, Ohio. This three-horsepower engine was equipped with tank cooling and a pump jack.

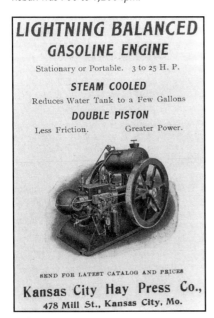

Left, above, right
These three photographs are of an extremely unusual engine. This engine was built by the Kansas City Hay Press Co. in Kansas City, Missouri. The Lightening engine was built in sizes from 3 to 25-horsepower. In some pictures, an actual working engine can be seen. The outside shape of the engine's cylinder is square. The illustration shows that originally the engine had a tank for cooling and a large round muffler.

Engine Manufacturer	Factory Location	Trade Name	Dates
Kansas City Eng. Works	Kansas City, MO	Kansas City	1900
Kansas City Univ.	Kansas City , MO	K. C. A. C.	na
Keating Mtr. Co.	Middletown, CT	Keating	1905
Kehoe & Kiss Boat & Mtr. Co.	Fort Wayne, IN	Kehoe & Kiss-Marine	1901
Keim, John	Buffalo, NY	Keim	na
Kelly Fdry. & Mach. Co.	Goshen, IN	Pease	na
Kelly Mfg. Co.	Waterloo, IA	Kelly	1915
Kelly Mfg. Co., O. S.	Iowa City, IA	Kelly	na
Kelly Mfg. Co., O. S.	Springfield, OH	Kelly	1901
Kelly-Western Mfg. Co.	Iowa City, IA	Kelly	1905
Kelly-Western Mfg. Co.	Iowa City, IA	Simplex	na
Kemp Mfg. Co.	Baltimore, MD	Kemp	na
Kemper-Odee Eng. Co.	Albert Lea, MN	Kemper	na
Kendall-Friday Co.	Peoria, IL	Kendall	1912
Kenney Machry. Co.	Indianapolis, IN	Square Deal	na
Kenton Gas Eng. Co.	Kenton, OH	Kenton	1898
Kenyon-Rosing Machry. Co.	Minneapolis, MN	na	
Kerby Mtr. Co.	Detroit, MI	Kerby-Marine	1910
Kermath Mfg. Co.	Detroit, MI	Kermath	na
Kerogas Eng. Co.	Detroit, MI	Kerogas	na
Kerosene Mtr. Co.	Peoria, IL	na	1916
Kerosene Oil Eng. Co.	New York, NY	na	1904
Kerosene Power Co.	Minneapolis, MN	Hero	na
Kerosene Power Co.	Minneapolis, MN	Viking	na
Kerosene Safety Eng. Co.	Jersey City, NJ	na	na
Kessler Mtr. Co.	Denver, CO	Kessler	1906
Ketchum & Co.	Marshalltown, IA	Lennox	1923
Kewanee Private Utilities Co.	Kewanee, IL	Kewanee Light & Power	na
Kewanee Water Supply Co.	Kewanee, IL	Kewanee	na
Keystone Driller Co.	Beaver Falls, PA	Keystone	1908
Keystone Eng. & Mfg. Co.	Dallastown, PA	Eastern	1909
Keystone Gas Eng. Co.	New Brighton, PA	Keystone	1907
Keystone Iron Works	Fort Madison, IA	Keystone	1893
Keystone Iron Works	Fort Madison, IA	Lamos	na
Kickasfer Corp.	Cedarburg, WI	Mercury	1943
Kimball Co.	Los Angeles, CA	Kimball	1914
Kimble Eng. Co.	Kalamazoo, MI	Kimble	1885
King & Hamilton Co.	Ottawa, IL	Ottawa	na
King Co., C. B.	Detroit, MI	King	1898
King Gas & Gasoline Eng. Co.	Battle Creek, MI	King	na
King Gas Eng. Co.	Iola, KS	King	1899
King Mach. Co.	Moline, IL	King	1899
Kingsland, A.	Hiscox, NY	Hydro Carbon	na
Kingsland Mfg. Co.	St. Louis, MO	Kingsland	na
Kinnard-Haines Co.	Minneapolis, MN	Flour City	1897
Kinne, W.	New Britain, CT	Kinne	na
Kinner Co.	Los Angeles, CA	Busy Bee	na
Kiser & Shellberger	Salamanaca, NY	Kiser & Shellberger	1907
Kissel Mfg. Co.	Hartford, WI	Kissel	1906–1931
Klemish Mfg. Co.	Kewanee, WI	Klemish	na
Kling Bros.	Chicago, IL	Chicago	na
Kling Bros.	Chicago, IL	Kling	na
Klumb & Sons Co.	Sheboygan, WI	Klumb	1919
Kneeland Mfg. Co.	Battle Creek, MI	Kneeland	na
Kneeland Mfg. Co.	Lansing, MI	Kneeland	1904
Kneeland Mfg. Co.	Battle Creek, MI	Maid Of All Work	na
Knight Mfg. Co.	Canton, OH	Canton	na
Knight Mfg. Co.	Canton, OH	Knight	1898
Knowlton Eng. Co.	Canton, SD	Eaton	1904–1915
Knowlton Eng. Co.	Canton, SD	Knowlton	na
Koban Mfg. Co.	Milwaukee, WI	Koban	1916
Kohler Co.	Kohler, WI	Kohler	1911–1936
Kollmyer & Talbot	Keokuk, IA	Kollmyer & Talbot	1907–1919
Kootz & Strachman Mach. Co.	Parkersburg, WV	Kootz & Strachman	na

The Kenton Gas Engine Co. located in
Kenton, Ohio built stationary and portable
horizontal engines in sizes from 3 to 30
horsepower. Shown here is a rear view of one
of their large stationary engines. Notice the
width of the flywheels. These engines may
have been designed for electrical generation,
which demanded a smooth, even-running
engine.

Kuhner Engine and Machine Co. built vertical engines in Rock Island, Illinois. The four-cycle
engines were manufactured in sizes from 2 1/2 to 16-horsepower. Shown here is their 2 1/2 and
4-horsepower portable tank-cooled model mounted on a factory cart.

The Lambert Gas Engine Co. in Anderson, Indiana was home to one of America's great men of
stationary engines, John Lambert. Lambert was building stationary engines as well as
automobiles in Indiana by the turn of the century. This nine-horsepower engine was pictured in
an advertisement in Gas Review magazine in 1914. The factory made engines in sizes from 1 to
35-horsepower.

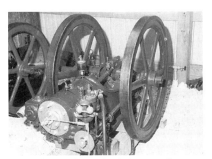

Shown here is a Kewanee Water Supply Co.
pumping outfit. The Kewanee engine and
pump are manufactured as one unit. The Co.
was located in Kewanee, Illinois.

This Krueger-Atlas eight-horsepower engine
uses hit-and-miss governing. A high-tension
magneto supplies current for spark plug
ignition. The fuel pump can be seen attached
to the engine's base with the fuel tank housed
within. This gasoline engine is tank-cooled.

This 1891 Lambert side-shaft engine has
been restored to running condition. Visible in
the photographs are the engine's vertical fly
ball governor low-tension hammer-break
igniter and side shaft as well as the engine's
round connecting rod. The crankshaft bearing
and journal are lubricated from the greaser
tapped into the connecting rod.

Left
A Lambert side-shaft engine in operation. This
portable engine is around eight-horsepower
and is screen cooled. The vertical flyball
governor can be seen just ahead of the
flywheel. A "pancake" magneto is operating
on the bracket that appears in front of the
governor.

The John Lauson Manufacturing Co. built engines in New Holstein, Wisconsin. Shown here is a throttle-governed kerosene engine. This engine is fitted with a make-and-break igniter and low-tension magneto ignition. The Lauson Co. built engines from 2 1/2 to 100 horsepower.

John Lauson also built the Baby Frost King one-horsepower engine. A battery box, batteries, and a coil were shipped from the factory with every hopper-cooled gasoline Baby Frost King engine.

This Lauson-Lawton side-shaft engine was equipped with high-tension spark plug ignition. The vertical flyball governor operates off of the engine's side-shaft. The engine burns gasoline and is hopper-cooled. This restored engine sold at action in 1995 for $6100.

The Lauson-Lawton Co. was located in DePere, Wisconsin. The Lauson-Lawton side-shaft engine pictured here sold for $6000 at a 1995 auction in Ohio. The spark plug is located tapped into the engine's heads on this model. The battery box and a vertical flyball governor are easy to spot on this hopper-cooled, gasoline engine.

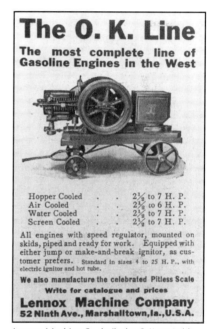

Lennox Machine Co. built the O.K. portable line of engines. The engine could be ordered with hopper, screen, and air cooling. O.K. engines were built in sizes from 2 1/2 to 7 horsepower. Lennox offered these engines equipped with either high-tension spark plug ignition or low-tension make-or-break ignition. Upon request, hot tubes would be fitted to engines equipped with electric ignition systems.

David Lennox started building engines at the Lennox Machine Co. in Marshalltown, Iowa during the early 1890s. Pictured here is a Lennox stationary engine mounted to a brick foundation. The engine is equipped with hot tube ignition and runs on gasoline. Lennox built engines in sizes from 2 to 30 horsepower.

This three-horsepower Model T engine was built by the Lincoln Gasoline Engine and Manufacturing Co. in Lincoln, Illinois. This reversible, two-cycle engine used only one flywheel. Equipped with a high-tension spark plug ignition and tank cooling, this cart-mounted unit could be moved from job to job.

Engine Manufacturer	Factory Location	Trade Name	Dates
Korting Gas Eng. Co.	New York, NY	Korting	na
Kowalsky, J.	Pittsburgh, PA	Kowalsky	na
Kreider Mach. Co.	Lancaster, PA	Lancaster	na
Kroger, J. M.	Stockton, CA	Kroger	1896
Krueger-Atlas Co.	San Antonio, TX	Samsco	na
Kuhner, L. C. Jr.	Chicago, IL	Kuhner Vanadiumized	1913
Kuhner Eng. & Mach. Co.	Rock Island, IL	Kuhner	1906–1911
Kuhner Eng. Co.	Oxford , IL	Kuhner	1911
Kumberger, Clemonts Co.	New York, NY	Vreeland	na
Kundsen Mtr. Corp.	Wilington, DE	Knudsen	1922
L-W-F Engnrg. Co.	College Point, NY	na	1919
Lackawanna Mfg. Co.	Newburgh, NY	Lackawanna-Marine	1899
Lackawanna Mtr. Co.	Buffalo, NY	Lackawanna	1904
LaCrosse Plow Co.	LaCrosse, WI	Hustler	na
LaCrosse Plow Co.	LaCrosse, WI	LaCrosse	na
LaCrosse Plow Co.	LaCrosse, WI	LaCrosse Hustler	na
Lacy Bros.	Toledo, OH	Lacy-Marine	na
Lake & Vaughn Bros.	Philadelphia, PA	na	1904
Lake Mtr. Co.	Milwaukee, WI	Lake	1919
Lake Shore Eng. Works	Marquette, MI	Lake Shore	na
Lake Shore Eng. Works	Marquette, MI	New Superior	1901
Lalley Light Corp.	Detroit, MI	Lalley Light Plant	na
Lamb Boat & Eng. Co.	Clinton, IA	Clinton	na
Lamb Boat & Eng. Co.	Clinton, IA	Lamb	1907
Lamb Gas Eng. & Power Co.	Portland, ME	Lamb	1901
Lambert Gas Eng. Co.	Anderson, IN	Hoosier Boy	na
Lambert Gas Eng. Co.	Anderson, IN	Hoosier Jr.	na
Lambert Gas Eng. Co.	Kalamazoo, MI	Lambert	1923
Lammert & Mann	Chicago, IL	Lammert & Mann	na
Landis Bros.	Rheems, PA	Columbus	1908
Langston & Co.	Philadelphia, PA	Climax	na
Lansing Boiler & Eng. Works	Lansing, MI	Lansing	1907
Lansing Mtr. & Pump Co.	Lansing, MI	Ebel	na
Lansing Mtr. & Pump Co.	Lansing, MI	Economy	na
Lansing Mtr. & Pump Co.	Lansing, MI	Lansing	1905
Lansing Wheel Barrow Co.	San Francisco, CA	Ideal	na
Larooke Co.	New York, NY	Larooke	1902
Latham Machry. Co.	Chicago, IL	na	na
Lathrop & Co.	Mystic, CT	Lathrop	na
Laubert & Nonnemacher	Youngstown, OH	na	na
Lauson Co.	Milwaukee, WI	na	na
Lauson Co., A. H.	Milwaukee, WI	Lauson	1896
Lauson Co., C. P. & J.	Milwaukee, WI	Badge	1914
Lauson Co., C. P. & J.	Milwaukee, WI	Badger	na
Lauson Co., C. P. & J.	Milwaukee, WI	Farmers Friend	na
Lauson Co., C. P. & J.	Milwaukee, WI	Lauson	1907
Lauson Mfg. Co., John	New Holstein, WI	Alpha	na
Lauson Mfg. Co., John	New Holstein, WI	Baby Frost King	na
Lauson Mfg. Co., John	New Holstein, WI	Frost King	na
Lauson Mfg. Co., John	New Holstein, WI	Frost King Jr.	na
Lauson Mfg. Co., John	New Holstein, WI	Peer Of Them All	na
Lauson Mfg. Co., John	New Holstein, WI	Uncle Sam	na
Lauson Mfg. Co., John	New Holstein, WI	Delaval	na
Lauson Mfg. Co., John	New Holstein, WI	Frost	1916
Lauson Mfg. Co., John	New Holstein, WI	Lauson	na
Lauson Mfg. Co., John	New Holstein, WI	Lauson Special	na
Lauson Mfg. Co., John	New Holstein, WI	Willing Helper	na
Lauson-Lawton Co.	De Pere, WI	Lauson-Lawton	na
Lauson-Lawton Co.	De Pere, WI	Wisconsin Light Plant	na
Lauson-Lawton Co.	De Pere, WI	Wisconsin	na
Laviene, Gill & Co.	Independence, MO	na	na
Lawrence Mach. Co.	Lawrence, MA	na	na
Lazier Co.	Plattsburgh, NY	Lazier-Marine	1907
Lazier Gas Eng. Co.	Buffalo, NY	Excelsior	na

Engine Manufacturer	Factory Location	Trade Name	Dates
Lazier Gas Eng. Co.	Buffalo, NY	Lazier	1903
Lazier Gas Eng. Co.	Buffalo, NY	Never Stop	na
Lazier Gas Eng. Co.	Buffalo, NY	Ohio	na
Le Roi Co.	Milwaukee, WI	Le Roi	na
Le Roi Co.	Milwaukee, WI	Roline	na
Le Roi Co.	Milwaukee, WI	Waukesha	na
Leader Eng. Co.	Grand Rapids, MI	Leader	na
Leader Gas Eng. Co.	Dayton, OH	Leader	1900–1904
Leader Iron Works	Decatur, IL	Leader Domestic	na
Leader Iron Works	Decatur, IL	Leader-Jobbed	na
Leader Iron Works	Decatur, IL	Novo-Jobbed	na
Leavitt Mfg. Co.	Urbana, IL	Leavitt	na
Leavitt Mfg. Co.	Urbana, IL	Success	na
Leco Engnrg. Co.	Lincoln, NE	Salsbury	na
Leland & Faulconer	Detroit, MI	na	na
Leland Elect.	Dayton, OH	Ready Power	na
Lenior Gas Eng. Co.	New York, NY	Lenoir	na
Lennox Mach. Co.	Marshalltown, IA	Lennox	1902–1914
Lennox Mach. Co.	Marshalltown, IA	O.K.	1908
Lennox Mach. Co.	Marshalltown, IA	Standard	na
Leon Berter Co.	Bradford, PA	Leon Berter	na
Leroie Co.	Milwaukee, WI	Leroie	na
Lester & Brundage	Albion, MI	Lester	1907
Levene Mtr. Co.	Philadelphia, PA	Ellis	na
Lewis Gas Eng. & Mach. Co.	Syracuse, NY	Lewis	1904
Lewis Gas Mtr. Co.	Baltimore, MD	Lewis	1897
Light Inspection Car Co.	Hagerstown, IN	na	1910
Lilly, A. L.	Rixford, PA	Lilly	na
Lima Eng. & Mfg. Co.	Lima, OH	Lima	1907
Lima Gas Eng. Co.	Lima, OH	Lima	na
Limbacher & Ternes	Detroit, MI	na	na
Lincoln Gasoline Eng. & Mfg. Co.	Lincoln, IL	Ladies Favorite	na
Lincoln Gasoline Eng. & Mfg. Co.	Lincoln, IL	Model T	1911–1912
Lindbury Co., C.	Bradford, PA	Lindbury	na
Linderman Steel & Mach. Co.	Dayton, OH	Electron Light Plant	na
Lindsay Bros. Co.	Minneapolis, MN	Haf A Hors-Jobbed	na
Lindsay Bros. Co.	Minneapolis, MN	Heer-Jobbed	na
Lindsay Bros. Co.	Minneapolis, MN	Lindsay-Alamo-Jobbed	na
Lindsay Bros. Co.	Minneapolis, MN	Lindsay-Jobbed	na
Lindsay Bros. Co.	Minneapolis, MN	Wolverine-Jobbed	na
Lininger Imp. Co.	Omaha, NE	Champion-Jobbed	na
Lininger Imp. Co.	Omaha, NE	Herr-Jobbed	na
Linquist & Havana Mfg. Co.	Chicago, IL	Webster	na
Lister, F.	Boston, MA	Lister	1907
Litchfield Eng. & Mach. Co.	Litchfield, IL	Litchfield	1903
Litchfield Mfg. Co.	Waterloo, IA	Litchfield	1903
Litscher Light Corp.	Grand Rapids, MI	Litscher-Lite Light Plant	na
Lizotte & Co.	Quincy, MA	Lizotte	na
Loane-Hiltz Eng. Co.	Baltimore, MD	Coaker	na
Loane-Hiltz Eng. Co.	Baltimore, MD	Fisherman	na
Loane-Hiltz Eng. Co.	Baltimore, MD	Loane-Hiltz	1910–1938
Lockwood-Ash Mtr. Co.	Jackson, MI	Motor-Go–Marine	na
Loffland Bros.	Woodsfield, OH	Loffland	na
Lombard Governor Co.	Ashland, MA	na	na
Long Mfg. Co.	Cherryville, KS	Long Log Saw	na
Longtime Gas Eng. Co.	Williamsport, PA	Longtime	1910
Look Mfg. Co.	Albion, MI	Look	na
Loomis, F. W.	New York, NY	Loomis	na
Loomis-Pettibone Machry. Co.	New York, NY	Crossley	na
Lorane & Trask Engnrg. Co.	Baltimore, MD	Fisherman Special	na
Lorimer Diesel Eng. Co.	Oakland, CA	Lorimer	na
Los Angeles Rotary Gas Eng. Co.	Los Angeles, CA	Los Angeles	1909
Losch Eng. Co.	Reading , PA	Losch	na
Louis-Allis Co.	Milwaukee, WI	L-A Generator	na

Engine Manufacturer	Factory Location	Trade Name	Dates
Lowe, E. L.	San Francisco, CA	Lowe	na
Lowe Bros. Mach. Works	Columbus, OH	Lowe	1905–1930
Lowe-Victorengine Co.	Chicago, IL	na	na
Lowell Model Co.	Lowell, MA	Lowell	1907
Lozier Mtr. Co.	New York, NY	Lozier	1904
Lozier Mtr. Co.	Plattsburg, NY	Lozier	na
Luitweiler Pumping Eng. Co.	Los Angeles, CA	Luitweiler	na
Lumbard Governor Co.	Ashland, MA	Lumbard	na
Lunt, Moss & Co.	Boston, MA	Lunt Moss	na
Lycoming Mfg. Co.	Williamsport, PA	na	na
Lykke Grand Island Fdry.	Grand Island, NE	Lykke	na
Lyons Eng. Co.	Lyons, MI	Lyons	1905
Lyons Eng. Co.	Lyons, MI	Simple Simplicity	na
Lyons-Atlas Co.	Indianapolis, IN	Atlas Diesel	na
Lyons-Atlas Co.	Indianapolis, IN	Lyons-Atlas	1912–1919
MacKadden Co.	St. Cloud, MN	MacKadden	na
MacClatchie Oil Tool Co.	Compton, CA	MacClatchie	na
Mach. Shop Equipment Co.	Grove City, PA	Gasoline-Kerosene	1933
Mackey Eng. Co.	Pontiac, MI	Mackey	1901
Macultivator Co.	Sandusky, OH	Motor Macultivator	na
Madison Gasoline Eng. Co.	Madison, WI	Drednaut	na
Madison Gasoline Eng. Co.	Madison, WI	Madison	1913
Maedler Eng. Corp.	Cleveland, OH	Maedler	1923
Maggowan & Finnigan Fdry. & Mach. Co.	St. Louis, MO	Perfect	na
Maggowan/Finnigan Fdry. & Mach Co.	St. Louis, MO	Success	na
Main Elect. Co.	Cleveland, OH	Main-Power Lite	na
Mainwaring & Havens	Sheffield, PA	Mainwarings & Haven	na
Majestic Gas Eng. Co.	Chicago, IL	Majestic	na
Major Marine Gas Eng. Co.	Detroit, MI	Major	na
Major Marine Gas Eng. Co.	Detroit, MI	Major Jones-Marine	na
Malin Eng. Co.	Vallejo, CA	na	na
Mallalieu & Conrey Co.	Philadelphia, PA	M & C	na
Mallalieu & Conrey Co.	Philadelphia, PA	Mallilieu	na
Maltby Automobile Co.	Brooklyn, NY	na	na
Mammert & Mann Co.	Chicago, IL	Mammert & Mann	na
Manelik, F. L.	Burton, OH	na	1907
Manhattan High-Powered Mtr. Co.	New York, NY	na	1907
Manhattan Oil Mtr. Co.	Newark, NJ	na	na
Manhattan Transit Co.	New York, NY	na	na
Manitowoc Mach. Co.	Manitowoc, WI	na	1904
Mansfield Mach. Works	Mansfield, OH	na	na
Manson Campbell Co.	Detroit, MI	Old Warhorse	na
Manufactors Construction Co.	Cincinnati, OH	Manufactor	na
Mfrs. Eng. Co.	Kansas City, MO	Meco-Jobbed	na
Mfrs. Eng. Co.	Kansas City, MO	Quincy-Jobbed	na
Marcellus Eng. Works	Marcellus, MI	Economizer	1915
Marcellus Eng. Works	Marcellus, MI	Chapman	na
Marco Power & Light Corp.	Chicago, IL	Marco Light Plant	na
Marine Eng. & Mach. Co.	Harrison, NJ	Alco-Vapor	1902
Marine Eng. & Mtr. Co.	Wilmington, DE	na	1904
Marine Oil Eng. Co.	New York, NY	na	na
Marine Power Co.	Milwaukee, WI	na	na
Marine Vapor Eng. Co.	Jersey City, NJ	na	na
Marinette Gas Eng. Co.	Chicago, IL	Marinette	1899–1907
Marinette Gas Eng. Co.	Chicago, IL	Marinette-Marine	1899–1907
Marinette Gas Eng. Co.	Chicago, IL	Walrath	1898
Marinette Iron Mfg. Co.	Marinette, WI	Marinette	1907
Marinette Iron Mfg. Co.	Marinette, WI	Marinette Queen	na
Marinette Iron Mfg. Co.	Marinette, WI	Marinette Special	na
Marinette Iron Mfg. Co.	Marinette, WI	Walrath	na
Marron Mfg. Co.	Rock Island, IL	Phelps	na
Marsh-Capron Mfg. Co.	Chicago, IL	Marsh-Capron	na
Marvel Mtr. Works	Kewaunee, WI	Marvel	1909
Marvel Mtr. Works	Kewaunee, WI	Marvel Air	na

The Lockwood-Ash Motor Co. in Jackson, Michigan built marine engines. Pictured here is their 1910 five- to six-horsepower two-cycle marine engine. This two-cylinder engine uses high-tension spark plug ignition.

The Major Marine Gas Engine Co. built the Major Jones stationary engines in sizes from 1 1/2 to 50 horsepower. Their stationary engines were equipped with low-tension ignition and a hammer-break igniter. Cooling was accomplished with an external tank.

The Maxwell and Fitch Co. built this two-cycle engine in Rome, New York. This semi-portable unit was manufactured in 1 1/2-, 2 1/2-, 5-, 8-, 10-, and 16-horsepower models. The engine was of the two-cycle design and used high-tension spark plug ignition. The engine was shipped from the factory with a battery, buzz coil, cooling tank, water circulation pump, belts, and a skid.

The Economizer engine was built by the Marcellus Engine Works in Marcellus, Michigan. The Economizer two-horsepower engine uses low-tension ignition and is equipped with a hammer-break igniter, battery and coil, and up-draft carburetor. The sheet metal hopper is an unusual feature found on this gasoline engine.

The throttle-governed Mecklenburg engine could be ordered in versions ranging from 2 to 50 horsepower. Mecklenburg Gas and Gasoline Engine Co. built their engines in South Bend, Indiana. High-tension spark plug or low-tension hammer-break ignition could be ordered.

The Major Marine Gas Engine Co. built marine engines in Detroit, Michigan. The Major Jones 1 1/2-horsepower two-cycle marine engine used high-tension spark plug ignition. In 1908, this engine came equipped with batteries, buzz coil, prop, and a starting crank, all for $48.50.

The Marvel air-cooled engine was manufactured by the Marvel Motor Works located in Kewaunee, Wisconsin. The Marvel side-shaft engines were made in five-, six- and eight-horsepower models. The cooling fins were shrouded inside a sheet-metal cover, and air was forced through this housing to cool the engine with a flywheel-driven fan.

Messinger Manufacturing Co. built engines in Tatamy, Pennsylvania. This restored Messinger engine is gasoline fueled, hit-and-miss-governed, and sports low-tension ignition with a hammer-break igniter.

Engine Manufacturer	Factory Location	Trade Name	Dates
Marvin, P. E.	Findlay, OH	Marvin	na
Marysville Mach. Works	Marysville, CA	na	1906
Mason Diesel Eng. Co.	Maywood, CA	Mason	na
Massey Harris, Ferguson	Racine, WI	Deya Massey	na
Massey-Harris Harvester Co.	Batavia, NY	Massey-Harris	na
Massey-Harris Gas Eng. Works	Milwaukee, WI	Massey-Harris	na
Mast, Foos & Co.	Springfield, OH	Buckeye	na
Mast, Foos & Co.	Springfield, OH	Buckeye Boy	na
Mathews & Co.	Bascom, OH	Mathews	1907
Mathews Boat Co.	Port Clinton, OH	Matthews	na
Mathews Co.	Port Clinton, OH	Ker-O-El Light Plant	na
Mathews Co.	Kansas City, MO	Mathews-Davis	1906
Mathews Engnrg. Co.	Sandusky, OH	Mathews Light Plant	na
Mathews Engnrg. Co.	Sandusky, OH	Plix	na
Maud S. Windmill & Pump Co.	Lansing, MI	Ideal	na
Maud S. Windmill & Pump Co.	Lansing, MI	Mauds	na
Maximotor Co.	Muskegon, MI	Maximotor	na
Maxwell & Fitch Co.	Rome, NY	Maxwell Fitch	1904–1912
Maxwell, Wyeth & Co.	Brooklyn, NY	Russ-Marine	na
Maxwell Gas Eng. Co.	New Castle, PA	na	1898
Mayer Bros. Co.	Mankato, MN	Mayer	na
Mayor, Lane & Co.	New York, NY	na	na
Maytag Co.	Newton, IA	Maytag	na
Maywood Fdry. & Mach. Co.	Maywood, IL	Maywood	na
McCadden Mach. Works	St. Cloud, MN	McCadden	1906
McClintock Eng. Co.	Detroit, MI	na	1912
McClure-Buchner Co.	Chicago, IL	na	na
McCullin Const. Co.	Chicago, IL	McCullin	na
McCullough Mtr. Corp.	Los Angeles, CA	McCullough	na
McDonald, A. H.	Chicago, IL	na	1904
McDuff, W. J.	Lakeport, NH	McDuff	na
McElroy Eng. Co.	Newark, NJ	na	1912
McElroy Eng. Co.	Newark, NJ	McElroy	1912
McElwaine & Co.	Bradford, PA	na	na
McEwen Bros.	Wellsville, KY	McEwen	1912
McFadden Mfg. Co.	Havana, IL	Marine	na
McFadden Mfg. Co.	Havana, IL	McFadden	1908
McGowan-Finnigan Fdry. & Mach. Co.	St. Louis, MO	na	na
McIntosh & Seymour Corp.	Auburn, NY	McIntosh	1908
McKinley Eng. Co.	Cincinnati, OH	Air Eng.	na
McLaughlin Mfg. Co.	North Boston, MA	Knox	na
McLaughlin Mfg. Co.	New York, NY	Knox	na
McLaughlin Mfg. Co.	North Boston, MA	McLaughlin	na
McLaughlin Mfg. Co.	New York, NY	McLaughlin	na
McManus Inc., Sandy	Waterloo, IA	McManus	na
McManus Inc., Sandy	Waterloo, IA	Power King	na
McManus Inc., Sandy	Waterloo, IA	Sandow	na
McManus Inc., Sandy	Waterloo, IA	Sandy McManus	na
McMullin Motive Power & Const. Co.	Chicago, IL	Little Mack	1906
McMullin Motive Power & Const. Co.	Chicago, IL	McMullin	na
McMyler Mfg. Co.	Cleveland, OH	na	na
McNaughton Bros.	Charlotte, MI	na	1901
McVickers Engnrg. Co.	Minneapolis, MN	McVickers	na
Mead Eng. Co.	Dayton, OH	Mead	1910
Mead Gas Eng. Co.	Providence, RI	Mead	1907
Mecklenburg Gas & Gasoline Eng. Co.	South Bend, IN	Mecklenburg	1907
Medford Fdry. & Mach. Shop	Medford, WI	Cyclone	na
Medford Fdry. & Mach. Shop	Medford, WI	Medford	na
Meriam, Abbott & Co.	Cleveland, OH	Medford	na
Meriam, Abbott & Co.	Cleveland, OH	Meriam	1909
Meriam, Abbott & Co.	Cleveland, OH	Meriam-Abbott	na
Merkel Mtr. Co.	Milwaukee, WI	Merkel	na
Merrell Co.	Toledo, OH	Merrell Elect. Sys.	na
Merrill & Barnwall	Eureka, CA	Little Wonder	na

Engine Manufacturer	Factory Location	Trade Name	Dates
Merrill Pneumatic Pump Co.	New York, NY	na	na
Merritt Co.	New York, NY	Merritt Light Plant	na
Messinger Mfg. Co.	Tatamy, PA	Messinger	na
Mesta Mach. Co.	Pittsburgh, PA	Mesta	1910
Metcalf Mfg. Co.	Quincy, PA	Metcalf	1897
Metzger, W. F.	Detroit, MI	na	na
Mianus Diesel Eng. Co.	New York, NY	na	na
Mianus Elect. Co.	Mianus, CT	Mianus	na
Mianus Elect. Co.	Mianus, CT	Plamer	na
Mianus Mtr. Works	Mianus, CT	Mianus	na
Michael Mtr. Co.	Grand Rapids, MI	Michael	na
Michael Mtr. Co.	Grand Rapids, MI	Michael-Marine	na
Michigan Brick & Tile Mach. Co.	Morency, MI	Michigan	na
Michigan City Mtr. Works	Michigan City, MI	Junior	na
Michigan City Mtr. Works	Michigan City, MI	Michigan	na
Michigan Mfg. Co.	Ypsilanti, MI	Michigan	na
Michigan Mtr. Co.	Grand Rapids, MI	Michigan	1907
Michigan Yacht & Power Co.	Detroit, MI	Michigan	na
Middleditch Eng. Co.	Detroit, MI	Middleditch	1911
Middleton Mach. Co.	Middleton, OH	Middleton	1908
Middletown Mach. Co.	Middletown, OH	Howe	na
Middletown Mach. Co.	Middletown, OH	Miami	1900
Middletown Mach. Co.	Middletown, OH	Schramm	na
Middletown Mach. Co.	Middletown, OH	Speedwell	na
Middletown Mach. Co.	Middletown, OH	Woodpecker	1886–1928
Midget Mach. Works	Camden, NJ	Midget	na
Midland Mtr. Co.	Moline, IL	na	na
Midwest Eng. Co.	Indianapolis, IN	Midwest	na
Midwest Eng. Co.	Indianapolis, IN	Utilite Power Plant	na
Mietz & Weiss	New York, NY	Mietz & Weiss	na
Mietz Corp.	New York, NY	Mietz & Weiss	1894–1922
Miller, H. A., Inc.	Los Angeles, CA	Miller	na
Miller, G. B. Co.	Waterloo, IA	American Boy	na
Miller, G. B. Co.	Waterloo, IA	Anicer	1925
Miller, G. B. Co.	Waterloo, IA	Faultless	na
Miller, G. B. Co.	Waterloo, IA	Jeffery	1926
Miller, G. B. Co.	Waterloo, IA	Miller	na
Miller, G. B. Co.	Waterloo, IA	Revenge	na
Miller Bros.	Chicago, IL	Miller	na
Miller Co.	Waterloo, IA	Revenoe	1926
Miller Improved Gas Eng. Co.	Springfield, OH	Miller	1897
Miller Improved Gas Eng. Co.	Springfield, OH	Miller Improved	na
Miller Improved Gas Eng. Co.	Springfield, OH	Watts Miller	na
Milwaukee-Rice Machry. Co.	Milwaukee, WI	Milwaukee	na
Milwaukee-Rice Machry. Co.	Milwaukee, WI	Reliance	na
Milwaukee Gas Eng. Works	Milwaukee, WI	Wonderful	na
Milwaukee Gas Eng. Works	Milwaukee, WI	Milwaukee	na
Milwaukee Machry. Co.	Milwaukee, WI	Hamilton	1898
Milwaukee Machry. Co.	Milwaukee, WI	Milwaukee	na
Miner & Peck Mfg. Co.	New Haven, CT	na	na
Miner's Gas Eng. & Mfg. Co.	Joplin, MO	na	1906
Mink, D. N.	Fresno, CA	Mink	1898
Minneapolis-Moline Eng. Co.	Russellville, AR	na	na
Minneapolis Brass & Iron Mfg. Co.	Minneapolis, MN	na	na
Minneapolis Steel & Mach. Co.	Minneapolis, MN	Muenzel	1907
Minneapolis Steel & Mach. Co.	Minneapolis, MN	Twin City	na
Minute Mfg. Co.	Newton Falls, IA	Minute	na
Model Gas Eng. Co.	Hillsdale, MI	Mogul Motor	na
Model Gas Eng. Works	Pittsburgh, PA	Model	1912
Model Gas Eng. Works	Peru, IN	Model	1905
Model Gas Eng. Works	Peru, IN	Mogul Motor	na
Modern Elevator Co.	Colfax, WA	na	na
Modern Elevator Co.	Colfax, WA	Modern	na
Modern Eng. & Supply Co.	Chicago, IL	Modern	na

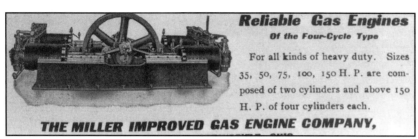

The Miller Improved Gas Engine Co. in Springfield, Ohio manufactured huge engines. This 150-horsepower four-cylinder engine used one center flywheel. Miller built engines in sizes ranging from 35 to 150 horsepower.

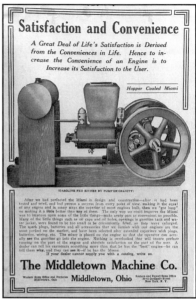

The Miami engines were built by the Middletown Machine Co. in Middletown, Ohio. High-tension spark plug ignition and hopper cooling were standard features on these gasoline engines. Fuel is fed by gravity to the engine's fuel mixer, located on the engine head.

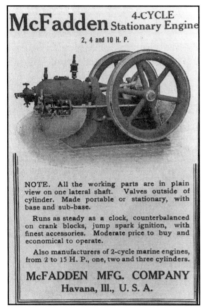

The McFadden four-cycle stationary engine was manufactured in Havana, Illinois by the McFadden Manufacturing Co. This side-shaft engine was built in 2-, 4-, and 10-horsepower models. McFadden gasoline engines were designed with external valves and jump spark ignition.

The Junior Motor built by the Michigan City Motor Works, Michigan City, Michigan, is a two-cylinder two-cycle marine engine. This 1908 engine illustration was published in a Gas Power magazine advertisement.

This is a Middletown Machine Co. Woodpecker engine. This restored Woodpecker four-horsepower gasoline engine uses hit-and-miss governing, high-tension spark plug ignition, and hopper cooling. Expect to pay a high price for the rare Woodpecker engine.

The Milwaukee engine was built by the Milwaukee Machinery Co. in Milwaukee, Wisconsin. Built in sizes from 2 to 30 horsepower, the Milwaukee side-shaft engines use low-tension ignition and a hammer-break igniter. Engine speed is regulated with a vertical flyball governor. These tank-cooled engines could be equipped to run on natural gas or gasoline.

National Engineering Company's New Model engine shown here is a two-horsepower version. It is hit-and-miss-governed and uses low-tension hammer-break ignition. Dry-cell batteries and coil came with the engine from the factory. This hopper-cooled gasoline engine and cart combination weighs well over 550 pounds.

The Moline Pump Co. advertised 30 reasons why you should buy their Eli engine. The company was located in Greenville, Illinois. Eli engines were built in several sizes from 2 to 10 horsepower. Gasoline and high-tension spark plug ignition turned the flywheels on this enclosed crankcase engine.

Engine Manufacturer	Factory Location	Trade Name	Dates
Modern Gas Eng. Co.	Buffalo, NY	na	1901
Modern Marine Equipment Co.	Cincinnati, OH	Modern-Marine	na
Modine Mfg. Co.	Racine, WI	Coldwell	na
Mohler & Degress Co.	Astoria, NY	Mohler	na
Moline Eng. & Pump Co.	Ottumwa, IA	Ottumwa	na
Moline Novelty Mfg. Co.	Moline, IL	na	1899
Moline Plow Co.	Moline, IL	Brown	na
Moline Plow Co.	Moline, IL	Duplex Superior	na
Moline Plow Co.	Moline, IL	Eli	na
Moline Plow Co.	Moline, IL	Flying Dutchman	na
Moline Plow Co.	Moline, IL	Moline	1905
Moline Pump Co.	Moline, IL	Eli	na
Monarch Duplex Eng. Co.	Cleveland, OH	na	na
Monarch Gas Eng. Co.	Indianapolis, IN	Monarch	1907
Monarch Gas Eng. Co.	Indianapolis, IN	Royal	na
Monarch Mach. Co.	Des Moines, IA	Monarch	na
Monarch Mach. Co.	Des Moines, IA	Standard	na
Monarch Mach. Works	Milwaukee, WI	Monarch	1919
Monarch Mtr. Co.	Chicago, IL	Monarch	na
Monitor Vapor Eng. & Power Co.	Grand Rapids, MI	Monitor	na
Monmouth Plow Factory	Monmouth, IL	Monmouth-Jobbed	1921
Montague Iron Works Co.	Montague, MI	na	na
Montgomery Ward & Co.	Chicago, IL	Holiday	na
Montgomery Ward & Co.	Chicago, IL	Rayner-Field	na
Montgomery Ward & Co.	Chicago, IL	Admiral	na
Montgomery Ward & Co.	Chicago, IL	Always Ready	na
Montgomery Ward & Co.	Chicago, IL	Big Giant	1908
Montgomery Ward & Co.	Chicago, IL	Bronson	na
Montgomery Ward & Co.	Chicago, IL	Bullseye-Jobbed	na
Montgomery Ward & Co.	Chicago, IL	Dairy Maid	na
Montgomery Ward & Co.	Chicago, IL	Hummer	na
Montgomery Ward & Co.	Chicago, IL	Little Giant	na
Montgomery Ward & Co.	Chicago, IL	Newark-Jobbed	na
Montgomery Ward & Co.	Chicago, IL	Power-Lite	na
Montgomery Ward & Co.	Chicago, IL	Racine-Sattley	na
Montgomery Ward & Co.	Chicago, IL	Sandow	na
Montgomery Ward & Co.	Chicago, IL	Sattley	na
Moon Bros.	Grove City, PA	Moon	na
Moore & Sons Corp.	Elizabethport, NJ	Crescent	na
Moore, C. A.	Westford, MA	na	na
Moore Plow & Imp. Co.	Greenville, MI	Moore	1909
Moore Plow & Imp. Co.	Greenville, MI	Sure Cool	na
Moore Power & Vehicles Co.	Philadelphia, PA	na	na
Moore Vehicle Power Co.	Philadelphia, PA	Moore	na
Morgan, C. H.	Worchester, MA	Morgan	1907
Morgan, C. H.	Worcester, MA	na	na
Morgan Construction Co.	New York, NY	Morgan	na
Morgan Mtr. Co.	Brooklyn, NY	Morgan	na
Morro Mtr. Co.	Morro, CA	na	na
Morton Gas Eng. Co.	Fresno, CA	Morton	na
Morton Gasolene Traction Co.	York, PA	Morton	1907
Mosler Co., A. R.	New York, NY	Mosler Valveless	1901
Mtr. Car Power & Equipment Co.	Milwaukee, WI	Evinrude	1915
Mtr. Vehicle Power Co.	Philadelphia, PA	na	na
Mtr. Vehicle Power Co.	Philadelphia, PA	Gasolene Motor	1901
Mtr.-Mower	Detroit, MI	Moto-Mower	na
Mound City Mtr. Co.	St. Louis, MO	na	na
Mr. Tom Mtr. Co.	Milwaukee, WI	Tom	na
Mudge & Co.	Chicago, IL	Mudge	na
Mullins Co., W. H.	Salem, OH	Mullins-Marine	na
Multonomah Iron Works	Portland, OR	Multonomah	na
Multonomah Mfg. Co.	Fort Worth, TX	Multonomah	na
Muncie Gas Eng. & Supply Co.	Muncie, IN	Muncie Oil Eng.	1908–1924
Muncie Oil Eng. Co.	Muncie Oil, IN	Muncie	1913

The National Engineering Co. built New Model and Michigan engines in Saginaw, Michigan. Michigan engines were built in 6-, 8-, and 10-horsepower models. Flywheel centrifugal governing and a removable water jacket were standard features. The engine could also be supplied with tank or screen cooling.

This two-cylinder 10 horsepower vertical engine was built by the National Meter Co. in New York, New York. The Nash engine line consisted of engines from 10 to 250 horsepower. The engines were designed for electric lighting, pumping, and powerplant applications.

The New Era Gas Engine Co. in Dayton, Ohio built quality engines. Engine building began in Dayton, Ohio in the mid-1890s. Their New Era natural gas or gasoline engines were built in sizes from 1 1/2 to 150 horsepower. A low-tension, hammer-break ignition system, vertical flyball governing, and tank cooling are standard features.

This is a restored 10-horsepower New Era engine. The engine was built in 1894 by the New Era Gas Engine Co. of Dayton, Ohio. This beautifully restored engine can be seen on display at the Coolsprings Power Museum in Coolsprings, Pennsylvania.

The Great Douglas engine was manufactured by the New Belle Isle Motor Co. in Detroit, Michigan. Two and six-horsepower Great Douglas two-cycle engines used high-tension spark plug ignition and are tank-cooled. The engine is designed to burn gasoline, kerosene, or distillate. The two-horsepower sold for $63.75 and the six-horsepower for $123.75. A 30-day free trial was offered by the company from the date of purchase.

Pictured here is a Little Jumbo engine manufactured by the Nelson Brothers Co. of Saginaw, Michigan. The Little Jumbo is equipped with low-tension hammer-break ignition, a flyball governor, and hopper cooling. A low-tension Webster oscillating magneto is mounted on the igniter bracket and is mechanically tripped as the engine's pushrod cycles. Nelson Brothers manufactured engines for jobbers as well as for themselves. Thousands of engines were produced by Nelson Brothers and many are still around today.

This is an original 1 1/2-horsepower New Holland engine. Notice that the engine is designed with only one flywheel. The hammer-break igniter can be seen attached to the head of the engine. Low-tension battery-and-coil ignition is used on this hopper-cooled engine. If a New Holland engine can be found today, expect to pay over $2,000 for one in the condition pictured here.

This is another New Holland Machine Co. engine. This engine is equipped with high-tension spark plug ignition. A Wico EK magneto can be seen attached to the engine's water hopper. The exhaust valves are actuated from underneath the engine's cylinder.

This unusual looking gasoline engine is a New Holland. It was manufactured by the New Holland Machine Co. in New Holland, Pennsylvania. These engines were built in 1/2-, 1 1/2-, 2-, 4-, and 5-horsepower models. They all use low-tension ignition and are hopper-cooled. New Holland claimed that their water hopper design was Burst Proof; collectors today have found out differently.

This is an Oil City Engine. The Oil City Boiler Works Co. was located in Oil City, Pennsylvania. A hot tube ignition system is installed on this engine to ignite its natural gas fuel charge.

The New Way Motor Co. manufactured this vertical engine in Lansing, Michigan. These engines were built in sizes from 2 1/2 to 7 horsepower. The engine could be ordered equipped to burn natural gas or gasoline. The air cooling system used a shroud around the cylinder and a flywheel-driven fan for cooling. High-tension spark plug ignition with a battery and buzz coil were standard equipment.

This is a picture of an early Olds Gasoline Engine Works vertical engine. The Olds factory was located in Lansing, Michigan. This restored Olds engine is equipped with hot tube ignition and is water-cooled. It was manufactured before 1900. R.E. Olds, the founder of Oldsmobile, controlled this company in its early years.

The New Way 8- and 12-horsepower opposed two-cylinder engines first appeared in 1910. These engines were built by the New Way Motor Co. in Lansing, Michigan. A high-tension spark plug magneto ignition system is installed on the engine pictured. Both cylinders are fan-cooled. The fans are belt driven off of the engine's flywheel.

The Ohio Motor Co. was located in Sandusky, Ohio. This restored Ohio 14-horsepower side-shaft engine weighs several tons. Its runs on gasoline and is fired by low-tension, hammer-break ignition. A vertical flyball governs engine speed and the tank cools the engine. The exhaust is piped to an exhaust pot. This device acts very much the same as a muffler, but could be mounted away from the engine.

Buffalo, New York was the home of the Olin Gas Engine Co. The Olin Standard engine line was built in 15 sizes from 2 1/4 to 100 horsepower. Both single- and twin-cylinder models were built. A single-cylinder, external tank-cooled model is illustrated here on a permanent foundation. It appears that the single-cylinder Olin Standard engine was designed with a round connecting rod. The engines could be ordered with hit-or-miss or throttle-governing and single or two cylinder models. Olin Standard engines could be equipped to burn gasoline, natural gas or producer gas.

Engine Manufacturer	Factory Location	Trade Name	Dates
Mundle Mfg. Co.	Peru, IN	Winner	na
Murphy Diesel Eng. Co.	Milwaukee, WI	na	na
Murray & Tregurtha Co.	Quincy, MA	Murray & Tregurtha	na
Murray Iron Works	Burlington, IA	Murray	na
Murray Mtr. Mfg. Co.	Newark, NJ	na	na
Muskegon Eng. Co.	Muskegon, MI	Muskegon	1917
Myrick Mach. Co.	Olean, NY	Eclipse	na
Myrick Mach. Co.	Olean, NY	Luther	na
Myrick Mach. Co.	Olean, NY	Myrick	na
Nadig & Bros.	Allentown, PA	Nadig	1907
Nadler-Fay & Mach. Co.	Plaque Mine, LA	Nadler	na
Nagel, O.	New York, NY	na	na
Napier Mtr. Co.	Portland, OR	Napier	1909
Nash Bros.	Vicksburg, MI	Nash	na
Natl. Dairy & Mach. Co.	Goshen, IN	Majestic	na
Natl. Elect. Lighting Co.	Wilton, IA	Natl.-Lite Light Plant	na
Natl. Eng. Co.	Rockford, IL	Herckenrath	na
Natl. Eng. Co.	Saginaw, MI	Junior	na
Natl. Eng. Co.	Saginaw, MI	Michigan	na
Natl. Eng. Co.	Waterloo, IA	Natl.	1913
Natl. Eng. Co.	Rockford, IL	Natl.	1903
Natl. Eng. Co.	Saginaw, MI	Natl.	na
Natl. Eng. Co.	Saginaw, MI	Natl. Jr.	1906
Natl. Eng. Co.	Saginaw, MI	New Model	na
Natl. Eng. Co.	Rockford, IL	Wellington	na
Natl. Eng. Co.	Rockford, IL	Winnebago Chief	1904
Natl. Engnrg. Co.	Saginaw, MI	Michigan	1917
Natl. Engnrg. Co.	Saginaw, MI	Natl.	1908
Natl. Farm Equip. Co.	New York, NY	Natl. Farmer	na
Natl. Farm Equipment Co.	New York, NY	Natl.	na
Natl. Farm Equipment Co.	New York, NY	Natl. Chief	na
Natl. Farm Equipment Co.	New York, NY	NFE	na
Natl. Free Piston Eng. Co.	Los Angeles, CA	na	1904
Natl. Gear Wheel & Fdry. Co.	Allegany, PA	Mertes Duplex	na
Natl. Gear Wheel & Fdry. Co.	Allegany, PA	Natl.	1907
Natl. Iron Works	San Francisco, CA	Natl.	1903
Natl. Mach. Co.	Hartford, CT	Natl.	1907
Natl. Mach. Works	Milwaukee, WI	Natl.	1907
Natl. Meter Co.	New York, NY	Nash	1888
Natl. Meter Co.	New York, NY	Natl.	na
Natl. Pitless Scale Co.	Kansas City, MO	Knodig-Jobbed	na
Natl. Pitless Scale Co.	Kansas City, MO	Natl.	na
Natl. Pulley & Mfg. Co.	Chicago, IL	Natl.	na
Natl. Pulley & Mfg. Co.	Chicago, IL	Natl. Pumper	na
Natl. Rotary Valve Co.	Dayton, OH	Natl.	1901
Natl. Sewing Mach. Co.	Belvidere, IL	Duro	na
Natl. Sewing Mach. Co.	Belvidere, IL	Eldridge	na
Natl. Sewing Mach. Co.	Belvidere, IL	Natl.	na
Natl. Steam Pump Co.	Upper Sandusky, OH	Natl.	1913
Natl. Steam Pump Co.	Upper Sandusky, OH	Natl. Oil	na
Natl. Transit Co.	Oil City, PA	Klein	na
Natl. Transit Co.	Oil City, PA	Little Hummer	na
Natl. Transit Co.	Oil Cit , PA	Natl.	1894–1948
Natl.-Superior Co.	Springfield, OH	Natl.	na
Natl.-Superior Co.	Springfield, OH	Superior	na
Natl.-Superior Co.	Springfield, OH	Superior Diesel	na
Neer Air Cooled Eng. Co.	Plain City, OH	Neer	na
Neilson, H. P.	St. Louis, MO	Neilson	1905
Nelson Bros. Co.	Saginaw, MI	Arcadia	na
Nelson Bros. Co.	Saginaw, MI	Bluffton	na
Nelson Bros. Co.	Saginaw, MI	Bohan	na
Nelson Bros. Co.	Saginaw, MI	Brown	na
Nelson Bros. Co.	Saginaw, MI	Dairy King	na

Engine Manufacturer	Factory Location	Trade Name	Dates
Nelson Bros. Co.	Saginaw, MI	Dan Patch	na
Nelson Bros. Co.	Saginaw, MI	Dazzle Patch	na
Nelson Bros. Co.	Saginaw, MI	Detroit	na
Nelson Bros. Co.	Saginaw, MI	Drew	na
Nelson Bros. Co.	Saginaw, MI	Dubuque	na
Nelson Bros. Co.	Saginaw, MI	Dunns	na
Nelson Bros. Co.	Saginaw, MI	Eaton	na
Nelson Bros. Co.	Saginaw, MI	Efficiency	na
Nelson Bros. Co.	Saginaw, MI	El Bros.	1926
Nelson Bros. Co.	Saginaw, MI	Essex	1906
Nelson Bros. Co.	Saginaw, MI	Essick	na
Nelson Bros. Co.	Saginaw, MI	Ever Ready	na
Nelson Bros. Co.	Saginaw, MI	Franklin	na
Nelson Bros. Co.	Saginaw, MI	Gray	na
Nelson Bros. Co.	Saginaw, MI	Gray-Aldrich	na
Nelson Bros. Co.	Saginaw, MI	Hapwood Plow	na
Nelson Bros. Co.	Saginaw, MI	Hertzler & Zook	na
Nelson Bros. Co.	Saginaw, MI	Hush	1925
Nelson Bros. Co.	Saginaw, MI	John M. Smythe	na
Nelson Bros. Co.	Saginaw, MI	Joy	na
Nelson Bros. Co.	Saginaw, MI	Jumbo	na
Nelson Bros. Co.	Saginaw, MI	Kracker Jack	na
Nelson Bros. Co.	Saginaw, MI	Lazier	na
Nelson Bros. Co.	Saginaw, MI	Little Jumbo	1920
Nelson Bros. Co.	Saginaw, MI	Little Trojan	na
Nelson Bros. Co.	Saginaw, MI	Lyons	na
Nelson Bros. Co.	Saginaw, MI	Macleod	na
Nelson Bros. Co.	Saginaw, MI	Majestic	na
Nelson Bros. Co.	Saginaw, MI	Mandt	na
Nelson Bros. Co.	Saginaw, MI	Matchless	na
Nelson Bros. Co.	Saginaw, MI	Maynard	1917
Nelson Bros. Co.	Saginaw, MI	Maynard Jr.	na
Nelson Bros. Co.	Saginaw, MI	Mendy	na
Nelson Bros. Co.	Saginaw, MI	Michigan	na
Nelson Bros. Co.	Saginaw, MI	Minneota	na
Nelson Bros. Co.	Saginaw, MI	Minnesoda	na
Nelson Bros. Co.	Saginaw, MI	Mohr	na
Nelson Bros. Co.	Saginaw, MI	Monarch	na
Nelson Bros. Co.	Saginaw, MI	Natl. Chief	na
Nelson Bros. Co.	Saginaw, MI	Natl. Farmer	na
Nelson Bros. Co.	Saginaw, MI	Nelson	na
Nelson Bros. Co.	Saginaw, MI	Nelson Royal	na
Nelson Bros. Co.	Saginaw, MI	New Model	na
Nelson Bros. Co.	Saginaw, MI	Northome	na
Nelson Bros. Co.	Saginaw, MI	Ohio	na
Nelson Bros. Co.	Saginaw, MI	Ontario	na
Nelson Bros. Co.	Saginaw, MI	P & O	na
Nelson Bros. Co.	Saginaw, MI	Page Fence	na
Nelson Bros. Co.	Saginaw, MI	Patch	na
Nelson Bros. Co.	Saginaw, MI	Royal	na
Nelson Bros. Co.	Saginaw, MI	Samsco	na
Nelson Bros. Co.	Saginaw, MI	Samson	na
Nelson Bros. Co.	Saginaw, MI	Sandow	na
Nelson Bros. Co.	Saginaw, MI	Sattley	na
Nelson Bros. Co.	Saginaw, MI	Savage	na
Nelson Bros. Co.	Saginaw, MI	Sheldon	na
Nelson Bros. Co.	Saginaw, MI	Slave	na
Nelson Bros. Co.	Saginaw, MI	Smyth-Desspard	na
Nelson Bros. Co.	Saginaw, MI	Standard Motor	na
Nelson Bros. Co.	Saginaw, MI	Stover	na
Nelson Bros. Co.	Saginaw, MI	Sun	na
Nelson Bros. Co.	Saginaw, MI	Sun Power	1926
Nelson Bros. Co.	Saginaw, MI	Thorndike	na
Nelson Bros. Co.	Saginaw, MI	Toronto	na

Pictured here is an O and S engine manufactured by Orr and Sembower Inc. located in Reading, Pennsylvania. The O and S vertical engine is designed with high-tension spark plug ignition and hopper cooling. Careful examination reveals that the water hopper is not round but has flat sides. This is an unusual characteristic of this gasoline engine.

The Otto Gas Engine Works of Philadelphia, Pennsylvania built the Otto portable gasoline engine in four sizes. These side-shaft engines could be ordered in 4-, 6-, 10-, or 15-horsepower. Otto portable engines were equipped with low-tension ignition, vertical flyball governing, and hopper cooling. The engine is shown mounted on an original horse-drawn steel-wheeled cart.

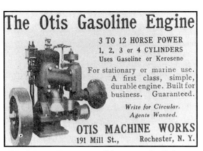
The Otis engine pictured here was built by the Otis Machine Works of Rochester, New York. It was designed for stationary or marine use. The Otis engines were built in one-, two-, three-, and four-cylinder models in sizes from 3 to 12 horsepower. The company assured prospective buyers that the engine would run on gasoline or kerosene.

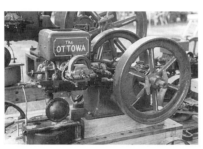

Ottawa Manufacturing Co. was located in Ottawa, Kansas. Pictured here is an Ottawa engine equipped with low-tension, hammer-break ignition, and hit-and-miss governing. The engine is designed with a flywheel centrifugal governor, and the head has no water jacket.

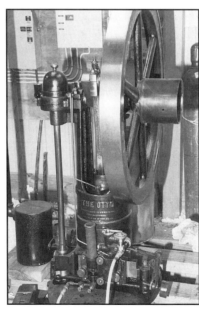

This is a picture of a beautifully restored 1876 inverted vertical Otto engine. The engine was fired with an open flame that used a slide valve to ignite the fuel charge inside the cylinder.

Ottawa Manufacturing Co. engines can be found fairly easily today. Ottawa engines were built in Ottawa, Kansas. This uses a Wico high-tension magneto for its spark plug ignition.

This two-horsepower skidded Otto engine first appeared in 1911. Its high-tension, spark plug ignition used a battery and buzz to generate ignition. The engine is throttle-governed and hopper-cooled.

During 1893, the Otto Gas Engine Works in Philadelphia, Pennsylvania built this Otto 14-horsepower side-shaft engine. It is on an original steel-wheeled cart. Low-tension hammer-break ignition and tank cooling are standard equipment on this gasoline Otto. The engine sports a round connecting rod.

Engine Manufacturer	Factory Location	Trade Name	Dates
Nelson Bros. Co.	Saginaw, MI	Trojan	na
Nelson Bros. Co.	Saginaw, MI	United Factories	na
Nelson Bros. Co.	Saginaw, MI	Unito	na
Nelson Bros. Co.	Saginaw, MI	Wilson	na
Nelson Bros. Co.	Saginaw, MI	Winnepeg Boy	na
Nelson Gas Eng. Co.	Harlan, IA	Nelson	na
Nelson Gas Eng. Works	Harlan, IA	Mathless	na
Nelson Mfg. Co.	Willmar, MN	Nelson	1907
New Belle Island Mtr. Co.	Detroit, MI	Great Douglas	1910
New Castle Eng. Co.	New Castle, PA	Duplex	na
New Castle Eng. Co.	New Castle, PA	New Castle	na
New Century Mtr. Co.	Camden, NJ	na	na
New Departure Mfg. Co.	Bristol, CT	na	na
New England Eng. & Supply Co.	Boston, MA	New England-Jobbed	na
New England Gas Eng. Co.	Boston, MA	New England	na
New England Gas Eng. Co.	Boston, MA	na	na
New Era Gas Eng. Co.	Dayton, OH	Little Giant	na
New Era Gas Eng. Co.	Portsmouth, OH	New Era	1904–1912
New Era Iron Works	Dayton, OH	New Era	1894–1903
New Hampton Mfg. Co.	New Hampton, IA	Lucky	na
New Hampton Mfg. Co.	New Hampton, IA	Lucky Star	na
New Hampton Mfg. Co.	New Hampton, IA	New Hampton	na
New Hampton Mfg. Co.	New Hampton, PA	New Hampton	na
New Holland Mach. Co.	New Holland, PA	New Holland	1901
New Idea Inc.	Coldwater, OH	New Idea	na
New Idea Inc.	Coldwater, OH	Vari-Speed	na
New Idea Spreader Co.	Coldwater, OH	New Idea	na
New Jersey Argi. Works	Trenton, NJ	Butterworth	na
New Jersey Mtr. Co.	Keyport, NJ	New Jersey Motor	na
New Light Heat & Power Co.	Salt Lake City, UT	na	1901
New London Ship & Eng. Works	New London, NJ	Nelseco	na
New London Ship & Eng. Works	New London, NJ	New London	na
New Way Mtr. Co.	Lansing, MI	Deya	na
New Way Mtr. Co.	Lansing, MI	Goes & Goes Right	na
New Way Mtr. Co.	Lansing, MI	Jewel	na
New Way Mtr. Co.	Lansing, MI	Little Giant	na
New Way Mtr. Co.	Lansing, MI	New Way	1905
New Way Mtr. Co.	Lansing, MI	Standard	na
New York Kerosene Eng. Co.	New York, NY	New York	1904
New York Mtr. Co.	New York, NY	New York Motor	na
Newark Gas Eng. Co.	Newark, NY	Newark	na
Newcomb Eng. Co.	New York, NY	Newcomb	1911
Newell Bros.	Cleveland, OH	na	na
Nichols & Wright Mtr. Co.	Buffalo, NY	na	1914
Nichols, C.	Buffalo, NY	Nichols	na
Nielson Co., H. P.	St. Joseph, MO	Nielson	1905
Niles Automobile & Gas Eng. Co.	Niles, MI	na	1903
Nordberg Mfg. Co.	Milwaukee, WI	Nordberg	1915
Norfolk Fdry. & Mach. Co.	Norfolk, NE	na	na
Norman Co., J. J.	Chicago, IL	Norman	na
Norris Mtr. Co.	Columbus, OH	Norris	1911
North & Co.	Jefferson, IA	na	na
North Am. Gas Eng. Works	Algona, IA	Road Boss	na
North Coast Machry. Co.	Seattle, WA	North Coast	na
North Dakota Gas Eng.	Lansford, ND	na	1912
North Star Mfg. Co.	Minneapolis, MN	North Star	na
Northern Engnrg. Works	Detroit, MI	Northern	na
Northern Engnrg. Works	Detroit, MI	Tandem	na
Northrup Co., B. D.	Washington, PA	Either	na
Northrup Gas Eng. Co.	Washington, PA	Northrup	na
Northwell Co., T. G.	Lansing, MI	United	1912
Northwestern Mach. Co.	Detroit, MI	Little Tiger-Marine	na
Northwestern Mtr. Co.	Eau Claire, WI	Casey Jones	na
Northwestern Steel & Iron Works	Eau Claire, WI	King Of All Farm Engs.	na

Engine Manufacturer	Factory Location	Trade Name	Dates
Northwestern Steel & Iron Works	Eau Claire, WI	Northwestern	1904–1917
Norwalk Launch Co.	Pittsfield, MA	Norwalk-Marine	1899
Novelty Iron Works	Mankato, MN	na	1905
Novelty Iron Works Co.	Dubuque, IA	Estes	na
Novo Eng. Co.	Lansing, MI	Farmers Helper	na
Novo Eng. Co.	Lansing, MI	Friend	na
Novo Eng. Co.	Lansing, MI	Hardie	na
Novo Eng. Co.	Lansing, MI	Hildreth	1913
Novo Eng. Co.	Lansing, MI	Novo	1897
Novo Eng. Co.	Lansing, MI	Novo Jr.	na
Novo Eng. Co.	Lansing, MI	Novo Roller	na
Novo Eng. Co.	Lansing, MI	Roll-R	na
Novo Eng. Co.	Lansing, MI	SSS	na
Noye Mfg. Co.	Buffalo, NY	na	na
NY Safety Steam Power Co.	New York, NY	Dock	na
NY Yacht, Launch & Eng. Co.	Morris Heights, NY	Nickelson-Marine	1910
NY Yacht, Launch & Eng. Co.	Morris Heights, NY	na	1910
Nye Gas Eng. Co.	Laporte, IN	na	1911
O & B Co.	Dravosburg, PA	O & B	1917
O'Neil Imp. Co.	Marseilles, IL	Flying Swede	na
O. K. Gas Eng. Co.	Marshalltown, IA	O. K.	na
O. K. Gas Eng. Co.	Winchester, OH	O. K.	1903
Oakland Mtr. Car Co.	Pontiac, MI	Stinger	1909
Ode Gas Eng. Co.	Albert Lea, MN	Ode	1913
Odee & Koto Mfg. Co.	Beloit, WI	Odee	1910
Odee & Koto Mfg. Co.	Beloit, WI	Odee & Kato	1910
Ofeldt & Sons	Brooklyn, NY	na	na
Ohio Elect. Works	Cleveland, OH	Ohio Light Plant	na
Ohio Eng. Sales Co.	Sandusky, OH	Joy-Jobbed	na
Ohio Gas Eng. Co.	Sandusky, OH	Ohio	1897–1920
Ohio Mfg. Co.	Upper Sandusky, OH	Ohio	1907
Ohio Mtr. Co.	Sandusky, OH	Excelsior-Jobbed	na
Ohio Mtr. Co.	Sandusky, OH	Joy-Jobbed	na
Ohio Mtr. Co.	Sandusky, OH	Lazier-Jobbed	na
Ohio Mtr. Co.	Sandusky, OH	Ohio-Jobbed	na
Ohio Mtr. Co.	Sandusky, OH	Sandusky-Jobbed	1904
Ohio Tractor Mfg. Co.	Marion, OH	Ohio	na
Ohio Valley Supply Co.	Marietta, OH	Ohio	1907
Oil City Boiler Works	Oil City, PA	Oil City Motor	1896
Oil Well Supply Co.	Pittsburgh, PA	Black Bear	na
Oil Well Supply Co.	Pittsburgh, PA	Oilwell	1902
Oil Well Supply Co.	Pittsburgh, PA	Simplex	na
Okay Mtr. Mfg. Co.	Brooklyn, NY	Okay	1916
Okmulgee Imp. & Mfg. Co.	Okmulgee, OK	na	1909
Olds & Hough Co.	Albion, MI	Olds & Hough	na
Olds & Son, P. F.	Lansing, MI	Olds	1880
Olds & Son, P. F.	Lansing, MI	Olds Safety Vapor Eng.	1897
Olds Gas Power Co.	Lansing, MI	Rumley Olds	na
Olds Gasoline Eng. Works	Lansing, MI	Olds	1890
Olds Gasoline Eng. Works	Lansing, MI	Reliance	na
Olds Gasoline Eng. Works	Lansing, MI	Seager	na
Olds Mtr. Works	Detroit, MI	Olds	na
Olin Gas Eng. Co.	Buffalo, NY	Olin	1896
Onan & Sons, D. W.	Minneapolis, MN	Onan	na
Onan & Sons, D. W.	Minneapolis, MN	Ten Life	na
Onan Corp.	Fridley, MN	Onan	na
Onan Corp.	Minneapolis, MN	Onan	na
One Minute Mfg. Co.	Newton, IA	One Minute	1911
Ontario Wind Eng. & Pump Mfg. Co.	Alexander, NY	Chapman	na
Ontario Wind Eng. & Pump Mfg. Co.	Alexander, NY	Toronto	na
Original Gas Eng. Co.	Lansing, MI	Ideal	na
Original Gas Eng. Co.	Lansing, MI	Original	na
Oriental Gas Eng. Co.	San Francisco, CA	Oriental	1902
Orleans Boat & Mach. Co.	West Derby, VT	na	1904
Orr & Sembower Inc.	Reading, PA	Junior Oil	na

Engine Manufacturer	Factory Location	Trade Name	Dates
Orr & Sembower Inc.	Reading, PA	O & S	na
Orr & Sembower Inc.	Reading, PA	O & S Jr.	na
Orr & Sembower Inc.	Reading, PA	Orr & Sembower	na
Osborne Machry. Co.	New Haven, CT	na	na
Oshkosh Mfg. Co.	Oshkosh, WI	Oshkosh	na
Oswald Mtr. Co.	Goshen, IN	Oswald	na
Otis Bros. & Co.	New York, NY	Baldwin	1883
Otis Mach. Works	Rochester, NY	Otis	na
Otis Mach. Works	Rochester, NY	Otis-Marine	na
Ottawa Mfg. Co.	Ottawa, KS	Gibraltar	na
Ottawa Mfg. Co.	Ottawa, KS	Ottawa	na
Otto Gas Eng. Works	Philadelphia, PA	Otto	na
Otto Gas Eng. Works	Philadelphia, PA	Otto Silent	na
Otto Gas Eng. Works	Philadelphia, PA	Superior	na
Owen & Co.	Chicago, IL	Owen	na
Owen & Co.	New York, NY	na	na
P & O Plow Co.	Canton , IL	Big 4 Pumper	na
P & O Plow Co.	Canton, IL	Big Chief	na
P & O Plow Co.	Canton, IL	P & O	na
P & O Plow Co.	Canton, IL	Parks Ball Bearing	na
P & O Plow Co.	Canton, IL	Wolverine-Jobbed	na
P. T. Mtr. Co.	New York, NY	P. T.	na
Pennsylvania Ready Mtr. Co.	Philadelphia, PA	Ready	na
Pacific Diesel Eng. Co.	Oakland, CA	na	na
Pacific Gas Eng. Co.	San Francisco, CA	Pacific	na
Padden & Pett Co.	Waterloo, IA	Padden & Pett	na
Page Co.	Chicago, IL	Page	na
Page Engnrg. Co.	Chicago, IL	Oriole	na
Page Engnrg. Co.	Baltimore, MD	Oriole	na
Page Engnrg. Co.	Chicago, IL	Page	na
Page Engnrg. Co.	Baltimore, MD	Page	na
Page Fence & Gas Eng. Co.	Adrian, MI	Church	na
Page Fence & Gas Eng. Co.	Adrian, MI	Page	na
Page Mfg. Co.	Richfield, WI	na	na
Palm Gas Eng. Co.	Butler, PA	Palm	na
Palmer & Rey Co.	San Francisco, CA	Hercules	na
Palmer & Rey Co.	San Francisco, CA	Improved Hercules	na
Palmer & Rey Co.	San Francisco, CA	New Hercules	na
Palmer & Rey Co.	San Francisco, CA	Palmer	na
Palmer Bros.	Cob, CT	Pal	na
Palmer Bros.	Cos Cob, CT	Palmer	na
Palmer Mtr. Co.	Cos Cob, CT	Palmer	na
Palmer Oil Eng. Co.	Cleveland, OH	Palmer	1908
Palmer-Moore Co.	Syracuse, NY	Moore	na
Pan-Am. Mtr. Co.	New York, NY	na	na
Paradox Gas Eng. Co.	Hartford, CT	Paradox	na
Paragon Utilities Co.	Chicago, IL	Paragon	na
Parcelle Eng. Co.	Elgin, IL	Elgin Comet	na
Parcelle Eng. Co.	Elgin, IL	Parcelle	na
Parker Co.	Fulton, NY	Parker	na
Parkersburg Eng. Co.	Parkersburg, WV	Spencer	na
Parkersburg Mach. Co.	Parkersburg, WV	Parkersburg	na
Parkersburg Mach. Co.	Parkersburg, WV	Parmaco	na
Parks Ball Bearing Mach. Co.	Cincinnati, OH	Parks Ball Bearing	na
Parlin & Orendoroff Plow Co.	Canton, IL	Big 4 Pumper	na
Parlin & Orendoroff Plow Co.	Canton, IL	Big Chief	na
Parlin & Orendoroff Plow Co.	Canton, IL	P & O	na
Parlin & Orendoroff Plow Co.	Canton, IL	Parks Ball Bearing	na
Parlin & Orendoroff Plow Co.	Canton, IL	Wolverine	na
Parsell & Weed Co.	New York, NY	Franklin	na
Parsell & Weed Co.	New York, NY	Parsell	na
Parson-Rich Co.	Newton, IA	Waterloo	na
Pasche Air Brush Co.	Chicago, IL	Pasche	na
Pass City Fdry. & Mach. Co.	El Paso, TX	na	na

Engine Manufacturer	Factory Location	Trade Name	Dates
Patterson, Gottfried & Hunter	New York, NY	na	1903
Patterson Supply Co.	Cleveland, OH	Domestic-Jobbed	na
Pattin Bros. Co.	Marietta, OH	Pattin	na
Pausin Engnrg. Co.	Newark, NJ	Arrow	na
Pausin Engnrg. Co.	Newark, NJ	Pausin	na
Pausin Engnrg. Co.	Newark, NJ	Waterous	na
Payne Eng. Co.	Elmira, NY	Payne	1899
Pearson Corp.	Cincinnati, OH	Cincinnati Elect. Light Plant	1925
Pearson Eng. & Mfg. Co.	Boston, MA	Pearson	1916
Pease Eng. & Mach. Works	Goshen, IN	Pease	na
Peerless Gas Eng.	Chicago, IL	Farmers Boy	na
Peerless Gas Eng.	Chicago, IL	Hercules	na
Peerless Gas Eng.	Chicago, IL	Peerless	na
Peerless Mfg. Co.	Springfield, OH	Peerless	na
Peerless Marine Eng. Co.	Detroit, MI	Peerless-Marine	na
Peerless Mtr. Co.	Lansing, MI	Acme	na
Peerless Mtr. Co.	Lansing, MI	Butcher Boy	1908
Peerless Mtr. Co.	Lansing, MI	Chicago	na
Peerless Mtr. Co.	Lansing, MI	Hercules	na
Peerless Mtr. Co.	Lansing, MI	Lazier	na
Peerless Mtr. Co.	Lansing, MI	Never Stop	na
Peerless Mtr. Co.	Lansing, MI	Noiseless	1904
Peerless Mtr. Co.	Lansing, MI	Parkersburg	na
Peerless Mtr. Co.	Lansing, MI	Peerless	na
Peerless Mtr. Co.	Lansing, MI	Special	na
Pelton & Sons	Lyons, IA	Pelton-Marine	na
Pelton Gasoline Works	Lyons, MI	Perfect	na
Pendleton Star Mfg. Co.	Pendleton, IN	Pendleton	1902
Peninsular Mtr. Co.	Grand Rapids, MI	Peninsular	na
Pennsylvania Iron Works	Philadelphia, PA	Globe	1898
Pennsylvania Iron Works	Philadelphia, PA	Pennsylvania	na
Penrose Mtr. Co.	Woodbury, NJ	na	1914
Percyprova Belt	Fredonia, KS	Belt	na
Perfection Gas Eng. Co.	Cedar Rapids, IA	Perfection	na
Perfection Storage Battery Co.	Chicago, IL	Perfection Light Plant	na
Perkin Bros.	Havana, IL	S & H	na
Perkins Windmill & Eng. Co.	Mishawaka, IN	Perkins	na
Perry Mfg. Co.	Lexington, OH	Star	1907
Peterson, C.	LaCrosse, WI	Peterson	1901
Petoskey Iron Works	Petoskey, MI	Petoskey	na
Phelps Light & Power Co.	Rock Island , IL	Phelps Power-Light	na
Phelps Mtr. Co.	Rock Island , IL	All Service	na
Phelps Mtr. Co.	Rock Island , IL	Phelps	na
Phillip's Drag Saw & Mfg. Co.	Kansas City, MO	Phillips	na
Phillips Gas Eng. & Mtr. Co.	Chicago, IL	Original Air Cooled	na
Phillips Gas Eng. & Mtr. Co.	Chicago, IL	De Moin	na
Phillips Gas Eng. & Mtr. Co.	Chicago, IL	Phillips	na
Phillips Gas Eng. & Mtr. Co.	Chicago, IL	Yellow Jacket	na
Phillips Gasoline Eng. & Mtr. Co.	Chicago, IL	Phillips Duplex	na
Phillips Gasoline Eng. & Mtr. Co.	Chicago, IL	Phillips Ready To Run	na
Phillips Mfg. Co.	Butler, PA	Phillips	na
Phoenix Gas Eng. Mfg. Co.	Seattle, WA	Phoenix	1917
Piera Vapor Eng. Co.	Racine, WI	Piera Vapor	na
Pierce Eng. Co.	Racine, WI	Pierce	na
Pierce Eng. Co.	Racine, WI	Pierce-Truscott	na
Pierce Eng. Co.	St. Joseph, MI	na	na
Pierce-Budd Co.	Bay City, MI	na	1914
Pierce-Crouch Eng. Co.	New Brighton, PA	Brighton	na
Pierce-Crough Eng. Co.	New Brighton, PA	Pierce	1894–1907
Piersen, Head & Co.	San Francisco, CA	Gray	na
Piersen Mfg. Co.	Topeka, KS	na	na
Pine Tree Milking Mach. Co.	Chicago, IL	Pine Tree-Jobbed	na
Pittsburgh Gas Eng. Co.	Pittsburgh , PA	Pittsburgh	1899
Pittsburgh Mach. Co.	New Brighton, PA	Pittsburgh	1907

The Otto Gas Engine Works was located in Philadelphia, Pennsylvania. Otto engines built in 1912 ranged in size from 1 to 150 horsepower. A hammer-break igniter and low-tension ignition fire this engine that could burn city gas, natural gas, producer's gas, gasoline, alcohol, or distillate if so equipped. A vertical flyball governor controls the engines speed.

Peerless Motor Co. was located in Lansing, Michigan. The Butcher Boy engine is a two-horsepower vertical engine. Fuel lines are seen running from fuel tank in the engine's base to the carburetor.

This 1910 Peerless two-horsepower side-shaft engine was built in Lansing Michigan by the Peerless Motor Co. These side-shaft engines were built in sizes from 2 to 15 horsepower. This engine and cart sold at auction in 1995 for $8,000.

Pictured here is an 1877 side-shaft Otto engine. The engine has only one flywheel and uses hot tube ignition. A wipe oiler was designed to run off of the side-shaft and automatically lubricate the cylinder.

This Peerless differs from the model shown above. Notice that the flywheels are almost as high as the engine's water hopper and the shape of the hopper has been changed. These engines were built in sizes from 2 to 15 horsepower.

This 1893 Otto inverted vertical engine used hot tube flame ignition. It is tank-cooled and was running when this photograph was taken.

Combination Pumper

Engine and jack on one skid. Sprocket chain connection makes it noiseless. Pull one pin to change from jack to windmill. Remove chain from engine sprocket and use engine for grinding, sawing, etc.

Farm engines 2½, 5, 7, 10 and 12 h. p. Feed grinders and crushers of the best kind. 54 kinds and sizes of wind mills, steel tanks, trucks, pump jacks, etc. Catalogues and prices to dealers on application.

Perkins Wind Mill & Engine Co.

6 Main St.   Mishawaka, Ind.

The Perkins Wind Mill and Engine Co. built vertical and horizontal stationary engines at 6 Main Street, in Mishawaka, Indiana. Their Farm Engines were built in 2 1/2, 5, 7, 10 and 12-horsepower sizes. The engine operates a pump jacket which is chain driven from a crankshaft gear.

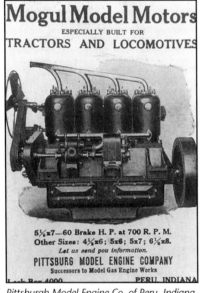

Mogul Model Motors

ESPECIALLY BUILT FOR

TRACTORS AND LOCOMOTIVES

5½x7—60 Brake H. P. at 700 R. P. M.
Other Sizes: 4½x6 ; 5x6 ; 5x7 ; 6½x8.
Let us send you information.

PITTSBURG MODEL ENGINE COMPANY

Successors to Model Gas Engine Works

PERU, INDIANA

Pittsburgh Model Engine Co. of Peru, Indiana built locomotive and tractor engines. This engine was designed with four cylinders and produced sixty horsepower at 700 rpm. High-tension magneto ignition fired the engine's fuel charges.

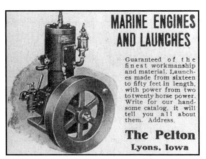

MARINE ENGINES AND LAUNCHES

Guaranteed of the finest workmanship and material. Launches made from sixteen to fifty feet in length, with power from two to twenty horse power. Write for our handsome catalog, it will tell you all about them. Address.

The Pelton

Lyons, Iowa

T.G. Pelton and Sons was located in Lyons, Iowa. These two-cycle marine engines were built in sizes from 2 to 20 horsepower. They used high-tension, spark plug ignition.

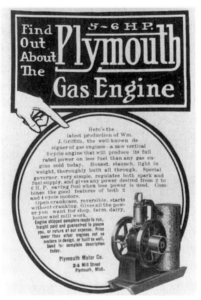

Find Out About The **Plymouth** 5-6 H.P. **Gas Engine**

Plymouth Motor Co. was built at 24 Mill Street in Plymouth, Michigan. The Plymouth, 2-six-horsepower, two-cycle vertical engine is illustrated here. These engines used high-tension, jump spark ignition and tank cooling. They were designed with an open crankcase.

Right
Essex, Iowa was the home of the Porter air-cooled engine. W. F. Porter built these engines in three sizes, 1 1/2, 2 1/2 and five-horsepower. A flywheel-driven fan aided air cooling. This gasoline engine is pictured connected to a pump jacket that cycles a water pump.

This is a restored Perkins pushrod-style engine. The Perkins Windmill and Engine Co. advertised this new line of engines during 1912. High-tension spark plug ignition and hopper cooling were standard features for this gasoline engine. The original muffler is quite unique.

Frost Proof—Sun Proof—Rain Proof
2—Phillips "Ready to Run"—H. P.

Simple—Reliable—Long-Lived

PHILLIPS GASOLINE ENGINE COMPANY,   41 N. Clinton Street, Chicago, Ill.

The Phillips Gasoline Engine Co. was located in Chicago, Illinois. The Ready to Run two-horsepower engine is air-cooled. This gasoline engine outfit was supplied from the factory with a skid, battery box, batteries and a coil.

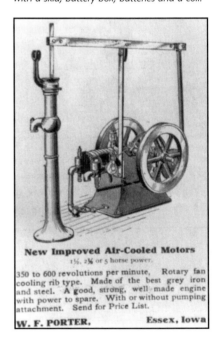

New Improved Air-Cooled Motors

1½, 2½ or 5 horse power.

350 to 600 revolutions per minute, Rotary fan cooling rib type. Made of the best grey iron and steel. A good, strong, well-made engine with power to spare. With or without pumping attachment. Send for Price List.

W. F. PORTER.   Essex, Iowa

George D. Pohl Manufacturing Co. manufactured their Advance engines in Vernon, New York. Advance side shaft engines were equipped with low-tension hammer-break ignition. A vertical flyball governed engine speed on these tank-cooled natural gas or gasoline engines.

In 1902, the Power Manufacturing Co. was located in Lima, Ohio. In 1916, the company was advertising their Primm crude oil engines. Their huge engines were built in sizes up to 150 horsepower.

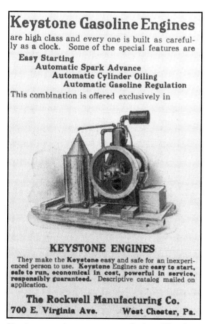

Keystone engines were manufactured by the Rockwell Manufacturing Co. of West Chester, Pennsylvania. The Keystone engine was built in sizes from 2 to 12-horsepower. Automatic spark advance, cylinder oiling, and fuel regulation were this engine's special features. High-tension, spark plug ignition and external tank cooling were standard equipment for these gasoline engines.

This portable Quincy hit-and-miss-governed engine is mounted on an iron-framed cart. Notice that two pedestals secure this engine to the cart. One is seen under the engine's cylinder, and the other is below the crankcase. A low-tension Webster oscillating magneto and a hammer-break igniter supply ignition for this gasoline engine.

Pictured here is a Rockford stationary engine. It was manufactured by the Rockford Engine Works. These side-shaft engines were built in sizes from 4 to 30 horsepower. Low-tension make-and-break ignition and a vertical flyball governing system were standard features.

Pictured here is a restored Quincy engine. It was manufactured by the Quincy Engine Co. located in Quincy, Pennsylvania. This style engine was also built in a smaller 1 1/2-horsepower model. Hit-and-miss governing, high-tension spark plug ignition and hopper cooling are standard features on this gasoline engine.

This very popular two-cycle engine was manufactured in Oil City, Pennsylvania by the Joseph Reed Gas Engine Co. This restored Reed two-cylinder engines uses hot tube ignition and external tank cooling.

This engine was built by the Reeves Pulley Co. in Columbus, Indiana. The Reeves built the one- and two-horsepower engines with hit-and-miss governing. Low-tension, hammer-break ignition was used on this hopper-cooled gasoline engine.

Engine Manufacturer	Factory Location	Trade Name	Dates
Pittsburgh Model Eng. Co.	Pittsburgh, PA	Model	na
Pittsburgh Model Eng. Co.	Pittsburgh, PA	Mogul	na
Pittsburgh Model Eng. Co.	Pittsburgh, PA	Pittsburgh	na
Pittsburgh Pump Co.	Pittsburgh, PA	Pittsburgh Pump	na
Pivert Mtr. Co.	Pittsburgh, PA	Pivert-Marine	na
Place Gas Eng. Co.	New York, NY	na	1884
Plunket, J. E.	Chicago, IL	Junior	na
Plunket, J. E.	Chicago, IL	Plunket	1906
Plunket, J. E.	Chicago, IL	Plunket Jr.	na
Plymouth Metal Products	Plymouth, WI	Plymouth	1917
Plymouth Mtr. Co.	Plymouth, MI	Plymouth-Jobbed	1911
Plymouth Mtr. Co.	Clinton, WI	Steiner	na
Pohl Mfg. Co.	Vernon, NY	Advanced	1904
Pohl Mfg. Co.	Vernon, NY	Farmers Favorite	na
Pohl Mfg. Co.	Vernon, NY	Pohl	1905
Polson Imp. Co.	Seattle, WA	Polson-Jobbed	na
Pontiac Tractor Co.	Pontiac, MI	Pontiac	na
Pormo-Portable Mfg. Co.	Chicago, IL	Pormo	na
Port Chester Mach. Works	Port Chester, NY	Port Chester	1907
Port Huron Eng. & Thresher Co.	Port Huron, MI	Port Huron	1901–1904
Portable Power Mfg. Co.	Chicago, IL	Pormo	na
Portage Boat & Eng. Co.	Portage, WI	na	na
Porter, W.F.	Essex, IA	Porter	1907
Portland Agricultural Works	Portland, PA	Portland	na
Portsmouth Eng. Co.	Portsmouth, OH	New Era	na
Potter Co.	Oelwein, IA	Potter	1910
Potts Machry. Co.	Columbus, OH	na	na
Powell Eng. Corp.	New York, NY	Powell	1910
Power & Mining Machry. Co.	New York, NY	American Crossley	na
Power Equipment Co.	Minneapolis, MN	Peco-Jobbed	na
Power Mfg. Co.	Lima, OH	Power	1915
Power Mfg. Co.	Marion, OH	Primm	na
Power Mfg. Co.	Lima, OH	Primm	na
Power Products Corp.	Grafton, WI	Power Products	na
Practical Gas Eng. & Mach. Works	Chicago, IL	Practical	1909
Premier Eng. Works	Seattle, WA	Premier	1917
Presler-Crawley Mfg. Co.	Cincinnati, OH	na	na
Presque Isle Gas Eng. Co.	Erie, PA	na	1899
Priestman & Co.	Philadelphia, PA	Priestman	1888
Priestman Eng. Co.	Philadelphia, PA	Priestman	na
Primm Eng. Co.	Marion, OH	Primm	na
Primm Oil Eng. Co.	Van Buren, IN	Primm Oil	na
Producers Supply Co.	Franklin, PA	Producers	1916
Progressive Mfg. Co.	Torrington, CT	Eagle	1906
Propulsion Eng. Corp.	Kansas City, MO	Pak	na
Propulsion Eng. Corp.	Kansas City, MO	Power Pak	na
Prouty Mtr. Co.	Chicago, IL	Prouty	na
Providence Engnrg. Works	Providence, RI	na	1907
Puget Sound Iron & Eng. Works	Tacoma, WA	na	na
Pugh & Tinsman Co.	Bruin, PA	Pugh & Tinsman	na
Pungs-Finch Auto & Gas Eng. Co.	Detroit, MI	Pungs-Finch	na
Quast Gas & Gasoline Eng. Co.	Bucyrus, OH	Quast	na
Quick Mfg. Co.	Patterson, NJ	Quick	na
Quincy Eng. Co.	Quincy, PA	Quincy	1912
Quincy Eng. Works	Quincy, IL	Quincy	na
Quincy Eng. Works	Quincy, IL	Williams	na
R. E. D. Eng. Co.	New York, NY	R.E.D.	1921
Racine Boat Mfg. Co.	Muskegon, MI	Racine-Marine	na
Racine Gas Eng. Co.	Racine, WI	Racine	1897
Racine Hardware Co.	Racine, WI	Racine-Jobbed	na
Racine-Sattley Co.	Springfield, IL	Hummer	na
Racine-Sattley Co.	Springfield, IL	Racine-Sattley	na
Racine-Sattley Co.	Jackson, MI	Racine-Sattley	na
Racine-Sattley Co.	Springfield, IL	Sattley	na

Engine Manufacturer	Factory Location	Trade Name	Dates
Radiant Mfg. Co.	Sandusky, OH	Radiant	na
Radiant Mfg. Co.	Sandusky, OH	Radiant Light Plant	na
Ralston Gas Eng. & Mfg. Co.	Newark, NJ	Ralston	1883
Rambrentner, Otto	Sheboygan Falls, WI	New Perfection	na
Randell, N. B.	Hancock, NY	na	na
Raser Gas Eng. Works	Ashtabula, OH	Raser	na
Raspberry Island Boat & Eng. Co.	St. Paul, MN	Fish	na
Raspberry Island Boat & Eng. Co.	St. Paul, MN	Raspberry	na
Rathbun Lacy Co.	Toledo, OH	na	na
Rathbun-Jones Engnrg. Co.	Toledo, OH	Price	1910
Rathbun-Jones Engnrg. Co.	Toledo, OH	Rathbun	1910
Rawleigh, W. T.	Freeport, IL	Rawleigh	1916
Rawleigh Mfg. Co.	Freeport, IL	Rawleigh-Jobbed	na
Rawleigh-Morton Gas Eng. Co.	Fresno, CA	Rawleigh-Morton	na
Rawleigh-Morton Gas Eng. Co.	Fresno, CA	Morton	na
Rawleigh-Schryer Co.	Freeport, IL	Excelsior	na
Rawleigh-Schryer Co.	Freeport, IL	Puritan	na
Rawleigh-Schryer Co.	Freeport, IL	Rawleigh	1912–1916
Rawleigh-Schryer Co.	Freeport, IL	Rawleigh-Schryer	na
Ray Mtr. Co.	Detroit, MI	Ray	na
Raymond Engnrg. Co.	Boston, MA	R-V	na
Raymond Engnrg. Co.	Boston, MA	Raymond	na
Raymond Mfg. Co.	San Francisco, CA	Raymond	na
Reading Iron Works	Reading, PA	Ilmer	1904
Reading Oil & Gas Eng. Co.	Reading, PA	Reading Oil	na
Reciprocity Mtr. Co.	New York, NY	Pearson	1911
Red Wing Boat Mfg. Co.	Red Wing, MN	Red Wing	na
Red Wing Boat Mfg. Co.	Red Wing, MN	Red Wing-Marine	1907
Reeves Bros.	Columbus, OH	Reeves	na
Reeves Engnrg. Co.	Mt. Vernon, OH	Reeves	na
Reeves Gas Eng. Co.	Columbus, OH	Reeves	1901–1906
Reeves Pulley Co.	Columbus, IN	Reeves	na
Regal Gasoline Eng. Co.	Coldwater, MI	Regal-Marine	na
Regal Gasoline Eng. Co.	Coldwater, MI	Regallite	na
Regan Vapor Eng. Co.	San Francisco, CA	Electro Vapor	na
Regan Vapor Eng. Co.	San Francisco, CA	Regan	1884
Reid Gas Eng. Co.	Oil City, PA	Reid	1898
Reid Gasoline Eng. Co.	Auburn, IN	Lycoming	na
Reilly Mfg. Co.	Louisville, KY	na	na
Reirson Machry. Co.	Portland, OR	King Of The Woods	na
Reirson Machry. Co.	Portland, OR	Waterloo Boy	na
Reiske Bros.	Dayton, OH	Reiske	1900
Reliable Eng. Co.	Portsmouth, OH	Reliable	na
Reliable Mach. Co.	Anderson, IN	Reliable	na
Reliable Mtr. Works	Toledo, OH	Reliable	na
Reliable Mtr. Works	Toledo, OH	Toledo	na
Reliable Tractor & Eng. Co.	Portsmouth, OH	Heer	1915–1933
Reliable Tractor & Eng. Co.	Portsmouth, OH	Reliable	na
Reliance Engnrg. Co.	Lansing, MI	Olds	na
Reliance Engnrg. Co.	Lansing, MI	Reliance	na
Reliance Engnrg. Co.	Lansing, MI	Seager	na
Reliance Gas & Oil Eng. Co.	Milwaukee, WI	Reliance	na
Reliance Gas Eng. Co.	Detroit, MI	na	na
Reliance Iron & Eng. Co.	Racine, WI	Reliance	1908
Reliance Iron & Eng. Co.	Racine, WI	Sta-Rite	1904–1910
Reliance Mfg. Co.	Providence, RI	Reliance	1907
Reliance Mfg. Co.	New York, NY	na	na
Remington Oil Eng. Co.	Stanford, CT	Crude Oil	na
Remington Oil Eng. Co.	New York, NY	Crude Oil	na
Remington Oil Eng. Co.	Stanford, CT	Remington	na
Remington Oil Eng. Co.	New York, NY	Remington	na
Remington Oil Eng. Co.	Stanford, CT	Remington-Marine	na
Remington Oil Eng. Co.	New York, NY	Remington-Marine	na
Remy Bros. Co.	Anderson, IN	na	1914

The Rockford Engine Works was located in Rockford, Illinois. This Rockford three-horsepower side-shaft engine was designed with low-tension make-and-break ignition. The vertical flyball governor is run off of the engine's side shaft. The engine base, cylinder, and water hopper are cast in one piece.

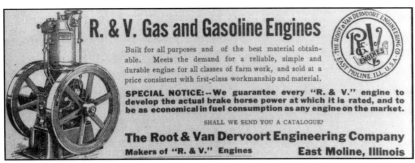
Root and Van Dervoort Engineering Co. built their R and V engines in East Moline, Illinois. The R and V vertical engine were manufactured in sizes from 1 1/2 to 6 horsepower. Low-tension, hammer-break ignition; hit-and-miss governing; and screen tank cooling were standard features.

The 1909 R and V six-horsepower engine was built by Root and Van Dervoort Engineering Co. in East Moline, Illinois. These horizontal stationary engines used low-tension, hammer-break ignition. A vertical flyball governor the external tank-cooled engine's speed.

The Rumely Products Co. was located in LaPorte, Indiana. Shown here is the Rumley Olds 1 1/2-horsepower engine. This hopper-cooled four-cycle gasoline engine uses hit-and-miss governing and high-tension spark plug ignition. A wooden battery box can be seen mounted to the engine crankshaft and connecting rod guard between the flywheels.

The E.L. Russell Co. manufactured the Silent Valve engine line in Indianapolis, Indiana. This electric lighting plant was built in 3/4-, 1 1/2-, and 5-kilowatt models. High-tension spark plug ignition and a single flywheel were standard features.

Engine Manufacturer	Factory Location	Trade Name	Dates
Renfrew Sta-Rite Eng. Co.	LaCrosse, WI	Hustler	na
Renfrew Sta-Rite Eng. Co.	LaCrosse, WI	LaCrosse	na
Renfrew Sta-Rite Eng. Co.	LaCrosse, WI	LaCrosse Hustler	na
REO Mtr. Co.	Lansing, MI	REO	na
Requa Mtr. Co.	Brooklyn, NY	na	1909
Reynolds Gas Eng. Co.	Detroit, MI	Reynolds	1909
Rice Co.	Bordentown, NJ	Rice	na
Richards Iron Works	Manitowoc, WI	Manitowoc-Marine	na
Richards Iron Works	Manitowoc, WI	Richards	na
Richardson Mfg. Co.	Worchester, MA	Simplicity-Jobbed	na
Richmond & Holmes	St. Johns, MI	Richmond	na
Richmond Gasoline Eng. Co.	Richmond, VA	Little Wonder	na
Richmond Standard	Richmond, IN	Granite	na
Rider-Ericsson Engnrg. Co.	New York, NY	Reeco	na
Rider-Ericsson Engnrg. Co.	New York, NY	Reeco Ericsson	na
Rider-Ericsson Engnrg. Co.	New York, NY	Reeco Rider	na
Rider-Ericsson Engnrg. Co.	New York, NY	Rider-Ericsson	na
Riley & Wayman Co.	Dayton, OH	Riley	1904
Riotte Co.	New York, NY	Empire	na
Risdon Iron/Locomotive Works	San Francisco, CA	na	1897
River Mach. & Boiler Works	Cleveland, OH	na	na
Riverside Eng. Co.	Oil City, PA	Riverside	1909
Robbins & Myers Co.	Springfield, OH	Dynamo	na
Robbins & Myers Co.	Springfield, OH	Lalley Light	na
Robbins Heavy Duty Distillate Engs.	San Diego, CA	Robbins	na
Roberts Gas & Gasoline Eng. Co.	Pittsburgh, PA	na	1914
Roberts Mtr. Co.	Clyde, OH	Roberts	na
Roberts Mtr. Co.	Sandusky, OH	Roberts	na
Roberts-Hamilton Co.	Minneapolis, MN	Rohaco Light	na
Robertson, J. G.	St. Paul, MN	na	na
Robertson Mfg. Co.	Buffalo, NY	Hero	1903
Robertson Mfg. Co.	Buffalo, NY	Robertson	1906
Robinson & Co.	Richmond, IN	Robinson	na
Robinson-Tilton Machry. Co.	Columbus, OH	Noxol	na
Rochester Gas Eng. Co.	Rochester, NY	Acme	1906–1907
Rochester Mach. Tool Works	Rochester, NY	Acme	1898–1900
Rock Island Plow Co.	Rock Island, IL	Chanticleer	na
Rock Island Plow Co.	Rock Island, IL	Frost King	na
Rock Island Plow Co.	Rock Island, IL	Frost Proof	na
Rock Island Plow Co.	Rock Island, IL	Great Western	na
Rock Island Plow Co.	Rock Island, IL	Rock Island	na
Rockefeller Mtr. Co.	Cleveland, OH	na	1913
Rockford Eng. Works	Rockford, IL	Emerson	na
Rockford Eng. Works	Rockford, IL	Rockford	1899
Rockford Mach. Co.	Rockford, IL	Little Giant	na
Rockland Mach. Co.	Rockland, ME	Rockland	na
Rockwell Mfg. Co.	West Chester, PA	Keystone	na
Rockwell Mfg. Co.	West Chester, PA	Rockwell	na
Rogers Gas Eng. Works	Chicago, IL	na	na
Rogers Iron Works	Springfield, OH	Bayley	na
Rollason Gas Eng. Co.	New York, NY	Rollason-Jobbed	na
Rollaway Co.	Toledo, OH	Rollaway	na
Rome Gas Eng. Co.	Rome, NY	na	na
Ronning Mtr. Co.	Minneapolis, MN	Ronning	na
Root & Vandervoort	East Moline, IL	Easy Cooler	na
Root & Vandervoort	East Moline, IL	Reindeer	na
Root & Vandervoort	East Moline, IL	Root & Vandervoort	1901
Root & Vandervoort	East Moline, IL	Triumph R & V	na
Rosalia Mfg. Co.	Rosalia, WA	Rosalia	na
Rotor Corp. Of America	Dayton, OH	Flame Licker	na
Rotor Corp. Of America	Dayton, OH	Vacuum Rotor	na
Rowell Co.	Menominee Falls, WI	Rowell	1903
Royal Eng. Co.	Saginaw, MI	Monarch	na
Royal Eng. Co.	Bridgeport, CT	Royal	1904–1912

Engine Manufacturer	Factory Location	Trade Name	Dates
Royal Eng. Co.	Saginaw, MI	Royal	na
Royal Equipment Co.	Bridgeport, CT	Royal	1904–1909
Ruger Mfg. Co.	Buffalo, NY	Great Niagara	na
Ruger Mfg. Co.	Buffalo, NY	Olin	na
Ruger Mfg. Co.	Buffalo, NY	Ruger	1897
Ruggles Mach. Co.	Poultney, VT	Ruggles	na
Rumely Co., M.	Laporte, IN	Falk	na
Rumely Co., M.	Laporte, IN	Oil Turn	na
Rumely Co., M.	Laporte, IN	Olds	na
Rumely Co., M.	Laporte, IN	Rumely	1912
Rumely Co., M.	Laporte, IN	Rumely Falk	na
Rumely Co., M.	Laporte, IN	Rumley Oil Turn	na
Rumely Co., M.	Laporte, IN	Rumley Olds	na
Rumsey Mach. Co.	Friendship, NY	Rumsey	1905
Rumsey Mfg. Co.	St. Louis, MO	Rumsey-Jobbed	na
Rumsey-Williams Co.	Johnsville, NY	Rumsey	na
Rumsey-Williams Co.	Johnsville, NY	Rumsey-Williams	1907
Rural Elect. Equip. Co.	Canton, PA	na	1921
Russell Automatic Gas Eng. Co.	Rockford, IL	Russell	1911
Russell Co.	Indianapolis, IN	Russell	na
Russell Co.	Indianapolis, IN	Silent Valve	na
Russell Grader Mfg. Co.	Minneapolis, MN	Russell	1909
Russell Grader Mfg. Co.	Minneapolis, MN	Russell Grader	1909
Ruterber Mfg. Co.	Logansport, IN	Rutenber	na
S.P.C. Eng. Co.	Des Moines, IA	S.P.C.	na
Safety Shredder Co.	New Castle, IN	Lawter	1907
Safety Vapor Eng. Co.	New York, NY	Safety Vapor	na
Sageng Threshing Mach. Co.	St. Paul, MN	Sageng	na
Salem Iron Works	Salem, NC	na	na
Salisbury Mtr. Co.	Pomona, CA	Salisbury	na
Salley Elect. Lighting Co.	Detroit, MI	Salley Elect.	na
Sammons, T. A.	Dayton, OH	na	1905
Samson Iron Works	Stockton, CA	Samsco	1903
Samson Iron Works	Stockton, CA	Samson	na
San Antonia Mach. & Supply Co.	San Antonio, TX	Krueger-Atlas	na
San Antonia Mach. & Supply Co.	San Antonio, TX	Atlas	na
San Antonia Mach. & Supply Co.	San Antonio, TX	Samsco-Jobbed	na
Sanderson Cyclone Drill Co.	Orrville, OH	Sanderson	na
Sands Mfg. Co.	Wheeling, WV	na	na
Sandusky Fdry. & Mach. Co.	Sandusky, OH	Sandusky	1904
Sandwich Mfg. Co.	Sandwich, IL	Big	na
Sandwich Mfg. Co.	Sandwich, IL	Big Six	na
Sandwich Mfg. Co.	Sandwich, IL	Cub	na
Sandwich Mfg. Co.	Sandwich, IL	Hasick	1925
Sandwich Mfg. Co.	Sandwich, IL	Light Six	na
Sandwich Mfg. Co.	Sandwich, IL	New Idea	na
Sandwich Mfg. Co.	Sandwich, IL	Parmaco	na
Sandwich Mfg. Co.	Sandwich, IL	Pine Tree	na
Sandwich Mfg. Co.	Sandwich, IL	Sandwich	1915
Sandwich Mfg. Co.	Sandwich, IL	Taylor Vacuum	na
Sargent Engnrg. Co.	Chicago, IL	Sargent	na
Sargent Engnrg. Co.	Indianapolis, IN	Sargent	1907
Sarvent Marine Eng. Works	Chicago, IL	Sarvent-Marine	na
Savage & Love Co.	Rockford, IL	na	na
Savage Factories	Minneapolis, MN	Casy Jones	na
Savage Factories	Minneapolis, MN	Dan Patch	na
Savage Factories	Minneapolis, MN	Dazzle Patch	1912
Savage Factories	Minneapolis, MN	Northome	na
Sawtelle Rotary Mtr. Co.	San Francisco, CA	na	1905
Sayer & Co.	New York, NY	Standard Rider	na
Scandia Pacific Eng. Co.	Oakland, CA	na	na
Schaefer, W. E.	Ripon, WI	Schaefer	na
Schafer Mfg. Co.	Berlin, WI	Berlin	1914
Scheppele Mach. Works	Dubuque, IA	Scheppele	na

Engine Manufacturer	Factory Location	Trade Name	Dates
Schilling, Adams & Sons	San Francisco, CA	Golden Gate	na
Schleicher, Schumm & Co.	Philadelphia, PA	Otto	na
Schleicher, Schumm & Co.	Philadelphia, PA	Schleicher	1877
Schleicher-Achman Co.	Philadelphia, PA	Otto	na
Schmid & Herckfeld	Allegheny, PA	Schmid	1897
Schmidt Bros. Eng. Works	Davenport, IA	Schmidt	1907
Schmidt Bros. Eng. Works	Davenport, IA	Schmidt White Lilly	na
Schmidt Bros. Eng. Works	Davenport, IA	White Lilly	na
Schmidt Bros. Eng. Works	Davenport, IA	Chilled Cylinder	na
Schoonmaker-Brennelsson Co.	Warren, PA	na	na
Schosser Mfg. Co.	New York, NY	na	na
Schramm & Sons	West Chester, PA	Dean	na
Schramm & Sons	Philadelphia, PA	Dean	na
Schramm & Sons	West Chester, PA	Domestic	na
Schramm & Sons	Philadelphia, PA	Domestic	na
Schramm & Sons	West Chester, PA	Keystone	1910–1917
Schramm & Sons	Philadelphia, PA	Keystone	1910–1917
Schramm & Sons	West Chester, PA	Miami	na
Schramm & Sons	Philadelphia, PA	Miami	na
Schramm & Sons	West Chester, PA	Rockwell	na
Schramm & Sons	Philadelphia, PA	Rockwell	na
Schramm & Sons	West Chester, PA	Schramm	na
Schramm & Sons	Philadelphia, PA	Schramm	na
Schramm & Sons	West Chester, PA	Schramm Domestic	1891
Schramm & Sons	Philadelphia, PA	Schramm Domestic	1891
Schramm & Sons	West Chester, PA	West Chester	na
Schramm & Sons	Philadelphia, PA	West Chester	na
Schroder Gasoline Eng. Co.	Evansville, IN	Schroder	na
Schug Elect. Mfg. Co.	Detroit, MI	Schug	na
Schwad Gas Eng. Co.	Springfield, OH	Schwad	na
Scientific Research Co.	New York, NY	na	na
Sciple, H. M.	Philadelphia, PA	na	na
Scott & Ewing Co.	Bluffton, OH	Scott & Ewing	na
Scott, C. A.	Cedar Rapids, IA	Scott	1899
Scott Bros. Co.	Detroit, MI	Robson	na
Scott Bros. Co.	Detroit, MI	Scott	na
Scott Eng. & Const. Co.	New York, NY	Scott	1911
Scott Gasoline Eng. Co.	Lamonite, IA	Scott	na
Scott Gasoline Eng. Co.	Kansas City, MO	Scott	na
Scott Two-Stroke Mtr. Co.	Kansas City, MO	Scott Motor	na
Scripps Mtr. Co.	Detroit, MI	Scripps	na
Seabury Co.	New York, NY	Seabury	na
Seager Eng. Works	Lansing, MI	Olds	1905
Seager Eng. Works	Lansing, MI	Rumley Olds	1912
Seager Eng. Works	Lansing, MI	Seager	na
Sears, Roebuck & Co.	Chicago, IL	Cascade Jr.-Jobbed	na
Sears, Roebuck & Co.	Chicago, IL	Economy-Jobbed	na
Sears, Roebuck & Co.	Chicago, IL	Fulton-Jobbed	na
Sears, Roebuck & Co.	Chicago, IL	Harvard-Jobbed	na
Sears, Roebuck & Co.	Chicago, IL	Improved Model- Jobbed	na
Sears, Roebuck & Co.	Chicago, IL	Kenwood-Jobbed	na
Sears, Roebuck & Co.	Chicago, IL	Little Wonder-Jobbed	na
Sears, Roebuck & Co.	Chicago, IL	Motor-Go-Jobbed	na
Sears, Roebuck & Co.	Chicago, IL	Otto-Jobbed	na
Sears, Roebuck & Co.	Chicago, IL	Sparta-Economy-Jobbed	1909–1912
Sears, Roebuck & Co.	Chicago, IL	Thermoil-Jobbed	na
Sears, Roebuck & Co.	Chicago, IL	Universal-Jobbed	na
Sebelin Mach. & Tool Works	Davenport, IA	Rival	na
Sebelin Mach. & Tool Works	Davenport, IA	Sebelin	1913
Secord & Orr	Jackson, MI	na	na
Seitz Co.	Newark, NJ	De Gress	na
Seitz Co.	Newark, NJ	Mohler & De Gress	na
Sensation Mower Co.	Ralston, NE	Sensation	na
Sensation Mower Co.	Ralston, NE	na	na

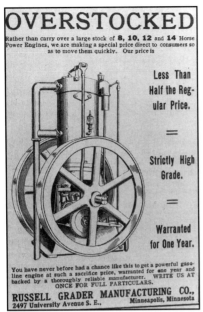

Russell Grader Manufacturing Co., 2497 University Avenue SE, in Minneapolis, Minnesota manufactured the Russell engines. The Russell vertical engine was built in 8-, 10-, 12-, and 14-horsepower. High-tension spark plug ignition and hit-and-miss governing were standard features on the tank-cooled gasoline engine.

The Sandwich Manufacturing Co. built engines in Sandwich, Illinois. This Sandwich engine is designed with low-tension, hammer-break ignition and hopper cooling. A plug oscillating Magneto can be seen attached to the igniter bracket.

The Samson Iron Works was located in Stockton, California. Samson hit-and-miss-governed engines used low-tension hammer-break ignition. These gasoline or kerosene burning engines were tank-cooled.

Sandwich, Illinois was the home of the Sandwich Manufacturing Co. Pictured here is an original Sandwich engine which was built in 1 1/4- to 10-horsepower models. This engine is equipped with a Webster oscillating low-tension ignition system and an up-draft carburetor and was hopper-cooled.

Sandusky Foundry and Machine Co. was built on the shores of Lake Erie in Sandusky, Ohio. The five-horsepower Sandusky engine had a single flywheel. Ignition was accomplished using a high-tension spark plug system. This gasoline engine was designed with an enclosed crankcase and weighed 225 pounds.

This Schmidt Chilled Cylinder engine was manufactured in sizes ranging from 4 to 7 1/2 horsepower. A high-tension spark plug ignition system was standard, with battery and buzz coil supplying the electric current. Schmidt Brothers Engine Works was located in Davenport, Iowa.

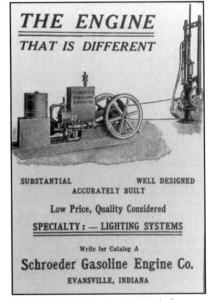

The Schroeder engine uses a side-shaft operated flyball governor to control engine speed. This hopper-cooled gasoline engine was built by the Schroeder Gasoline Engine Co. in Evansville, Indiana. Electric light and pumping outfits were this company's specialty.

Engine Manufacturer	Factory Location	Trade Name	Dates
Shadegg Eng. Co.	Minneapolis, MN	Brown	na
Shaefer, W. E.	Ripon, WI	na	na
Shaefer Mfg. Co.	Berlin, WI	Berlin	1914
Shamburg & Allen Co.	Coraopolis, PA	Shamburg	na
Sharp Mfg. Co.	Albert Lea, MN	Sharp	1902
Sharples Separator Co.	West Chester, PA	Sharples	1916
Sharples Separator Co.	West Chester, PA	Sharples Olds	na
Sharples Separator Co.	West Chester, PA	Triumph	na
Shaw Mfg. Co.	Galesburg, KS	Shaw	na
Shawd Gas Eng. Co.	Springfield, OH	Bull Dog	na
Sheboygan Mach. Co.	Sheboygan, WI	Sheboygan	1912
Sheffer Gales Co.	Emlenton, PA	Sheffer	na
Sheffield Car Co.	Three Rivers, MI	Sheffield	na
Sheffield Gas Power Co.	Kansas City, MO	Sheffield	1898
Sheffield Gas Power Co.	Kansas City, MO	Weber	na
Sheffield Tool & Supply Co.	Sheffield, PA	Barnes	na
Sheffield Tool & Supply Co.	Sheffield, PA	Main Waring	na
Sheffield Tool & Supply Co.	Sheffield, PA	Sheffield	na
Shelby Eng.	Shelbyville, IN	Shelby	na
Shelbyville Fdry. & Mach. Works	Shelbyville, IN	Shelby	1910
Sheldon Concrete Mixer Mfg. Co.	Nahauka, NE	Sheldon	na
Sheldon Eng. & Sales Co.	Waterloo, IA	Sheldon	1915
Sheldon Eng. & Sales Co.	Waterloo, IA	Sheldon Light Plant	na
Shepard, C. G.	Buffalo, NY	na	na
Sheppard Co.	Hanover, PA	Sheppard	na
Sherman & Smith Mfg. Co.	Independence, IA	Sherman & Smith Jr.	na
Sherman & Smith Mfg. Co.	Independence, IA	Sherman & Smith	1912
Sherman & Smith Mfg. Co.	Stanley, IA	Sherman & Smith	1908
Shipman Eng. Co.	Boston, MA	na	1887
Shone Co.	Chicago, IL	Shone	1897
Shorthill Co.	Marshalltown, IA	Marshall	na
Shuger's Gasoline Eng. Works	Coldwater, MI	na	na
Sibley-Houfley Mach. Co.	Detroit, MI	Peerless-Marine	1908
Sibley-Houfley Mach. Co.	Detroit, MI	Sibley-Houfley	1908
Sieverkropp Eng. Co.	Racine, WI	Sieverkropp	1908
Silberzahn Gas Eng. Works	Marinette, WI	Silberzahn	1907
Simple Gas Eng. Co.	Menasha, WI	Simple	1917
Simple Oil Eng. Co.	Los Angeles, CA	Simple	na
Simple Oil Eng. Co.	Denver, CO	Simple	1911
Simplex Gas Eng. Co.	Menasha, WI	Simplex	1917
Simplex Utilities Corp.	New York, NY	Simplex System	na
Simpson Mfg. Co.	Homer, MI	Simpson	na
Sinclair Eng. Corp.	Indianapolis, IN	Sinclair	1917
Sinker-Davis & Co.	Indianapolis, IN	Sinker-Davis	1878
Sinning Mach. Works	St. Louis, MO	Sinning	1908
Sintz Eng. Mfg. Co.	Marshall, MI	Sintz	1909
Sintz Gas Eng. Co.	Grand Rapids, MI	Sintz	1892
Sintz Mfg. Co.	Grand Rapids, MI	Leader	1905
Sintz Mfg. Co.	Marshall, MI	Sintz	na
Sintz Mfg. Co., Clark	Grand Rapids, MI	Sintz	1891
Sintz Mfg. Co. Charles	Springfield, OH	Sintz	na
Sintz-Wallin Co.	Grand Rapids, MI	Leader	na
Sintz-Wallin Co.	Grand Rapids, MI	Little Giant	na
Sioux City Cement Mach. Co.	Sioux City, IA	na	1913
Sioux City Engnrg. & Mach. Co.	Sioux City, IA	Stickney Hunter	na
Sipp Elect. & Mach. Co.	Patterson, NJ	Sipp	na
Sipp Elect. & Mach. Co.	Patterson, NJ	Weed	1905
Sipp Mach. Works	Patterson, NJ	Sipp	na
Skagit Steel & Iron Works	Sedro Wooley, WA	Mac	na
Skillin & Richards Mfg. Co.	Chicago, IL	Burrell	na
Skinner Automatic Device Co.	Sacramento, CA	na	1925
Slater Eng. Co.	Warren, PA	Slater	na
Sloane Mtr. Co.	Chicago, IL	Sloane-Marine	1910
Smalley Bros. Co.	Bay City, MI	Smalley	1904

In Bluffton, Ohio, the Scott and Ewing and Co. manufactured gasoline engines. Pictured here is their Scott and Ewing water-cooled engine. The engine is equipped with low-tension hammer-break ignition. The engine is designed with an open crankcase.

The Seager Engine Works in Lansing, Michigan bought the rights to manufacture Olds engines. Pictured here is an original 1 1/2-horsepower, hit-and-miss-governed gasoline engine. The engine is equipped with high-tension spark plug ignition and is hopper-cooled. A hand crank can be seen housed in a flywheel recess. The wooden battery box in mounted on the engine's crank guard. This engine sold for about $2,500 in 1995.

Right
The 1908 Sinning four- and six-horsepower engines were manufactured by the Sinning Machine Works of St. Louis, Missouri. High-tension spark plug ignition and tank cooling are features found on Sinning gasoline engines.

This Seager Engine Works Olds engine is equipped with hit-and-miss governing, high-tension spark plug ignition, and hopper cooling. This is probably an eight-horsepower engine. The circuit breaker can be seen attached to the side of the cylinder casting.

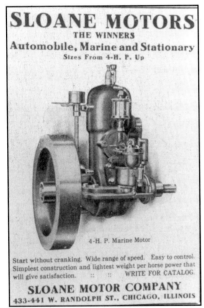

The Sloane Motor Co. manufactured the Sloane marine engine. The company was located in Chicago, Illinois. This four-horsepower, two-cycle marine engine uses high-tension spark plug ignition.

The Sherman and Smith Manufacturing Co. of Stanley, Iowa manufactured engines in sizes from 1 1/4 to 15 horsepower. This 1908 engine was equipped with low-tension hammer-break ignition and used dry-cell batteries and a coil. The gravity feed fuel tank is mounted in front of the engine's water hopper. The battery box is mounted on an original factory cart.

This external tank-cooled gasoline engine was built in Stanley, Iowa by the Sherman and Smith Manufacturing Co. The fuel tank is mounted to a the stand on the engine's original skid. The battery and coil are protected underneath the fuel tank.

The Siberzahn Gas Engine Works was located in Marinette, Wisconsin. This Siberzahn engine was designed with high-tension spark plug ignition. Dry-cell batteries and buzz coil supplied the electrical current for ignition on this air-cooled gasoline engine. The company advertised them for use with cream separators, pumps, churns, washing machines, and ice cream freezers.

This restored Spotless side-shaft engine was manufactured by the Spotless Engine Co. in Richmond, Virginia. This small side-shaft engine uses low-tension hammer-break ignition and hopper cooling. The crankshaft spiral gear can been seen inside the flywheel. This gasoline engine's side shaft is rotated by the crankshaft spiral gear.

The Springfield Gas Engine Co. was located in Springfield, Ohio. This restored 1900 Springfield engine is equipped with hot tube ignition. The engine is cooled with an external tank.

Above and left
These pictures show a restored Springfield cross-shaft engine. The Springfield Gas Engine Co. was located in Springfield, Ohio. The Springfield engine is equipped with a cross-shaft which operates the hammer-break igniter and intake and exhaust valves. This engine is tank-cooled and runs on gasoline. Springfield cross-shaft engines are very rare.

The St. Mary's Machine Co. engines were manufactured in sizes from 2 1/2 to 100 horsepower. Engines could be ordered equipped to burn natural gas, producers gas, gasoline, distillate, or oil.

Sta-Rite Engine Co. was located in LaCrosse, Wisconsin. The Sta-Rite engine was built in sizes from 1 1/2 to 10 horsepower. It is designed with low-tension hammer-break ignition and hopper cooling. This restored Sta-Rite gasoline engine is hit-and-miss-governed.

The Standard engines were built by the Standard Gas Engine Co. in Milwaukee, Wisconsin. Standard engines were built in a 1 1/2- and 2 1/2-horsepower models. High-tension spark plug ignition and hopper cooling are featured on these gasoline engines.

Engine Manufacturer	Factory Location	Trade Name	Dates
Smalley Mfg. Co.	Manitowoc, WI	Smalley	na
Smelser Eng. Co.	Frankton, IN	na	1903
Smisor Bros.	Webster City, IA	na	1899
Smith Co., Geo.	St. Louis, MO	Sulton	1914
Smith & Baldridge Mach. Co.	Detroit, MI	S & B	na
Smith & Son Mfg. Co.	Kansas City, MO	Smith	na
Smith & Sons Mfg. Co.	Kansas City, MO	Royal	na
Smith, G. W.	Milford, CT	na	1903
Smith Cement Mixer Co., T. L.	Milwaukee, WI	Smith-Jobbed	na
Smith Co., John	Chicago, IL	Smith	na
Smith Longmaid Co.	Portland, ME	Smith Longmaid	na
Smith Mfg. Co.	Chicago, IL	Chicago	na
Smith Mfg. Co.	Chicago, IL	Frost King	na
Smith Mfg. Co.	Chicago, IL	Great Western	1909
Smith Mfg. Co.	Chicago, IL	Rock Island	na
Smith-Courtney & Co.	Richmond, VA	Smith-Courtney	na
Smydor Pump & Well Co.	Richmond, VA	na	na
Smyth-Despard Co.	Utica, NY	Kracker Jack	na
Smythe Merchandising Co.	Chicago, IL	Faultless-Jobbed	na
Smythe Merchandising Co.	Chicago, IL	Little Marvel-Jobbed	na
Smythe Merchandising Co.	Chicago, IL	Smythe-Jobbed	na
Snow Mfg. Co.	Batavia, IL	Snow	na
Snow Steam Pump Works	Buffalo, NY	Snow	na
Sombart Gas Eng. Co.	New York, NY	Sombart	na
South Penn Oil Co.	Clarksburg, WV	South Penn	na
Southern Eng. & Boiler Works	Jackson, TN	Southern	na
Southern Gasoline Eng. Co.	Spartanburg, SC	na	1911
Southern Mtr. Works	Nashville, TN	Marathon	na
Southwork Fdry. & Mach. Co.	Philadelphia, PA	Harris Valveless	na
Spade Eng. Co.	Vicksburg, MI	na	na
Sparks Mach. Co.	Alton, IL	na	1904
Sparta Iron Works	Sparta, WI	Sparta	na
Spaulding Gas Eng. Works	St. Joseph, MI	Spaulding	1905
Spayd Bros.	Van Wert, OH	Spayd	1915
Spayde Eng. Co.	Vicksburg, MI	Spayde	na
Spear Gas Eng. Co.	Northfield, MN	Spear	na
Spears & Riddle	Wheeling, WV	na	na
Speed Change Pulley Co.	Indianapolis, IN	Degamable	na
Speedway Boat Mtr. Co.	Freeport, IL	Speedway-Marine	na
Spence, H. M.	Parkersburg, WV	Spence	na
Sperry Engnrg. Co.	Cleveland, OH	Sperry	na
Spotless Co.	Richmond, VA	Blue Ribbon	na
Spotless Co.	Richmond, VA	Spotless	na
Springfield Gas Eng. Co.	Springfield, OH	Springfield	1905
Sorg, W. A.	Minneapolis, MN	na	na
St. Clair Mtr. Co.	Detroit, MI	Baird	na
St. Joseph Mtr. Co.	St. Joseph, MI	Miss Simplicity	na
St. Joseph Mtr. Co.	St. Joseph, MI	St. Joseph	na
St. Louis Gasoline Mtr. Co.	St. Louis, MO	St. Louis	na
St. Marys Mach. Co.	St. Mary's, OH	Duplex	1903–1915
St. Marys Mach. Co.	St. Mary's, OH	Heavy Oil	na
St. Marys Mach. Co.	St. Mary's, OH	Rumsey	na
St. Marys Mach. Co.	St. Mary's, OH	St. Marys	na
St. Marys Mach. Co.	St. Mary's, OH	Super Diesel	na
St. Marys Oil Eng. Co.	St. Charles, MO	Fairbanks	na
St. Marys Oil Eng. Co.	St. Charles, MO	Heavy Oil	na
St. Marys Oil Eng. Co.	St. Charles, MO	St. Marys Oil	na
St. Marys Oil Eng. Co.	St. Charles, MO	Standard	1916
St. Marys Oil Eng. Co.	St. Charles, MO	Super Diesel H.O.	na
Sta-Rite Eng. Co.	LaCrosse, WI	LaCrosse	na
Sta-Rite Eng. Co.	LaCrosse, WI	Renfrew	na
Sta-Rite Eng. Co.	LaCrosse, WI	Sta-Rite	1911–1917
Stamford Mtr. Co.	Stamford, CT	na	na
Standard Auto Gas Eng. Co.	Youngstown, OH	na	na

Engine Manufacturer	Factory Location	Trade Name	Dates
Standard Automatic Gas Eng. Co.	Oil City, PA	Raymond	na
Standard Eng. Co.	Schiesinger, WI	Standard	1916
Standard Gas Eng. Co.	Oakland, CA	Frisco Standard	1923
Standard Gas Eng. Co.	San Francisco, CA	Frisco Standard	na
Standard Gas Eng. Co.	Schleislingerville, WI	Slinger	na
Standard Gas Eng. Co.	San Francisco, CA	Standard	1909
Standard Gas Eng. Co.	Newark, NJ	Standard	na
Standard Gas Eng. Co.	Milwaukee, WI	Standard	na
Standard Iron Works	Chicago, IL	Standard	na
Standard Machry. Co.	Schieisingerville, WI	Slinger	1916
Standard Mtr. Const. Co.	Jersey City, NJ	Standard	1907
Standard Pattern & Mfg. Co.	Richmond, IN	Richmond Standard	na
Standard Pattern & Mfg. Co.	Richmond, IN	Standard	1910
Standard Pump & Eng. Co.	Cleveland, OH	Standard	na
Standard Scale & Supply Co.	Pittsburgh, PA	S.S.S.-Jobbed	na
Standard Scale & Supply Co.	Pittsburgh, PA	Standard Scale-Jobbed	na
Standard Scale & Supply Co.	Pittsburgh, PA	Standard-Jobbed	na
Standard Separator Co.	Milwaukee, WI	Automatic-Jobbed	na
Standard Separator Co.	Milwaukee, WI	Standard Farm -Jobbed	na
Standard Separator Co.	Milwaukee, WI	Standard-Jobbed	na
Standish, S.	Gridley, CA	Standish	1887
Stang Eng. Co.	Harvey, IL	Stang	na
Stanley Co.	Salem, MA	Stanley	na
Star Drilling Mach. Co.	Akron, OH	Star	na
Star Fdry. & Mach. Co.	Oshkosh, WI	Star	1907
Star Gas Eng. Co.	New York, NY	Star	1897
Star Mfg. Co.	Wabash, IN	Star	na
Star Mfg. Co.	New Lexington, OH	Star	1909
Staub, A. W.	Philadelphia, PA	Quaker City	na
Std. Engnrg. & Mfg. Co.	Detroit, MI	na	1908
Std. Mfg. Co.	Canton, MI	na	1898
Stearns Automobile Co.	Syracuse, NY	na	na
Stearns Co.	New York, NY	Stearns	1909
Stearns Eng. Co.	Chicago, IL	Stearns	na
Stearns Gas Eng. Works	Los Angeles, CA	Stearns	1907
Stearns Mfg. Co.	Adrian, MI	Stearns Light Plant	na
Stearns Mtr. Mfg. Co.	Ludington, MI	Stearns Deluxe Light Plight	na
Stearns Mtr. Mfg. Co.	Ludington, MI	Stearns Light Plant	na
Stearns Mtr. Mfg. Co.	Ludington, MI	Stearns Simplex Light Plight	na
Steavens & Co.	New York, NY	Roberts	na
Steel King Mfg. Co.	Spokane, WA	na	1910
Steelton Machry. Co.	Kansas City, MO	Steelton	1910
Steelton Machry. Co.	Kansas City, MO	Teddy	na
Steffey Mfg. Co.	Philadelphia, PA	na	na
Stehling Co., C. H.	Milwaukee, WI	Sieverkropp	1926
Steiner & Co.	Dayton, OH	Steiner	1902–1930
Steiner Mfg. Co.	Chilton, WI	Gasolene/Kerosene	1914
Steiner Mfg. Co.	Chilton, WI	Steiner	1914
Sterling Eng. Co.	Buffalo, NY	Sterling	na
Sterling Eng. Co.	Buffalo, NY	Viking	na
Sterling Iron Works	Stockton, CA	Sterling	na
Sterling Mach. & Stamping Co.	Vermillion, OH	Little Samson	na
Sterling Mach. & Stamping Co.	Vermillion, OH	Sterling	na
Sterling Mfg. Co.	Sterling, IL	Sterling	na
Sterling Marine Eng. Co.	Detroit, MI	Little Giant	na
Sterling Marine Eng. Co.	Detroit, MI	Little Giant-Marine	na
Sterling Marine Eng. Co.	Detroit, MI	Major	na
Sterling Marine Eng. Co.	Detroit, MI	Strelinger	na
Sterling Oil Eng. Co.	Pittsburgh, PA	Sterling	1910
Sterlinger, Chas. A.	Detroit, MI	Sterlinger	1907
Sterne Bros. Co.	San Diego, CA	West Coast	na
Stickley-Hunter Gas Eng. Co.	New Hampton, IA	Lucky Star	1910
Stickney, Charles A.	St. Paul, MN	Fulton	na
Stickney, Charles A.	St. Paul, MN	Harvard	na

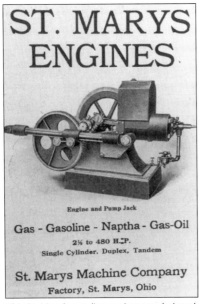

This is a Star engine built in 1894. The Star six-horsepower engine was manufactured by the Star Gas Engine Co. in New York, New York. It is equipped with a low-tension hammer-break ignition system and a removable head.

In 1908, the Star Manufacturing Co. in New Lexington, Ohio began building their Star engines. This restored Star side-shaft engine is designed with high-tension magneto spark plug ignition. It is a screen tank-cooled engine and runs on gasoline. The engine is mounted on the original factory cart.

This St. Mary's gasoline engine was designed for use with a direct-drive pump jack. The engine is equipped with an up-draft carburetor that receives fuel from a tank housed in the engine's base. A single flywheel is attached to one end of the crankshaft, and a pump drive gear is attached to the other. The engine's cooling hopper has an unusual shape.

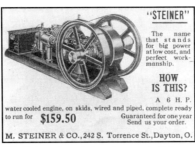

This Steiner air-cooled engine was built by Steiner and Co. of Dayton, Ohio. The Steiner engine runs on gasoline and is equipped with high-tension spark plug ignition. The engine is equipped with a flywheel-driven fan to aid cooling and is shown on an original skid with a mounted battery box. Steiner also made a six-horsepower, water-cooled gasoline engine that sold for $159.

The Steiner Manufacturing Co. was located in Chilton, Wisconsin. Steiner Long Life engines were built in sizes from 3 to 16 horsepower. A hammer-break igniter and low-tension magneto ignition fired these hopper-cooled gasoline-burning engines. The engine's valves were set in valve cages for easy removal. Skidded or portable truck-mounted units could be ordered.

The Stover Engine Works was located in Freeport, Illinois. Stover manufactured an extensive line of stationary engines during its years in business. Pictured here is a six-horsepower Stover gasoline engine. It is designed with low-tension hammer-break ignition and tank cooling. A huge subbase has been bolted to the engine's base to provide ground clearance for the flywheels. Stover built thousands of engines and they are commonly found today.

One of the most unusual stationary engine designs belongs to the Charles A. Stickney Co. in St. Paul, Minnesota. Charles A. Stickney sold many of his early engines to Sears, Roebuck and Co. for resale. A restored three-horsepower Stickney engine is shown here. Low-tension hammer-break ignition and a cast iron hopper cooling were standard design features. The engines burned gasoline and a pedestal mounted the engine's cylinder.

Engine Manufacturer	Factory Location	Trade Name	Dates
Stickney, Charles A.	St. Paul, MN	Junior	na
Stickney, Charles A.	St. Paul, MN	Kenwood	1905–1915
Stickney, Charles A.	St. Paul, MN	Lucky Star	na
Stickney, Charles A.	St. Paul, MN	New Line	na
Stickney, Charles A.	St. Paul, MN	St. Paul	na
Stickney, Charles A.	St. Paul, MN	Stickney	na
Stickney, Charles A.	St. Paul, MN	Stickney Jr.	na
Stickney, Charles A.	St. Paul, MN	Stickney-Hunter	na
Stickney, Charles A.	St. Paul, MN	Trinity	na
Stickney, Charles A.	St. Paul, MN	Universal	na
Stickney, H. R.	Portland, ME	Stickney	1887
Stickney-Hunter Gas Eng. Co.	New Hampton, IA	Lucky Star	na
Stintz-Wallin Co.	Grand Rapids, MI	Leader	na
Stinz, Claude	Grand Rapids, MI	Sintz	na
Stoddard Mfg. Co.	Rutland, VT	Stoddard	na
Stohr-Freund Co.	Muscatine, IA	Stohr-Freund	na
Storle Eng. Co.	Algoma, WI	na	1914
Stover Eng. Works	Freeport, IL	Easy	1939
Stover Mfg. & Eng. Co.	Freeport, IL	Alpha	na
Stover Mfg. & Eng. Co.	Freeport, IL	Duro	na
Stover Mfg. & Eng. Co.	Freeport, IL	Eaton	na
Stover Mfg. & Eng. Co.	Freeport, IL	Economy	1939
Stover Mfg. & Eng. Co.	Freeport, IL	Excelsior	na
Stover Mfg. & Eng. Co.	Freeport, IL	Fletcher	na
Stover Mfg. & Eng. Co.	Freeport, IL	Fuel Oil	na
Stover Mfg. & Eng. Co.	Freeport, IL	Regular	na
Stover Mfg. & Eng. Co.	Freeport, IL	Steward	na
Stover Mfg. & Eng. Co.	Freeport, IL	Sandwich	na
Stover Mfg. & Eng. Co.	Freeport, IL	Champion	na
Stover Mfg. & Eng. Co.	Freeport, IL	Crude Oil	na
Stover Mfg. & Eng. Co.	Freeport, IL	De Laval	na
Stover Mfg. & Eng. Co.	Freeport, IL	Freeport	na
Stover Mfg. & Eng. Co.	Freeport, IL	Frick	na
Stover Mfg. & Eng. Co.	Freeport, IL	Judson	na
Stover Mfg. & Eng. Co.	Freeport, IL	Junior	na
Stover Mfg. & Eng. Co.	Freeport, IL	Lister	na
Stover Mfg. & Eng. Co.	Freeport, IL	Mitchell	na
Stover Mfg. & Eng. Co.	Freeport, IL	Multi-Motor	na
Stover Mfg. & Eng. Co.	Freeport, IL	Pilter	na
Stover Mfg. & Eng. Co.	Freeport, IL	Rawleigh	na
Stover Mfg. & Eng. Co.	Freeport, IL	Refrew	na
Stover Mfg. & Eng. Co.	Freeport, IL	Sandow	na
Stover Mfg. & Eng. Co.	Freeport, IL	Stover	1890–1942
Stover Mfg. & Eng. Co.	Freeport, IL	Stover-Lanova	na
Stover Mfg. & Eng. Co.	Freeport, IL	Taylor Vacuum	na
Stover Mfg. & Eng. Co.	Freeport, IL	Victor	1897
Stowe Supply Co.	Kansas City, MO	Trojan-Jobbed	na
Strait Mfg. Co.	Kansas City, MO	Monarch	na
Strang Eng. Co.	Harvey, IL	Strang	1905
Straub Co.	Philadelphia, PA	Quaker City	na
Strauble Mach. Co.	Green Bay, WI	Strauble	na
Streit Mach. Co.	Cincinnati, OH	na	na
Strelinger Marine Eng. Co.	Detroit, MI	Ohio-Jobbed	na
Strelinger Marine Eng. Co.	Detroit, MI	Brush-Jobbed	na
Strelinger Marine Eng. Co.	Detroit, MI	Bull Dog-Jobbed	na
Strelinger Marine Eng. Co.	Detroit, MI	Little Giant	na
Strelinger Marine Eng. Co.	Detroit, MI	Little Giant-Jobbed	na
Strelinger Marine Eng. Co.	Detroit, MI	Strelinger-Marine	na
Stroben, John	Davenport, IA	Stroben	1905
Stroble, F.	Marion, OH	Stroble	na
Stroud-Humphrey Mfg. Co.	Hastings, MN	Stroud	1908
Stroud-Humphrey Mfg. Co.	Hastings, MN	Stroud Valveless Vapor	na
Strudy Jack Eng. Mfg. Co.	Warren, PA	Sturdy Jack	na
Strudy Jack Eng. Mfg. Co.	Warren, PA	Sturdy Jack Pumper	na

Engine Manufacturer	Factory Location	Trade Name	Dates
Struthers-Wells Co.	Warren , PA	Struthers	1899
Struthers-Wells Co.	Warren , PA	Warren	1893
Sturtevant Co.	Boston, MA	na	1921
Suburban Lighting Co.	Toledo, OH	na	1921
Sumner Eng. Co.	Fairmont, MN	na	1919
Sumner Eng. Co.	Seattle, WA	na	na
Sumter Telephone Mfg. Co.	Sumter, SC	Sumter	na
Sun Power Eng. Co.	Detroit, MI	Sun	na
Sun Power Eng. Co.	Detroit, MI	Sun Power	na
Sunbeam Elect. Mfg. Co.	Evansville, IN	Farm Lite	na
Sunbeam Elect. Mfg. Co.	Evansville, IN	Sunbeam Farm Lite	na
Sunnyhome Elect. Co.	Detroit, MI	Sunnyhome Light Plant	na
Super-Diesel Tractor Co.	New York, NY	na	1917
Superior Duplex Co.	Superior, WI	Bridgeport	na
Superior Duplex Co.	Superior, WI	Duplex	na
Superior Duplex Co.	Superior, WI	Superior	na
Superior Gas Eng. Co.	Springfield, OH	Superior	na
Superior Gas Eng. Co.	Springfield, OH	Superior Special	na
Superior Gas Eng. Co.	Springfield, OH	Superior Standard	na
Superior Gas Eng. Works	Marquette, MI	na	1899
Superior Mfg. Co.	Ann Arbor, MI	Ann Arbor Lighting Sys.	na
Superior Mfg. & Mill Co.	Springfield, OH	na	1911
Superior Mtr. Co.	Lansing, MI	Superior	1913
Swain Hardware Mfg. Co.	San Francisco, CA	na	na
Swan Co., J. D.	Lima, OH	Swan	na
Swan Elect. Co.	Middletown, CT	Swan	na
Swartz Elect. Co.	Indianapolis, IN	Swartz Pioneer Plant	na
Swartz Elect. Co.	Indianapolis, IN	Swartz-Light	na
Swarzenburg Mfg. Co.	Minneapolis, MN	Swartzenburg	na
Sypher Mfg. Co.	Toledo, OH	Sypher	na
Syphere Mfg. Co.	Toledo, OH	Junior-Jobbed	na
Syphere Mfg. Co.	Toledo, OH	Wolverine-Jobbed	na
Syracuse Gas Eng. Works	Syracuse, NY	Easy	na
Syracuse Gas Eng. Works	Syracuse, NY	Little Six	na
Syracuse Gas Eng. Works	Syracuse, NY	Syracuse	na
Syracuse Washing Mach. Corp.	Syracuse, NY	Easy	na
Talley Co., C. H.	Lincoln, IL	Ladies Favorite	na
Talley Co., C. H.	Lincoln, IL	Talley	1910
Talyor Eng. Co.	Oakland, CA	Taylor	na
Talyor, Hough	St. Paul, MN	na	na
Talyor, Stiles & Co.	Riegelsville, NJ	Taylor	1910
Tanners Mach. Shop	Jefferson City, MO	Tanner	na
Tate, Jone & Co.	Pittsburgh, PA	na	na
Taylor Eng. Co.	Elgin, IL	Taylor	na
Taylor Engnrg. & Mfg. Co.	Allentown, PA	Taylor	1914
Taylor Gas Eng. Co.	Mechanicsburg, PA	Taylor	na
Temple Machry. Co.	Denver, CO	na	na
Temple Mfg. Co.	Cicero, IL	Temple	1914
Temple Pump Co.	Chicago, IL	Extra Ordinary	na
Temple Pump Co.	Chicago, IL	Favorite	na
Temple Pump Co.	Chicago, IL	Master Workman	1905
Temple Pump Co.	Chicago, IL	Pacemaker	na
Temple Pump Co.	Chicago, IL	Temple	1913
Temple Pump Co.	Chicago, IL	Temple Pump Jack	1905
Temple Pump Co.	Chicago, IL	Wizard	1905
Termaat & Monahan Co.	Oshkosh, WI	R & P	na
Termaat & Monahan Co.	Oshkosh, WI	Rice & Phelan	na
Termaat & Monahan Co.	Oshkosh, WI	T & M Light Plant	na
Termaat & Monahan Co.	Oshkosh, WI	T & M-Marine	na
Termaat & Monahan Co.	Oshkosh, WI	Termaat & Monahan	1913
Termaat & Monahan Co.	Oshkosh, WI	Wiscona Pep	na
Terry Eng. Co.	Columbus, OH	Cook	na
Thames Mtr. Co.	New London, CT	na	1904
Theim & Co.	St. Paul, MN	Theim	na

Engine Manufacturer	Factory Location	Trade Name	Dates
Thermo Eng. Co.	Chicago, IL	Thermo	na
Thomas & Co.	Baltimore, MD	Thomas	na
Thomas & Smith Co.	Chicago, IL	Thomas & Smith	na
Thomas, A. B.	Bradford, PA	Thomas	na
Thomas Engnrg. Works	Portland, OR	Bear Cat	na
Thomas Engnrg. Works	Portland, OR	Thomas	na
Thomas Mtr. Co.	Buffalo, NY	Thomas	na
Thompson & Sons Mfg. Co.	Beloit, WI	Favorite	na
Thompson & Sons Mfg. Co.	Beloit, WI	Lewis	1893
Thompson & Sons Mfg. Co.	Beloit, WI	Lunt-Moss	na
Thompson & Sons Mfg. Co.	Beloit, WI	Thompson-Gearless	na
Thompson & Sons Mfg. Co.	Beloit, WI	Thompson-Lewis	na
Thompson & Sons Mfg. Co.	Beloit, WI	Thompson-Tiger	na
Thompson, A.	New York, NY	Thompson	na
Thompson Bros.	Salisbury, NC	Jack Rabbit	na
Thompson Plow & Eng. Works	Beloit, WI	Thompson	na
Thor & Kabat Gas Eng. Co.	Manitowoc, WI	Thor & Kabat	1909
Thorndike Mach. Co.	Portland, ME	Thorndike	na
Thrall Mtr. Co.	Detroit, MI	Refined Motor	na
Three Rivers Elect. Co.	Three Rivers, MI	na	na
Tillinghast, B. D.	McDonald, PA	D.C. & U.	na
Tillinghast, B. D.	McDonald, PA	Tillinghast	1899
Tips Eng. Works	Austin, TX	Tips	1923
Titusville Iron Co.	Titusville, PA	Abel	na
Titusville Iron Co.	Titusville, PA	Acme Diesel	na
Titusville Iron Co.	Titusville, PA	JC	na
Titusville Iron Co.	Titusville, PA	Olin	na
Titusville Iron Co.	Titusville, PA	Tico	na
Titusville Iron Co.	Titusville, PA	Titusville	na
Titusville Iron Co.	Titusville, PA	Titusville-Olin	na
Tod, William	Youngstown, OH	Tod	1909
Toledo Gas Eng. Works.	Toledo, OH	Toledo Special	na
Toledo Gas Eng. Works.	Toledo, OH	Toledo	1911
Topeka Signal Co.	Topeka , KS	Pierson Cushman	na
Toquet Mtr. Co.	New York, NY	Toquet-Marine	na
Torbenson Mtr. Car Co.	Bloomfield, NJ	na	na
Torrington Co.	Torrington, CT	na	1914
Tower Engnrg. Co.	Buffalo, NY	Tower	1909
Trachcan Pump Co.	Rockford, IL	Trachcan-Jobbed	na
Trask, C. A.	Jackson, MI	na	na
Trebert Gas Eng. Co.	Butler, IN	Trebert	1911
Trebert Gas Eng. Co.	Rochester, NY	Trebert	na
Trees Mfg. Co.	Greenfield, IN	Trees	1901–1904
Triplex Gas Eng. Co.	New York, NY	Triplex	1907
Triumph Gas Eng. Co.	Dayton, OH	Triumph	1907–1917
Troy Eng. & Mach. Co.	Troy, MI	Troy	na
True Blue Mtr. Co.	Detroit, MI	True Blue	1910
Trumbull Mfg. Co.	Warren, OH	Trumbull	na
Truscott Boat Mfg. Co.	St. Joseph, MI	Truscott-Marine	1904
Tryor-Fox Eng. Co.	Seattle, WA	Tryor-Fox	na
Tubular Corp.	Chicago, IL	na	1921
Tunison, M. C.	Los Angeles, CA	Success	1903
Turner & Moore Co.	Detroit, MI	Turner & Moore-Marine	na
Turner & Swarzenburg Co.	Lawrence, MA	Turner & Swarzenburg	na
Turner Bros. Eng. Works	Sycamore, IL	Uniflo	na
Turner Fricke Mfg. Co.	Pittsburgh, PA	Turner Fricke	na
Turner Mfg. Co.	Port Washington, WI	Napoleon	na
Turner Mfg. Co.	Port Washington, WI	Simplicity	1910
Turner Mfg. Co.	Port Washington, WI	Suprise	na
Turner Mfg. Co.	Port Washington, WI	Turner	na
Turner Mfg. Co.	Port Washington, WI	Turner Simplicity	na
Tuttle Mtr. Co.	Canastota, NY	Tuttle	1910
Tuttle Mtr. Co.	Canastota, NY	Tuttle-Marine	na
Twin Energy Eng. Corp.	Albany, NY	Twin Energy	na

Engine Manufacturer	Factory Location	Trade Name	Dates
Twombly Mtr. Co.	New York, NY	Twombly	1912
Tygard, J. W.	Plainfield, NJ	Tygard	1906
Tyson Eng. Co.	Philadelphia, PA	Vase	na
Ubuelhuer Bros.	Upstate, NY	Ubuelhuer	na
Uhler, F. M.	Lincoln, NE	Uhler	na
Ulysses Eng. Co.	Ulysses, NE	Ulysses	na
Underwood Gas Eng. & Mtr. Co.	Elmore, OH	Elmore	na
Underwood Gas Eng. & Mtr. Co.	Elmore, OH	Underwood	na
Underwood Mach. Co.	Minneapolis, MN	Underwood	na
Unielectric Corp.	Detroit, MI	Uni-Elect. Light Plant	na
Union Eng. Co.	Pontiac, MI	Union	na
Union Fdry. & Mach. Co.	Ottawa, KS	Giant	na
Union Fdry. & Mach. Co.	Ottawa, KS	Union	na
Union Fdry. & Mach. Co.	Ottawa, KS	Union Giant	1915
Union Fdry. & Mach. Co.	Ottawa, KS	Warner	na
Union Gas Eng. Co.	San Francisco, CA	Pacific	na
Union Gas Eng. Co.	San Francisco, CA	Regan Vapor	na
Union Gas Eng. Co.	San Francisco, CA	Union	1885
Union Iron Works	Oshkosh, WI	Doman	na
Union Iron Works	Memphis, TN	Union	na
Union Iron Works	Minneapolis, MN	Union Iron	1902
Union Mach. & Boiler Works	Cleveland, OH	Union	na
Union Steam Specialty Co.	Scranton, PA	Union	na
Union Steel Products Co.	Albion, MI	Cook	na
Union Steel Products Co.	Albion, MI	Union	na
Union Tool Co.	Torrance, CA	Ideal	na
Unit Mtr. Co.	Kansas City, MO	Unit	na
United Const. & Eng. Co.	Portland, ME	United	1900
United Eng. Co.	Lansing, MI	Associated	na
United Eng. Co.	Lansing, MI	Banner	na
United Eng. Co.	Lansing, MI	Majestic	na
United Eng. Co.	Lansing, MI	U. M. A.	na
United Eng. Co.	Lansing, MI	United	na
United Eng. Co.	Lansing, MI	United Light Plant	na
United Eng. Co.	Lansing, MI	Weil	na
United Eng. Mfg. Co.	Hanover, PA	Manley	1914
United Engnrg. Co.	San Francisco, CA	United	na
United Engnrg. Works	San Francisco, CA	United	1914
United Factories Co.	Cleveland, OH	United	na
United Factories Co.	Cleveland, OH	Unito	na
United Mach. Works	Racine, WI	United	na
United Mfrs.	New York, NY	United	na
United Mfrs. Assoc.	Jackson, MI	U. M. A.	na
United Mfrs. Assoc.	Lansing, MI	U. M. A.	na
United Mfrs. Assoc.	Jackson, MI	United	1911
United Mfrs. Assoc.	Lansing, MI	United	na
United Mfg. Co.	Detroit, MI	Little Giant	na
United Mfg. Co.	Detroit, MI	United	1907–1910
United States Const. & Eng. Co.	Boston, MA	United	1903
United States Eng. Co.	Parkersburg, WV	United	1901
United States Eng. Co.	Lansing, MI	Unito	na
United States Eng. Works	Oshkosh, WI	Doman	na
United States Eng. Works	Chicago, IL	Pacemaker	na
United States Eng. Works	Chicago, IL	U.S.	na
United States Eng. Works	Chicago, IL	Uncle Sam	na
United States Eng. Works	Chicago, IL	United States	1915
United States Gasoline Eng. Co.	Chicago, IL	Uncle Sam	na
United States Mtr. Co.	Detroit, MI	United	na
United States Switch Co.	Eau Claire, WI	Keller	na
Universal Valveless Four Cycle Mtr. Co.	Muskegon, MI	Universal Valveless	1917
Universal Battery Co.	Chicago, IL	Universal Light Plant	na
Universal Engnrg. Co.	Maywood, IL	Universal	1920
Universal Kerosene Eng. Co.	New York, NY	Universal	1905
Universal Mach. Co.	Bowling Green, OH	Toledo	na

Engine Manufacturer	Factory Location	Trade Name	Dates
Universal Mach. Co.	Bowling Green, OH	Universal-Marine	na
Universal Mfg. Co.	Oshkosh, WI	Universal	1915
Universal Milking Mach. Co.	Syracuse, NY	Taylor-Jobbed	1923
Universal Milking Mach. of MN	Albert Lea, MN	Universal-Jobbed	na
Universal Mtr. Co.	Oshkosh, WI	Universal	na
Universal Products	Sandusky, OH	Doman	na
Universal Products	Oshkosh, WI	Doman	na
Universal Products	Sandusky, OH	Universal	na
Universal Products	Oshkosh, WI	Universal	na
Universal Products	Sandusky, OH	Universal Products L/P	na
Universal Products	Oshkosh, WI	Universal Products L/P	na
Universal Products	Sandusky, OH	Upco	na
Universal Products	Oshkosh, WI	Upco	na
Universal Products	Sandusky, OH	Upco Lite	na
Universal Products	Oshkosh, WI	Upco Lite	na
US Eng. Works	Chicago, IL	U.S.	na
US Mtr. Corp.	Oshkosh, WI	U/S Elect. Plant	na
Utica Gas Eng. Works	Utica, NY	Utica	na
Utopian Eng. Co.	Chicago, IL	Upco	na
Valentine Bros. Mfg. Co.	Minneapolis, MN	Imperial	na
Valentine Gas Eng. Co.	Westfield, NJ	Valentine	1904
Valley Boat & Eng. Co.	Baldwinsville, NY	Saginaw	na
Valley Boat & Eng. Co.	Baldwinsville, NY	Valley	na
Valley Boat & Eng. Co.	Saginaw, MI	Valley-Marine	na
Van Aken Mtr. & Mach. Works	Yonkers, NY	Van Aken	1907
Van Blerck Mtr. Co.	Detroit, MI	Van Blerck-Marine	na
Van Duzen, Ben C.	Winston Place, OH	Van Duzen	na
Van Duzen, Roys & Co.	Columbus, OH	Van Duzen	1913
Van Duzen Crude Oil Eng. Co.	Marion, OH	Van Duzen	na
Van Duzen Gas & Gasoline Eng. Co.	Cincinnati, OH	Van Duzen	1891
Van Horne, Burger & Co.	Dayton, OH	Van Horne, Burger	1899
Van Nouhuys Mach. Works	Albany, NY	Van Nouhuys	1905
Vanderbloom, J. C.	Milwaukee, WI	Vanderbloom	1913
Vapor Gas Eng. Mfg. Co.	Perth Amboy, NJ	Vapor	1907
Vaughn Eng. Co.	Tippecanoe, OH	Vaughn	na
Vaughn Mtr. Works	Portland, OR	Light Weight	na
Vaughn Mtr. Works	Portland, OR	Vaughn	na
Venn-Severin Mach. Co.	Chicago, IL	Venn	na
Venn-Severin Mach. Co.	Chicago, IL	Venn-Severin Oil Eng.	na
Vermont Farm Machry. Co.	Bellows Falls, VT	United States L/P-Jobbed	na
Vermont Farm Machry. Co.	Bellows Falls, VT	United States-Jobbed	na
Victory Mtr. Co.	Niles, CA	Victory	1915
Vim Mtr. Co.	Sandusky, OH	Vim	1913
Vim Mtr. Co.	Sandusky, OH	Vim-Marine	na
Vim Tractor Co.	Schleislingerville, WI	Slinger	na
Vim Tractor Co.	Schleislingerville, WI	Standard	na
Vincennes Tractor Co.	Vincennes, IN	Vincennes	na
Vreeland Gas Eng. Co.	New York, NY	Vreeland	1897
W.H.W. Mach. & Tool Co.	Lansing, MI	Chore Boy	na
W.H.W. Mach. & Tool Co.	Lansing, MI	Colt	na
W.H.W. Mach. & Tool Co.	Lansing, MI	Iowa	na
W.H.W. Mach. & Tool Co.	Lansing, MI	Iowa Oversize	na
W.L.P. Co.	Chicago, IL	WLP	1912
Wabash Eng. Co.	Wabash, IN	Wabash	na
Wachusett Mach. Co.	Fitchburg, MA	Fenner	na
Wade & Co., R. M.	Portland, OR	Wade	na
Waite Gas Eng. Co.	Milwaukee, WI	Waite	1904
Walke, G. Jacksonville	Jacksonville, IL	Walke	1909
Walker, H. E.	Clinton, IA	Walker	na
Walker Mfg. Co.	Council Bluff, IA	Boss	na
Walker Mfg. Co.	Council Bluff, IA	Boss Farmer	na
Walker Mfg. Co.	Omaha, NE	Boss Farmer	na
Wall Mfg. Co.	Philadelphia, PA	Wall	1903
Waller & Sons	Council Bluff, IA	na	na

The Strang Engine Co. built engines in Chicago, Illinois. This 1910 vertical oil engine used compression ignition.

This 1909 15-horsepower side-shaft engine was built by the Superior Gas Engine Co. in Springfield, Ohio. This stationary natural gas or gasoline engine uses a vertical flyball governor to control engine speed and is tank-cooled. The engine is equipped with a hot tube ignition system that appears to have poppet valves working off of the engine's side-shaft.

This 1910 Ladies Favorite engine was manufactured by C.H. Talley of Lincoln, Illinois. The engine is of the two-cycle design and uses high-tension spark plug ignition. Ladies Favorite engines were of the single-flywheel design, tank-cooled, and weighed only 200 pounds.

This marine engine was manufactured by the Strelinger Marine Engine Co. at West 169 to 177 Woodbridge Street, Detroit, Michigan. This Strelinger two-cycle marine engine is a 1 1/2-horsepower model.

This is an illustration of the Stroud Valveless Vapor Engine that was manufactured by the Stroud-Humphrey Manufacturing Co. in Hastings, Minnesota. Little is known of this company outside of advertisements found in period trade magazines.

Engines of 35 to 200 horsepower were manufactured by the Struthers-Wells Co. in Warren, Pennsylvania. These engines were designed with huge single flywheels. The engines were built in one-, two-, and four-cylinder models.

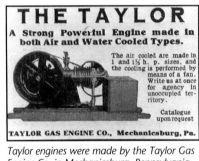

Taylor engines were made by the Taylor Gas Engine Co. in Mechanicsburg, Pennsylvania. The Taylor fan air-cooled engines were made in 1 and 1 1/2-horsepower models.

The T and M engine line was manufactured by the Termaat and Manahan Co. located in Oshkosh, Wisconsin. This two-horsepower engine is designed with a single flywheel. The two-cycle engine is coupled to a plunger type pump that had a 27-barrel per hour capacity.

Pictured here is a Monarch hit-and-miss-governed engine. The Monarch engine was manufactured by the Grand Rapids Engine Co. in Grand Rapids, Michigan. Low-tension hammer-break ignition is a standard feature on this air-cooled gasoline engine.

This Harrisburg 2 1/4-horsepower engine is designed with hit-and-miss governing and high-tension spark plug ignition. The engine is hopper-cooled and runs on gasoline.

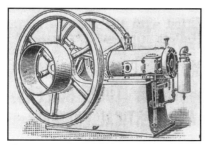

Illustrated here is a Thompson tank-cooled engine. They were manufactured in sizes from 4 to 18 horsepower. Thompson and Sons Manufacturing Co. was located in Beloit, Wisconsin.

The Triumph Gas Engine Co. built engines in Dayton, Ohio. Pictured here is a 1905 Triumph six-horsepower engine. These engines were equipped with a low-tension ignition system featuring a dynamo and tank cooling. The fuel tank is mounted on a stand between the engine and the cooling tank.

The Tiger engine line was manufactured by Thompson and Sons Manufacturing Co. in Beloit, Wisconsin. Pictured here is their 1 1/2-horsepower air-cooled engine. It is equipped with an up-draft carburetor, a flyball flywheel governor, and is exhausted out the top of the engine's head.

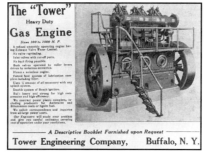

Tower Engineering Co. located in Buffalo, New York, built their Tower engines in sizes from 100 to 1,000 horsepower. These multicylinder vertical engines used a dual Bosch high-tension ignition system.

This Triumph side-shaft engine is equipped with high-tension spark plug ignition and uses a side-shaft flyball governor to control engine speed. This is an extremely rare Triumph engine.

Left
The United Engine Co. built their engines in Lansing, Michigan. The engines were available in sizes from 1 1/2 to 12 horsepower. A hammer-break, low-tension ignition system and hit-and-miss governing were standard features on this hopper-cooled gasoline engine. The water-cooled engines could be ordered as portable, skidded, or stationary units from the factory. United's 1 1/2-horsepower engine sold for $28 in 1913.

Tiger engines were manufactured in sizes from 1 1/2 to 8 horsepower. The engines were equipped with high-tension spark plug ignition. Dry cell batteries and a buzz coil were supplied from the factory with this hopper-cooled gasoline engine.

The U.S. Engine Works was located in Chicago, Illinois. These inverted vertical engines were built in sizes from 1 3/4 to 10 horsepower. They were built in one- and two-cylinder models. Engines could be ordered equipped to run on natural gas, gasoline, or kerosene. An original, restored engine sold at an Ohio auction during 1995 for $5,750.

Engine Manufacturer	Factory Location	Trade Name	Dates
Walrath-Maxim Gas Eng. Co.	Jersey City, NJ	Walrath-Maxim	1910
Waltham Mfg. Co.	Waltham, MA	Waltham	na
Wandscheer Bros. Co.	Sioux Center, IA	Wandscheer	1910–1917
Warden, Henry	Philadelphia, PA	Atkinson	na
Warden, Henry	Philadelphia, PA	Cycle	na
Warden, Henry	Philadelphia, PA	Nash	1890
Warman Marine Mtr. Co.	Detroit, MI	Conoe Motor	na
Warner Elect. Co.	Pasadena, CA	Simplex Light	na
Warner Elevator Co.	Warner, IL	Warner	na
Warner Kite Co.	Pasadena, CA	Simplex Light Plant	na
Warner Mfg. Co.	Ottawa, KS	Giant	na
Warner Mfg. Co.	Ottawa, KS	Ottawa	na
Warner Mfg. Co.	Ottawa, KS	Union Giant	na
Warner Mfg. Co.	Ottawa, KS	Warner	na
Warnerlite Products Co.	Davenport, IA	Warnerlite	1921
Washington Iron Works	Seattle, WA	Washington	na
Washington Iron Works	Seattle, WA	Washington-Estep	na
Wat Eng. Co.	Port Huron, MI	Wat	1907
Waterloo Cement Mach. Co.	Waterloo, IA	Wander	na
Waterloo Cement Mach. Co.	Waterloo , IA	Yale	1908
Waterloo Cement Mach. Co.	Waterloo, IA	Wonder-Jobbed	na
Waterloo Cement Mach. Co.	Waterloo, IA	Yale-Jobbed	na
Waterloo Const. Machry. Co.	Waterloo, IA	Wonder	na
Waterloo Eng. Works	New York, NY	Mogul	na
Waterloo Fdry. Co.	Waterloo, IA	Waterloo Chief	1911
Waterloo Gasoline Eng. Co.	Waterloo, IA	Harris	na
Waterloo Gasoline Eng. Co.	Waterloo, IA	Jackson	na
Waterloo Gasoline Eng. Co.	Waterloo, IA	Woodruff Up To Date	na
Waterloo Gasoline Eng. Co.	Waterloo, IA	All Purpose	na
Waterloo Gasoline Eng. Co.	Waterloo, IA	American Boy	na
Waterloo Gasoline Eng. Co.	Waterloo, IA	Banner	na
Waterloo Gasoline Eng. Co.	Waterloo, IA	Beat Em All	na
Waterloo Gasoline Eng. Co.	Waterloo, IA	Big Chief	na
Waterloo Gasoline Eng. Co.	Waterloo, IA	Cray	na
Waterloo Gasoline Eng. Co.	Waterloo, IA	Downes	na
Waterloo Gasoline Eng. Co.	Waterloo, IA	Drednaut	na
Waterloo Gasoline Eng. Co.	Waterloo, IA	Eaton	na
Waterloo Gasoline Eng. Co.	Waterloo, IA	Economy	na
Waterloo Gasoline Eng. Co.	Waterloo, IA	Faultless	na
Waterloo Gasoline Eng. Co.	Waterloo, IA	Gault	na
Waterloo Gasoline Eng. Co.	Waterloo, IA	Hartman	na
Waterloo Gasoline Eng. Co.	Waterloo, IA	Hustler	na
Waterloo Gasoline Eng. Co.	Waterloo, IA	Imperial	na
Waterloo Gasoline Eng. Co.	Waterloo, IA	Iowa	na
Waterloo Gasoline Eng. Co.	Waterloo, IA	John Deere	na
Waterloo Gasoline Eng. Co.	Waterloo, IA	Knowlton	na
Waterloo Gasoline Eng. Co.	Waterloo, IA	Lester	na
Waterloo Gasoline Eng. Co.	Waterloo, IA	Little Marvel	na
Waterloo Gasoline Eng. Co.	Waterloo, IA	Newark	na
Waterloo Gasoline Eng. Co.	Waterloo, IA	Omaha Chief	na
Waterloo Gasoline Eng. Co.	Waterloo, IA	Overtime	na
Waterloo Gasoline Eng. Co.	Waterloo, IA	Sandow	na
Waterloo Gasoline Eng. Co.	Pasadena, IA	Sheldon	na
Waterloo Gasoline Eng. Co.	Waterloo, IA	Special	na
Waterloo Gasoline Eng. Co.	Pasadena, IA	Uniflo	na
Waterloo Gasoline Eng. Co.	Waterloo, IA	Unito	na
Waterloo Gasoline Eng. Co.	Waterloo, IA	Up To Date	na
Waterloo Gasoline Eng. Co.	Waterloo, IA	Van Duzen	na
Waterloo Gasoline Eng. Co.	Waterloo, IA	Vapor Cooled	na
Waterloo Gasoline Eng. Co.	Waterloo, IA	Waterloo	1895
Waterloo Gasoline Eng. Co.	Waterloo, IA	Waterloo Boy	1894–1911
Waterloo Gasoline Eng. Co.	Waterloo, IA	Waterloo Boy-Kerosene	na
Waterloo Gasoline Eng. Co.	Waterloo, IA	Waterloo Chief	na
Waterloo Gasoline Eng. Co.	Waterloo, IA	Waterloo Vapor Cooled	na

Engine Manufacturer	Factory Location	Trade Name	Dates
Waterloo Gasoline Eng. Co.	Waterloo, IA	Weil	na
Waterloo Gasoline Eng. Co.	Waterloo, IA	Wonder	na
Waterloo Mtr. Works	Waterloo, IA	Davis	1902
Waterman Marine Mtr. Co.	Detroit, MI	Porto-Marine	na
Waterman Mtr. Co.	Detroit, MI	Arrow	na
Waterman Mtr. Co.	Detroit, MI	Uni-Elect.	na
Waterman Mtr. Co.	Detroit, MI	Waterman	na
Waterour Eng. Works	St. Paul, MN	Waterour	1900
Watertown Mtr. Works	Watertown, NJ	Watertown	na
Watkins Mfg. Co.	Wichita, KS	Little Pet-Jobbed	na
Watkins Mfg. Co.	Cincinnati, OH	Sumner	na
Watkins Mfg. Co.	Cincinnati, OH	Watkins	1900
Watkins Mfg. Co.	Cincinnati, OH	Watkins Special	na
Watkins Mtr. Co.	Cincinnati, OH	Toledo	na
Watkins Mtr. Co.	Cincinnati, OH	Watkins Special-Marine	na
Watt Mtr. Co.	Detroit, MI	Watt	na
Waukesha Mtr. Co.	Waukesha, WI	Hesselman Oil	na
Waukesha Mtr. Co.	Waukesha, WI	Waukesha	na
Waukesha Mtr. Co.	Waukesha, WI	Waukesha Ice Motor	na
Wausau Fdry. & Mach. Co.	Wausau, WI	Simplex	na
Weatherholt, William	Columbus, OH	Weatherholt	na
Weaver & Little Co.	Lebanon, PA	Nanzy	1903–1910
Weaver & Little Co.	Lebanon, PA	Weaver	1903–1910
Webber & Richer Mach. Works	San Francisco, CA	Webber	na
Weber Eng. Co.	Kansas City, MO	Weber	1917
Weber Gas & Gasoline Eng. Works	Kansas City, MO	Sheffield	na
Weber Gas & Gasoline Eng. Works	Kansas City, MO	Weber	1891
Weber Gas & Gasoline Eng. Works	Kansas City, MO	Weber Jr.	na
Webster Eng. Works	Waterloo, IA	Webster	1895
Webster Mfg. Co.	Chicago, IL	Webster	na
Webster Mfg. Co.	Chicago, IL	Webster Handy Man	na
Webster Mfg. Co.	Chicago, IL	Handy Man	na
Weeber Mfg. Co.	Albany, NY	Weeber	na
Welch & Lawson	New York, NY	Lawson	1897
Wellman, Seaver & Morgan Co.	Cleveland, OH	Cockerill	na
Wellman, Seaver & Morgan Co.	Cleveland, OH	Weaver	na
Wellman, Seaver & Morgan Co.	Cleveland, OH	Wellman	na
Wells Mfg. Co.	Fond du Lac, WI	Pony Power	na
Wendel, Jacob	Atkins, IA	Wendel	1912
Werner & Co.	Pine Grove, PA	Werner	na
Wesco Cable & Light Co.	Baldwin, WI	Wesco	na
West Chester Eng. Co.	West Chester, PA	West Chester	na
West Coast Eng. Co.	San Diego, CA	West Coast	na
Westbend Aluminum Co.	West Bend, WI	West Bend	na
Westerfield, G. G.	Anderson, IN	Westerfield	na
Westerfield Co.	Indianapolis, IN	Westerfield	na
Westerfield Gas Eng. Co.	Vincennes, IN	Westerfield	1911
Western Elect. Co.	New York, NY	Western Elect.	na
Western Gas Const. Co.	Fort Wayne, IN	Western	na
Western Gas Eng. Co.	Los Angeles, CA	Western	na
Western Gas Eng. Co.	Mishawaka, IN	Western	na
Western Gas Eng. Works	Grand Rapids, MI	Western	1898
Western Harness & Supply Co.	Waterloo, IA	Knox	na
Western Iron Works	Los Angeles, CA	Western	1905
Western Launch & Eng. Works	Michigan City, IN	Western-Marine	1904
Western Machry. Co.	Los Angeles, CA	Western	na
Western Mfg. Co.	Iowa City, IA	Kelly	1905
Western Mtr. Co.	Logansport, IN	Rutenber	na
Western Mtr. Co.	Detroit, MI	Uni-Lectric Light	na
Westinghouse Co.	Schenectady, NY	Schenectady	na
Westinghouse Co.	Schenectady, NY	Westinghouse	na
Westinghouse Mach. Co.	East Pittsburgh, PA	Westinghouse	1895
Wheeler Eng. Works	Bridgeport, CT	Wheeler	na
Whitcomb Mach. Co.	Albany, WI	Hustler	na

In 1912, the President of the United Manufacturers Association in Lansing, Michigan was C.L. Sprinkle. This United two-horsepower engine uses make-and-break low-tension battery and coil ignition. The valves were operated by walking beam and the gasoline engine is hopper-cooled. The engine had a 4 inch bore and a 5 1/2 inch stroke. The flywheels are 22 inches in diameter. The engine is shown attached to an original factory skid. A battery box, complete with dry-cell batteries and a coil, is attached to the front of the skid. This unit weighed 500 pounds.

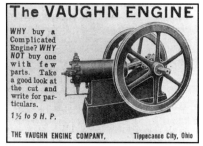

The Vaughn Engine Co. was located in Tippecanoe City, Ohio. This stationary engine was built in sizes from 1 1/2 to 9 horsepower. Make-and-break low-tension ignition and tank cooling were used on these engines.

Illustrated here is a Waterloo Boy Model H engine. It uses low-tension ignition with hit-and-miss governing. A plug oscillating magneto is attached to the engine's igniter bracket. The Waterloo Boy Model H engine is hopper-cooled and runs on gasoline.

This restored United engine is equipped with a hit-and-miss governing and low-tension hammer-break ignition. A rotary low-tension magneto is used to supply the electrical current for this hopper-cooled engine. The engine is exhausted out of the top of the engine's head. An up-draft carburetor mixes the engine's fuel charge.

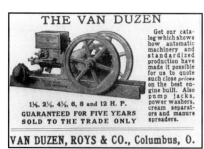

Van Duzen, Roys and Co. manufactured engines in Columbus, Ohio. Their engines were built in sizes from 1 1/2 to 12 horsepower. Hammer-break low-tension ignition and hopper cooling are standard features. Their engines were marketed for use with pump jacks, washing machines, and manure spreaders.

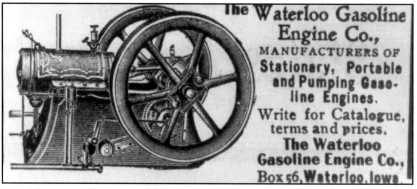

One of the most prolific engine builders in early stationary engine manufacturing was the Waterloo Gasoline Engine Co. in Waterloo, Iowa. This 1897 Waterloo stationary engine is tank-cooled and runs on gasoline. It features low-tension make-and-break ignition.

Pictured here is a skid-mounted Waterloo Boy engine. Waterloo engines were built in sizes from 2 to 10 horsepower. They are equipped with a hammer-break igniter, low-tension ignition, hit-and-miss governing, and hopper cooling. The Waterloo Gasoline Engine Co. was located in Waterloo, Iowa.

Very little is known about the Wenco engine pictured here. The Wenco engine is equipped with a vertical flyball governor and tank cooling. The engine runs on gasoline.

178

Engine Manufacturer	Factory Location	Trade Name	Dates
White Eng. Works	Kansas City, MO	Aristocrat	1890
White Gas Eng. Co.	Baltimore, MD	White	na
White Gas Eng. Co.	Milwaukee, WI	White	na
White Gas Eng. Co.	Baltimore, MD	White-Middletown	1897
White Gas Eng. Co., Charles	Baltimore, MD	White	na
White Gas Eng. Co., Charles	Baltimore, MD	Middleton	na
White Gas Eng. Co., Charles	Baltimore, MD	Schram	na
White Lilly Mfg. Co.	Davenport, IA	White-Lilly	na
White Lilly Washer Co.	Davenport, IA	White-Lilly	1906
White Mfg. Co.	New York, NY	White	1899
White-Blakeslee Mfg. Co.	Birmingham, AL	Blakeslee	na
White-Blakeslee Mfg. Co.	Birmingham, AL	Birmingham	na
White-Blakeslee Mfg. Co.	Birmingham, AL	White	1907
Whitfield Co.	Memphis , TN	Whitfield	1899
Whitman Agricultural Co.	St. Louis, MO	Novo	na
Whitman Agricultural Co.	St. Louis, MO	Sultan	na
Whitman Agricultural Co.	St. Louis , MO	Whitman	1913
Whitney, F. E.	Boston, MA	Whitney	na
Whitney, J. C.	Ovid, NY	Whitney	na
Wisconsin Machry. & Mfg. Co.	Milwaukee, WI	Wisconsin-Marine	na
Wilcox, Stephen	Westerly, RI	Wilcox	na
Wile Power Gas Co.	Rochester, NY	Wile-Jobbed	na
Willard & Co.	Chicago, IL	Simplex-Marine	na
Willard Co., Charles P.	Chicago, IL	Willard	1897
Williams & Orton Mfg. Co.	Sterling , IL	Charter	na
Williams Stores	New York, NY	Maynard Jr.-Jobbed	na
Williams Stores	New York, NY	Maynard-Jobbed	na
Williams, G. F.	Dexter, NY	Williams	1902
Williamson Mtr. Co.	Philadelphia, PA	Williamson	na
Williamsport Gas Eng. Co.	Williamsport, PA	Economy	na
Williamsport Gas Eng. Co.	Williamsport, PA	Williamsport	1907
Willmar Gas Eng. Co.	Willmar, MN	Willmar	na
Wilson Mach. Co.	Des Moines, IA	Matchless	1911
Wilson Mach. Co.	Des Moines, IA	Old Warhorse	na
Wilson Mach. Co.	Des Moines, IA	Wilson	1911
Wilson Mach. Co.	Des Moines, IA	Wilson-Des Moines	na
Winfield, E.	Los Angeles, CA	Winfield	na
Wing & Co.	New York, NY	Wing	1897
Winkley Eng. Co.	Lynn, MA	Winkley	1907
Winnebago Gas Eng. & Const. Co.	Faribault, MN	Winnebago	na
Winton Eng. Works	Cleveland, OH	Winton	na
Wiscona Pep Mtr. Co.	Oshkosh, WI	Diro	na
Wiscona Pep Mtr. Co.	Oshkosh, WI	Wiscona Pep	na
Wisconsin Eng. Co.	Corliss, WI	Adams Kero	1912
Wisconsin Eng. Co.	Corliss, WI	Wisconsin	1908
Wisconsin Mtr. Corp.	Milwaukee, WI	Wisconsin	na
Wisconsin Wheel Works	Racine, WI	Wisconsin	na
Wittaker-Up Co.	Kansas City, MO	Little Pal	na
Witte Eng. Works	Kansas City, MO	Daltex	na
Witte Eng. Works	Kansas City, MO	H & P	na
Witte Eng. Works	Kansas City, MO	H & R	na
Witte Eng. Works	Kansas City, MO	Meco	na
Witte Eng. Works	Kansas City, MO	Sprayer	na
Witte Eng. Works	Kansas City, MO	Standard	1890
Witte Eng. Works	Kansas City, MO	Surplus 6	na
Witte Eng. Works	Kansas City, MO	Trojan	na
Witte Eng. Works	Kansas City, MO	Winner	na
Witte Eng. Works	Kansas City, MO	Witte	1885
Witte Eng. Works	Kansas City, MO	Witte Jr.	na
Witte Iron Works	Kansas City, MO	Witte	na
Witte Iron Works	Kansas City, MO	Witte Jr.	na
Witte Iron Works	Kansas City, MO	Witte Standard	na
Wogamon Bros. Co.	Greenville, OH	Sure Go	na
Wogamon Bros. Co.	Greenville, OH	Wogamon	na

White and Middleton Gas Engine Co. built engines in Baltimore, Maryland. This restored 1891 White and Middleton engine is equipped with hot tube ignition and a vertical flyball governor to control its speed.

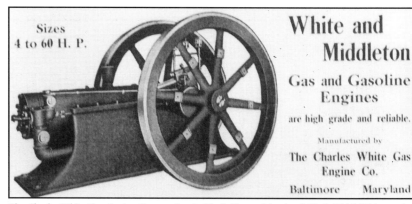

Sizes 4 to 60 H. P.

White and Middleton

Gas and Gasoline Engines

are high grade and reliable.

Manufactured by

The Charles White Gas Engine Co.

Baltimore   Maryland

The Charles White Gas Engine Co. was located in Baltimore Maryland. Their 1912 White engines were built in sizes from 4 to 60 horsepower. The engines were equipped with hot tube ignition and external tank cooling.

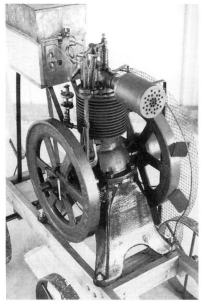

The White Lily Manufacturing Co. built washing machine engines in Davenport, Iowa. Shown here is their one-horsepower vertical air-cooled gasoline engine that uses high-tension spark plug ignition. The engine is designed with an open crankcase. A White Lily engine recently sold in Ohio for $2,700.

The Sultan engine line was manufactured in sizes from 2 1/2 to 6 1/2 horsepower. The Sultan was built by the Whitman Agricultural Co. in St. Louis, Missouri. These gasoline engines are equipped with high-tension spark plug ignition and are hopper-cooled. The Sultan name appears on the engine's crankcase cover.

The Wilson Machine Co. was located in Des Moines, Iowa. The Matchless one-horsepower engine weighed in at 135 pounds. This little water-cooled gasoline engine sold for $39.75 new.

This one-horsepower New Matchless engine was manufactured by the Wilson Machine Co. in Des Moines, Iowa. This air-cooled gasoline engine is equipped with a float-fed carburetor and high-tension spark plug ignition.

The Sure Go engine was manufactured by Wogamon Brothers in Greenville, Ohio. Pictured here is a Sure Go 3 1/2-horsepower engine. It uses high-tension spark plug ignition and is tank-cooled. The fuel tank is mounted on top of the cooling tank piping and supplies gasoline to the engine's carburetor by gravity.

Worthington engines were manufactured by Worthington Pump and Machinery Corporation in Cudahy, Wisconsin. Low-tension ignition and a hammer-break igniter were fitted to this hopper-cooled gasoline engine. A Webster oscillating magneto is seen attached to the engine's igniter bracket.

Engine Manufacturer	Factory Location	Trade Name	Dates
Wolverine Mtr. Co.	Albion, MI	Wolverine	1912
Wolverine Mtr. Works	Grand Rapids, MI	Junior	na
Wolverine Mtr. Works	Bridgeport, CT	Wolverine	na
Wolverine Mtr. Works	Grand Rapids, MI	Wolverine	1897
Wonder Mfg. Co.	Syracuse, NY	Wonder-Marine	na
Wood & Co.	Philadelphia, PA	Wood	1905
Wood & Co.	Philadelphia, PA	Woodie	na
Wood & Spencer Co.	Cleveland, OH	Casalux	na
Wood Co.	Hassick Falls, NY	Wood	na
Wood Elect. & Mfg. Co.	South Bend, IN	Wemco	na
Woodin & Little	San Francisco, CA	Freeport-Jobbed	1905
Woodin & Little	San Francisco, CA	Woodin & Little-Jobbed	1905
Woodmanse Mfg. Co.	Freeport, IL	Mogul	na
Woodmanse Mfg. Co.	Freeport, IL	Oil Rite	na
Woodmanse Mfg. Co.	Freeport, IL	Woodmanse Mogul	na
Woods Gas Eng. Co.	Salida, CO	Woods	1910
Woodsman Power Saw Co.	Eureka, CA	Little Woodsman	na
Woodward Co.	Fresno, CA	Steiner Long Life	na
Woodward Co.	Fresno, CA	Woodward	na
Woolery Mach. Co.	Minneapolis, MN	Wooley	na
Wooley Fdry. & Mach. Works	Anderson, IN	Burger	1905
Wooley Fdry. & Mach. Works	Anderson, IN	Burger Auto	1905
Woolf Valve Gear Co.	Minneapolis, MN	Woolf	1907
Worfolk Bull Eng. Works	Detroit, MI	Worfolk	na
Worth Mfg. Co.	Benton Harbor, MI	Worth	1897
Worthington Pump & Mach. Co.	Cudahy, WI	Portable	na
Worthington Pump & Mach. Co.	Cudahy, WI	Worthington	na
Worthington Pump & Mach. Co.	Cudahy, WI	Worthington Light Plight	na
Worthington Pump & Mach. Co.	Cudahy, WI	Ingeco	na
Worthington Pump & Mach. Co.	Cudahy, WI	Ingeco Light Plant	na
Wright Eng. Co.	Greenville, MI	C. T. Wright	na
Wright Eng. Co.	Pittsburgh, PA	Wright	1909
Wright Mach. Co.	Owensboro, KY	Wright	1915
Wright Mtr. Co.	Buffalo, NY	Valveless	na
Western Malleable/Gray Iron Mfg. Co.	Port Washington, WI	Western	na
Western Malleable & Gray Iron Mfg. Co.	Port Washington, WI	Simplicity	1908
Western Malleable & Gray Iron Mfg. Co.	Port Washington, WI	Simplicity Jr.	1908
Wyandotte Eng./Novelty Works	Wyandotte, MI	Wyandotte	na
Wygodsky Eng. Co.	New York, NY	Wygodsky	1910
Xander Mach. & Supply Co.	Reading , PA	Xander	na
Xargill Mfg. Co.	St. Utica, NY	Utica	na
Yacht Gas Eng. & Launch Co.	Philadelphia, PA	Baby Crown-Marine	na
Yacht Gas Eng. & Launch Co.	Philadelphia, PA	Yacht-Marine	na
Yale Eng. & Mtr. Co.	Portland, ME	Yale	na
Yale Gas Eng. Co.	Cedar Falls, IA	Yale	1899
Yocom & Co.	Reading , PA	Yocom	na
Yonker Mfg. Co.	Fulton, NY	Parker-Marine	na
Yonkers Machry. Co.	Yonkers, NY	Parker-Jobbed	na
Yonkers Mfg. Co.	New York, NY	Parker	1885
York Eng. & Fdry. Co.	York, NE	York	1900–1910
Young & Co.	Titusville, PA	Young	na
Young Mach. Co.	San Francisco, CA	Young	na
Young Machry. Co.	Lynn, MA	Essex	na
Yuba Mfg. Co.	Benicia, CA	Hicks-Marine	na
Zenith Gas Eng. & Power Co.	San Francisco, CA	Zenith	na
Ziegler-Schryer Mfg. Co.	Freeport, IL	Duplex	na
Ziegler-Schryer Mfg. Co.	Freeport, IL	Little Giant	na
Ziegler-Schryer Mfg. Co.	Freeport, IL	Ziegler-Schryer	na

Literature Guide

This appendix is devoted to recommended books and magazines as well as sources for manuals and other literature for stationary engines. Many of the magazines, journals, and books mentioned here are out of print. However, hobbyists interested in engine history, manufacturers' advertising, and technical articles will find that old out of print trade magazines and manuals are the best source for this type information. Swap meets and literature dealers that specialize in out of print books are the best places to buy these books and magazines. Reprinted stationary gas engine manuals can run from $1 to about $5. Original manufacturers manuals can cost anywhere from $10 to $100 each. out of print books on gas engines are currently running from about $15 to $200 a copy. Many reprinted manufacturers manuals can be purchased from the literature dealers listed here.

Recommended Magazines

The following in- and out of print magazines are good sources for information on stationary engines. Some of these titles are devoted entirely to the gas engine. Others, such as *Technical World*, had limited coverage of the stationary engine. Magazines that are highly recommended will be noted.

American Machinist
Out of print
This is a machine trade magazine. However, in early issues coverage was given to the engine companies. The huge machine shops that produced engines made for great stories in this publication. Check each issue before purchasing; the issues from 1890 to 1930 may be most useful. Priced from $4 to $10 each.

Antique Gas Engine & Tractor Magazine
Antique Gas Engine & Tractor
122 Magnolia Avenue
Scarborough, Ontario, Canada M1K 3K8
Out of print
Antique Gas Engine & Tractor is a magazine that covered the

engine trade in the late 1970s and 1980s. out of print issues are interesting and cover the entire trade. Many great photographs and stories are packed into each issue. Priced from $2 to $6 each.

Antique Power
P. O. Box 1000
Westerville, OH, 43081-7000
Phone: 614-848-5038
In print
This bimonthly magazine covers early farm tractors in detail. Limited coverage of gas engines. It has a classified section and some "how to" articles. Subscription rate is $18 per year.

Bessemer Monthly
Bessemer Gas Engine Co.
Grove City, PA
Out of print
This magazine was printed each month by the Bessemer Company and detailed what was happening in their business. Bessemer engines and factory projects were covered in each issue. Priced from $4 to $10 each.

Bores and Strokes
Coolspring Power Museum
P. O. Box 19
Coolspring, PA 15730
Phone: 814-849-6883
In print
The Museum has published a series of softbound magazines called *Bores & Strokes* on various engines. There are approximately eight issues of highly recommended reading.

Cassier's
Out of print
This magazine covered a wide range of articles. It is not an engine specific magazine. However, if issues can be found they should be reviewed, as engines and new improvements were covered. Look for issues from 1885 to 1915. Priced from $10 to $20 each.

Engineering News and American Railway Journal
Out of print
This is a technical magazine dealing with railroads. However, the magazine does have great classified and advertising information

in each of the weekly issue. Look for issues from 1885 to 1910. Priced from $2 to $8 each.

Engineering Record and The Sanitary Engineer
Out of print

This is another technical magazine with interesting classified and advertising information in each issue. Look for issues from 1895-1910. Priced from $2 to $8 each.

Engineers & Engines
Published by Engineers & Engines
1118 North Raynor Avenue
Joliet, IL 60435
Phone: none
In print

EEM covers gas, steam, railroads, farm machinery, and tractors. Recommended reading.

Farm Engineering
The Farm Engineering Publishing Co.
Chicago, IL
Out of print

Large-format magazine that covers the entire farm scene. Many issues have articles related to gas engines. Classified and advertising information in each issue. Check issues before purchasing. Priced from $2 to $6 each.

Gas Energy
Gas Energy Company
24 Murry Street
New York, NY
Out of print

Great technical magazine devoted entirely to the gas engine trade. A must-read for any interested hobbyist. Search for magazines printed from 1906 to 1920. Priced from $10 to $25 each.

Gas Engine Magazine
P. O. Box 328
Lancaster, PA 17608
Phone: 717-392-0733
Fax: 717-392-1341
In print

A monthly magazine covering the gas engine hobby in detail. Articles each month on history, identification of engines, shows, and engine manufacturers. Each month has a great classified section as well as a listing of upcoming events. This is a highly recommended magazine, a must-read!

Gas Power
Gas Power Publishing Co.
St. Joseph, MI
Out of print

The best magazine on the gas engine trade. Each issue covered the gas engine in detail. Articles on running, maintenance, improvements, manufacturers and patents. Search for issues from 1902 to 1918. Priced from $10 to $25 each.

Gas Review
Madison, WI
Out of print

This is my second choice in magazines on the early engine trade. This monthly magazine covered all facets of engine trade but did not have quite the advertising base as did Gas Power. Look for issues from 1908 to 1918. Priced from $10 to $25 each.

Home Study
Out of print

This is a large-format magazine that was published for educating people at their leisure at home. There are not many issues that deal with gas engines; however the issues published between 1897 to 1898 had great coverage of the gas engine. A must-read, if you can find them. Check each issue before purchasing. Priced from $6 to $12 each.

Iron-Men Album
Iron-Men Album
P. O. Box 328
Lancaster, PA 17608-0328
Phone: 717-392-0733
Fax: 717-392-1341
In Print

This magazine covers gas and steam shows. Articles cover steam-related equipment. The classified section is a good source of gas-engine-related items.

Power
Power Publishing Co.
New York, NY
Out of print

Power magazine is a technical monthly magazine that covered the steam trade in early years. Gas engines are seen in every issue in the classified section and ads. Limited gas engine coverage; check each issue before purchasing. Priced from $10 to $20 each.

Scientific American
Out of print

This is another magazine that occasionally published articles on the gas engine trade. Early issues are best, look for issues from 1895 to 1915. Check each issue before purchasing. Priced from $8 to $25 each.

Stationary Engine
Kelsey Publishing Ltd.
Kelsey House
77 High Street
Beckenham, Kent, England BR3 1AN
Phone: 081-658-3531
In print

This is a 28-page monthly magazine that covers Europe's stationary gas and steam engines and shows. Recommended.

Technical World
Out of print

This is another magazine I have used in doing research for the book. It has limited articles on the gas engine, but should be checked if issues are found. Articles in the magazine are generally excellent reading. Priced from $8 to $20 each.

The Gas Engine
The Gas Engine Publishing Company
Cincinnati, OH
Out of print

A must-read magazine if it can be found. Covers the engine trade in detail each month. Look for issues from 1905 to 1920, which are excellent reading. Priced from $10 to $25 each.

The Thresherman's Review
The Thresherman Review Company
St. Joseph, MI
Out of print

This is a large-format magazine that covers the entire farm-trade market. Some issues contain information on stationary engines. Most issues cover steam- and gas-powered farm machinery. The magazine has extensive advertising throughout. Recommended informational reading; look for issues from 1900 to 1920. Priced from $10 to $20 each.

The Veteran Farmer
Veteran Farmer
P. O. Box 98827
Sloane Park, 2152, South Africa
In print

A gas engine magazine from South Africa! It covers tractors, stationary engines, and steam power. Informative, excellent reading. Classified ads and events are well covered.

Tractor and Gas Engine Review
The Clark Publishing Co.
Madison, WI
Out of print
　　This is the magazine that carried on where *Gas Review* left off. Has the same coverage of gas engine articles, slowly being replaced with tractor-related articles. Look for issues from the late teens to about 1925. Priced from $8 to $20 each.

Recommended Books
　　The following book list should be used as a starting point for building your reference library on early stationary gas engines. It would be impossible to include the thousands of original manufacturers' catalogs, and operator's and owner's manuals that were published. I would recommend that you check with dealers and search the flea markets for the titles that you're looking for. Many of the books deal with specific areas, such as ignition or batteries, while others cover the engine as a whole. Original, out of print books on stationary engines are not cheap. They can cost in excess of $100 per copy. Reprinted books generally cost from $3 to $45.

Adams, H.W. *Common Sense Instruction on Gas Tractor Operation,* 1920. Out of print

Audel, Theo., & Co. *Hawkins Electrical Guide, Questions, Answers and Illustrations,* Theo. Audel & Co. Publishers, 1919. Out of print

Audel, Theo. *Gas Engine Manual,* Theo. Audel & Co. Publishers, 1907. Out of print

Brate, H. R. *Farm Gas Engines* , 1913. Out of print

Brooks, L. Elliott. *The Practical Gas and Oil Engine Handbook,* Frederick J. Drake & Company, 1905. Out of print

Brooks, L. Elliott. *The Practical Gas and Oil Engine Handbook,* Frederick J. Drake & Company, 1913. Out of print

Carhart, Henry S. *Primary Batteries,* Allyn and Bacon Publishers, 1891. Out of print

Cummins, C. Lyle. *Diesel's Engine, Volume One From Conception to 1918,* Carnot Press, 1993. In print as of 1996

Cummins, C. Lyle. *Internal Fire,* Society of Automotive Engineers, Inc., 1989. In print as of 1996.

Edgington, David. *Amanco Engines: The Story of Associates Manufacturers' Company LTD.,* Published by David Edgington, 1996. In print as of 1996

Edgington, David. Old *Stationary Engines,* Shire Publications Ltd., 1980. In print as of 1996

Graham, Frank D. *Audel's Handy Book of Practical Electricity,* Theo. Audel & Co. Publishers, 1924. Out of print.

Graham, Frank D. *Audel's Engineers & Mechanics Guide # 4,* Theo. Audel & Co. Publishers, 1927. Out of print.

Gray, R. B. *The Agricultural Tractor, 1855-1950,* 1975. Out of print.

Hebert, Luke. *Gas & Air Engines,* Lindsay Publications Inc., 1985. In print as of 1996

Hiscox, Gardner D. *Gas, Gasoline and Oil Engines,* Norman W. Henley & Company, 1911. Out of print

Hiscox, Gardner D. *Gas, Gasoline and Oil Engines,* Norman W. Henley & Company, 1902. Out of print

Karch, Glen. *Hercules Engines & The Hercules Mfg. Co.,* Glen Karch. In print as of 1996

Karch, Glen. *Sparta Economy Gasoline Engines,* Glen Karch. In print as of 1996

Kindschi, Verne W. *The Fuller & Johnson Story,* Giegerich's Son Inc., 199?. In print as of 1996

King, Alan. *Gasoline Engines 1909-1962,* Independent Print Shop Company Inc., 1994. In print as of 1996.

King, Alan. *Gasoline Engines Vol. 1 through 8,* Independent Print Shop Company Inc., 1976 to 1983. Out of print.

King, Alan. Gasoline *Engines 1884-1934,* Independent Print Shop Company Inc., 1994. In print as of 1996.

Kushlan, Max. *The Gas Motor,* Branch Publishing Company, 1918. Out of print

Lucke, Charles E. *The Use of Alcohol and Gasoline in Farm Engines,* 1907. Out of print

Lunkenheimer. *Lunkenheimer* (Catalogs 1 - 72), Lunkenheimer Company, 1890 to 1971. Out of print

Marks, Lionel S. *Gas & Oil Engines,* American School of Correspondence, 1915. Out of print

Morrison, L. H. *Diesel Engines Operation and Maintenance,* American Technical Society, 1942. Out of print

Motry, Bud. *Guide to Antique Engine Repair,* Bud Motry, In print as of 1996

Norris, Earle B. *Gas Engine Ignition,* McGraw-Hill Book Company, 1916. Out of print

Osborne, E. L. *Plain Gas Engine Sense,* Gas Power Publishing Company, 1905. Out of print

Page, V. W. The *Modern Gas Tractor,* The Norman W. Henley Publishing Company, 1918. Out of print

Pfanstiehl, Carl A. *Ignition,* Penton Publishing Company, 1912. Out of print

Poole, Cecil P. *The Gas Engine,* McGraw-Hill Book Company, Inc., 1910. Out of print

Rathbun, J. B. *Gas Engine Troubles and Installation,* Charles C. Thompson Company, 1911. In reprint as of 1996

Roberts, E. W. *Gas Engine Secrets,* Lindsay Publications Inc., 1986. In print as of 1996

Roberts, E. W. *The Gas-Engine Handbook,* The Gas Engine Publishing Company, 1903. Out of print

Roberts, E. W., *The Gas-Engine Handbook,* The Gas Engine Publishing Company, 1917. Out of print

Sommerville, Bill. *A History of the Cushman Motor Works.* In print as of 1996

St. John, Lawrence. *How to Run the Gas Engine–Simplified,* 1915. Out of print

Verrill, A. H. *Harper's Gasoline Engine Book,* Harper & Brothers Publishers, 1914. Out of print

Warwick, B. P. *The Gas Engine,* Bubier Publishing Company, 1897. Out of print

Wendel, C. H. *American Gasoline Engines Since 1872,* Crestline Publishing Co., 1983, In print as of 1996

Wendel, C. H. *Fairbanks Morse: 100 Years of Engine Technology,* Stemgas Publishing Co., 1993. In print as of 1996

Wendel, C. H. *Power in The Past, Vol. 1, 2, 3,* Old Iron Book Company, 1982. In print as of 1996

Wright, F. B. *The Small Single-Cylinder Gas Engine,,* Reprinted by Hit & Miss Enterprises. In print as of 1996.

The Official Gazette of the United States Patent Office, United States Patent Office, 1870 - 1925. Out of print

Literature Sources

Listed here are places of business and individuals that sell both in- and out-of-print literature on gas engines. Original manufacturer's engine manuals are recommended for hobbyists that require detailed information on a specific engine. Books that cover the stationary engine in general are great sources for overall engine knowledge. Many dealers have free catalogs or lists that will allow you to browse the titles available at your leisure.

Broken Kettle Books
702 E. Madison Street
Fairfield, IA 52556
Phone: none
New and out of print books, magazines, and manuals on stationary engines. A catalog or list is available upon request.

Carnot Press
P. O. Box 1544
Lake Oswego, OR 97035
Phone: none
Fax: 503-694-5353
Publishes *Internal Fire* and *Diesel's Engine Vol. I.*

Clarence Goodburn
101 West Main
Madelia, MN 56062
Phone: 507-642-3281
A list of original manufacturer's literature is available upon request.

Hit & Miss Enterprises
P. O. Box 157
Orwell, OH 44076
Phone: 216-272-5335
Fax: 216-272-5333
Hit & Miss sells parts, engines, books, and literature. A catalog is available that features reproduced and original parts and accessories. A current sales list of engines may also be requested.

Jean Metcalf
7924 Depot Road
Ashtabula, OH 44004
Phone: none
Reprinted books, manuals, and engine literature can be purchased from a free listing, which is available upon request.

Jim Meister
3520 S.R. 98
Bucyrus, OH44820
Phone: 419-562-3094
Jim has an extensive collection of original tractor and stationary engine literature for sale. Because of the nature of original literature sales, a catalog is not applicable.

Kings Books
P. O. Box 86
Radnor, OH 43066-0086
Phone: none
Reprinted engine manuals and literature are available. A catalog will be sent upon request.

M. W. Tichenor
RR#1 Box 213AA
Charleston, IL 61920
Phone: 217-923-5138
Original tractor and stationary engine literature dealer. Because of the nature of original literature sales a catalog is not applicable.

Mark Meincke
P. O. Box 12
Avon, OH 44011
Phone: 216-937-5630 (evenings only)
Author of *The Complete Guide to Stationary Gas Engines.*Sells reprinted and original engine literature and books.

Motorbooks International
729 Prospect Avenue
Osceola, MN 54020
Phone: 800-826-6600
Publisher and distributor of transportation-related books and reference manuals; catalog available.

Ohio Windmill & Pump Company
P. O. Box 157
Berlin Center, OH 44401-0157
Phone: 330-547-6300
Fax: 330-547-8213
Some original and reprinted engine literature available.

Lee W. Pedersen
78 Taft Avenue
Lynbrook , NY., 11563
Phone: none
Lee carries an extensive list of reprinted original literature. A catalog or list is available upon request.

Ron Lachniet
9690 Downes NE
Lowell, MI 49331
Phone: none
Reprinted copies of *Gas Engine Troubles and Installation* by J. B. Rathbun, 1911, are available for $27.95 each, which includes shipping. Recomended book.

Rusty Iron Monthly
P. O. Box 342
Sandwich , IL 60548
Phone: none
Monthly classified ad magazine where you can find engines and parts for sale; $14.00 per year.

Stationary Engine Magazine
Kelsey Publishing Ltd.
Kelsey House 77 High Street
Beckenham, Kent, England BR3 1AN
Phone: none
Publishers of a monthly engine magazine from England. Each issue is about 28 pages. Air-mailed subscription rate is $39.00 per year.

Stemgas Publishing Company
P. O. Box 328
Lancaster, PA 17603
Phone: 717-392-0733
Fax: 717-392-1341
Publishers of two monthly magazines: *Gas Engine* ($30.00 per year) and *The Iron Men Album* ($15.00 per year). Show directories,

books and reprinted manuals and engine literature. Catalog available upon request. *Gas Engine* is highly recommended for all engine buffs. The magazine covers articles on specific engines, history, shows, and auctions. Classified and wanted information in each issue.

Verle Decker
Rt#2 Box 151
Hollenberg, KS 66946
Phone: 913-337-2923
Sells new and out of print engine literature. List upon request.

Verne Kindschi
S9008B U. S. HWY 12
Prairie du Sac, WI 53578
Phone: 608-643-3915
Author of *The Fuller & Johnson Story*. Copies are available along with several other Fuller & Johnson manuals, catalogs. and literature. List upon request.

Parts and Supplies

The following list of suppliers service or sell engines and parts. Most of these companies and individuals advertise their services or products in the monthly trade magazines. There are a few places where restored or original condition engines can be purchased. Parts and services are generally dedicated to the more common engines. You will need to inquire with specific needs for rarer engines. Many times, parts are available but are not listed in a catalog.

Bailey Craftsman Supply
P. O. Box 276
Fulton, MO 65251-0276
Phone: 314-642-5998
    Scale engine models can be purchased from them.

Branson Enterprises
7722 Elm Avenue
Rockford, IL 61115
Phone: 815-633-4262
    Branson's has a great service department for engine magnetos. New and used magnetos are available.

Calvin and Ted Brookover
4801 East Red Bridge Road
Kansas City, MO. 64137
    Brookover's do igniter repairing or remanufacturing, new magnetos and magneto repairing. Custom made igniters can be purchased as well. Excellent work on all projects.

Cornelius Bergbower
Louie Avenue, Box 144
Bluford, IL 62814
    You can buy, sell, or swap antique spark plugs with Mr. Bergbower. He also has three books that contain spark plug photographs and history. Catalog is available on request.

D & V Iron Works
P. O. Box 618
Allyn, WA 98524-0618
    Hobbyists can purchase new drip oilers here. Write for list or wants.

Dale Nickerson
8670 Glasgow Road
Cassadaga, NY 14718
Phone: 716-595-3260
    Magneto repairing service.

Dan Steding
1119 Kramme Drive
Fort Dodge, IA 50501
Phone: 515-955-3749
    Dan carries an extensive line of parts and new custom-made fuel tanks. A listing of his products and services will be sent upon request.

Debolt Machine Inc.
4206 West Pike
Zanesville, OH 43701
Phone: 614-454-8082
    Manufacturers of model stationary engines. They also carry a complete line of parts for models. A catalog is available upon request.

Don Oberholtzer
603 South Main Street
Columbiana, OH 44408
Phone: 216-482-4097
    Don does an excellent job on casting new parts. Castings of IHC parts are his specialty.

Ed Strain
400 2nd Avenue NE
St. Petersburg, FL 33701
Phone: 813-896-1623
    Magneto repair service and sale of reconditioned magnetos.

Fildes Electric Motor Company
Ken Fildes
1014 Cleveland Street
Grafton, OH 44044
Phone: 216-926-2641
    Repairs antique electrical devices, motors, and fans, manufactures some parts. Great work and fair prices.

Forest Glidewell
6934 State Rt. # 121
Greenville, OH 45331
Phone: 513-548-1084
    Manufactures new piston rings and carries a line of engine parts and supplies. A catalog is available upon request.

George Kempher
110 Seventh Street
Emporium, PA 15834
Phone: 814-486-2605
    Manufactures new high- and low-tension coils.

Gibbs Brand
P. O. Box 256
Carthage, TN 37030
Phone: 1-800-GIBBS YA
    Oil products for stuck engines; works great to free up rusted engines.

Hartville Magnetos
297 Pleasant Valley Road
Hartville, WY 82215
Phone: 307-836-2960
    High-tension magnetos manufactured new. A catalog is available upon request.

Irvine's Model Shop
P. O. Box 126
Burbank, OH 44214
Phone: 330-624-2132
    Manufacturer of scale engine models. A catalog is available upon request.

J & M Carousel
Jack Hurt
1711 Calavaras Drive
Santa Rosa, CA 95405
Phone: 1-800-789-1026
    Coils and magneto repair service which I can recommend. Reconditioned units for sale.

Jerry Terrell
9831 State Rt. #138
Leesburg, OH 45135
Phone: 513-981-7189
    McCormick-Deering "M" Parts. A listing is available upon request.

John Brillman
Box 333
Tatamy, PA 18085
    Deals and sells new and antique spark plugs. A listing is available upon request.

John Wanat
Box 275
West Redding, CT 06896
Phone: 203-938-3771
    Manufactures new low- and high-tension coils. Builds new custom gas tanks. A listing is available upon request.

Keith Blaho
RD #1 Box 55
Enon Valley, PA 16120
Phone: 412-336-6529
    Engine moving and transporting services.

Kohnke's Machine
Box 21
Clare, IA 50524
Phone: 515-546-4551
    Bearing rebabbitting services.

Lightning Magneto
Mitch Malcolm
RT. #1, Box 564
Ottertail, MN 56571
Phone: 218-367-2819
    Repairs magnetos, sells reconditioned mags as well.

M & E Products
P. O. Box 37
Simpsonville, SC 29681
Phone: 803-288-1992
    Manufacturers of scale model stationary engines. A catalog is available upon request.

Magnetos
3132 Carson
Indianapolis, IN 46227
Phone: 1-800-255-4084
    Repairs magnetos, sells reconditioned mags as well.

Mark Meincke
34361 Schwartz Road
Avon, OH 44011
Phone: 216-937-5630 (evenings)
    Buys, sells, trades engines, literature, and related items.

Mark Minzel
233 East 2nd Street
Waconia, MN 55387-1508
Phone: 612-442-5234
    Deals in engines parts. Must contact him with your needs.

Musky Machine
Carl Martin or Mike Sanderson
1435 270th Street
Garwin, IA 50005
Phone: 515-488-2453
    High-quality reproduction fuel mixers (Lunkenheimer style) $80.00 to $155.00 each.

Olsen's Gaskets
3059 Opdal Road East
Port Orchard, WA 98366
Phone: 206-871-1207
    Makes gaskets, 1910s to 1960s.

Paul Weaver
680 Sylvan Way
Bremerton, WA 98310
Phone: 206-373-7870
    Manufactures new custom piston rings 1 to 10 inches. A listing is available upon request.

Robert Kubisch
2111 Gilbride Road
Martinsville, NJ 08836
    Maytag & Aermotor parts and magnetos. A catalog is available upon request.

Robert Whitaker
2102 Ken Court
Mt. Dora, FL 32757
Phone: 904-383-1402
    Mags and coils, both new and used, can be purchased here.

Scholl Engine Shop
Raymond Scholl
202 Bryan Combs Road
Sugar Grove, NC 28679
Phone: 704-297-4406
    Sells restored and original engines and engine carts and related items. A listing is available upon request. I recommend working with Raymond!

Shamrok Specialties Inc.
3503 West Oak
Palestine, TX 75801
Phone: 1-800-658-1188
    Oil products for stuck engines. A catalog is available upon request.

Simpson Motors
3306 Amherst Pike
Madison Hts., VA 24572
Phone: 804-929-4468
    Maytag engine parts. A listing is available upon request.

Starbolt Engine Supplies
3403 Buckeystown Pike
Adamstown, MD 21710
Phone: 301-694-6840
    Bill carries a line of parts, supplies, and literature for stationary engines. A catalog is available upon request. I can recommend Starbolt!

T. Scheltema
6912 84th Street
Caledonia, MI 49316
    Supplies new drip oiler glass. A listing is available upon request.

The Shop
P. O. Box 279
Creston, CA 93432
Phone: 1-800-525-9188
    Paint and painting supplies for restoring stationary engines. A listing is available upon request.

Tip Tools and Equipment
7075 Rt. #446
P. O. Box 649
Canfield, OH 44406
Phone: 1-800-321-9260
    Manufacturers of new sandblasting equipment. A catalog is available upon request.

William Damewood
4600 North Urbana-Lisbon Road
Mechanicsburg, OH 43044
Phone: 513-828-1149
    Magneto repair servicing.

WJW Magnetos
Box 29
Maida, ND 58255
Phone: 204-822-5672
    Magneto repair and servicing. A listing is available upon request.

Index